FIFTH EDITION

Elementary Harmony

Theory and Practice

ROBERT W. OTTMAN

University of North Texas

PRENTICE HALL, Upper Saddle River, New Jersey 07458

Library of Congress Cataloging-in-Publication Data

Ottman, Robert W.
Elementary harmony : theory and practice / Robert W. Ottman. — 5th ed.
p. cm.
Includes index.
ISBN 0-13-281610-5 (paper)
1. Harmony. I. Title.
MT50.0924 1998
781.2'5—dc21 97-25707
CIP
MN

Editorial director: *Charlyce Jones Owen*
Publisher: *Norwell F. Therien*
Editor: *Marion Gottlieb*
Project manager: *Carole R. Crouse*
Prepress and manufacturing buyer: *Bob Anderson*
Copy editor: *Carole R. Crouse*
Marketing manager: *Sheryl Adams*

This book was set in 10.5/12 Times Roman by Thompson Type and was printed and bound by Courier Companies, Inc.
The cover was printed by Courier Companies, Inc.

Simon & Schuster / A Viacom Company
Upper Saddle River, New Jersey 07458

Printed in the United States of America

10 9 8 7 6 5 4 3 2 1

ISBN 0-13-281610-5

Prentice-Hall International (UK) Limited, *London*
Prentice-Hall of Australia Pty. Limited, *Sydney*
Prentice-Hall Canada Inc., *Toronto*
Prentice-Hall Hispanoamericana, S.A., *Mexico*
Prentice-Hall of India Private Limited, *New Delhi*
Prentice-Hall of Japan, Inc., *Tokyo*
Simon & Schuster Asia Pte. Ltd., *Singapore*
Editora Prentice-Hall do Brasil, Ltda., *Rio de Janeiro*

Contents

Preface

Elementary Harmony: Theory and Practice, fifth edition, and its accompanying workbook present materials for study covering the first year of a two-year program. Preceded by a preliminary review of those fundamentals prerequisite to a study of harmony, the principal chapters of the text cover diatonic harmony, dissonance treatments, secondary dominant harmony, and elementary modulation.

In addition to the usual presentation of this subject matter through the study of chord constructions, chord successions, harmonic analysis, and part-writing, this text also emphasizes the study of melody, including melodic constructions (form) and the characteristic elements of successful melodic writing. As the text progresses in its cumulative study of harmonic practices, application of this knowledge is continually applied to the analysis of the implications of harmony in a melodic line and to the harmonization of given melodic lines.

Further, all harmonic studies are supplemented by exercises in keyboard performance. This tactile and aural experience is invaluable in the reinforcement of harmonic knowledge. Early abstract exercises in keyboard harmony are so designed that they can be easily accomplished even by students without previous keyboard experience. Later studies include melody harmonization, first through the use of "lead sheet" symbols, followed by the students' own interpretation of the harmony implied in the melodic line.

A complete course in music theory can be achieved through the use of correlating studies in sight singing and ear training as found in the author's *Music for Sight Singing,* fourth edition, 1996, and *Basic Ear Training Skills* (with Paul Dworak), 1991, available with supplementary computer disks, both published by Prentice Hall.

New to the fifth edition are many assignments that are followed by references to answers found either in Appendix 5, in the workbook, or in both. Although use of the workbook in conjunction with this text is not required, an explanation of the dual system of answers is appropriate here.

For a given assignment in the text, answers are usually given to selected items, thereby allowing the student to receive both immediate reinforcement and the opportunity for independent solutions. In the workbook, many of these exercises are found in a programmed format, questions and answers side by side, whereby a student can work out a problem and immediately check the solution for accuracy. In both the text and the workbook, those exercises for which answers are given are so crafted that only one solution is possible when staying within the procedures presented in the particular chapter. This experience furnishes a strong foundation for later assignments that require more freedom in writing techniques. Answers are not given where multiple solutions are possible (as in an extended part-writing exercise), since a single given answer can be misleading.

Of further interest in this edition is the use of excerpts from the works of women composers of the nineteenth century. Included are Clara Schumann, Fanny Mendelssohn Hensel, Elizabeth-Claude Jacquet, and Maria Szymanowska.

That the study of harmony not be considered a subject unrelated to music history and performance, a series of twelve articles assists in relating concepts of the tonal era under study to pre-seventeenth- and post-nineteenth-century musical styles and practices. Finally, a series of appendixes includes the articles *Instrumentation, Elementary Acoustics, The Medieval Modes,* and *The Essentials of Part-Writing,* the last a condensation of the conventional procedures of part-writing as gathered from the individual presentations in chapters throughout the text.

Robert W. Ottman

1

Basics I

pitch on the staff and the keyboard; scales; key signatures

For many college-level students, most of Chapters 1 through 3 will constitute a review of basic materials already learned from previous musical experience. Additional practice is available in the Workbook, *where exercises correlate closely with the presentation in these three chapters. Most of these exercises include a section with answers given, followed by a section without answers. Students requiring more extensive and rigorous review are referred to either of two texts designed to precede* Elementary Harmony. *They are* Rudiments of Music, *third edition (Prentice Hall, 1995), and* Programmed Rudiments of Music, *second edition (Prentice Hall, 1994), both by Robert W. Ottman and Frank D. Mainous.*

Let us assume that you have just heard a single musical sound, perhaps a note on the piano or on some other instrument. What did you hear? Within this one sound, you should be able to distinguish four properties.

1. *Pitch:* How high or low is the sound?
2. *Duration:* How long is the sound held?
3. *Intensity:* How loud or soft is the sound?
4. *Timbre:* What is the quality of the sound; that is, does it sound like a piano, a trumpet, a violin, or what?

As you can see (or hear), even a single sound is complex; but in listening to music, we hear many sounds simultaneously and in rapid succession. For maximum comprehension of these combined musical events, we need to know how the pitches are grouped, how the durations are related to each other, and how these are combined with intensity and timbre to form a musical composition. To accomplish that, we must first know the symbols used to represent these four characteristics, how those symbols are placed on paper, and how they are interpreted.

Chapters 1 through 3 cover elementary considerations in the areas of *pitch* and *duration.* The *timbre* of a musical sound is a function of acoustics (see Appendix C). Terms indicating *intensity* and *tempo* can be found in the appendixes of each of the *Rudiments* texts listed at the beginning of this chapter, as well as in general music dictionaries and dictionaries of musical terms.

For the student of harmony, knowledge of the basics is essential. In regard to pitch, the student should be able to do the following with absolute accuracy and without hesitation:

1. Name both the major and the minor key for any key signature.
2. State the number of sharps or flats in the signature of a given key and spell these accidentals in their correct order on the staff.
3. Spell all the major scales and the three forms of each minor scale, ascending and descending.

Pitch on the Staff

To indicate pitch on paper, we use a *staff* (plural *staves*) consisting of five parallel horizontal lines and four intervening spaces.

FIGURE 1.1 *The Staff*

Lines and spaces are named using the letters A B C D E F G. Where on the staff these letter names are placed is determined by a *clef* sign. A clef sign is ordinarily placed at the beginning of each staff in a music composition.[1] See page 37 for the origin of the staff and the clefs.

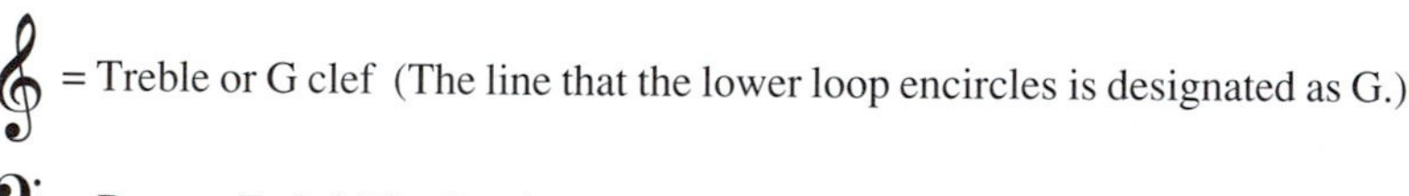

Once these pitches are established, adjacent lines and spaces use adjacent letter names.

[1]The C clefs and their staff spellings are presented in Chapter 8.

FIGURE 1.2 *Staff Spellings*

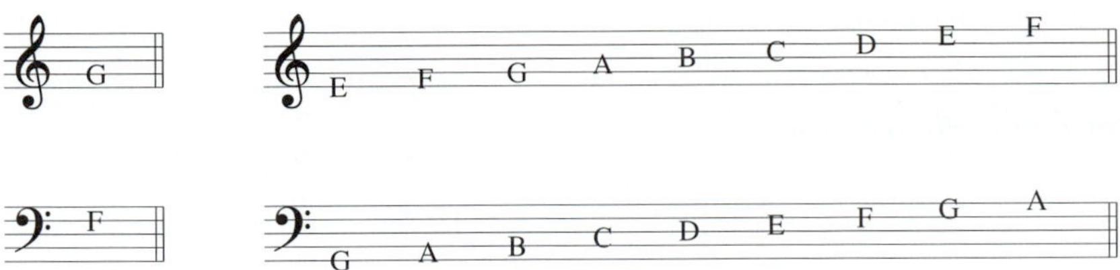

We can also place notes above or below the staff by using *ledger (leger) lines,* short lines equidistant from each other.

FIGURE 1.3 *Ledger Lines*

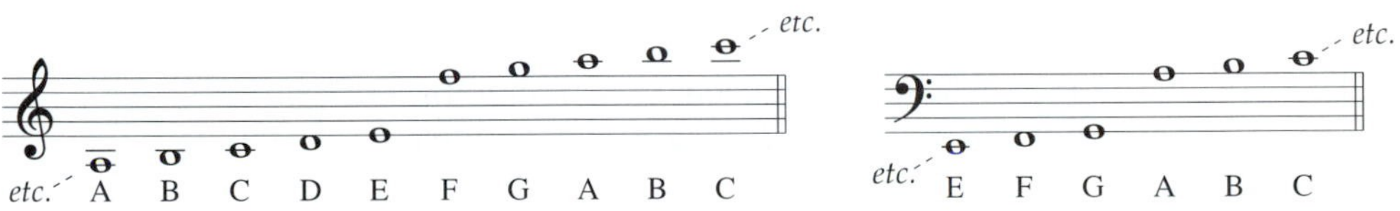

The treble and bass clefs can be joined together by a *brace* to produce a *grand staff (great staff, piano staff). Middle C* is a special name given to that C occuring between the staves.

FIGURE 1.4 *The Grand Staff*

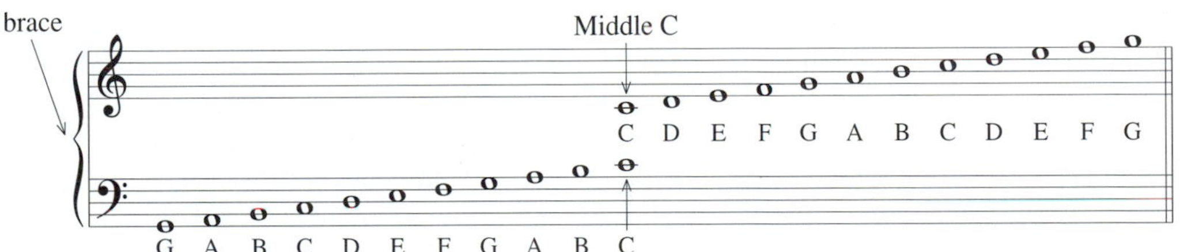

Observe that middle C occurs both above the bass staff and below the treble staff. Placing it midway between the staves, as in Figure 1.5, is incorrect.

FIGURE 1.5 *Incorrect Placement of Middle C*

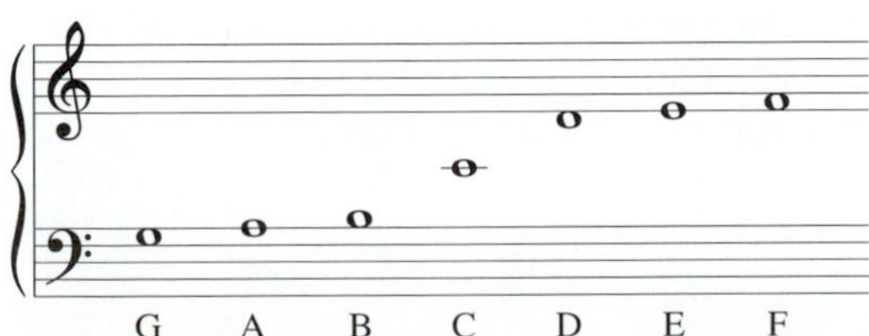

The correct placement of middle C allows us to continue the ledger lines downward in the treble clef and upward in the bass clef. The two notes above each letter name in Figure 1.6 are identical in pitch.

FIGURE 1.6 *Ledger Lines between Staves*

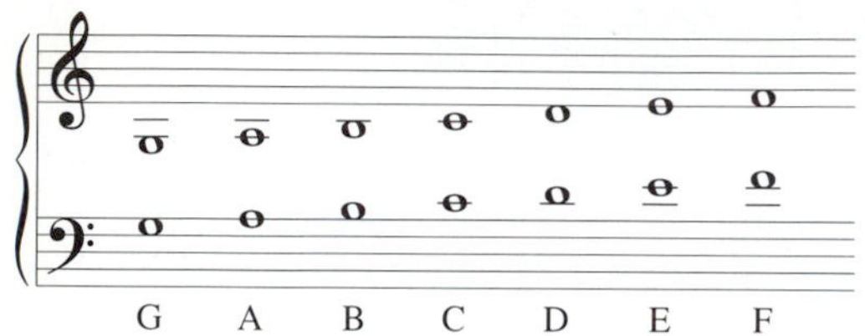

Pitch on the Keyboard

Pitch names for the keys on the keyboard are conveniently figured from the pitch C. You can easily find any C on the keyboard by finding the white key immediately to the left of any group of two black keys.

FIGURE 1.7 *Location of C on the Keyboard*

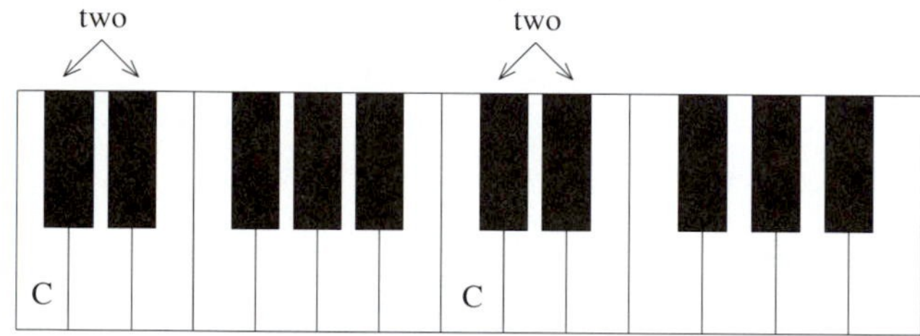

When you sit at the center of the keyboard, middle C is immediately before you. The keys to the right are named in alphabetical order ascending to the next C: C D E F G A B C. The distance from C to the next C, up or down, is called an *octave* (from the Latin *octo,* meaning "eight"), since eight letter names or keys are spanned. The same is true for any letter name and its repetition eight letter names away. A up to A, for example, is an octave.

In Figure 1.8, you see that there are eight C's (the sign *8va* means that these notes sound an octave higher than written). To the right of each C, the letters of the musical alphabet extend to the next C, except, of course, for the last C. In addition, there are two extra keys—A and B—at the left of the keyboard. How are these successive octaves, C to C, differentiated from each other? In a system known as *octave registers,* each C has its own designation and, to the right of any C, each of the other letter names carries the same designation. (There are several systems; the one shown here is the most widely used.)

FIGURE 1.8 *Names of the Keys on the Keyboard (Octave Registers)*

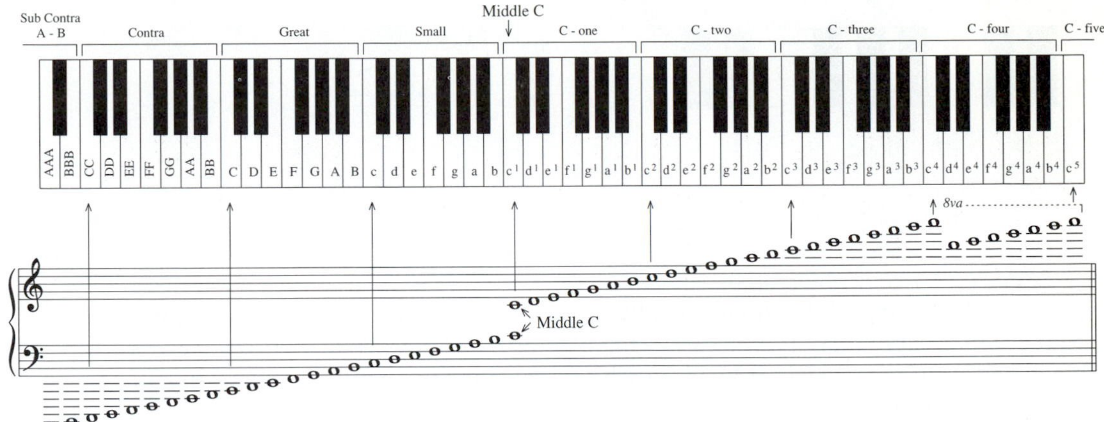

The octave register designations are spoken thus:

AAA = Sub Contra
CC = Contra
C = Great
c = small
c^1 = c-one
c^2 = c-two
c^3 = c-three
c^4 = c-four
c^5 = c-five

Intervals: Half Steps and Whole Steps

An interval is the distance between two pitches, either as heard or as represented by two notes on the staff or two keys on the keyboard. The octave described on page 4 is an interval. For the present, we will consider only the two intervals used in writing or playing a scale: the half step and the whole step.

A *half step* consists of two pitches as close together as possible. See Figure 1.9.

On the keyboard: Look at the white keys on the keyboard (Figure 1.9*a*), and you will see half steps between E and F and between B and C. A half step may also occur between any white key and an adjacent black key.

On the staff: The white-key half steps occur on the staff as shown in Figure 1.9*b*.

FIGURE 1.9 *Half Steps*

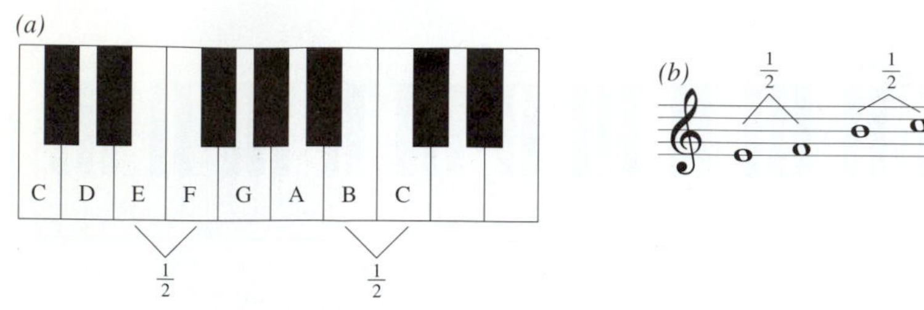

A *whole step* is made up of two half steps.

On the keyboard: Each pair of adjacent white keys, except E–F and B–C, is a whole step because there is a black key intervening. A whole step may also include a black key—white-to-black or black-to-white—provided that only two adjacent half steps are involved.

On the staff: Any adjacent line and space except E–F and B–C constitute a whole step. To create other half steps and whole steps—for example, a whole step above E—use *chromatic alterations* (also called *accidentals*) to raise or lower the pitch of a given note. Listed here are the accidentals and how each alters a pitch.

Sharp (♯)	Raises the pitch of a tone one half step (C♯ is one half step higher than C).
Flat (♭)	Lowers the pitch of a tone one half step.
Double sharp (𝄪)	Raises the pitch of a tone one whole step.
Double flat (𝄫)	Lowers the pitch of a tone one whole step.
Natural (♮)	Cancels a previously used accidental.

Figure 1.10 illustrates how accidentals are used. To change a whole step to a half step, shown in Figure 1.10*a,* raise the lower note one half step or lower the upper note one half step. Raising the lower note of the whole step G–A produces the half step G♯–A; lowering the upper note produces the half step G–A♭. In a similar manner, explain the intervals in Figure 1.10*b*.

To change a half step to a whole step, raise the upper note one half step or lower the lower note one half step. In Figure 1.10*c,* raising the upper note of the half step E–F produces the whole step E–F♯; lowering the lower note produces the whole step E♭–F. In a similar manner, explain Figure 1.10*d*.

FIGURE 1.10 *Use of Accidentals*

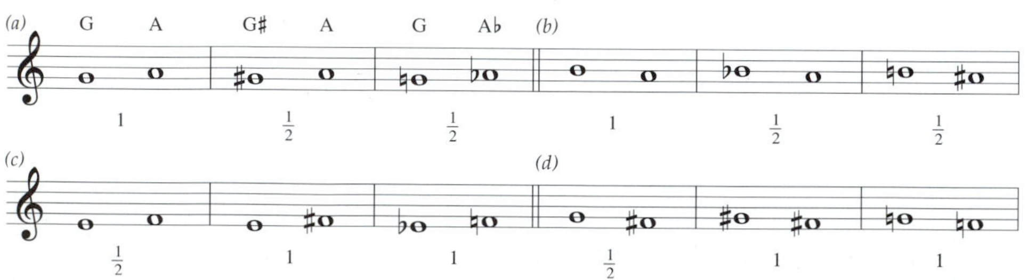

Major Scales

A *scale* is a series of eight pitches using eight consecutive letter names extending from a given pitch to its octave, ascending or descending. The series usually consists of whole steps and half steps, and it is the location of the half steps within the scale structure that determines the type of scale (major, minor, Dorian, Mixolydian,[2] and so forth). In the major scale, the half steps are located between $\hat{3}$ and $\hat{4}$ and between $\hat{7}$ and $\hat{8}$. (The symbol ˆ means *scale degree*. $\hat{3}$–$\hat{4}$ means *scale degrees three and four.* This designation of scale degrees will continue throughout the text.)

When a major scale begins on C, the half steps $\hat{3}$–$\hat{4}$ and between $\hat{7}$–$\hat{8}$ coincide with the half steps E–F and B–C on the keyboard (Figure 1.9*a*). Consequently, the C major scale uses only the white keys on the keyboard. On the staff, $\hat{3}$–$\hat{4}$ and $\hat{7}$–$\hat{8}$ in C mjaor also coincide with E–F and B–C (Figure 1.11).

FIGURE 1.11 *C Major Scale on the Staff*

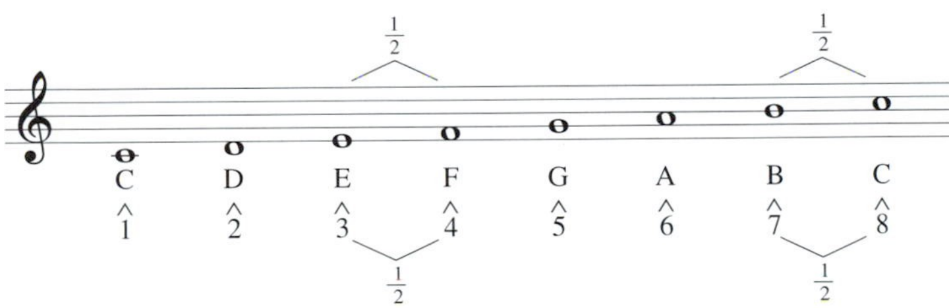

When a major scale begins on any other letter name, accidentals are necessary to provide the correct arrangement of half steps and whole steps. In a white-key scale starting on G, for example, there is a half step between $\hat{6}$ and $\hat{7}$ and a whole step between $\hat{7}$ and $\hat{8}$. If F is raised to F♯, $\hat{7}$–$\hat{8}$ becomes a half step, $\hat{6}$–$\hat{7}$ becomes a whole step, and the scale becomes major.

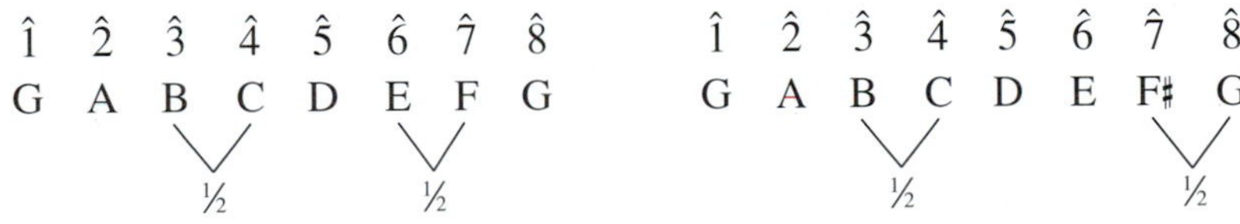

A scale can begin on a note with an accidental. Figure 1.12*a* shows the E♭ major scale on the staff, and in *b* we see the same scale on the keyboard.

[2] See page 15 for a Mixolydian scale and melody; see Appendix D for a discussion of modal scales.

FIGURE 1.12 *The E♭ Major Scale*

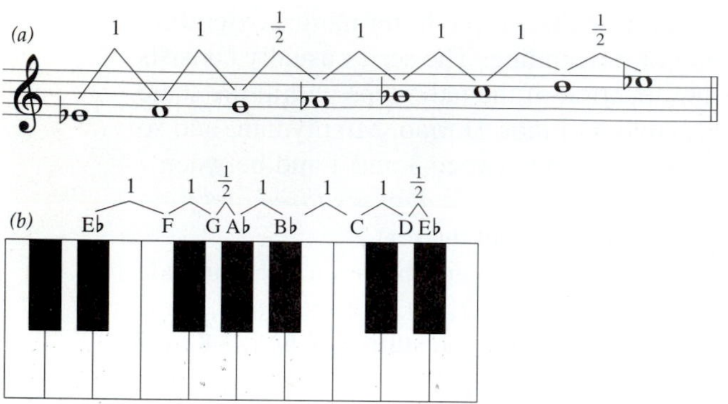

Scale-Degree Names

Scale degrees are known by name as well as by number. Instead of saying "first scale degree," we can say "tonic scale degree" or "tonic note."

Scale degree	*Name*	*Meaning*
$\hat{1}$	Tonic	The tone that identifies the key
$\hat{2}$	Supertonic	The tone a whole step above the tonic
$\hat{3}$	Mediant	The tone midway between the tonic and the dominant
$\hat{4}$	Subdominant	The tone five tones below the tonic
$\hat{5}$	Dominant	The tone five tones above the tonic
$\hat{6}$	Submediant	The tone halfway between the tonic and the subdominant (or five tones below the mediant)
$\hat{7}$	Leading tone	The tone that leads to the tonic

Major Key Signatures

Music could be written with accidentals throughout the piece, placed as needed. The beginning of "Joy to the World," Figure 1.13*a,* consists of a descending D major scale, with sharps on F and C. Instead of putting a sharp before every F and C in the piece, we use a *key signature,* simplifying the problem by placing the accidentals at the beginning as in Figure 1.13*b,* thus indicating that all F's are F♯ and all C's are C♯.

FIGURE 1.13 *Use of a Key Signature*

Therefore, we say that two sharps in the key signature indicates the key of D major. In the same way, a system of fifteen key signatures will name each major key and identify its tonic note.

FIGURE 1.14 *Major Key Signatures*

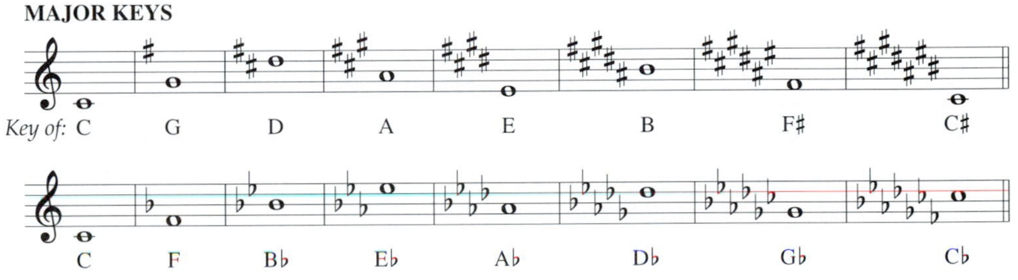

In the bass clef, the accidentals are arranged in the same way.

FIGURE 1.15 *Key Signatures in the Bass Clef*

After the first sharp or flat, each additional accidental is added in a certain pattern. For sharps, it is down four lines and spaces, F–(E)–(D)–C, up five, C–(D)–(E)–(F)–G, down four, and so forth; for flats it is up four, down five, up four, and so forth. There is one exception: The fifth sharp, A♯, breaks the pattern by its placement a fourth down from D♯. That avoids placing sharps on ledger lines.

Minor Scales

Like major scales, minor scales show a succession of eight scale steps. They differ from major scales in that (a) there are three forms of the minor scale in a given key; (b) the placement of half steps differs from that in major scales; and (c) the analysis symbols $\sharp\hat{6}$ and $\sharp\hat{7}$ each indicate that the natural tone of the scale has been raised one half step, such as G to G♯ or B♭ to B.

1. *Natural (pure) minor scale:* The half steps are between $\hat{2}$ and $\hat{3}$ and between $\hat{5}$ and $\hat{6}$. The natural minor scale with no accidentals starts on A.

FIGURE 1.16 *Natural Minor Scale*

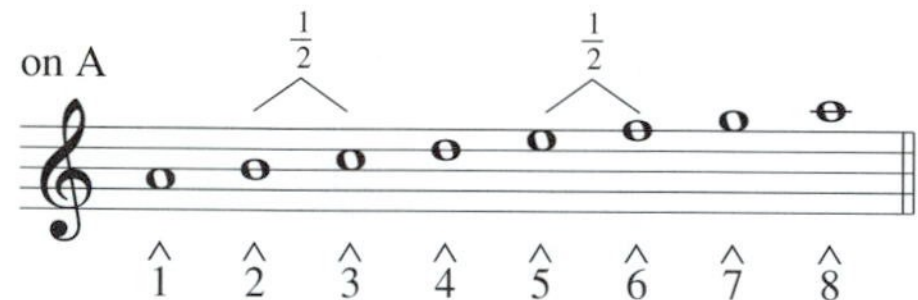

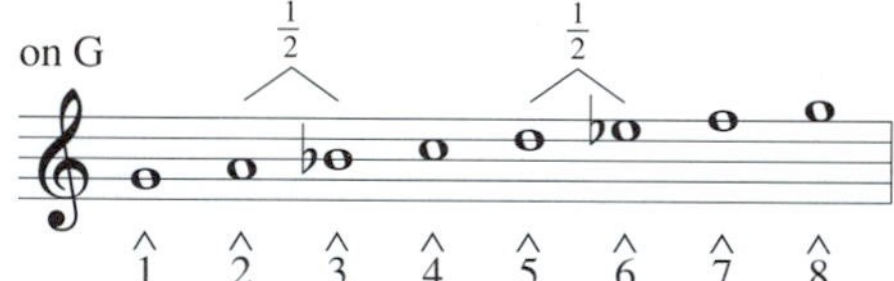

2. *Harmonic minor scale:* Raising $\hat{7}$ of the natural minor scale one half step ($\sharp\hat{7}$) supplies a leading tone not present in the natural minor scale. The half steps are now between $\hat{2}$ and $\hat{3}$, $\hat{5}$ and $\hat{6}$, and $\sharp\hat{7}$ and $\hat{8}$. Note also that the interval from $\hat{6}$ to $\sharp\hat{7}$ is a step and a half (called an augmented second).

FIGURE 1.17 *Harmonic Minor Scale*

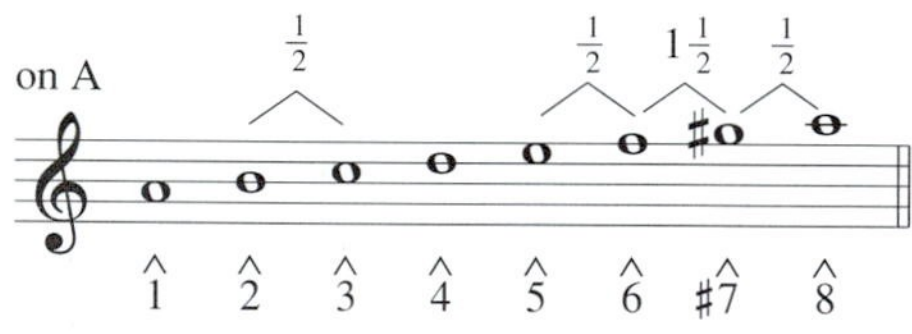

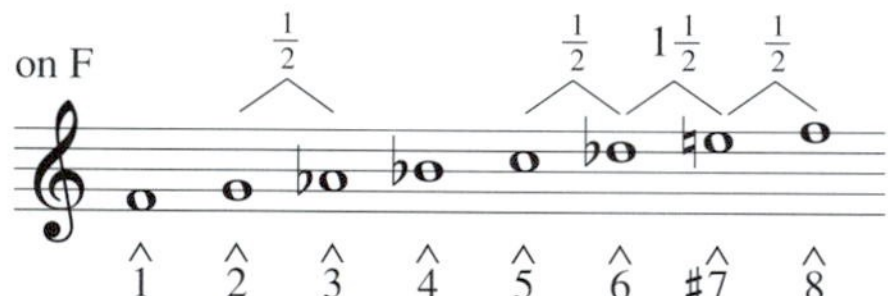

3. *Melodic minor scale:* In the ascending form of this scale, both $\hat{6}$ and $\hat{7}$ are raised one half step, indicated as $\sharp\hat{6}$ and $\sharp\hat{7}$. The half steps are now between $\hat{2}$ and $\hat{3}$ and between $\sharp\hat{7}$ and $\hat{8}$, and the awkward step and a half is eliminated. Descending, the form of the scale is the same as that of the natural minor scale. Though $\hat{7}$ and $\hat{6}$ descending are correct, $\flat\hat{7}$ and $\flat\hat{6}$ are commonly used to avoid confusion.

FIGURE 1.18 *Melodic Minor Scale*

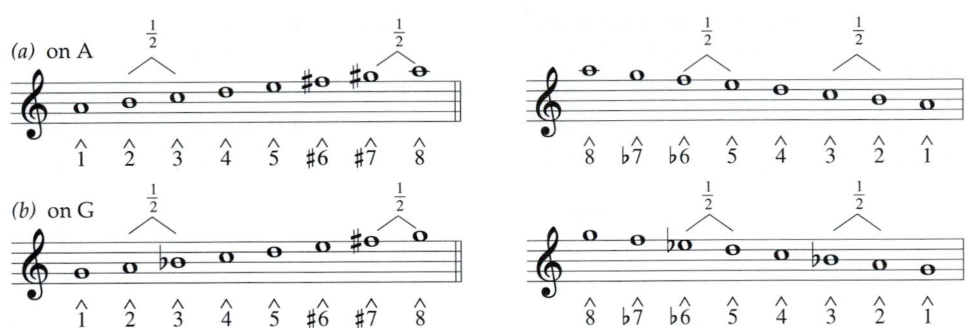

Any minor scale with the same tonic as a major scale can easily be spelled as follows:

Minor scale	*To change from major scale*
Melodic minor	lower $\hat{3}$
Harmonic minor	lower $\hat{3}$ and $\hat{6}$
Natural minor	lower $\hat{3}$, $\hat{6}$, and $\hat{7}$

FIGURE 1.19 *Spelling Minor Scales on E♭*

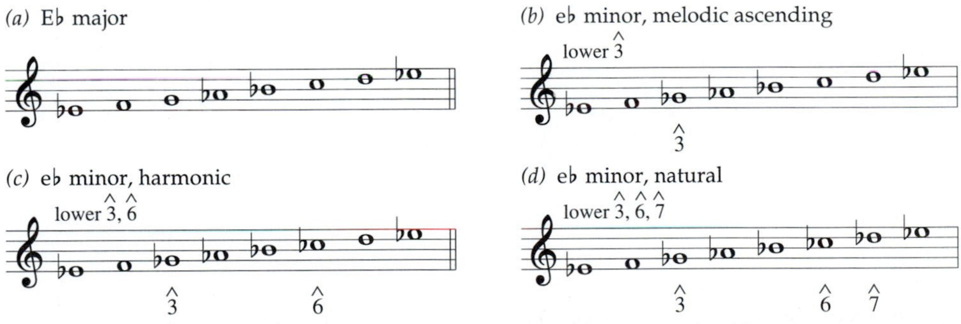

Three minor scales, G♯, D♯, and A♯, must be spelled by whole steps and half steps, since no major scale has a tonic on these pitches. The leading tone in each requires a double sharp (𝄪).

Scale-Degree Names in Minor

For $\hat{1}$ through $\hat{5}$, scale-degree names are the same in major and minor. These are names for $\hat{6}$ and $\hat{7}$:

Scale degree	*Name*
Lowered $\hat{6}$ (or ♭$\hat{6}$)	Submediant
Raised $\hat{6}$ (♯$\hat{6}$)	Raised submediant
Lowered $\hat{7}$ (♭$\hat{7}$)	Subtonic
Raised $\hat{7}$ (♯$\hat{7}$)	Leading tone

Minor Key Signatures

Minor key signatures use the accidentals found in the natural minor scale. Thus, the key signature of the e♭ minor scale shown in Figure 1.19 is six flats. In Figure 1.20, note that lowercase letters are used for key names in minor (a minor, f♯ minor, and so forth).

FIGURE 1.20 *Minor Key Signatures*

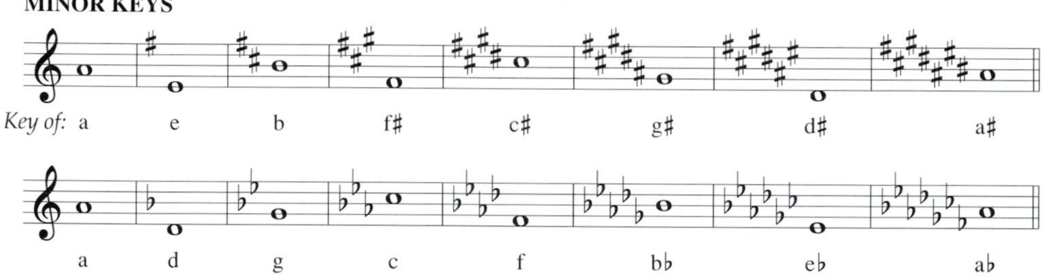

The Circle of Fifths

You may have observed in Figures 1.14 (major key signatures) and 1.20 (minor key signatures) that when you read the key names from left to right, $\hat{5}$ of any *sharp* key is $\hat{1}$ of the next key to the right; for example, $\hat{5}$ of G major is $\hat{1}$ of D major, and $\hat{5}$ of c♯ minor is $\hat{1}$ of g♯ minor.

Similarly, $\hat{4}$ of any *flat* key is $\hat{1}$ of the next key; for example, $\hat{4}$ of E♭ major is $\hat{1}$ of A♭ major, and $\hat{4}$ of d minor is $\hat{1}$ of g minor. This information is incorporated in a simple diagram called the *circle of fifths,* in which

reading clockwise:	Each tonic is the fifth scale step of the preceding tonic.

reading counterclockwise: Each tonic is the fourth scale step of the preceding tonic.

FIGURE 1.21 *The Circle of Fifths*

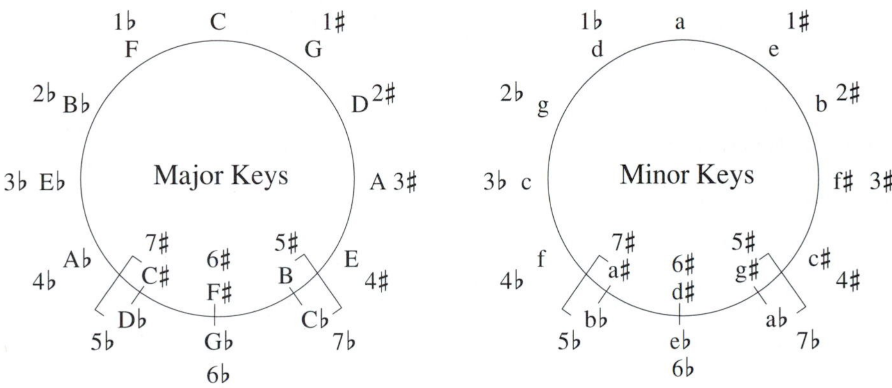

The bracketed keys are known as *enharmonic keys.* The two pitch names of a bracketed pair (for example, B and C♭) represent the same pitch and are the same key on the keyboard.

FIGURE 1.22 *Enharmonic Keys*

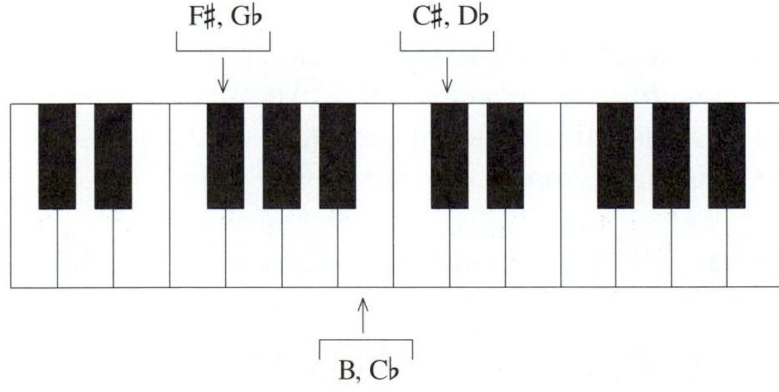

Relative and Parallel Keys

Relative Keys The two circles of fifths, major and minor, can be superimposed so that C major and A minor coincide (both have no ♯'s or ♭'s), with the other pairs of keys with the same key signatures also aligning. These coinciding keys are known as *relative keys.* B♭ major and g minor, for example, are relative keys, since both have a key signature of two flats.

FIGURE 1.23 *Circle of Fifths for Major and Minor Keys Together*

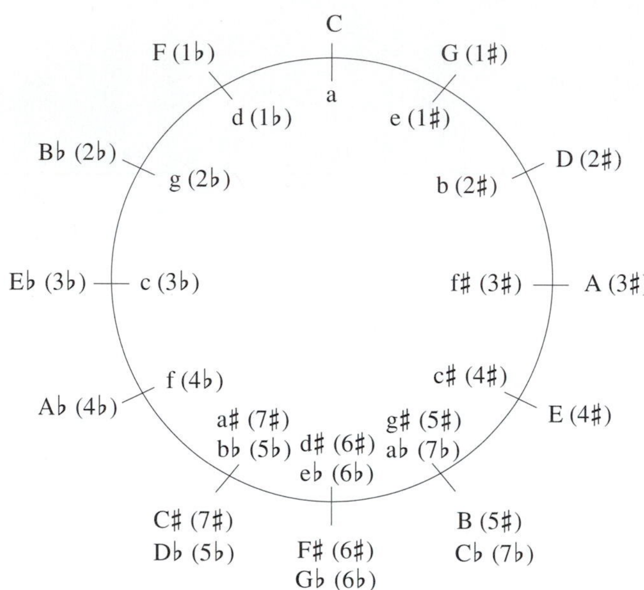

Parallel Keys Two keys employing the same tonic tone are known as *parallel keys.* B♭ major and B♭ minor are parallel keys.

Scales and Keys

With so much emphasis placed on the learning of scales in music lessons, one might be led to believe that music is derived from scales. Just the opposite is true. The scale is simply a pattern formed by an arrangement in alphabetical order of the pitches used in a composition. An obvious example is the Christmas hymn "Joy to the World" (Figure 1.13).

The first eight notes of the tune encompass all the pitch names and are in descending alphabetical order: D C♯ B A G F♯ E D. This is the descending form of the D major scale, usually stated in the ascending alphabetical form: D E F♯ G A B C♯ D. In most melodies, however, the scale structure is not so obvious, as in Figure 1.24.

FIGURE 1.24 *Scale: D E F♯ G A B C♯ D*

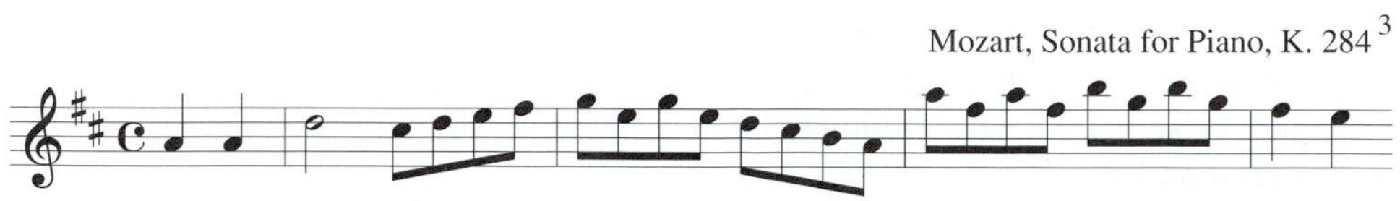

[3]K.: abbreviation for Köchel. Ludwig von Köchel in 1862 catalogued and assigned numbers to Mozart's works. Mozart did not number his compositions.

Here is the same D scale tones are present but in a more random order. Note that the Mozart example neither begins nor ends on D. Why, then, is this scale a D scale? Because all the notes seem to gravitate toward the single pitch D. Note the strength of the first D you hear and notice how the last note "wants" to continue to D (as it does in the sonata). A pitch with this quality of stability and finality is called the *tonic,* and it functions as the first note of a scale. It is usually found at or near the beginning of a composition and more often than not is also the last pitch. Music from which the scale is derived is said to be in the key of the tonic note. In the preceding two cases, it is in the key of D.

Whether the scale is major or minor depends on the arrangement of whole and half steps. The scale of the previous piece is major, whereas the scale in Figure 1.25 is minor.

FIGURE 1.25 *Scale: G A B♭ C D E♭ F♯ G*

Bach, *English Suite,* III, Gigue, BWV 809[4]

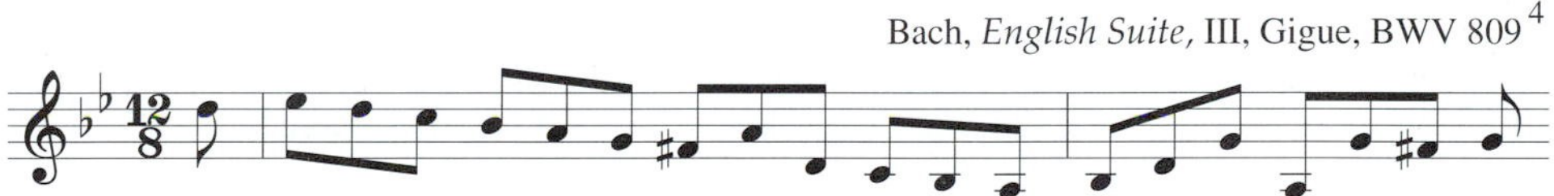

Not all scales are major or minor. The note F in the melody of Figure 1.26 possesses the quality of tonic, but this F scale shows half steps between $\hat{3}$ and $\hat{4}$ and between $\hat{6}$ and $\hat{7}$. The effect is that of major but with a lowered $\hat{7}$. It is called a Mixolydian scale, one of several scales in common use in composed music before about 1650 and found universally in folk music. (See Appendix D.)

FIGURE 1.26 *Scale: F G A B♭ C D E♭ F*

England

A key signature is nothing more than the accidentals of the scale placed at the beginning of a composition. It does not determine the key; it merely reports the accidentals used, although for convenience we commonly do use the key signature to identify the key. A key signature of two flats, for example, usually indicates B♭ major or g minor, but in the preceding English folk song it indicates F Mixolydian.

The "Basics Quiz"

These short examinations are offered in Chapters 1–3. If you encounter any difficulty, review the problem thoroughly before proceeding to more advanced study.

[4]BWV: abbreviation for *Bach-Werke-Verzeichnis,* a compilation and numbering of Bach's works by Wolfgang Schmieder in 1950. Sometimes "S." (for "Schmieder") is used instead of BWV.

BASICS QUIZ #1

In Appendix E: Answers to all questions in this quiz are given.

1. Name each of these pitches, using octave register symbols.

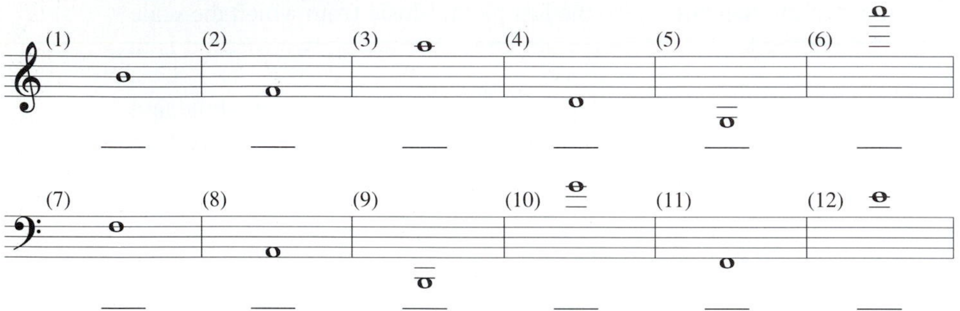

2. From this keyboard, identify each key name marked with an X, using octave register names. The letter name f^1 is already placed for you.

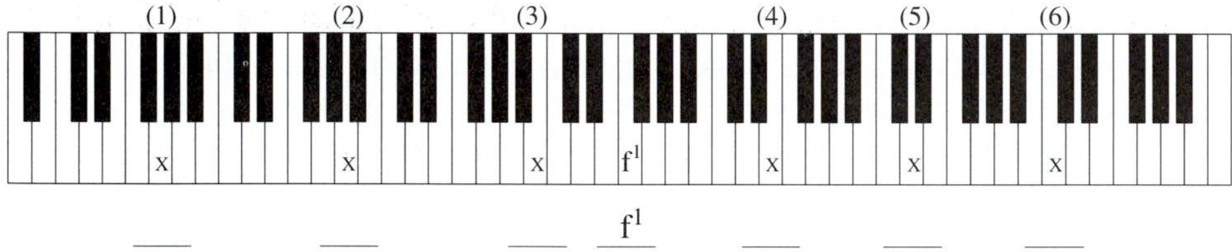

3. Identify each pair of pitches as a half step or a whole step.

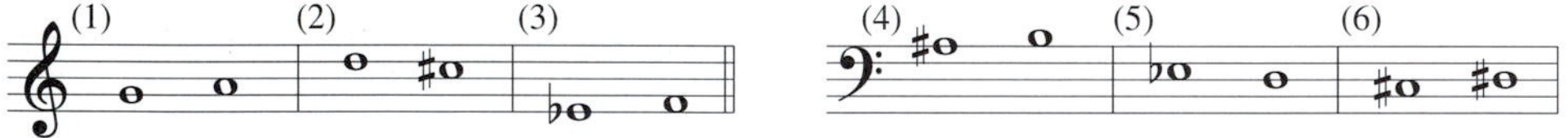

4. Write the second note of these half steps and whole steps. Always use an adjacent letter name.

a. Half steps

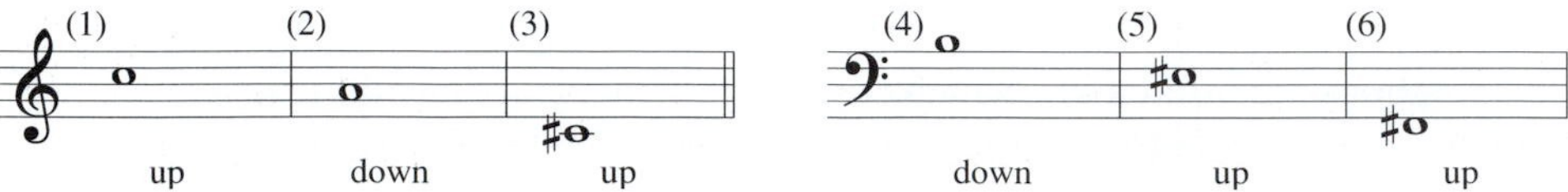

b. Whole steps

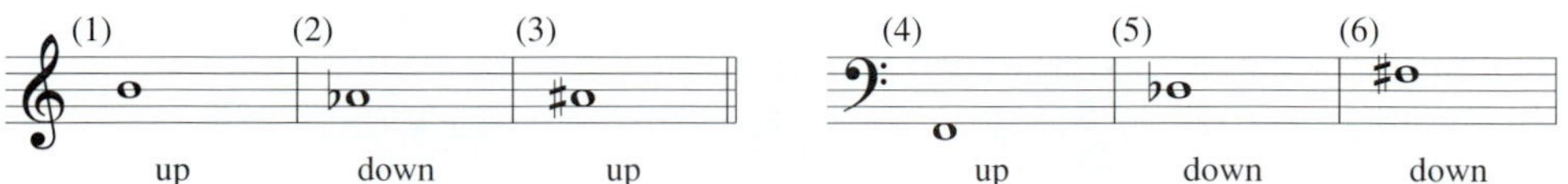

5. Add accidentals to convert these scales to major scales.

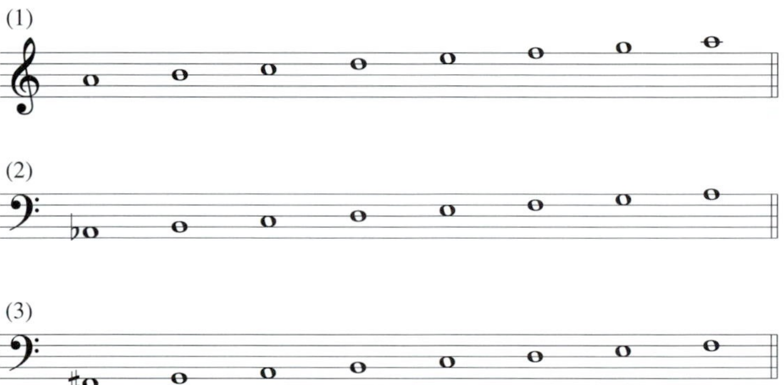

6. Name the major key for each of these key signatures.

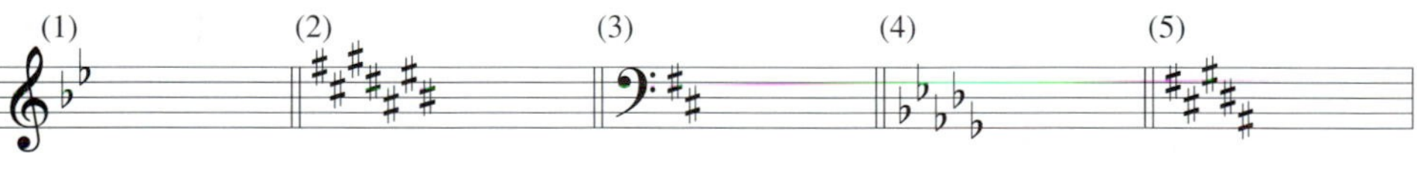

7. Add accidentals to convert these scales to minor scales in the form given.

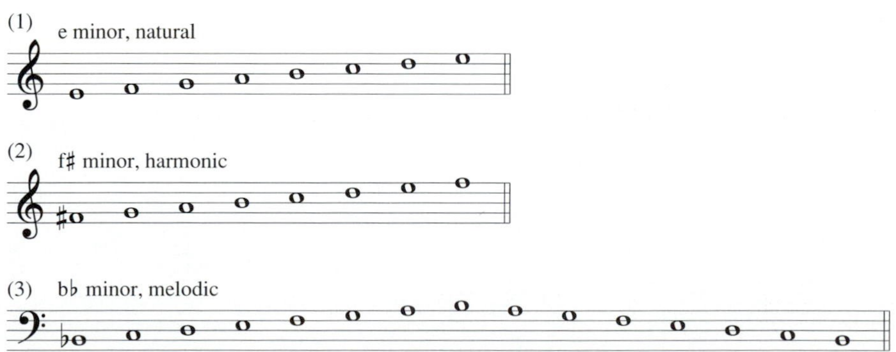

8. Name the minor key for each of these signatures. Place the tonic note on the staff.

(1) (2) (3) (4) (5)

_____ _____ _____ _____ _____

9. Name the relative and parallel keys of the given keys. Write "none" if there is no parallel key.

	Relative	***Parallel***
(1) D	_______	_______
(2) E♭	_______	_______
(3) d	_______	_______
(4) g♯	_______	_______
(5) b	_______	_______
(6) A♭	_______	_______

10. Enharmonic keys

a. The key enharmonic with F♯ is _______.

b. The key enharmonic with D♭ is _______.

c. The key enharmonic with B is _______.

2

Basics II

intervals; chords; staff notation

When you listen to music, you are hearing, as it were, in two directions at once. You hear the melody, one note after another in an imaginary horizontal line, and you orient yourself at any given moment by relating the melody tone you are hearing to the one you have already heard, or even to what you expect to hear next. At the same time, you are hearing harmony, a vertical composite of several simultaneous sounds.

Figure 2.1 shows this concept graphically, using the opening of the well-known chorale "Now Thank We All Our God." The arrow over the soprano line indicates single pitches heard one after the other (melody), which in notation looks horizontal. (Where are the three other horizontal lines?) The arrows below the staff point to groups of notes heard simultaneously (harmony), which in notation looks vertical.

FIGURE 2.1 *Horizontal and Vertical Analysis*

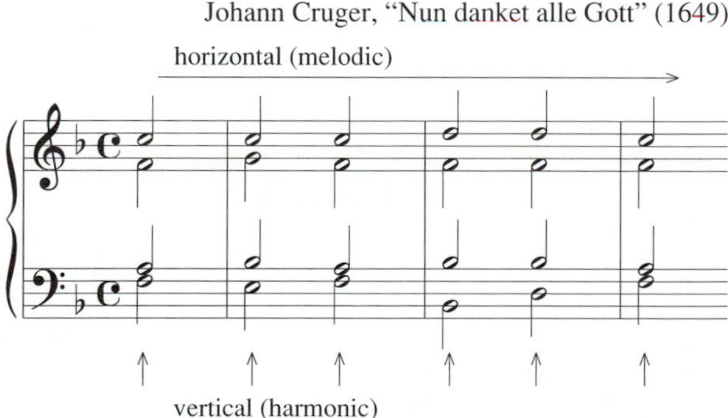

Intervals

Both melody and harmony make constant use of intervals. In melody, the distance horizontally between each pair of notes is a *melodic interval* (Figure 2.2*a*). In harmony, the distance vertically between any two notes is a *harmonic interval* (Figure 2.2*b*). Combining two or more harmonic intervals produces a chord.

FIGURE 2.2 *Melodic and Harmonic Intervals*

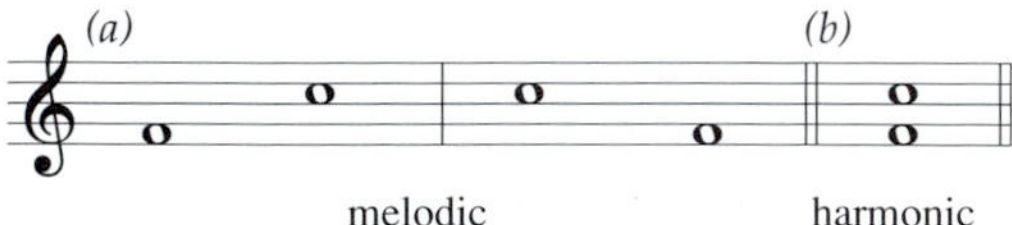

An interval is described by its *quantity* and its *quality.* Its quantity is measured by the number of letter names encompassed. For example, C up to E is a *third* because three letter names (C, D, and E) are encompassed. C♯ up to E is also a third, since only letter names determine quantity.

FIGURE 2.3 *Measurement of Intervals*

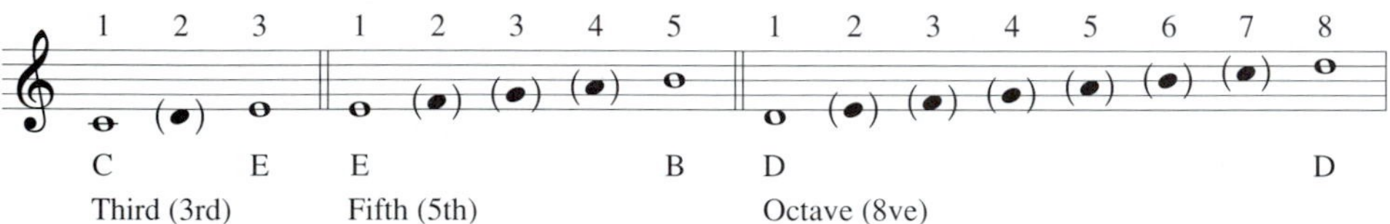

Since the distance between two letter names may vary, as in C–E and C♯–E, numerical size is qualified by terms indicating the quality of the interval: *perfect* (P), *major* (M), *minor* (m), *diminished* (d), and *augmented* (A).

Spelling Ascending Intervals[1]

Perfect and Major Intervals Any interval above the tonic note will be a perfect or a major interval, as shown in the key of C in Figure 2.4. A P5 (perfect fifth) above C, for example, is $\hat{5}$, or G, from the C major scale.

FIGURE 2.4 *Perfect and Major Intervals*

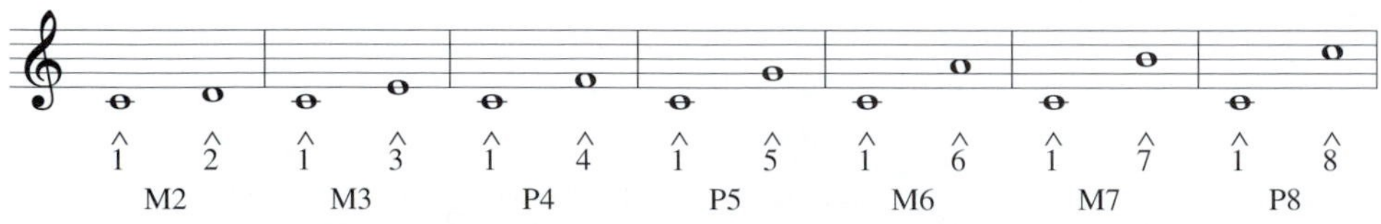

[1]Descending intervals will be easier to work with once you have studied "Inversion of Intervals," page 24.

Here is another example: Calculate a M6 above E. Call E the tonic of a major scale and count up to the sixth scale step, C♯. E up to C♯ is a M6.

DRILL #1 (INTERVALS) Place the second note of the interval above the given note.

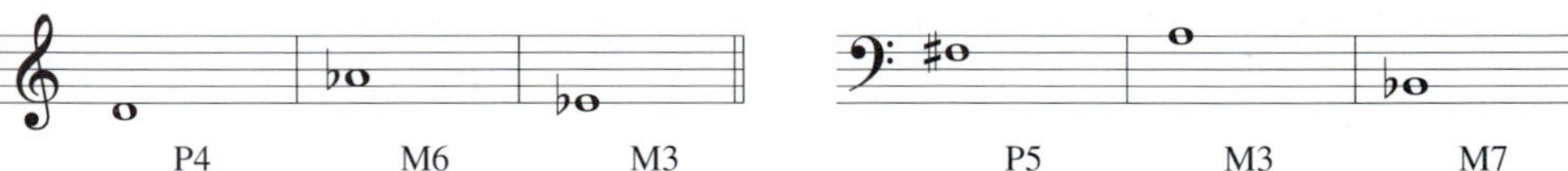

In Appendix E: Answers to Drill #1 are given.

The other intervals, minor (m), diminished (d), and augmented (A), can be calculated and identified by comparing them with perfect (P) or major (M) intervals. For example, "M" reduced by one half step becomes "m"—as shown in the following chart:

Reduce by	P	M	m
one half step	d	m	d
two half steps	–	d	–

Increase by	P	M	m
one half step	A	A	M
two half steps	–	–	A

Minor Intervals These are one half step smaller than major intervals. The decrease is accomplished when the upper note of a major interval is lowered one half step or the lower note is raised one half step, *using the same letter names.* Altering the M3 C–E, for example, will produce the minor third C–E♭ or C♯–E. Spelling C–D♯ instead of C–E♭ produces an augmented second (A2), since only two letter names are involved.

Note that the half step and the whole step described in Chapter 1 have the numerical names of m2 and M2, respectively, as seen in Figure 2.5.

FIGURE 2.5

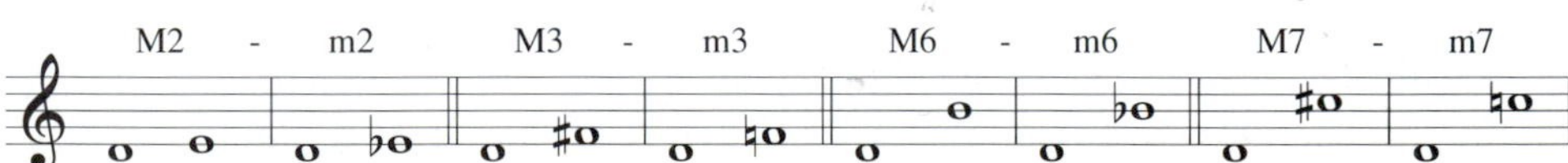

DRILL #2 (INTERVALS) Place the second note of the interval above the given note.

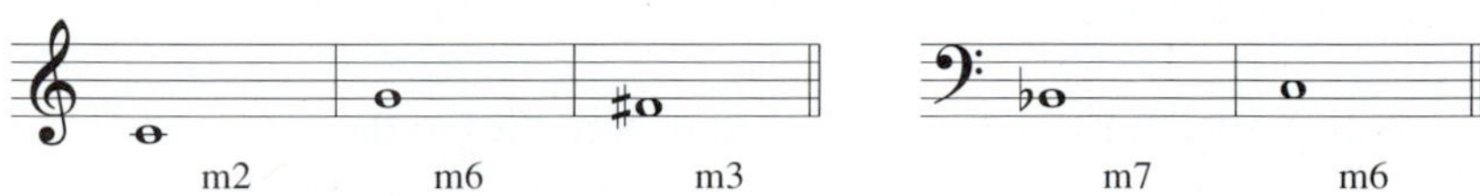

In Appendix E: Answers to Drill #2 are given.

Diminished Intervals These are one half step smaller than minor or perfect intervals; they are accomplished by lowering the upper note or raising the lower note, but *always using the same letter names.* When you compute a d interval from a M interval, be sure to reduce the M interval by *two half steps (same letter names),* M to m, then m to d, as in Figure 2.6*b*.

FIGURE 2.6 *Diminished Intervals*

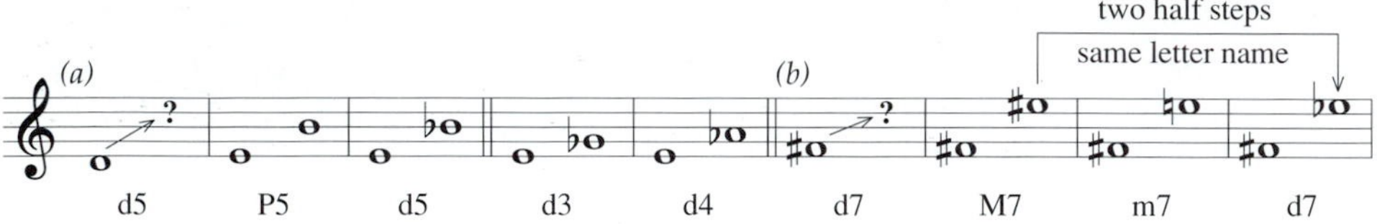

Augmented Intervals These are one half step larger than perfect or major intervals, *using the same letter names.* If the C to F♯ in Figure 2.7 were changed to C♭ to F, an A4 would also be produced.

FIGURE 2.7 *Augmented Intervals*

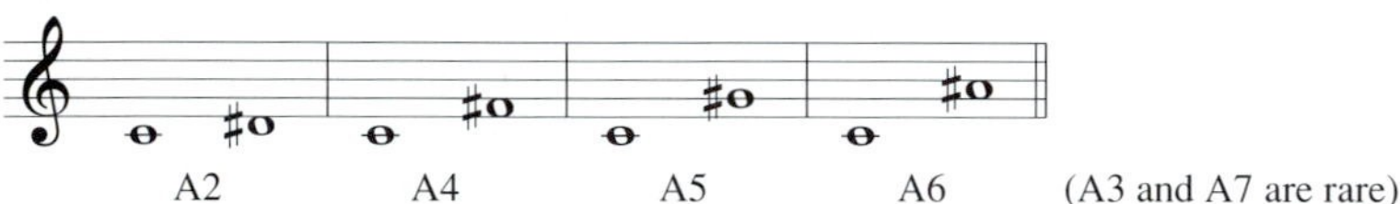

(A3 and A7 are rare)

DRILL #3 (INTERVALS) Place the second note of the interval above the given note.

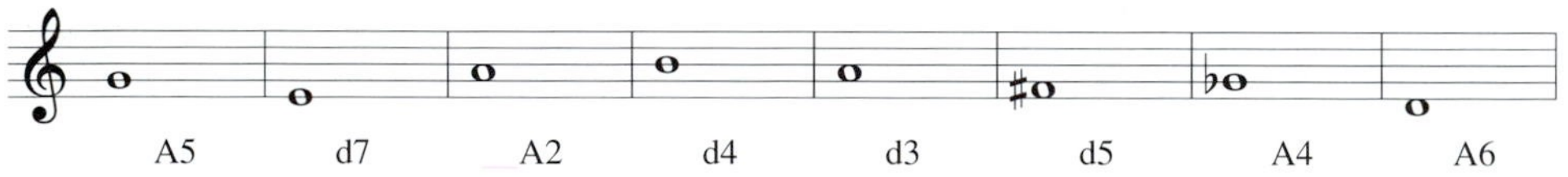

In Appendix E: Answers to Drill #3 are given.

Some letter names with an accidental are not the tonic of any major scale. These are G♯, D♯, A♯, E♯, and B♯. (Only one flatted note, F♭, cannot be tonic. Its use is not common.) To spell intervals above the sharped notes:

1. For P, M, and A intervals, remove the ♯, spell the interval, then raise both notes one half step (Figure 2.8*a*).
2. For m intervals, remove the ♯, spell a M interval, then restore the ♯ to the lower note (Figure 2.8*b*).
3. For d intervals, remove the ♯, spell a P or m interval, then restore the ♯ to the lower note (Figure 2.8*c*).

FIGURE 2.8 *Spelling Intervals above Notes That Cannot Be Tonic in a Major Key*

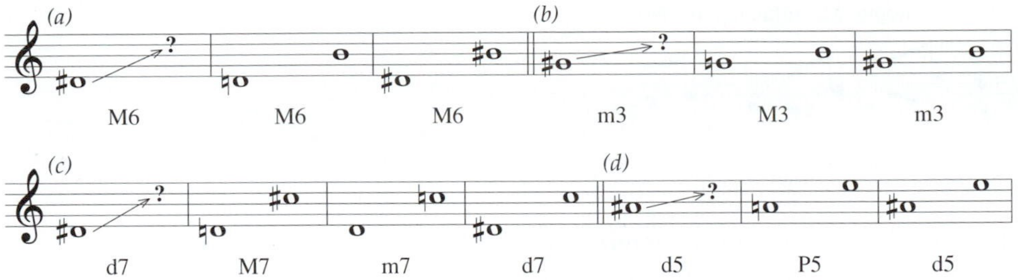

DRILL #4 (INTERVALS) Place the second note of the interval above the given note.

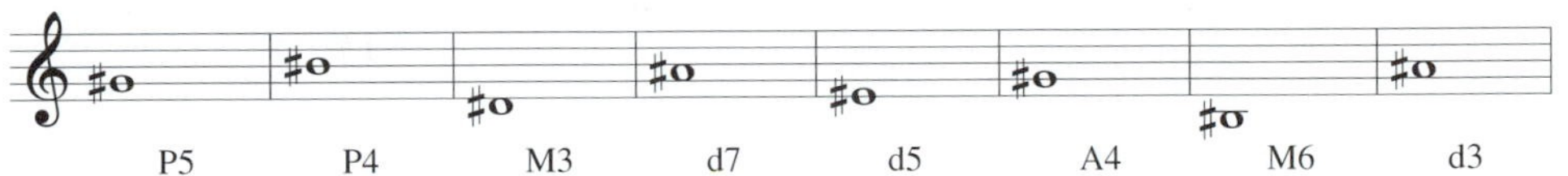

In Appendix E: Answers to Drill #4 are given.

Terminology for Other Intervals

In addition to the terms just discussed, the following are also used.

Unison (P1) or *perfect prime* (PP): Two identical pitches sounding simultaneously (such as a flute and a clarinet playing the same pitch).

Diatonic and chromatic half steps: In a diatonic half step, the two tones are spelled with adjacent letter names, such as C to D♭. In a chromatic half step, the two tones are spelled with the same letter name, such as C to C♯. The term *diatonic* refers to those tones as spelled in the scale of a given key.

Tritone: Refers to each of the enharmonic intervals of the augmented fourth and the diminished fifth. Each interval includes three whole steps (discussed further in Chapter 10).

Identifying Intervals

You should now be able to identify almost any interval you may find in a music score, using procedures similar to the preceding. Here are two measures of a melody by Chopin. What are the names of the marked intervals?

FIGURE 2.9 *Intervals in a Score*

Work from the lower note of each interval: (1) G♯ up to C, (2) D♯ up to A, and (3) E up to G. In (1) the given interval is G♯–C. Lower G♯ to G; the result is G–C, a P4. Since a d4 is a half step smaller than a P4, raising G to G♯ creates a d4.

FIGURE 2.10 *Calculating Intervals from Figure 2.9*

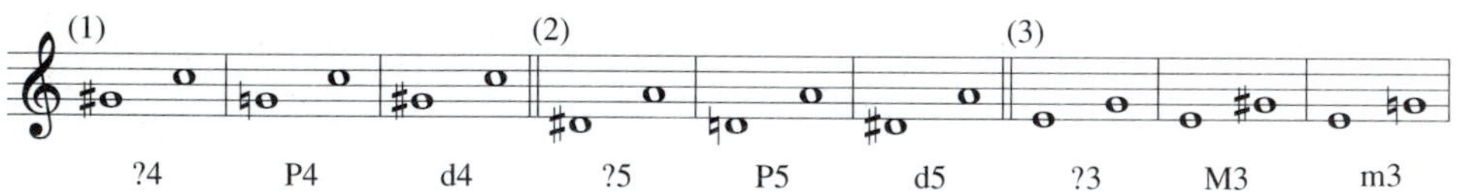

DRILL #5 (INTERVALS) Name each interval in this melodic line. Note the change of key signature. Look for the use of a chromatic half step.

In Appendix E: Answers to Drill #5 are given.

Inversion of Intervals

By inversion of an interval, we mean that we have moved the lower note up an octave or the upper note down an octave. In the process, no pitch names have been changed, but the size of the interval is different. In Figure 2.11, each interval is composed of the pitches C and G, but the octave displacement changes the P5 (C to G) to a P4 (G to C).

FIGURE 2.11 *Interval Inversion*

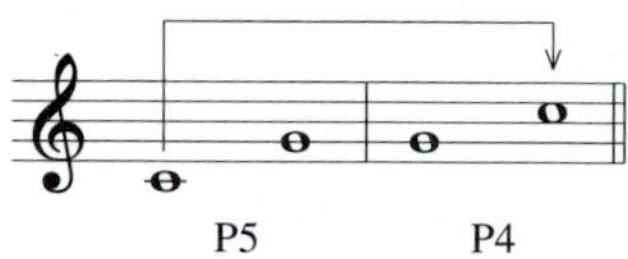

When inverted, any interval will have a different quantity numerical measurement. The quality of a perfect interval when inverted, however, always remains perfect (hence the name "perfect"); major and minor intervals reverse their designations (P5 inverts to P4, but M3 inverts to m6).

FIGURE 2.12 *Table of Inversions*

	Quantity (interval size)								*Quality*				
Original	1	2	3	4	5	6	7	8	P	M	m	d	A
Inversion	8	7	6	5	4	3	2	1	P	m	M	A	d

1 = unison; 8 = octave

You will notice that when any interval is inverted, the sum of the two numbers is always 9; for example, P5 + P4 = 9. You might have expected 8 because there is an octave (8) between the lowest and highest notes, but the number is 9 because one note is counted twice, as in Figure 2.11 where the G of C–G (P5) and G–C (P4) is counted twice. Thus, to find the numerical inversion of an interval, subtract its number from 9: The inversion of a third is 9 minus 3—a sixth.

Figure 2.13 shows inversions of P, M and m intervals only. Other intervals invert in the same way (A2–d7, d4–A5, and so forth).

FIGURE 2.13 Inversions of Intervals

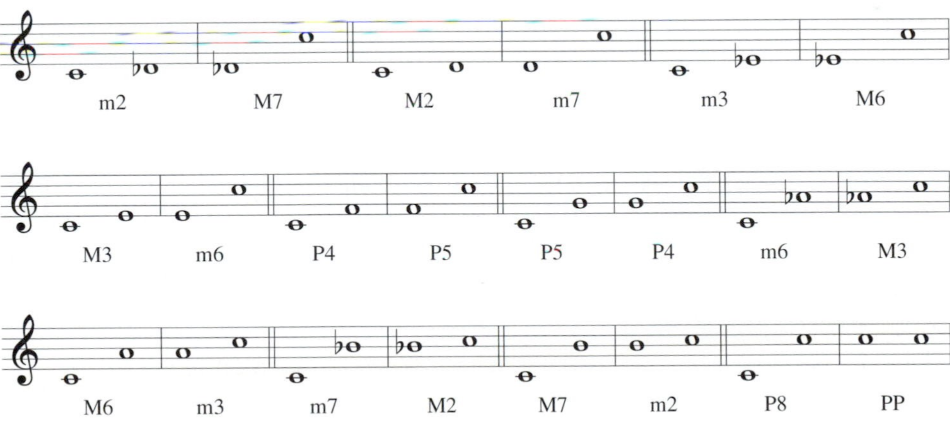

Spelling Descending Intervals

The principle of inversion is helpful in spelling descending intervals.

To spell descending perfect and minor intervals: Example: m6 below E♭ (Figure 2.14*a*).

1. Find the inversion of a m6: 9 minus m6 down = M3 up.

2. Spell a M3: M3 above E♭ is G.
3. Place the upper note an octave lower: m6 below E♭ is G.

To spell descending major, diminished, and augmented intervals: An extra step (step 2) is required for these. Example: M6 below C (Figure 2.14*b*).

1. 9 minus M6 down = m3 up.
2. To find a m3 up, first spell a M3 up. M3 above C is E.
3. m3 above C is E♭.
4. M6 below C is E♭.

FIGURE 2.14 *Finding the Lower Note of an Interval*

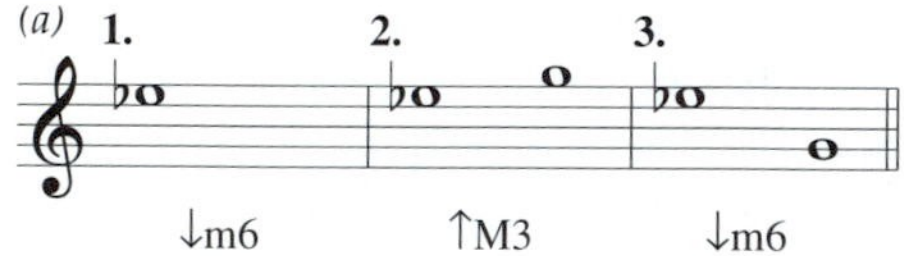

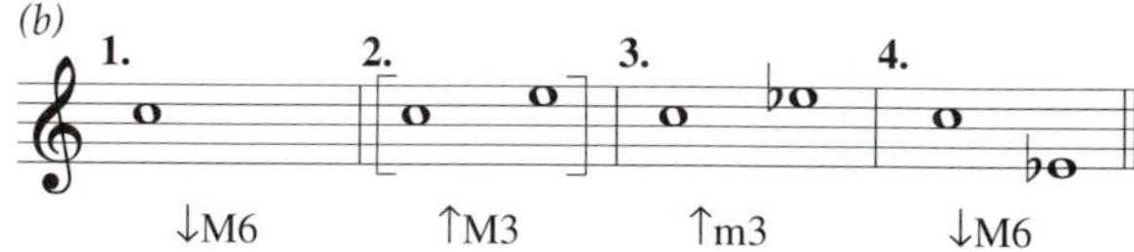

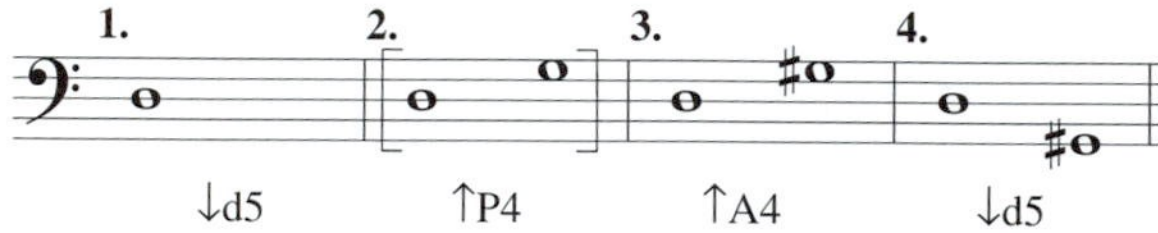

DRILL #6 (INTERVALS) Place the second note of each interval, all descending, on the staff.

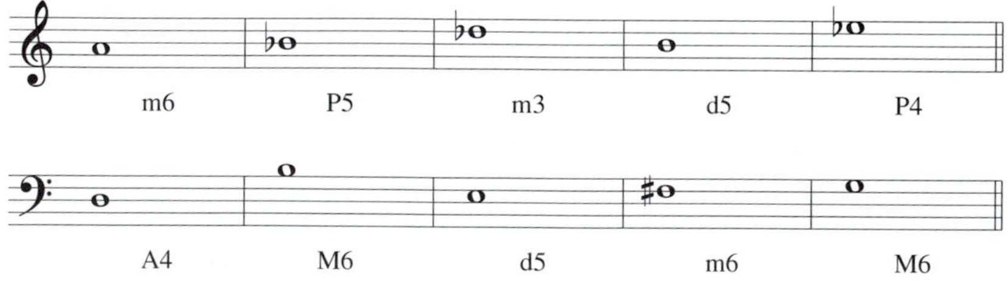

In Appendix E: Answers to Drill #6 are given.

Compound Intervals

Intervals larger than an octave are known as *compound intervals.* Except when the distinction is necessary, a compound interval is usually referred to by the name of its simple form; for example, a tenth is a third plus an octave but is often simply called a third.

FIGURE 2.15 *Compound Intervals*

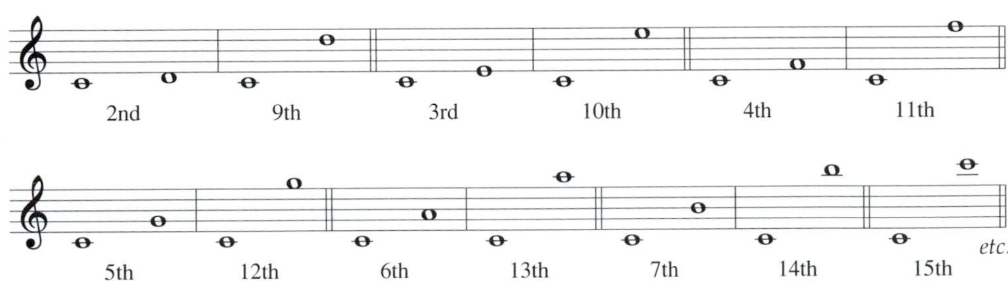

Consonance and Dissonance

These are subjective terms. *Consonance* is supposed to mean a "pleasant sound," and *dissonance* is supposed to mean an "unpleasant sound." Theorists have argued about which sounds are which as long as there has been music in two or more voices. About 1300, Franco of Cologne described the M6 and the m6 as dissonances, and M and m thirds were at best imperfect consonances.

By commonly accepted definition, consonances in the Baroque, Classical, and Romantic periods (ca. 1600–ca. 1900) are the perfect intervals and their inversions, and the major and minor thirds and their inversions (except for one particular use of the P4, described in Chapter 9). All other intervals are dissonances, though in our century many hardly seem to sound that way. Still, this is a valuable distinction for study because it provides reasons for the ways some chord tones are handled as well as an explanation of any tones that are not part of a chord. A chord containing only the "consonant" intervals above its root (see the following section entitled "Chords") is considered to be a consonant chord. All other vertical structures are termed "dissonant."

A more liberal interpretation avoids placing intervals or chords in specific categories. Intervals can be listed linearly, where any given interval is more consonant than the one to its right, or more dissonant than the one to its left, but no interval is specifically consonant or dissonant.

More consonant ⟷ More dissonant

P8 P5 P4 M3 m6 m3 M6 M2 m7 m2 M7 tritone

Music of the twentieth century generally disregards any distinction between consonance and dissonance, except perhaps in a relative way as above.

Chords

A *chord* is a group of notes sounding simultaneously or in close succession. In our study of harmony, we will be particularly interested in those chords built in thirds. Such chords are called *tertian chords,* and music based on tertian chords is known as *tertian harmony.*

When chord members sound simultaneously, a *block chord* is produced. Chord members may also sound in succession, resulting in a *broken* or *arpeggiated chord.* In addition, a limitless variety of configurations can occur, two of which are shown in Figure 2.16*c* and *d.*

FIGURE 2.16 *Chord Configurations*

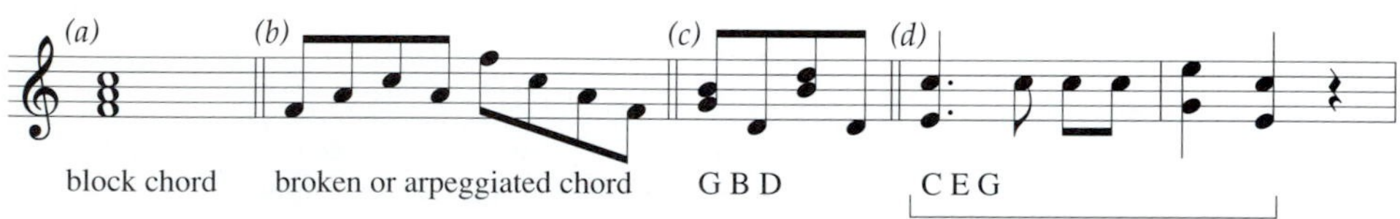

Triads

The simplest chord is the *triad,* a three-note group formed by two consecutive thirds. The lowest note is called the *root,* above which are the *third* and the *fifth.* Since both major and minor thirds exist, four different combinations are possible.

1. A *major triad* consists of a major third and a perfect fifth above the root, or a major third and a minor third from the root upward.
2. A *minor triad* consists of a minor third and a perfect fifth above the root, or a minor third and a major third from the root upward.
3. A *diminished triad* consists of a minor third and a diminished fifth above the root, or two minor thirds from the root upward.
4. An *augmented triad* consists of a major third and an augmented fifth above the root, or two major thirds from the root upward.

FIGURE 2.17 *Triad Types*

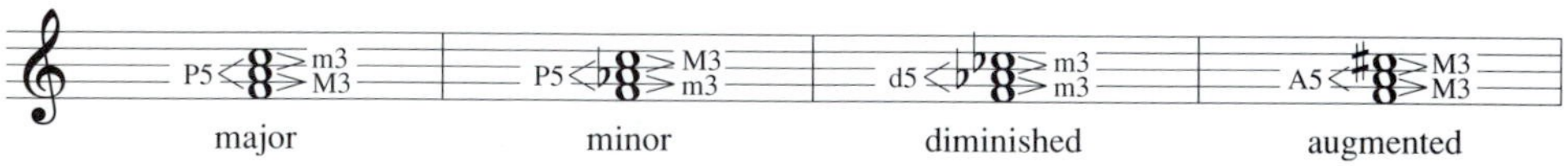

Triads in a Key

Triads can be built above each note of any major or minor scale. When only scale tones are used, any note or combination of notes, including triads, is called *diatonic.*

When a tone of a scale is modified by an accidental, it becomes an *altered tone,* and the chord in which it is found is an *altered chord,* except that ♯6̂ and ♯7̂ in minor are considered diatonic.

A triad in a key is identified by the scale-step number of its root and expressed by a roman numeral.

FIGURE 2.18 *Triad Identification*

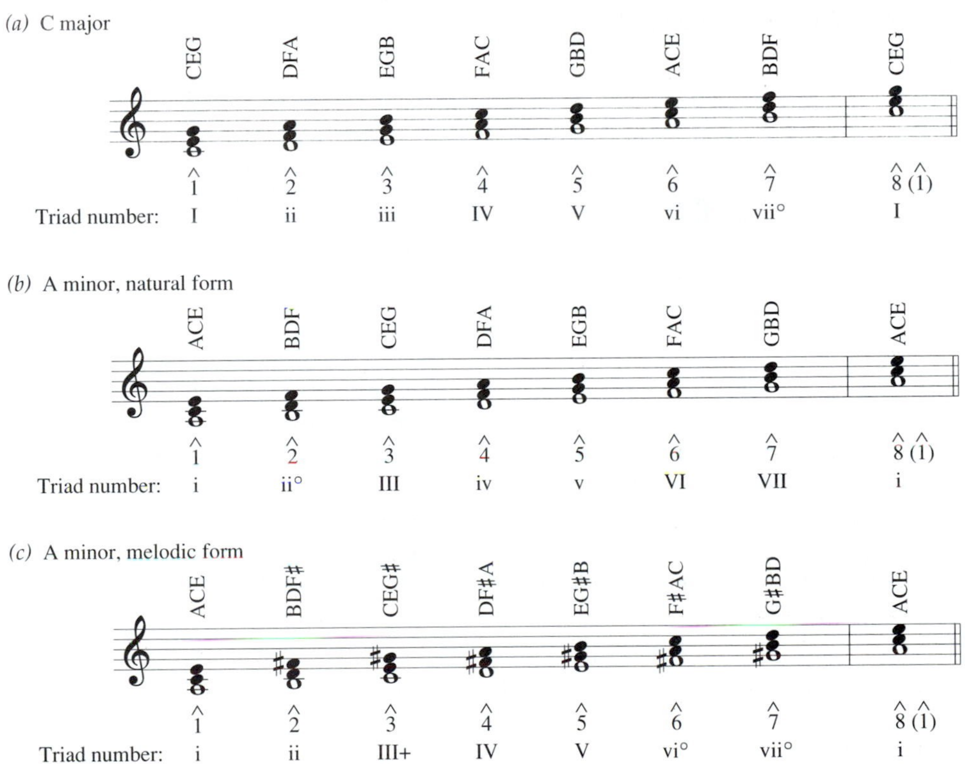

The roman numeral not only designates the scale-step location of the root of the triad but also indicates triad construction.

> Large numeral = major triad (I in C major = C E G)
>
> Small numeral = minor triad (ii in C major = D F A)
>
> Small numeral with small ° = diminished triad (vii° in C major = B D F)
>
> Large numeral with + = augmented triad (III+ in A minor = C E G♯)

Thus, IV indicates a major triad built on the fourth scale degree, and iv indicates a minor triad built on the fourth scale degree. A triad in a key may also be designated by the name of the scale step on which it is built; for example: I = tonic triad; V = dominant triad.

Chords Larger Than a Triad

The presentation of these chords at this time is meant only for reference. Of the chords listed, the V^7 in major and minor, the ii^7 in major, and the ii^{ø7} in minor are included for study in *Elementary Harmony.* The remaining chords will be found in *Advanced Harmony.*

Like triads, these chords are built in thirds. They are named according to the interval from the root to the final note in the series of thirds. Figure 2.19 shows all the possibilities above C. The thirteenth chord is the largest possible diatonic chord, since the next third higher is the same pitch as the root.

FIGURE 2.19 *Chords Larger Than a Triad*

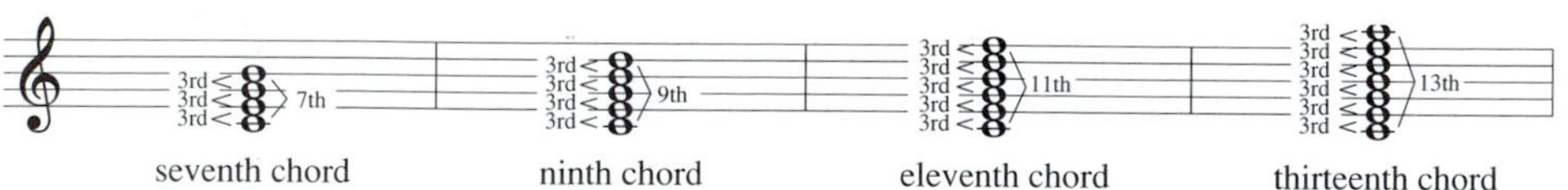

Seventh Chords

Of the chords in Figure 2.19, only the seventh chord is commonly used. The use of seventh chords is important because the "dissonant" interval of the seventh provides a necessary contrast to the "purity" of the triads. Seventh chords are identified by the type of triad plus the quality of the seventh above the root. For example, a major triad plus a minor seventh is called a major–minor seventh chord. But shorter names are commonly used. Commonly used names, followed by the full name in parentheses, are listed in Figure 2.20.

FIGURE 2.20 *Names of Seventh Chords*

Triad type	*Interval (root to 7th)*	*Seventh chord name (Abbr.)*	*Example in C*
Major	m7	Major–minor seventh chord[2] (Mm7)	V^7 G B D F
Minor	m7	Minor seventh chord (m7) (Minor–minor seventh chord)	ii^7 D F A C
Major	M7	Major seventh chord (M7) (Major–major seventh chord)	I^7 C E G B
Diminished	d7	Diminished seventh chord (°7) (Diminished–diminished seventh chord)	vii^{o7} B D F A♭
Diminished	m7	Half-diminished seventh chord (^{ø}7) (Diminished–minor seventh chord)	vii^{ø7} B D F A
Augmented		[rare]	

[2]The major–minor seventh chord is often casually called a "dominant seventh" because it is frequently built on the dominant of the key or used as a "secondary dominant," the same chord relationship as that between dominant and tonic, but applied to chords other than the tonic (see Chapter 18).

FIGURE 2.21 *Diatonic Seventh Chords*

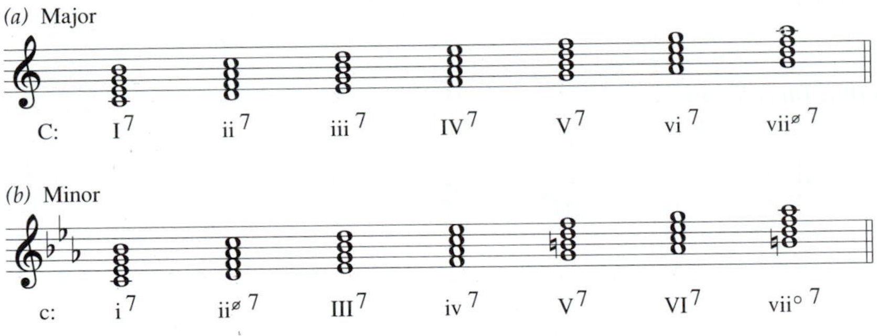

Other seventh chords in minor caused by the variable sixth and seventh scale degrees are used only infrequently and will be discussed when the need arises.

Inversion of Chords

Chords, like intervals, can be inverted, changing their intervallic content and the way they sound but without changing their spellings.

Lowest note	*Inversion*
1	(Root position)
3	First
5	Second
7	Third (seventh chords only)

Figure 2.22 shows the inversions of the D major triad and the A dominant seventh chord (I and V^7) in D major.

FIGURE 2.22 *Chords in Inversion*

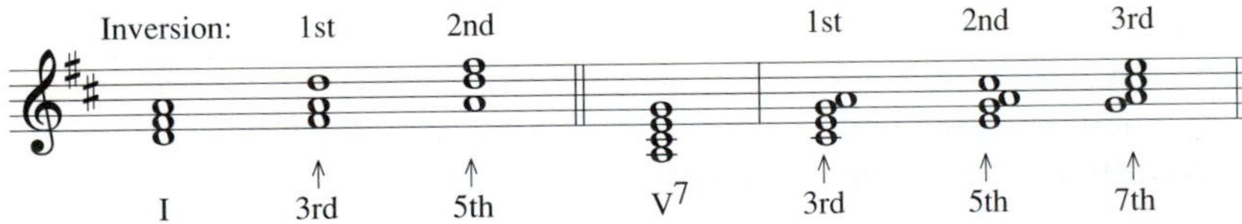

Figured Bass

A symbol indicating the inversion of a chord can be included with its roman numeral. Although "1" for first inversion, "2" for second inversion, and so forth, would seem logical, we use instead figured bass symbols. These are arabic numbers which, in a music score, appear below the lowest note to indicate the intervals above it. Thus, if we see $^6_4$ below the note G, we know that above G is a sixth (E) and a fourth (C). The complete chord, therefore, is C E G in second inversion. Its complete symbol in C major is I^6_4.

FIGURE 2.23 *Figured Bass Symbols*[3]

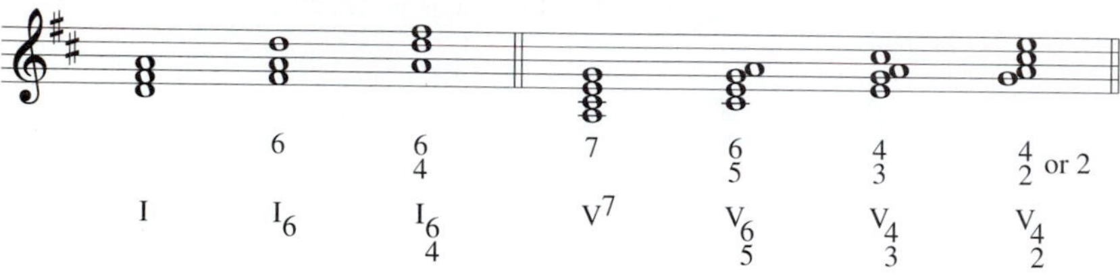

When chord members are chromatically altered, alterations are indicated in these ways:

1. A ♯, ♭, or ♮ standing alone refers to the third above the bass note.
2. A number preceded by a ♭ lowers the note one half step.
3. A number preceded by a ♯ (such as ♯6) or found with a slash (such as 6̸) indicates that the interval above the bass is to be raised one half step.

FIGURE 2.24

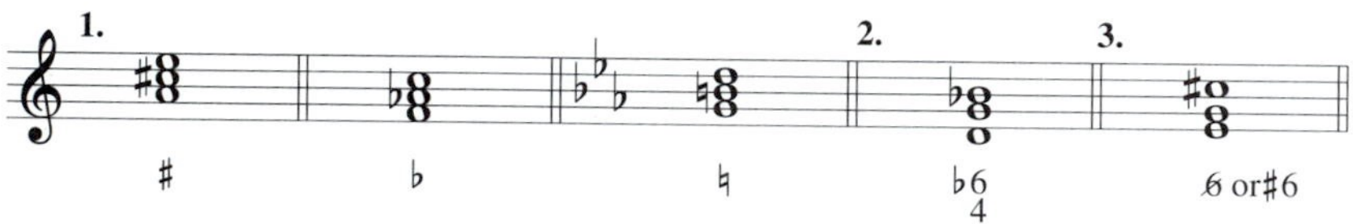

Performance of music using figured bass was a common practice in the Baroque period (ca. 1600–1750). A fuller description of figured bass with examples in music score will be found in an article on page 202. In the study of harmony, we will encounter frequent use of figured bass as a valuable pedagogical tool.

DRILL #7 (CHORD IDENTIFICATION) From the following music example: (*a*) find a chord that matches the symbol and place its number in the blank, and (*b*) find the chord that requires the given figured bass symbol and place its number in the blank.

[3]A complete figured bass symbol would account for all the notes above the lowest note. The shortened symbols in Figure 2.23 are generally used, with the remaining numbers being understood. For triads, the complete numbers are (used vertically): root in bass—5, 3; first inversion—6, 3; second inversion—6, 4. For seventh chords: root in bass—7, 5, 3; first inversion—6, 5, 3; second inversion—6, 4, 3; third inversion—6, 4, 2. When used under a bass line, any of these numbers may appear as circumstances dictate, as discussed in later chapters.

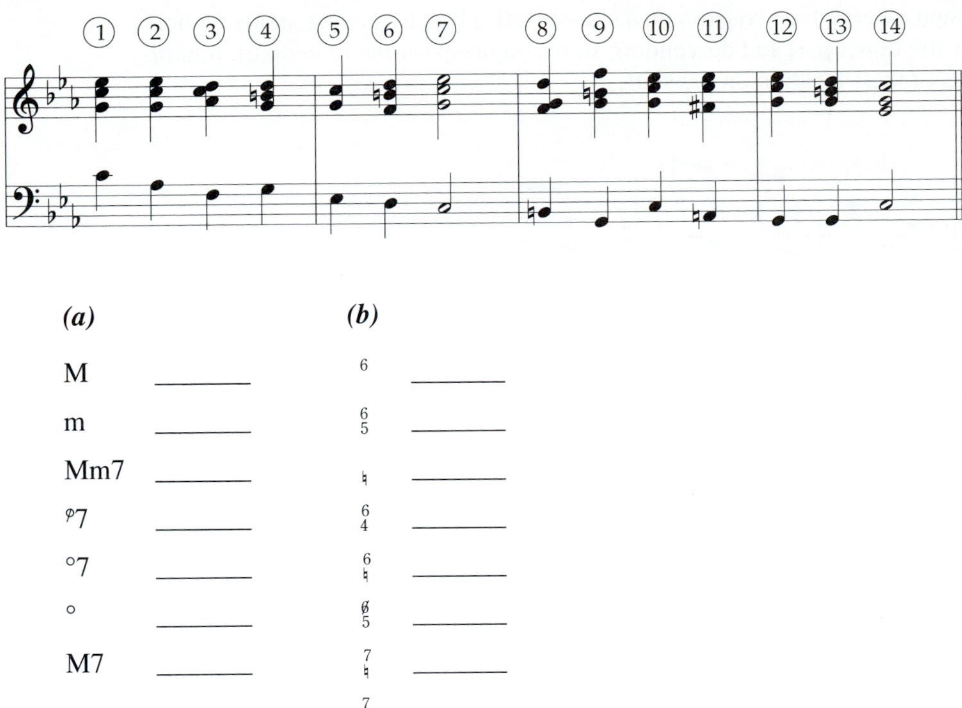

Staff Notation

For clear and legible notation, certain practices are universally used. To become completely proficient, make it a habit to carefully observe how music is notated in the scores you are studying and practicing. The following list presents the most common notational practices.

1. *The Single Note.* A note is drawn with one, two, or three parts:

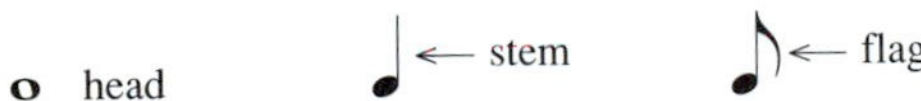

An ascending stem is found on the right side of the head:
A descending stem is found on the left side of the head:

2. *Notes on the Staff.*

   a. When writing notes for a single part (one voice or one instrument) on the staff, place descending stems on notes found on the middle line or above and ascending stems on notes below the middle line.

b. When writing for two parts on a single staff, place ascending stems on notes for the upper part and descending stems on notes for the lower part, regardless of their location on the staff.

c. To indicate two parts performing the same pitch on a single staff (unisons), use a single note head with both ascending and descending stems. For two whole notes in unison, use two overlapping whole notes.

3. *Notes Using Ledger Lines or Spaces.* Above the staff, do not write ledger lines above the highest note. Below the staff, do not write ledger lines below the lowest note.

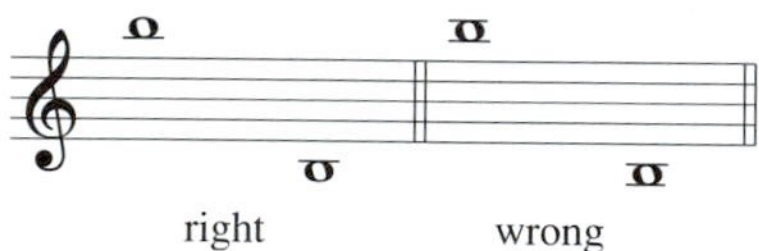

4. *Dotted Notes.* When the note head is in a space, the dot is found in the same space. When the note is on a line, the dot is usually found in the space above, though it is sometimes in the space below.

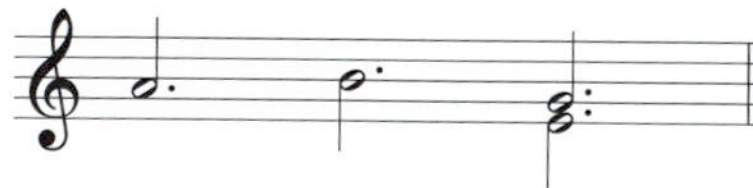

5. *Vertical Arrangement of Notes.* All notes sounding simultaneously must be written so that a line drawn through the note heads will be perpendicular to the lines of the staff.

6. *Horizontal Arrangement of Notes.* Space between notes should be in approximate proportion to their time values.

7. *Placement of Accidentals.* Accidentals are placed directly before the affected note and on the same line or space as the note head.

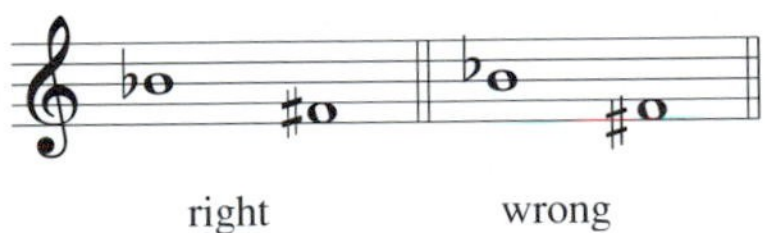

The effect of an accidental lasts until the following bar line, unless it is cancelled by a natural sign or the note is tied into the following measure or measures.

BASICS QUIZ #2

1. Write the second note of these ascending intervals.

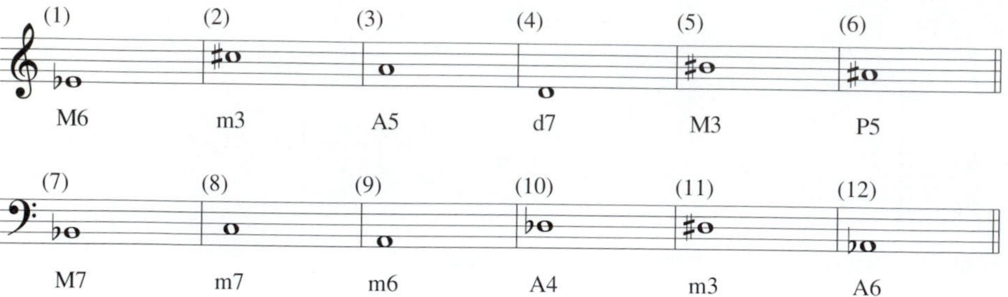

2. Name the inversion of each interval.

a. M3 _______ *e.* M6 _______

b. P5 _______ *f.* M2 _______

c. M7 _______ *g.* d5 _______

d. A4 _______ *h.* A2 _______

3. Write the second note of these descending intervals.

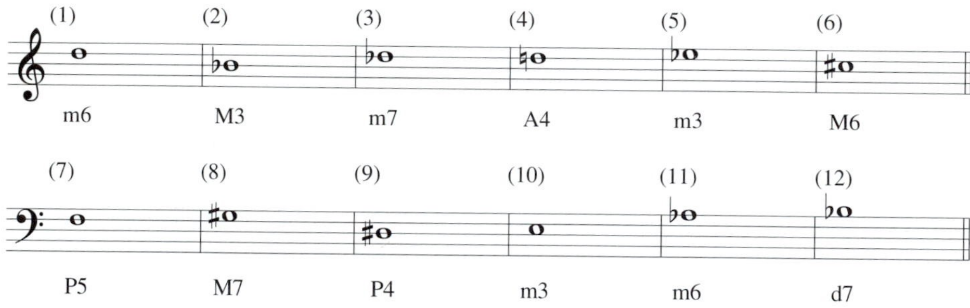

4. Name each triad: M, m, d, or A.

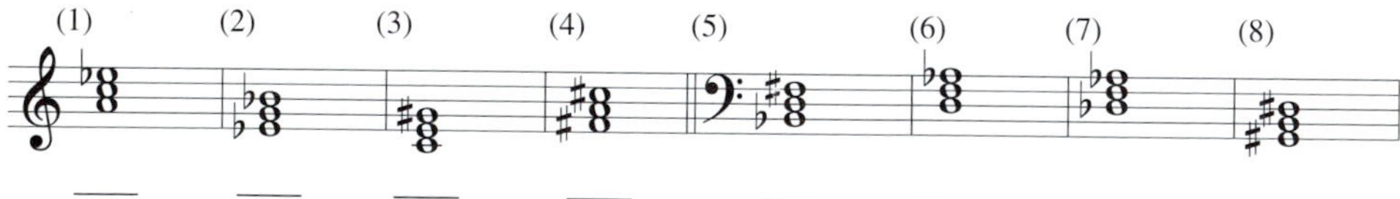

5. In D major, place the correct roman numeral under each chord.

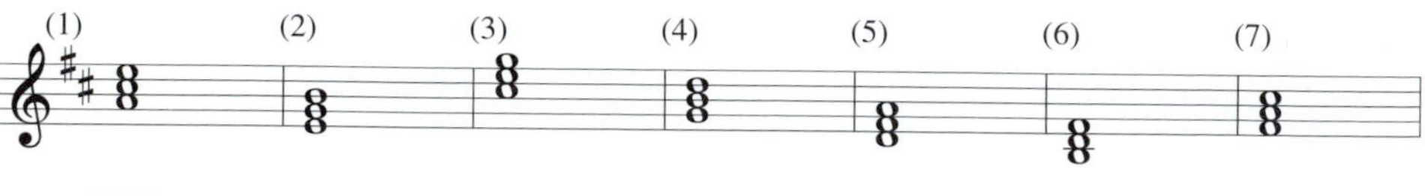

6. In F minor, place the correct roman numeral under each chord.

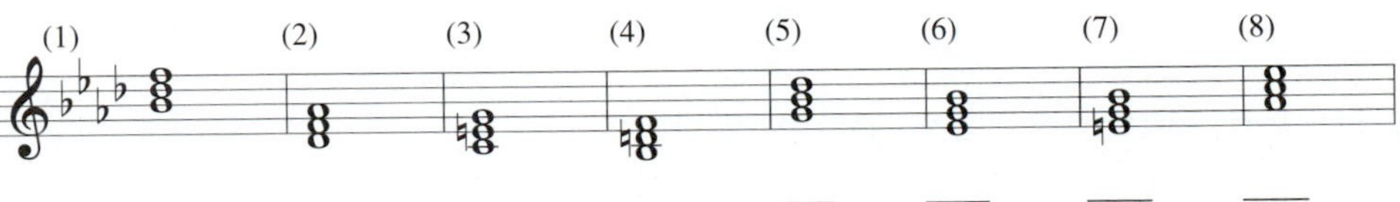

In Appendix E: Answers to all questions in Basics Quiz #2 are given.

ARTICLE #1

Pitch Notation from Earliest Times

We know that music existed in ancient times from sources such as pictures, artifacts, and literary works (Psalm 150 from the Bible, for example). However, because there was no music notation in those times, we will never know exactly how ancient music sounded.

The earliest known notation is that of pre-Christian Greece, in which letters of the alphabet were used to represent pitches. Because very little of this notation survives, we know only a little about the sound of their music, despite the fact that the Greeks were prolific in writing about music.

The beginnings of our present notation date back to approximately the eighth century A.D., when the object of notation was to indicate pitch levels and directions in singing the chants of the church service. This was done with signs, called *neumes,* placed directly over the words of the chant. The result was a vague indication of the movement of the melody—helpful, probably, only to someone already acquainted with the melody.

Neumes, circa 8th century

It occurred to someone in the tenth century that pitch could be indicated by drawing a line indicating a certain pitch (usually F) and placing neumes on, above, and below it. Staves with more lines followed, with four- and five-line staves appearing in the thirteenth century. By that time, neumes had evolved into note shapes more readily recognizable as precursors of our present notation. Notation was all black until the fifteenth century, when white notation appeared with the black to form a system that was used until approximately 1600 (see "Early Rhythmic Notation" on page 56).

One-line staff, circa 10th century

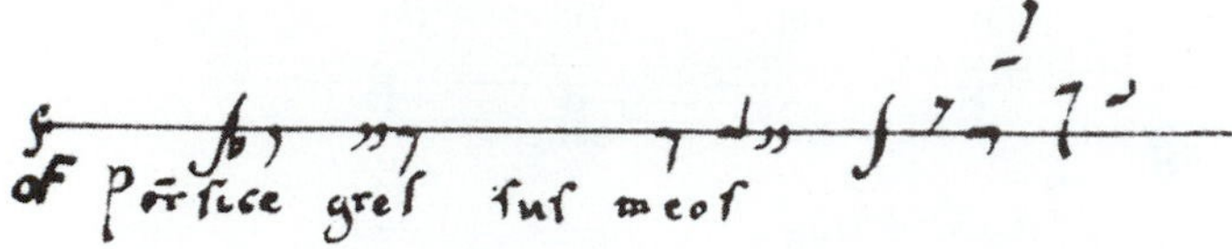

Two-line staff, circa 11th century

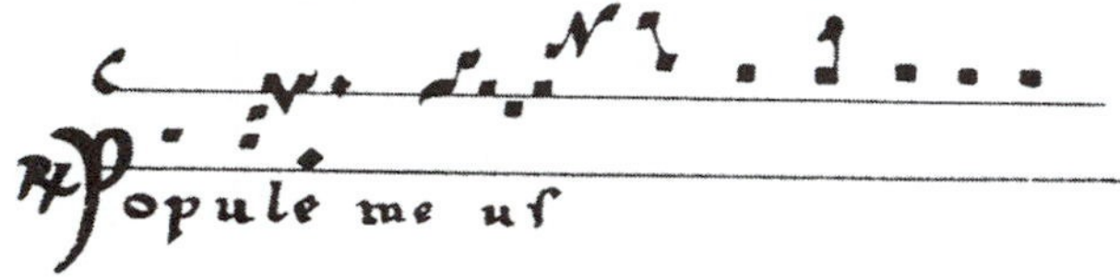

Four-line staff, circa 13th century

Five-line staff with white notation, 16th century

Clef signs developed from the need to designate the pitch names of the lines and spaces of the staff. The earliest clefs were representations of the letter names needed. These changed over the centuries to the forms used today.

Clefs

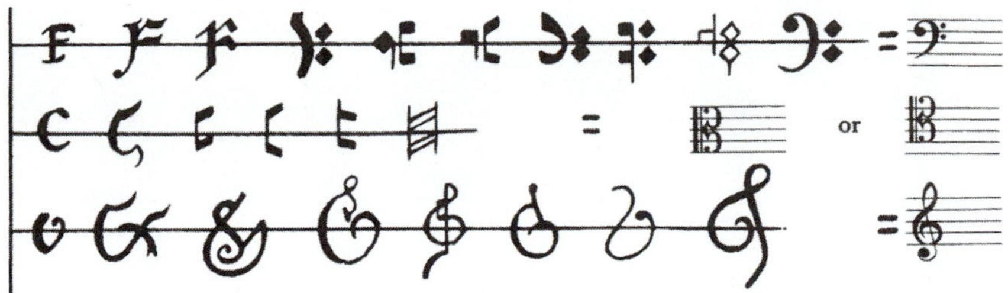

From Music Notation: A Manual of Modern Practice *by Gardner Read, Second Edition (Taplinger/Crescendo, 1979). © 1969 by Crescendo Publishing Company. Reprinted by permission.*

From 1600 to the present century, notation has undergone few developments. Contemporary composers express new ideas with a variety of notational devices, including conventional notation displayed in unconventional ways, new notational symbols accompanied by their own written directions, and graphic representations of the sounds the composer wishes to have produced.

The wide variety of notational devices, too numerous to be shown here, will be considered in *Advanced Harmony: Theory and Practice,* third edition. Further information can also be found in these texts: Reginald Smith Brindle, *The New Music* (London: Oxford University Press, 1975); Kurt Stone, *Music Notation in the Twentieth Century* (New York: W. W. Norton & Co., Inc., 1980); and Gardner Read, *Music Notation: A Manual of Modern Practice* (Taplinger/Crescendo, 1979).

3

Basics III

duration; time signatures

Note and Rest Values

Durations of pitch or silence may be indicated by characteristic note shapes and rest signs.

FIGURE 3.1 *Notes and Rests*[1]

Note		Value	Rest	
Double Whole Note	𝅜	2	Double Whole Rest	
Whole Note	𝅝	1	Whole Rest	
Half Note	𝅗𝅥	1/2	Half Rest	
Quarter Note	♩	1/4	Quarter Rest	𝄽
Eighth Note	♪	1/8	Eighth Rest	𝄾
Sixteenth Note	𝅘𝅥𝅯	1/16	Sixteenth Rest	𝄿
Thirty–second Note	𝅘𝅥𝅰	1/32	Thirty–second Rest	𝅀
Sixty–fourth Note	𝅘𝅥𝅱	1/64	Sixty–fourth Rest	𝅁

[1]The double whole note and rest are little used in post-sixteenth-century music. In many older or foreign editions of music, the quarter rest is written as 𝄾 (opposite of the eighth rest, 𝄾).

These notes do not indicate any specific duration of sound. Rather, their fractional names indicate relative durations: Any note value is twice as long as the next smaller value (𝅘𝅥𝅮 = 𝅘𝅥𝅯 + 𝅘𝅥𝅯) or half as long as the next higher value (𝅘𝅥 = one half of 𝅗𝅥).

Placing a dot after a note increases its value by one half—for example, 𝅘𝅥. = 𝅘𝅥‿𝅘𝅥𝅮; 𝅗𝅥. = 𝅗𝅥‿𝅘𝅥. (The curved line is a *tie;* tied notes are performed as a single note value.) Although rests may be dotted, it is common practice to use two signs—for example, 𝄽𝄾 instead of 𝄽. When a note is dotted, it is three times longer than the next lower undotted value (𝅘𝅥. = 𝅘𝅥𝅮𝅘𝅥𝅮𝅘𝅥𝅮); or an undotted note is one third the length of the next higher dotted value (𝅘𝅥 = one third of 𝅗𝅥.).

DRILL #1 Fill in each blank with the appropriate note value or values.

		Division of 2		*Division of 4*				*Division of 3*
(1)	𝅘𝅥	= 𝅘𝅥𝅮𝅘𝅥𝅮	=	𝅘𝅥𝅯𝅘𝅥𝅯𝅘𝅥𝅯𝅘𝅥𝅯	(6)	𝅘𝅥.	=	________
(2)	𝅘𝅥𝅮	= ________	=	________	(7)	𝅘𝅥𝅮.	=	________
(3)	___	= 𝅗𝅥 𝅗𝅥	=	________	(8)	___	=	𝅘𝅥 𝅘𝅥 𝅘𝅥
(4)	___	= ________	=	𝅘𝅥𝅰𝅘𝅥𝅰𝅘𝅥𝅰𝅘𝅥𝅰	(9)	𝅘𝅥𝅯.	=	________
(5)	___	= 𝅘𝅥 𝅘𝅥	=	________	(10)	___	=	𝅗𝅥 𝅗𝅥 𝅗𝅥

Tempo

How long a sound or a rest is actually held can either be suggested or be specified by a *tempo (time) marking*. Most music before 1750 included no indication at all. It was assumed that a musician would understand from the character of the music itself how fast or how slow the music should be performed.

The first tempo indications were Italian words placed at the beginning of a piece, words such as *presto* (very fast), *allegro* (joyfully), *andante* (rather slow), and *largo* (very slow). Similar indications in other languages soon followed. As you can see, these words indicate tempo only in a general way.

To indicate a specific duration, a marking such as M.M. 𝅘𝅥 = 60 often appears, meaning in this case that a quarter note has a duration of one second. M.M. stands for *Maelzel's metronome,* a ticking mechanism that Johann Maelzel claimed to have invented about 1816, and that can be set at numerous points between 40 and 208 beats per minute. Beethoven was the first composer to take advantage of metronome markings.

Although the metronome provides exact durations, exclusive reliance on it produces only mechanical results. Its use must be tempered by the performer's insight regarding the best artistic expression of the composer's ideas.

The Beat

The *beat* is a measurement that divides time into units of equal length, commonly moving you to tap your foot or your finger while listening to music. To illustrate this concept, sing "Jingle Bells" and tap as indicated in Figure 3.2. In so doing, you are dividing time into equal units, or beats, regardless of the staff notation used.

FIGURE 3.2 *Demonstration of Beats*

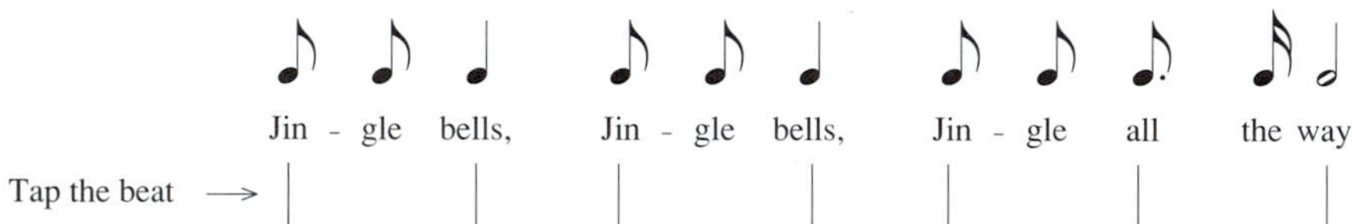

Grouping of Beats

As you listen for beats, as in Figure 3.2, you will note that they tend to group themselves, with one beat assuming more importance than the others. To experience this, sing "Jingle Bells" again. You should feel a grouping of two, a strong beat followed by a weaker beat (Figure 3.3*a*). Follow this by singing "America" (Figure 3.3*b*). Do you feel a three-beat grouping?

FIGURE 3.3 *Beat Groupings*

(*a*) Jin-gle bells, Jin-gle bells,

(*b*) My coun-try, 'tis of thee,

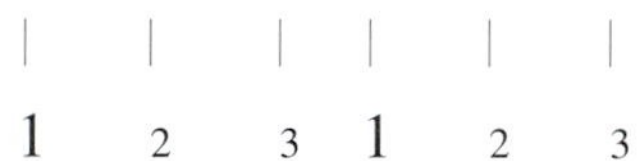

Groupings of four, commonly used in music composition, are more difficult to illustrate, since each grouping tends to sound like two groupings of two, although the third beat receives somewhat less emphasis than the first: 1 2 3 4.

Varieties of the Beat (Simple and Compound)

Two varieties of the beat exist: *simple beat* and *compound beat.* To illustrate the simple beat, sing "Jingle Bells" (Figure 3.2) once more. Notice that each beat has two divisions, easily demonstrated by making *two* taps instead of one at each beat. Then try tapping beats with the right hand while tapping the two simple divisions of each beat with the left hand.

FIGURE 3.4 *Tapping Simple Divisions*

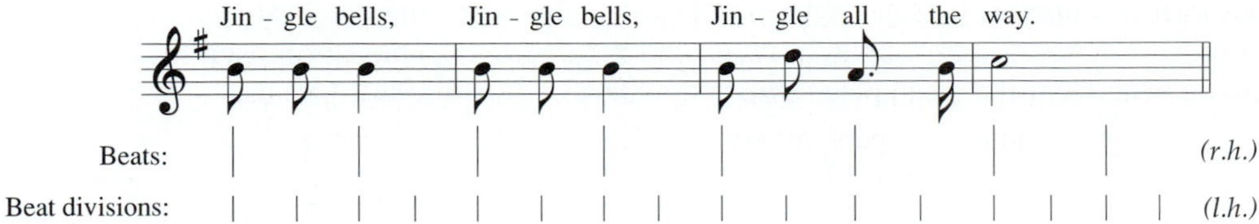

The compound beat can be illustrated in the same way. Sing "When Johnny Comes Marching Home Again" (Figure 3.5). First listen for the beats and tap them. They are in groups of two. Then listen for the beat divisions and tap them. This time, there are *three* divisions for each beat.

FIGURE 3.5 *Tapping Compound Divisions*

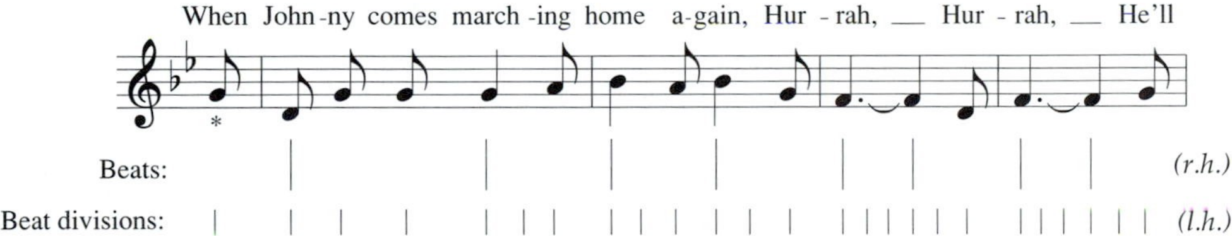

*The first beat of a measure is known as a *downbeat*. A preceding beat or part of a beat is an *upbeat*.

In summary, beats tend to group themselves in patterns of two, three, or four. In each pattern, the beat division may be either two or three.

FIGURE 3.6 *Beat Groupings and Beat Divisions*

<table>
<tr><td></td><td>Duple</td><td>Triple</td><td>Quadruple</td></tr>
<tr><td></td><td>1 2</td><td>1 2 3</td><td>1 2 3 4</td></tr>
<tr><td>Simple division</td><td>ǀ ı ǀ ı
> ></td><td>ǀ ı ǀ ı ǀ ı
> > ></td><td>ǀ ı ǀ ı ǀ ı ǀ ı
> > > ></td></tr>
<tr><td>Compound division</td><td>ǀ ı ı ǀ ı ı
> ></td><td>ǀ ı ı ǀ ı ı ǀ ı ı
> > ></td><td>ǀ ı ı ǀ ı ı ǀ ı ı ǀ ı ı
> > > ></td></tr>
</table>

Time Signature (Meter Signature)

A time signature consists of two numbers, one above the other (for example, $\frac{2}{4}$), at the beginning of a composition. It tells us

1. the number of beats in each grouping;
2. the division of the beat, simple or compound;
3. the notation to be used.

Simple Time Music in which the beat is divisible into two parts is said to be in *simple time*. The numerator (upper number) 2, 3, or 4 indicates the grouping of beats, and the denominator (lower number) indicates the simple note value receiving one beat.

In Figure 3.4, beats are grouped in twos, and the quarter ($\frac{1}{4}$) note is chosen to represent one beat. Hence, we can place a time signature of $\frac{2}{4}$ on the staff because

$\frac{1}{4} + \frac{1}{4} = \frac{2}{4}$, or 2 (beats) times $\frac{1}{4} = \frac{2}{4}$.[2]

The time signature appears immediately after the key signature on the staff. When notes are placed on the staff, each beat grouping is separated by a *bar line (bar)*. The distance between two bar lines is a *measure,* and a *double bar* marks the end of a composition or the end of a major section of a composition.

FIGURE 3.7 *Bar Lines and Measures*

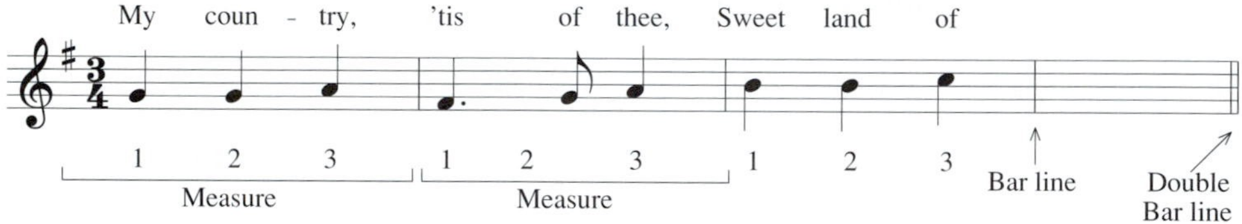

In simple time, any simple note value may be chosen to represent the beat—for example, a half note ($\frac{1}{2}$): $\frac{1}{2} + \frac{1}{2} = \frac{2}{2}$, or 2 (beats) times $\frac{1}{2} = \frac{2}{2}$. Notice in Figure 3.8 that the pattern below the staff is identical to that in Figure 3.4. This change in notation does *not* affect performance, assuming the duration of the beat is the same in each case.

FIGURE 3.8 *The Half Note as the Beat*

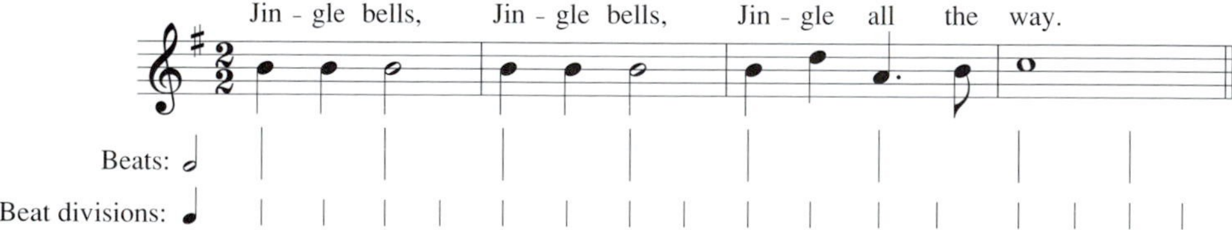

You will observe from Figure 3.9, a table of simple time signatures, that the numerators of simple time signatures are 2, 3, and 4.

2 = duple simple time (meter)

3 = triple simple time

4 = quadruple simple time

[2]The horizontal line is used for fractions but not in a time signature. Though they are arithmetical terms, "numerator" and "denominator" are convenient to describe members of the time signature.

FIGURE 3.9 *Simple Time Signatures*

Beat note	*2 beats per measure (Duple)*	*3 beats per measure (Triple)*	*4 beats per measure (Quadruple)*
(1/1)	2/1	3/1	4/1
(1/2)	*2/2 or ₵	*3/2	*4/2
(1/4)	*2/4	*3/4	*4/4 or C
(1/8)	2/8	*3/8	*4/8
(1/16)	2/16	3/16	4/16
(1/32)	2/32	3/32	4/32

* indicates the most commonly used time signatures

DRILL #2 Fill in the blanks, using number 1 as a guide.

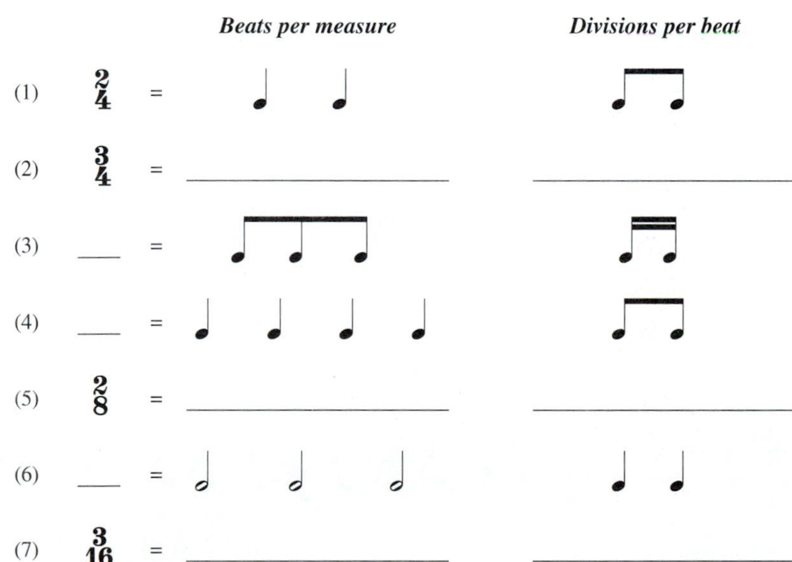

Compound Time Music using compound beat values (notes with three divisions) is said to be in *compound time.* The numerators 6, 9, and 12 also represent 2, 3, and 4

beats per measure, as we will see by working out the time signature exactly as we did for simple time.

First, repeat the tapping exercise in Figure 3.5. Sing the tune and tap the beats. Result: beat groupings of two. Next, tap the beat divisions. Result: three divisions for each beat.

Next, choose a note to represent the beat. Only a dotted note can have three divisions. Choosing a commonly used dotted-note value, the dotted quarter note (♩.), we find its fractional value to be $\frac{3}{8}$. The time signature must be $\frac{6}{8}$ because

$$\frac{3}{8} + \frac{3}{8} = \frac{6}{8}, \text{ or 2 (beats) times } \frac{3}{8} = \frac{6}{8}.$$

Confusion about compound time signatures stems from the fact that the numerator, instead of indicating how many beats per measure, actually shows the number of *beat divisions* per measure, and the denominator indicates the *note value of the beat division,* as shown in Figure 3.10*a* and on the staff in Figure 3.10*b*.

FIGURE 3.10 *Compound Time Signature ($\frac{6}{8}$ Time)*

(a)

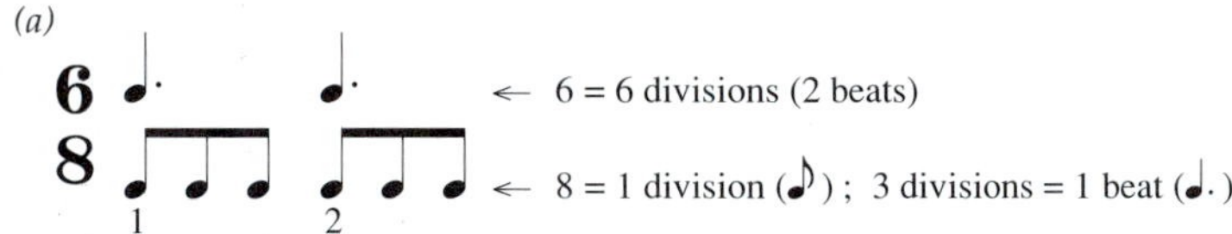

(b)

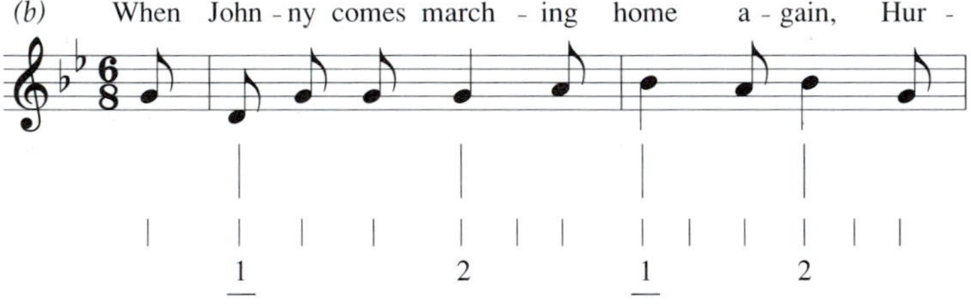

Again, we could have chosen a different note value to represent the beat—for example, a ♪.: $\frac{3}{16} + \frac{3}{16} = \frac{6}{16}$. The pattern below Figure 3.11 is identical to that in Figure 3.5.

FIGURE 3.11 *Example of $\frac{6}{16}$ Time Signature*

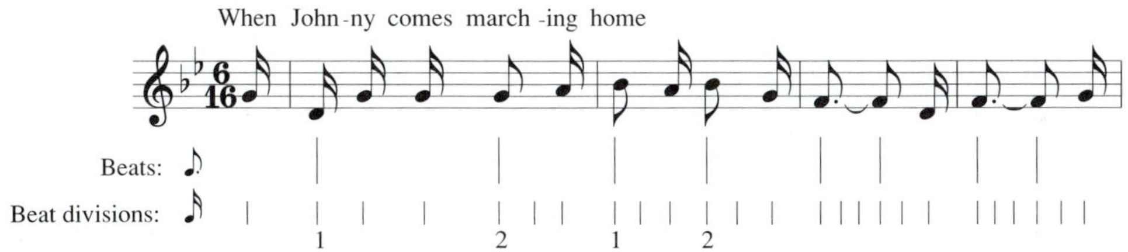

Observe from the table of Compound Time Signatures in Figure 3.12 that the numerators of signatures are 6, 9, and 12, representing 2, 3, and 4 beats per measure.

6 = duple compound time
9 = triple compound time
12 = quadruple compound time

FIGURE 3.12 *Compound Time Signatures*

Beat note		*2 beats per measure (Duple)*	*3 beats per measure (Triple)*	*4 beats per measure (Quadruple)*
𝅝.	(3/2)	6/2	9/2	12/2
𝅗𝅥.	(3/4)	*6/4	*9/4	12/4
♩.	(3/8)	*6/8	*9/8	*12/8
♪.	(3/16)	*6/16	*9/16	*12/16
𝅘𝅥𝅯.	(3/32)	6/32	3/32	12/32

* indicates the most commonly used time signatures

DRILL #3 Fill in the blanks, as in Drill #2 (page 45).

			Beats per measure	*Divisions per beat*
(1)	6/8	=	________	________
(2)	9/8	=	________	________
(3)	___	=	𝅗𝅥. 𝅗𝅥.	♩ ♩ ♩
(4)	12/8	=	________	________
(5)	6/16	=	________	________
(6)	___	=	♪. ♪. ♪.	𝅘𝅥𝅯𝅘𝅥𝅯𝅘𝅥𝅯
(7)	___	=	𝅗𝅥. 𝅗𝅥. 𝅗𝅥. 𝅗𝅥.	♩ ♩ ♩

An example of a better but little used way of writing compound time signatures is seen in Figure 3.13, in which the composer has used 2/𝅗𝅥. instead of 6/4. In the same way, the common time signature 6/8 would be written 2/♩. and 2/4 would be written 2/♩. If all time signatures, both simple and compound, were written in this manner, interpretation of any time signature would be much easier.

FIGURE 3.13

Other Interpretations of Time Signatures

In any time signature the upper number always indicates how many of the note values expressed by the lower number will be found in one measure. Although interpretations of time signatures such as those just presented are generally useful, there are occasions when a very fast or a very slow tempo requires a different interpretation.

In a Fast Tempo In music in a fast tempo with a signature of 4/4, there may actually be two half-note beats rather than four beats per measure. This is often indicated by a metronome marking, such as 𝅗𝅥 = 88 as used by Beethoven in Figure 3.14.

FIGURE 3.14

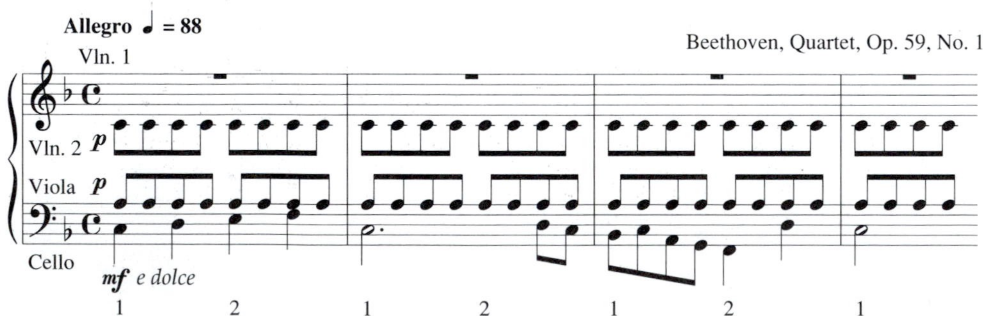

When a fast tempo is indicated but no metronome marking is present, any decision to interpret 4/4 or **c** as two beats in a measure must depend upon a subjective evaluation of the composer's intent. In the case of many well-known works, such interpretations have become traditional, as can be heard in the final movement of Mendelssohn's

Symphony No. 4 (*Italian*), Op. 90 (tempo marking *Presto*), or in the final movement of Tchaikovsky's Symphony No. 4, Op. 64 (tempo marking *Allegro con fuoco*).

Similarly, a fast tempo with a signature of $\frac{3}{4}$ or $\frac{3}{8}$ is often performed with one beat per measure. In Figure 3.15, each dotted half note receives one beat with a division of three quarter notes. The aural effect is that of compound time, one beat per measure.

FIGURE 3.15

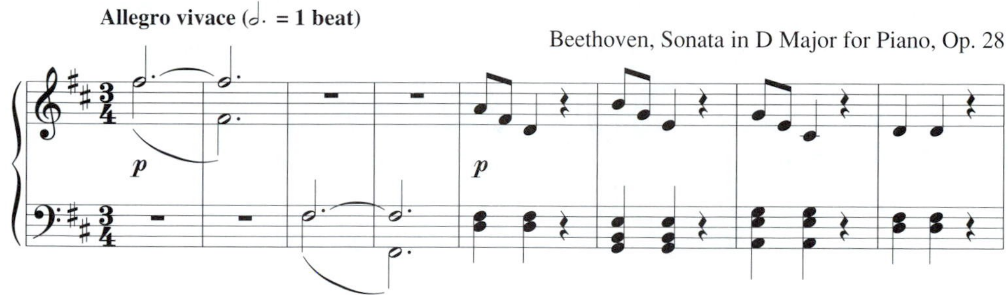

Why did Beethoven write this example in $\frac{3}{4}$, rather than using the duple compound time signature of $\frac{6}{4}$ 𝅗𝅥. 𝅗𝅥. | 𝅗𝅥. 𝅗𝅥. | ? Composers use $\frac{3}{4}$ instead of $\frac{6}{4}$ (or $\frac{3}{8}$ instead of $\frac{6}{8}$) in those fast tempi in which every third division has an equally strong accent like that in Figure 3.15, in contrast to $\frac{6}{4}$ (or $\frac{6}{8}$) in which the first division is stronger than the fourth:

The same is true of the popular tune "Take Me Out to the Ball Game," in which the composer has used $\frac{3}{4}$ instead of a duple compound signature to emphasize the strong accent on each third division.

FIGURE 3.16

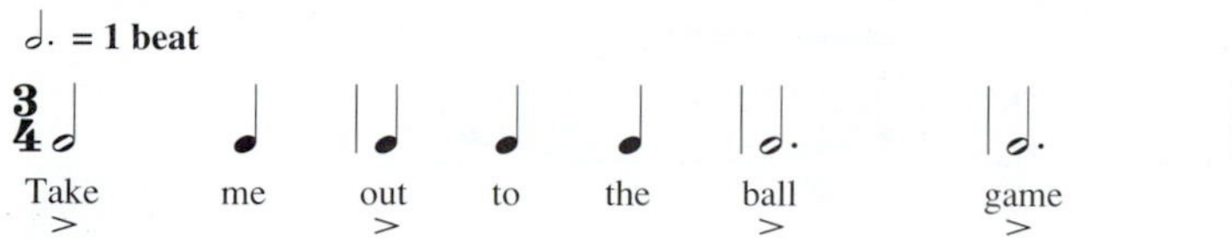

In a Slow Tempo In simple time, the division of the note value indicated in the denominator of the signature may sound as the beat value. In the slow $\frac{4}{4}$ of Figure 3.17, the aural effect is that of eight beats per measure.

FIGURE 3.17

In compound time with a very slow tempo, the lower number of the time signature indicates the note value receiving one beat.

FIGURE 3.18

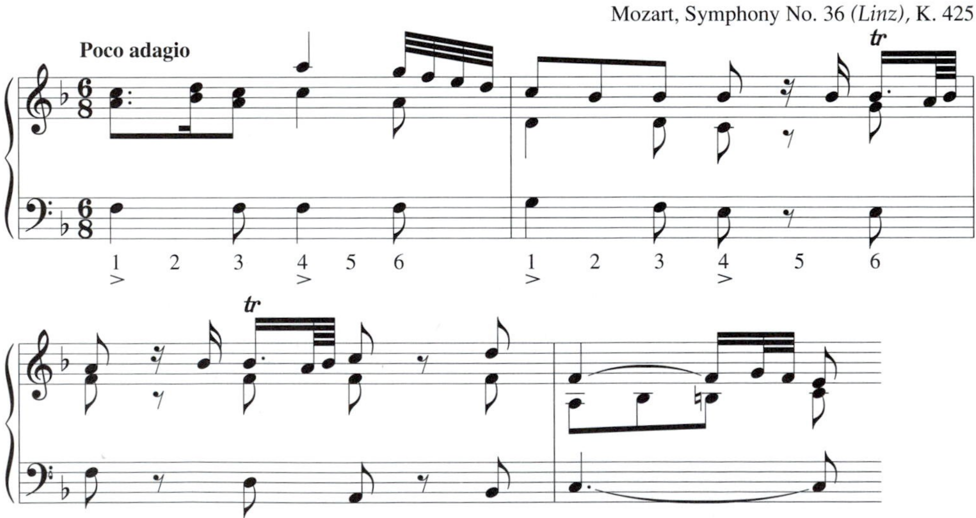

Observe that the numerator 6 in a very slow tempo still represents duple compound time because of the stress placed on the first and fourth beat divisions. The numerator 3 in a very slow tempo also has six beat divisions but represents triple simple time because the stress is on the first, third, and fifth beat divisions.

FIGURE 3.19

Numerators of 5 and 7; Other Numerators A numerator of 5 usually indicates simple time in which each measure includes a group of two beats and a group of three beats—for example, $\frac{5}{4}$ or . A numerator of 7 similarly indicates various groups of two beats and three beats: 3 + 2 + 2, 2 + 2 + 3, or 2 + 3 + 2—for example $\frac{7}{8}$ or $\frac{7}{4}$.

The desired grouping can be indicated in several ways: by beaming notes, by using phrase marks or accent marks, and by separating the groups with a vertical dotted bar line.

FIGURE 3.20

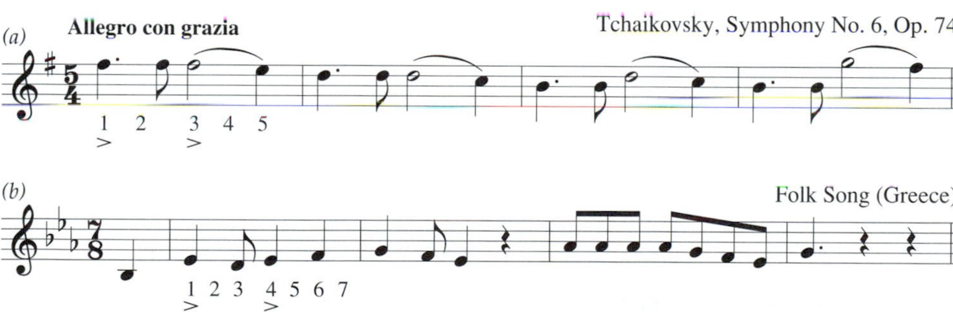

Many other signatures exist, used primarily in twentieth-century music. Some examples are $\frac{10}{4}$, $\frac{8}{8}$, $\frac{15}{8}$, $\frac{3\frac{1}{2}}{4}$, $\frac{3+2+2}{4}$, and $\frac{6}{8}\frac{2}{4}$.[3]

These examples point out the difficulty the composer often encounters in choosing a time signature that best represents the rhythmic and metric intentions of the music. Consequently, it is most important that the performer not rely solely on the time signature but make sufficient study of the music to determine the time signature's intent.

[3] See Gardner Read, *Music Notation* (Boston: Allyn & Bacon, 1969), chap. 10.

Beaming Notes for Rhythmic Clarity

Notes employing flags may be grouped together with beams.

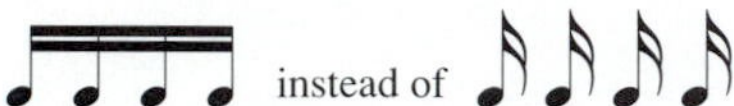

Notes ordinarily should be beamed according to beat units. In the following example, |______| indicates a beat unit.

FIGURE 3.21

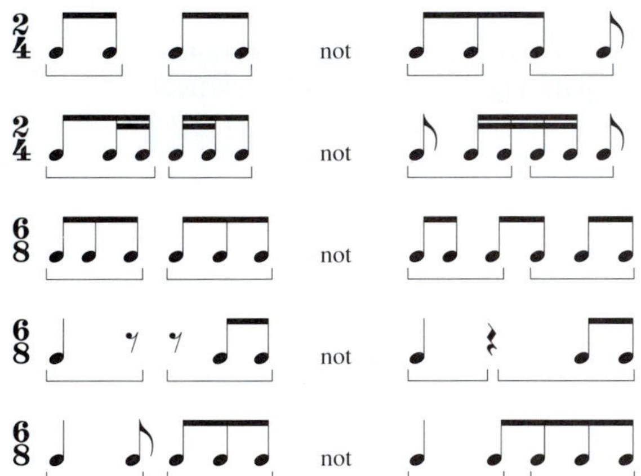

When you place a group of beamed notes on the staff, use a stem direction that is correct for the majority of notes in the group.

In vocal music, beams traditionally are used only when two or more notes are found on a single syllable. Recent practice allows beaming when syllables are carefully placed below beamed notation (beamed sixteenth notes in measure 2 of Figure 3.22). The curved line (*slur*) under "glow-" shows that the two notes are sung on a single syllable.

FIGURE 3.22

Triplets, Duplets, and Quadruplets

A *triplet* is a group of three notes dividing a simple note value into three equal parts (♪♪♪ = ♩; ♩♩♩ = 𝅗𝅥). Since the division is not mathematically accurate, a "3" is placed above the beam or the stems of the group. The triplet ♪♪♪ in $\frac{2}{4}$, for example, has the same duration as a ♩ or ♫. Other examples are 𝅘𝅥𝅯𝅘𝅥𝅯𝅘𝅥𝅯 = 𝅘𝅥𝅯𝅘𝅥𝅯 = ♪ (three sixteenths have the same duration as two sixteenth notes) and ♩♩♩ = ♩♩ = 𝅗𝅥 (three quarter notes have the same duration as two quarter notes).

Similarly, a *duplet* is a group of two notes dividing a compound note value into two equal parts (♫ = ♪♪♪ = ♩.). A *quadruplet* is a combination of two duplets (♪♪♪♪ = ♩.‿♩. or 𝅗𝅥.).

FIGURE 3.23

Rhythmic Transcription

Now that you have studied the derivation of time signatures, it should be obvious that any two or more time signatures with identical numerators designate the same meter.

If, for example, you hear music that you can identify as being in duple compound time, you can assume that the numerator of the time signature is 6, but it would be absolutely impossible to tell which of the possible denominators the composer had used. It could be any of them, since the denominator affects only the notation to be used. The same music with like numerators but with differing denominators will sound identical when the tempo of the beat is equal in each.

FIGURE 3.24

DRILL #4 Rewrite each of these melodies using the time signatures indicated.

1. In $\frac{4}{2}$ and $\frac{4}{8}$

2. In $\frac{3}{4}$ and $\frac{3}{16}$

3. In $\frac{12}{16}$ and $\frac{12}{4}$

BASICS QUIZ #3

1. Write the single note value equivalent to the given group. Example: ♫ = ♩

a.  (four sixteenth notes) ______

b.  ♩ ♩ ♩ ______

c.  (two thirty-second notes) ______

d.  ♩ ♩ ♩ ♩ ______

e.  (three sixteenth notes) ______

f. 𝅗𝅥 𝅗𝅥 ______

g.  (three thirty-second notes) ______

h.  (four sixty-fourth notes) ______

2. Describe each time signature as shown in the example.

			Description		*Beat note*	*Divisions*
Example:	2/4	=	duple	simple	 ♩	 ♫
a.	3/4	=	______	______	______	______
b.	6/8	=	______	______	______	______
c.	4/2	=	______	______	______	______
d.	9/8	=	______	______	______	______
e.	12/4	=	______	______	______	______
f.	2/2	=	______	______	______	______
g.	12/16	=	______	______	______	______
h.	3/16	=	______	______	______	______

In Appendix E: Answers to all questions in Quiz #3 are given.

ARTICLE #2

Early Rhythmic Notation

In the history of the notation of rhythm, the time signature made its appearance at a comparatively late date. One reason for this is that music before the seventeenth century did not make use of bar lines, and another is that a note value did not come to indicate a specific division (such as 𝅗𝅥 = ♩♩) until about the same time.

The earliest notation, as found in the religious chants of the eighth and ninth centuries, represented pitch only. How the rhythmic element of this plainchant notation was interpreted is still not entirely clear.

The first measurable rhythmic notation was produced in the thirteenth century. In this system, the duration of each note depended upon what note value or values followed it. The system, called *mensural notation* and developed by Franco of Cologne about 1280, was used to represent the rhythmic modes—a series of six rhythmic patterns, each representing the triple division in which the music of the time was composed.

Observe in the figure that the *longa* (𝆷) equals a quarter note at some times and a dotted quarter note at others, depending on the context. The same principle holds true for the *breve* (■). This music needed no time signatures. Its symbols were often combined into groups called *ligatures;* for example, 𝆷■ , ■■ , and ■𝆷■ . Another example can be seen in the article "Pitch Notation from Earliest Times," on page 37.

Mensural notation

About 1320, Philippe de Vitry, in his treatise *Ars Nova (The New Art),* recognized duple rhythm (note values divisible by two) as well as triple rhythm. Also at this time, white notation was gradually replacing much of the black notation. To indicate division of note values into two or three, a system of *mensural signatures* was devised about 1450. But in this system, the actual value of a given note was still determined by its relation to the preceding or following note (again, review page 37).

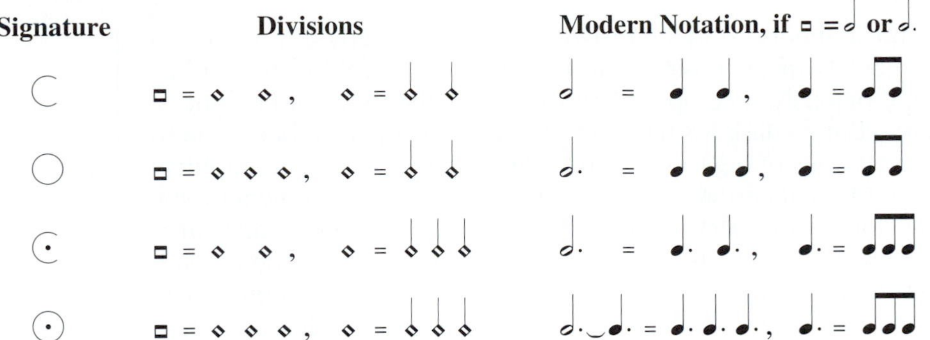

Of these four signatures, the time signature **C** still remains, indicating duple division at all levels and now used to indicate $\frac{4}{4}$ meter. Another mensural signature, **¢** indicated that all notes following it were to be taken twice as fast as before. Known as *cut time* or *alla breve* (the symbol ⊨ in the preceding table is called a *breve*), it is still used today to indicate $\frac{2}{2}$ meter. The time signatures we use today had developed by the early seventeenth century, and they have remained virtually unchanged since that time.

ARTICLE #3

What Is Music Theory?

A Prelude to the Study of Harmony

Music is universal. It exists in some form in every part of the world inhabited by humans. Its existence for thousands of years is attested to by references to music in humankind's earliest writing, pictures, and artifacts. During all this time, and in all these places, music has developed in a multitude of ways, each expressing the historical era and the local culture of its creators. In our own day, the number of ways in which the music of Western culture is expressed makes an impressive list: symphonic, folk song, military march, rock and roll, liturgical mass, jazz, and electronic music, to name only a few.

These diverse forms of musical expression have one characteristic in common: All use as their raw material the resources of sound—pitch, duration, intensity, and timbre. The art of composing music is dependent upon the skill of the composer in making choices from the raw materials of sound and in organizing those choices in ways that produce a successful composition.

The study of music theory is, in the broadest sense, the study of how sound has been organized to make music, regardless of geographical location or historical period. Obviously, a complete study of music theory would be one of great magnitude. But the task is simplified somewhat by the fact that throughout music history, ways of organizing musical sound in a given geographical area or a given historical period are often similar, making it convenient for the scholar or the student to concentrate on one such area or period at a time. Our present study will focus on music composed in western Europe and the areas under its influence, particularly the Americas, between the approximate dates 1600 and 1900, with comparative references to earlier styles, culminating in a survey of twentieth-century music. The era chosen encompasses the Baroque, Classical, and Romantic periods of music history and includes many of the best-known names in present-day concert repertoire, from J. S. Bach through such composers as Mozart, Beethoven, and Chopin, and at the end of the era, Brahms and Wagner.

It was during this period that harmony was a predominant characteristic of music composition. Harmony, defined broadly, results when two or more pitches sound simultaneously or in close succession. In this sense, most music of any period could be described as harmonic. But music of the period from about 1600 to about 1900 makes almost exclusive use of a system of tonal harmony so pervasive that the era is often known as the *common practice period.* Its principal characteristics are

1. chords built in thirds, such as C E G, called *tertian* harmony;
2. two scale systems, major and minor;
3. a tonal center represented by the tonic tone of a major or minor scale and a triad built on that tone, to which all tones and chords gravitate;
4. a certain predictability in the order of the various chords as they gravitate toward the tonic, a process often called *functional harmony.*

Before about 1600, music composition was based upon a system of six different scales, called *modes* (see Appendix D), and upon the concept of *counterpoint*—the simultaneous sounding of two or more melodic lines, their juxtaposition dependent upon the interval between any upper voice and the lowest sounding voice (see the example in the article on page 198). Counterpoint has been used extensively since 1600 but in addition to harmonic or other bases.

Since about 1900, composers of "serious" music have experimented with new ways of musical expression through nontertian and nontonal harmony, nontraditional uses of melody and rhythm, and use of new sound resources such as synthesizers and computers. Tonal music, however, is still widely used in the twentieth century and can commonly be heard in commercial music (radio, TV, motion pictures, "elevator music," and so forth) and in much educational and popular music.

4

Tonic and Dominant I

cadences

Beginning in this chapter, many assignments will be followed by one or two references to the locations of their answers. One of these references, In Appendix E, *indicates that answers are given in whole or in part, as indicated. The other,* In the Workbook, *indicates that a similar assignment using the same assignment number, such as* Assignment 4.1, *will provide additional practice, with answers. At appropriate places, there will be reference to additional assignments with given answers for closely related material; these are identified with a reference such as* Assignment 4A. *Lack of reference to an assignment in the* Workbook *indicates that no answers are given for that assignment.*

The Cadence

We will begin our study of harmony with an excerpt from the music of Bach, the well-known "Jesu, Joy of Man's Desiring," to illustrate the concept of *cadence,* a universal characteristic of music composition. First, listen to the music in Figure 4.1.

After you have listened to the music, sing the melody line of Figure 4.1, with or without the piano accompaniment. As you arrive at the final note, you should feel satisfied that you have come to a good stopping place and that there is no necessity to continue.

The sensation of arriving at a stopping place indicates the location of a cadence. You may have noticed another stopping place at the end of measure 4. But in this case, the cadence seems to be only temporary, requiring that the music continue. Poetry also exhibits these traits. In this stanza from an American folk ballad, note the two temporary pauses and the final stop at the end:

When the curtains of night
Are pinned back by the stars, *(pause)*
And the beautiful moon sweeps the sky, *(pause)*
I'll remember you, love, in my prayers. *(final stop)*[1]

[1]From Carl Sandburg's *The American Songbag* (1927).

FIGURE 4.1

Bach, *Herz und Mund und That und Leben,* "Jesu, Joy of Man's Desiring," BMV 147

As you read the poem or sing the melody above, the function of the cadence is clear: to mark a pause, complete or incomplete, in the poetic or musical thought being expressed. In this way, cadences make it possible for poetry or music to be a true structure, rather than just a nonstop flow of words or pitches.

The Cadence in Relation to Form

The structure of a piece of music is known as its *form.*[2] The terminology of music form describes all aspects of musical structure, from the smallest unit of pitch or rhythm to the complete composition. In Figure 4.1, a cadence appears at the end of each group of four measures, and each marks the end of a "form," which in this case is called a *phrase.* The two phrases together, one with a temporary cadence and the other with a full stop, constitute a form known as a *period,* as shown in Figure 4.2, the melody line from Figure 4.1.

[2]Form is presented in more detail in Chapter 7.

FIGURE 4.2 *Form in a Melodic Line*

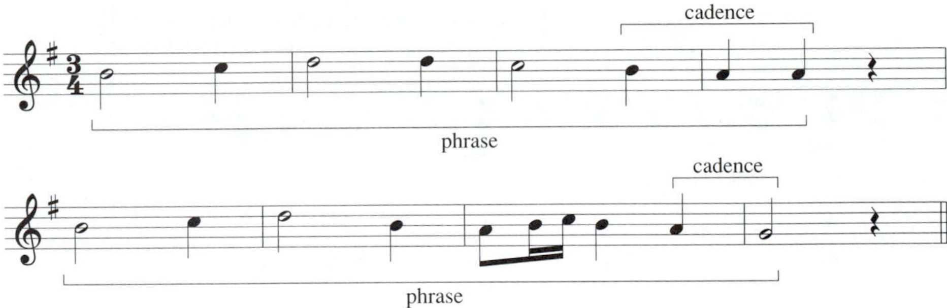

The final goal of a melodic line is commonly the tonic note of the key, as shown in Figure 4.2. The same is true in harmony: The ultimate goal of a series of chords is almost invariably the tonic triad. It is this feeling of reaching a goal, the tonic, that establishes aurally a sense of key in a composition. The pitch name of this tonic tone is also the name of the key. In listening to the Bach example (Figure 4.1), we recognize the sound of the final melody note and the final bass note as being tonic. By looking at the score and seeing that both notes are G, we know that G represents finality and, therefore, that the music is in the key of G.

Harmony at the Cadence (Major Keys)

In harmony, a cadence is usually found as the last two chords of a formal structure.[3] Most commonly, the chords dominant, V or V^7, and tonic constitute the cadence (review page 27 for roman numeral symbols). Looking at the final cadence of Figure 4.3, we see that the final two chords, the cadence, make use of the triads V and I (D F♯ A and G B D). In Figure 4.1, also in G major, the cadence is V^7–I (D F♯ A C–G B D). The two cadences are shown side-by-side for comparison in Figure 4.4.

[3]Cadences in the music of any historical era or geographical location fulfull the same function as those described here. For a few examples of cadences from music of other times and places, see the article "The Universality of the Cadence," on page 82

FIGURE 4.3

FIGURE 4.4 *Comparison of Cadences*

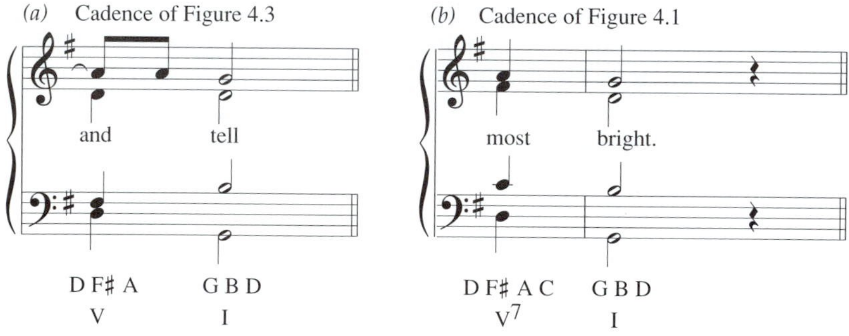

Both cadences in Figure 4.4 are called *authentic* cadences, a term describing a cadence with a root movement from dominant to tonic. The presence or absence of a seventh in the chord is not relevant. It might seem that we should study the easier chord, V, before V^7. But since V^7 is used far more frequently than V, we need to consider both.

When a cadence ends on any chord other than the tonic triad, it is called a *half cadence.* Figure 4.5 shows the half cadences, I–V, from the music of Figures 4.1 and 4.3.

[4]The number is that of the chorale in the collected editions of chorales of J. S. Bach, such as *The 371 Chorales of Johann Sebastian Bach,* edited, with the original instrumental obbligatos and with English texts, by Frank D. Mainous and Robert W. Ottman (New York: Holt, Rinehart & Winston, 1966). Excerpts from these chorales will be used extensively in this text.

FIGURE 4.5 *Half Cadences*

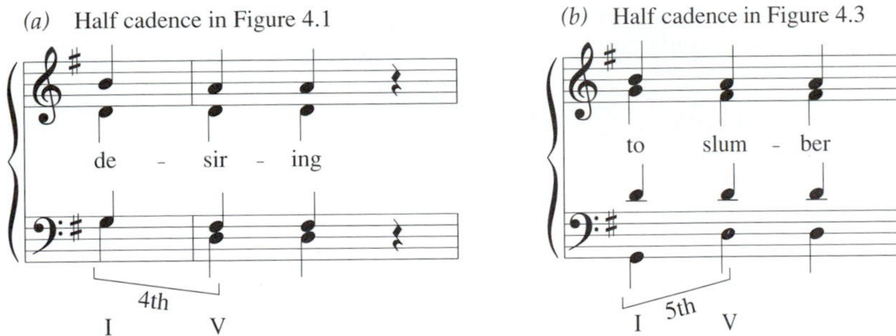

Is there a difference in these half cadences? Look again at the two half cadences in Figure 4.5. Both are I–V, but the root movement in the first is G down to D, a perfect fourth, whereas in the other the root movement is up a perfect fifth, but still G to D. Here is an example of the *inversion* of intervals as discussed on page 24. Since each interval is the inversion of the other, there is no change in the harmonic structure, so the two cadences are analyzed identically.

Root relationship by perfect fifth, as illustrated in cadential harmony, is probably the most important element delineating the character of tonal harmony. Chord movements based on roots a fifth apart are more common than others, and the most common key relationships are based on this interval, as in the circle of fifths (page 13).

As a diversion, we wish to point out that there is a strong similarity other than in cadences between Figures 4.1 and 4.3. Look at these figures carefully; sing or listen to both. Can you see or hear the similarity? They use the same melody![5] In devising the melody of "Jesu, Joy of Man's Desiring" from the chorale tune of Figure 4.3, what changes did Bach make? Sing or play the melody of each again and it should be obvious.

Spelling Tonic and Dominant Chords (Major Keys)

Further study of cadences will be easier if you are sure that you can spell the I, V, and V^7 chords quickly and accurately in any key. Here are two ways to do this:

1. For any diatonic chord, the chord number is the same as the scale step upon which it is built. From that letter name, spell in thirds by skipping over every other note of the scale. In these examples, the letter names skipped are in parentheses.

C major: I = C (d) E (f) G = C E G
B major: V = F♯ (g♯) A♯ (b) C♯ = F♯ A♯ C♯
V^7 = F♯ (g♯) A♯ (b) C♯ (d♯) E = F♯ A♯ C♯ E♯

[5]This melody was originally a hymn tune written by Johann Schop in 1642. Bach's harmonization of this melody is one of five to be found in *The 371 Chorales;* the others are 95, 121, 233, and 365.

2. Any major triad, diatonic or altered, can easily be spelled by using the following groups. Since there are but seven letter names, there are only seven possible triad spellings without accidentals. Three of these are already major, three are minor, and one is diminished; the triads can be grouped accordingly.

Group I *(major)*	Group II *(minor)*	Group III *(diminished)*
C E G	D F A	B D F
F A C	E G B	
G B D	A C E	
- - -	- ↑ -	- ↑ ↑

Group I. Triads in Group I will always be major when each member carries no accidental or when each carries the same accidental, as indicated by the symbol - - -.

C E G, C♯ E♯ G♯, C𝄪 E𝄪 G𝄪, C♭ E♭ G♭, C𝄫 E𝄫 G𝄫
\- - -   - - -   - - -   - - -   - - -

Group II. Triads in Group II will be major when the third carries an accidental one half step higher than the root and the fifth (- ↑ -).

A C♯ E, A♯ C𝄪 E♯, A♭ C E♭, A𝄫 C♭ E𝄫
\- ↑ -   - ↑ -   - ↑ -   - ↑ -

Group III. This single triad on the pitch name B is major when the third and the fifth carry an accidental one half step higher than the root (- ↑ ↑).

B D♯ F♯, B♯ D𝄪 F𝄪, B♭ D F, B𝄫 D♭ F♭
\- ↑ ↑   - ↑ ↑   - ↑ ↑   - ↑ ↑

This system is especially helpful when spelling a triad from its third or its fifth. For example, how would you spell a major triad whose third is F𝄪?

1. If F𝄪 is 3, the basic triad is D F A.
2. D F A is in Group II, - ↑ -, in which the third carries an accidental one half step higher than the root or the fifth.
3. The accidental 𝄪 is a half step higher than the accidental ♯; therefore, the root and the fifth are D♯ and A♯. The complete triad is D♯ F𝄪 A♯.

ASSIGNMENT 4.1 *(a)* Spell major triads when the given name is the root.

From Group I: F, F♯, F♭; G, G♯, G♭

From Group II: D, D♯, D♭; E, E♯, E♭

ARTICLE #4

The "Difficult" Triad Spellings

When spelling triads, you may feel that some are too complex to be useful. As your knowledge of harmony expands, you will find more and more of these triads in the music you study. Here are two examples: (1) F♭ A♭ C♭, the enharmonic of E G♯ B and used as the triad built on $\flat\hat{6}$ (F♭) in the key of A♭ major; and (2) D♯ F𝄪 A♯, used as the dominant triad in G♯ minor.

EXAMPLE 1

Schubert, *Moment Musical,* D. 780, No. 6

F♭ A♭ C♭

EXAMPLE 2

Chopin, Mazurka, Op. 33, No. 4

(*b*) Spell major triads when the given name is the third.

G♯, B, F♯, B♭, D, F𝄪, C♯, D♭, B, A♯

(*c*) Spell major triads when the given name is the fifth.

C, B, F♯, A♭, F, G♯, B♭, A♭, E♯, G♭

In Appendix E: Answers to the entire assignment are given.
In the Workbook: Do Assignment 4.1a–c. Answers are given.

ASSIGNMENT 4.2 Spell the I, the V, and the V^7 in each major key. Start with C major and work through the circle of fifths (review page 13) as begun for you below. In V^7, the seventh is $\hat{4}$. In C major, $\hat{4}$ is F. Adding F to G B D produces the V^7, G B D F.

	I	V	V^7
C:	C E G	G B D	G B D F
G:	G B D	D F♯ A	D F♯ A C
D:	D F♯ A	A C♯ E	A C♯ E G

In the Workbook: Do Assignment 4.2. Answers are given.

Cadences Incorporating Dominant Harmony

Perfect Authentic (PA) These are the characteristics of the perfect authentic cadence:

1. The progression is V–I or V^7–I, each chord with its root in the bass.
2. In the tonic triad (I), $\hat{1}$ is found in both soprano and bass.
3. The soprano line is usually $\hat{7}$–$\hat{1}$ or $\hat{2}$–$\hat{1}$.

The cadences of Figure 4.6*a* are perfect authentic, V–I, soprano lines $\hat{7}$–$\hat{1}$ and $\hat{2}$–$\hat{1}$. The cadences of 4.6*b* are the same except for the use of V^7. Review Figures 4.1 and 4.3; both show perfect authentic final cadences.

FIGURE 4.6 *Perfect Authentic Cadences*

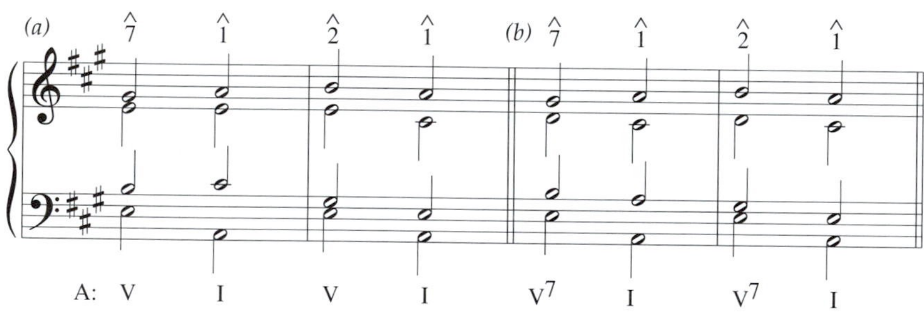

Imperfect Authentic (IA) These are the characteristics of the imperfect authentic cadence:

1. The progression V–I or V^7–I deviates in some way from a perfect authentic cadence; for example,
   a. The soprano note in the final tonic triad is $\hat{3}$ or $\hat{5}$.
   b. One or both chords are in inversion (review "Inversion of Chords," page 24).
2. The soprano line is usually $\hat{2}$–$\hat{3}$, $\hat{5}$–$\hat{5}$, or $\hat{5}$ down to $\hat{3}$ (Figure 4.7).

Figure 4.8, the first and last phrases of a chorale, shows two different imperfect authentic cadences.

FIGURE 4.7 *Imperfect Authentic Cadences*

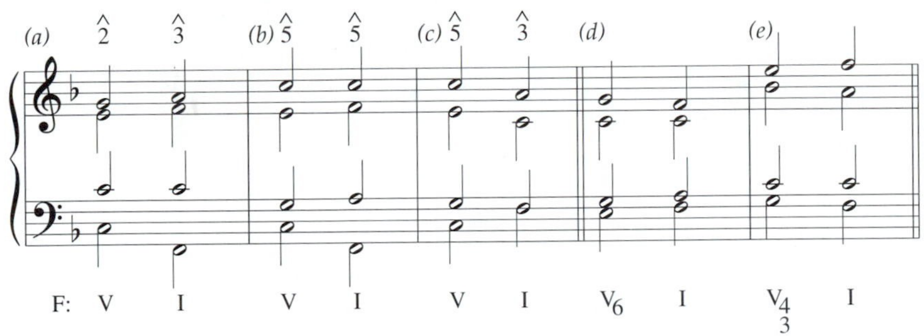

FIGURE 4.8

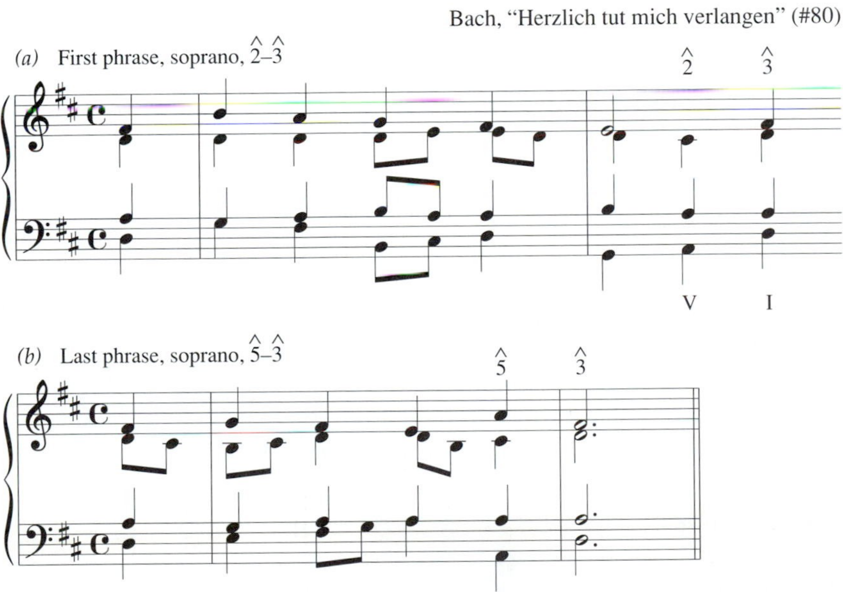

Half Cadence (HC) Any cadence ending on a chord other than the tonic triad is a half cadence, the most common being I–V. (Note that this cadence is *not* called an "authentic half" cadence.) The cadences of Figure 4.5 are half cadences. There are several soprano movements: $\hat{1}$–$\hat{7}$, $\hat{1}$–$\hat{2}$, $\hat{3}$–$\hat{2}$, $\hat{5}$–$\hat{5}$, and by various skips. Figure 4.9 illustrates two half cadences, each closing a two-measure idea.

FIGURE 4.9

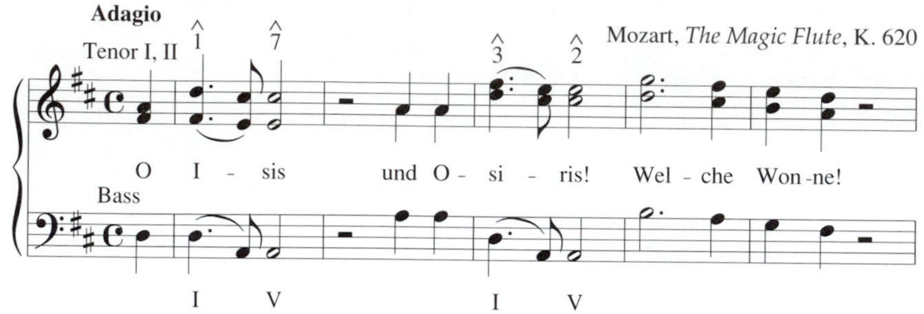

ASSIGNMENT 4.3 Describe the cadence in each of these excerpts, naming the key and the cadence (PA, IA, HC) and indicating the scale steps of the melodic line. For Figure 4.8*b*, the answer is: Key __D__; Cadence __IA__; Melody line __$\hat{5}$–$\hat{3}$__.

(1)

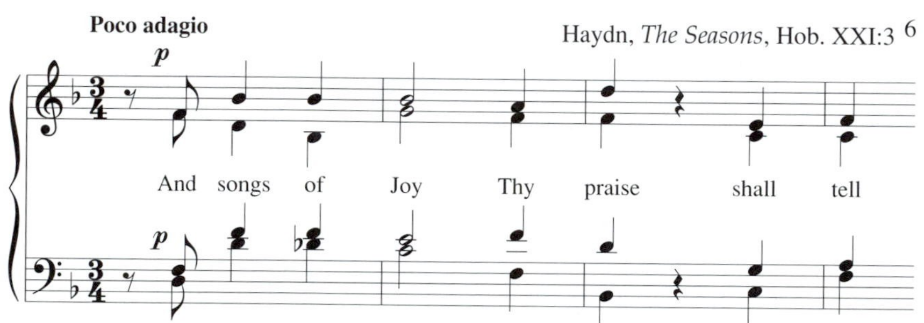

Key ______ Cadence ______ Melody line ______

(2)

Key ______ Cadence ______ Melody line ______

[6]Hob.: abbreviation for Anthony von Hoboken, who in 1957 catalogued Haydn's works.

[7]WoO: abbreviation for "Work without opus number."

(3)

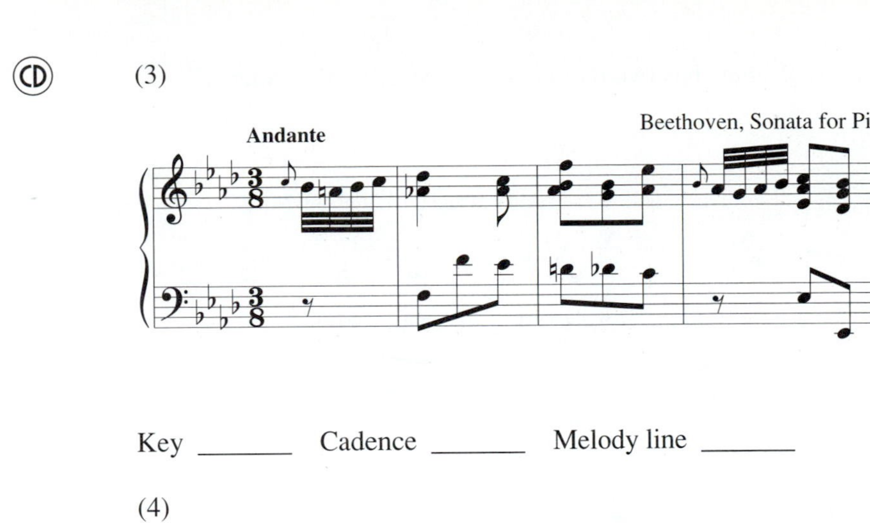

Key _______ Cadence _______ Melody line _______

(4)

Key _______ Cadence _______ Melody line _______

(5) Where is the melody line in this excerpt? Describe the movement of the soprano line during the four measures. Which line do you think you should use when describing the cadence? (There is no right or wrong answer. In analysis, we will encounter many similar situations for which alternative explanations are possible.)

Key _______ Cadence _______ Melody line _______

[8]D.: abbreviation for Otto Deutsch, who in 1951 catalogued Schubert's works.

(6) This familiar song by Brahms has two melody lines. Describe the cadence for each.

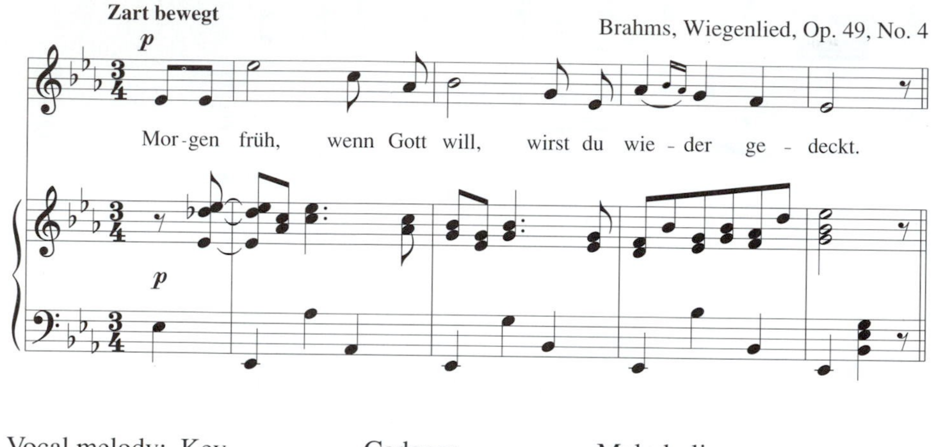

Vocal melody: Key _______ Cadence _______ Melody line _______

Piano melody: Key _______ Cadence _______ Melody line _______

In Appendix E: Answers to the entire assignment are given.

The Cadence in Minor Keys

Authentic cadences and the half cadence in a minor key are similar to those in a major key. The tonic triad is usually minor (i), whereas the dominant triad is usually major (V), requiring an accidental to provide a leading tone for the key. In Figure 4.10, V–i in A minor is spelled E G♯ B–A C E. Can you name the two cadences and explain the formal structure?

FIGURE 4.10

Spelling Tonic and Dominant Triads (Minor Keys)

You should be able to spell quickly and accurately the cadence chords in minor keys.

1. In the tonic (i) triad, the third is lowered in relation to the spelling of the major triad. Whereas I in C major is C E G, i in C minor is C E♭ G. Where there is no parallel major key, spell a major triad above the tonic tone and then lower the third a half step. Example: In G♯ minor, a major triad above the tonic is G♯ B♯ D♯; therefore, the tonic minor is G♯ B D♯.

   The tonic triad is also easily spelled by locating $\hat{1}$, $\hat{3}$, and $\hat{5}$ in the scale of the key. In G♯ minor, $\hat{1}$, $\hat{3}$, and $\hat{5}$ are G♯, B, and D♯.
2. In all major and minor keys, V and V^7 are major triads and major–minor seventh chords, respectively. In minor, the third of the chord is ♯$\hat{7}$, raised in relation to the key signature to provide a leading tone.

ASSIGNMENT 4.4 Spell these minor triads when
- *a.* the root is given: A, B♭, B, C♯, F♯
- *b.* the third is given: G, E♭, B♭, A♭, B
- *c.* the fifth is given: F♯, G♯, D, B♭, A♯

In Appendix E: Answers to the entire assignment are given.
In the Workbook: Do Assignment 4.4. Answers are given.

ASSIGNMENT 4.5 Locate, identify, and describe the cadences in each of these examples. Follow the same procedure as in Assignment 4.3.

CD (1)

Bach, "Helft mir Gotts güte Preisen" (#23)

Key ______ Cadence ______ Melody line ______

(2)

Key ______ Cadence ______ Melody line ______

(3)

Key ______ Cadence ______ Melody line ______

In Appendix E: Answers to the entire assignment are given.

Cadences Incorporating Dissonances

Music does not consist solely of triads and seventh chords. Tones other than chord tones are so frequent that it is necessary to investigate them to understand even simple music scores. These tones are dissonances (as defined on page 27) that sound simultaneously with a chord structure, and are called *nonharmonic tones.* For the present, it will be sufficient to simply recognize the presence of nonharmonic tones. Study of their nomenclature and use will follow in Chapters 11 and 12.

In the cadence of Figure 4.11, the alto D is not part of the A C♯ E triad, nor is the G in the tenor. But note that the G is the seventh of A C♯ E G. When the seventh is found this way, moving down by step from the root, it is called a *passing seventh.* You should be able to find more nonharmonic tones in the triads preceding the cadence of this example.

FIGURE 4.11

More complex is the cadence in Figure 4.12*a*, showing the V^7 triad extended for two measures, during which there are four nonharmonic tones, as well as one more in the tonic triad. In *b*, the texture is simplified to show the nonharmonic tones more clearly.

Note that the first circled note, F♯, is a *chromatic* nonharmonic tone, meaning that the tone is not part of the scale of the key in which it is found (F♯ is not a member of the C major scale). The remaining nonharmonic tones are *diatonic.*

FIGURE 4.12

Other Cadences: The Picardy Third and the "Empty Fifth"

The next two examples show not only nonharmonic tones in the cadence, but also two other features found in some minor cadences, especially in music written from about 1600 to 1750.

In the first (Figure 4.13), the final tonic chord in E minor is the major triad E G♯ B. This final major triad in a minor key is known as a *Picardy third* (or *tierce de Picardie*), for reasons unknown. Notice that the uppercase roman numeral "I" is used.

FIGURE 4.13 *The Picardy Third*

The "empty fifth" is shown as the final tonic chord in Figure 4.14. Without a third, it is neither major nor minor. We still use "i" to identify the structure because it was used almost exclusively in minor. Use of both this structure and the Picardy third dates from an earlier time when a major triad or an empty fifth was considered more consonant and therefore more suitable as a final cadence in a minor key.

FIGURE 4.14 *The "Empty Fifth"*

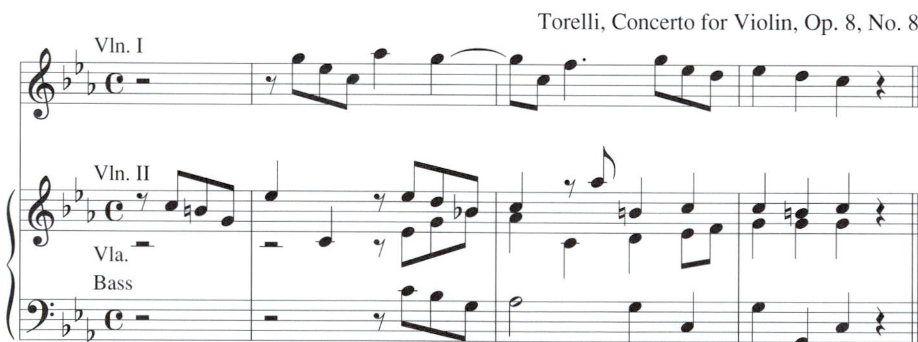

ASSIGNMENT 4.6 Name each cadence (PA, IA, HC) in each excerpt.

(1)–(3): Circle only those nonharmonic tones included with the cadence.

(4)–(6): Circle all nonharmonic tones in the entire excerpt (each excerpt includes only tonic and dominant harmony).

In any of the above, look for a V^7 cadence with the soprano line 4–3.

(1)

Handel, Concerto Grosso in B Minor, Op. 6, No. 12

Key ______ Cadence ____________

(2)

Bach, Cantanta No. 78, "Jesu, der du meine Seele"

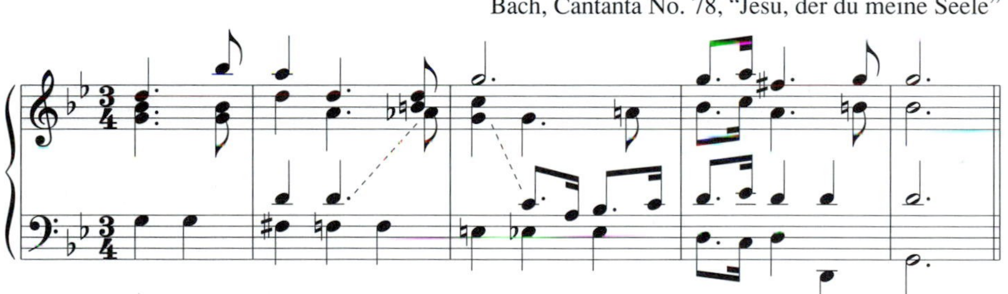

Key ______ Cadence ____________

(3)

Tchaikovsky, Symphony No. 5, Op. 64

Key ______ Cadence ____________

(4)

Key ______ Cadence ______________

(5)

Key ______ Cadence ______________

(6)

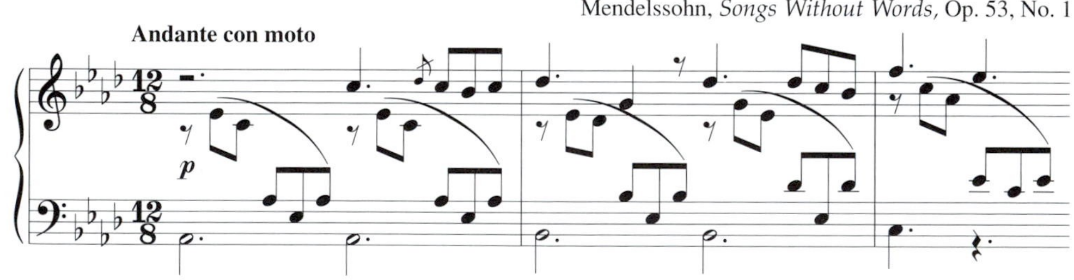

Key ______ Cadence ______________

In Appendix E: Answers to (1)–(3) are given.

Cadences in a Melodic Line

Cadences for one voice can usually be identified by the scale-step numbers of the melody at the point of the cadence. Figure 4.15, in B♭ major, shows two cadences: $\hat{3}$–$\hat{2}$ (D–C) implies I (B♭ D F)–V (F A C), whereas the final cadence, $\hat{2}$–$\hat{1}$ (C–B♭), implies V–I.

FIGURE 4.15

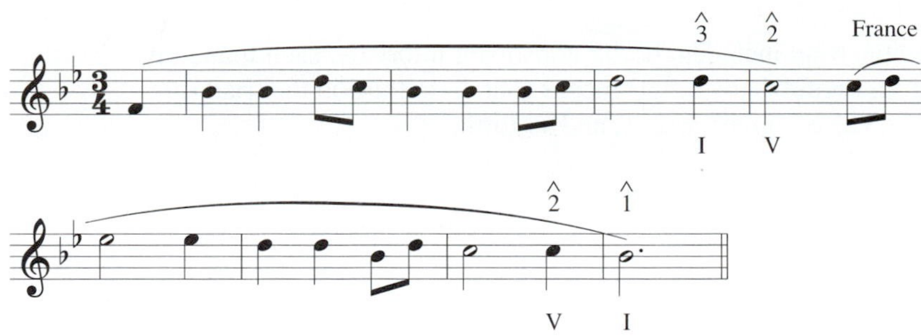

ASSIGNMENT 4.7 Analyze the final cadence in each example as in Figure 4.15. Also analyze those interior cadences located by the asterisk.

In Appendix E: Answers to the entire assignment are given.

Spelling Intervals from Major Triads

In Chapter 2, we learned to compute sizes and spellings of intervals, first by finding the major and perfect intervals above the tonic note, then by adjusting these by half-step manipulations to find other intervals. If you have now learned to spell major triads quickly and accurately, it will be even easier, in this optional method, to recognize and spell perfect, major, and minor intervals, especially those difficult ones with 𝄪's and 𝄫's.

Each major (or minor) triad includes the six consonant intervals, each made up of two notes of the triad. In Figure 4.16, 1 ↑ 3 means root up to third in the triad (not scale-step numbers). 1 ↑ 3 also implies 3 ↓ 1, and so forth.

FIGURE 4.16 *Intervals in a Major Triad*

1 ↑ 5 P5	1 ↑ 3 M3	3 ↑ 1 m6
5 ↑ 1 P4	3 ↑ 5 m3	5 ↑ 3 M6

Here are sample problems:

"easy":	P5 below D = ?	"difficult":	M6 below C𝄪 = ?
	P5 is 5 ↓ 1		M6 is 3 ↓ 5
	If D is 5, its triad = G B D		If C𝄪 is 3, its triad = A♯ C𝄪 E♯
	5 ↓ 1 = D ↓ G		3 ↓ 5 = C𝄪 ↓ E♯

ASSIGNMENT 4.8 *Spelling intervals.* Following the steps just given, name the second note of these intervals:

(1) m3 above F♯	(4) m6 above G𝄪
(2) M6 below G	(5) M3 below B♭
(3) P4 above A♭	(6) P5 below G♭

In Appendix E: Answers to the entire assignment are given.
In the Workbook: Do Assignment 4.8. Answers are given.

ASSIGNMENT 4.9 *Writing intervals.* Place the second note of the given interval on the staff.

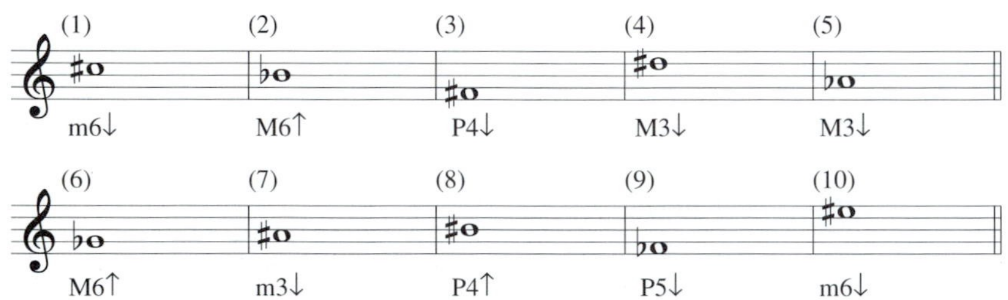

In Appendix E: Answers to the entire assignment are given.
In the Workbook: Do Assignment 4.9 a–b. *Answers are given.*

Triads Outlined in Melodies

Intervals in a melodic line often outline a triad. The melodies of Assignment 4.10 show more triad intervals than you would normally expect, but all are of typical usage.

ASSIGNMENT 4.10 Bracket any intervals in the I, i, or V chords and identify the triad as shown in the example. Be sure to spell the tonic and dominant triads before looking for the intervals.

Keyboard Harmony

In the study of keyboard harmony, you will learn to play chords and chord progressions as they are presented in each chapter. Playing harmonies, rather than just listening to them, will give you a more intimate acquaintance with their sounds and their relationships, and will help prepare you for practical application of your harmonic knowledge.

No previous keyboard skill is required. You will find your first experience in keyboard harmony easy if you have accomplished these prerequisites:

1. You know the names of the keys on the keyboard.
2. You have learned to spell quickly and accurately in all keys the chords presented in each chapter.

To begin the keyboard experience, you are asked to play only a single triad. The five steps below are illustrated in Figure 4.17 using a D major triad with its third in the soprano. Steps 1–4 show you how to find the correct keys before actually playing, so that at step 5 the triad will sound without error. With continued practice, you will soon be able to play any triad without the first four steps.

1. Spell the triad (D F♯ A).
2. Place a left-hand finger on the root of the triad (D). Do not play.
3. Place the little finger of the right hand on 3 (F♯). Do not play.
4. Find the two nearest notes of the triad below F♯ (D and A). Do not play.
5. Play all four notes of the triad simultaneously.

After sufficient practice, use step 5 only.

FIGURE 4.17 *Playing a Single Triad*

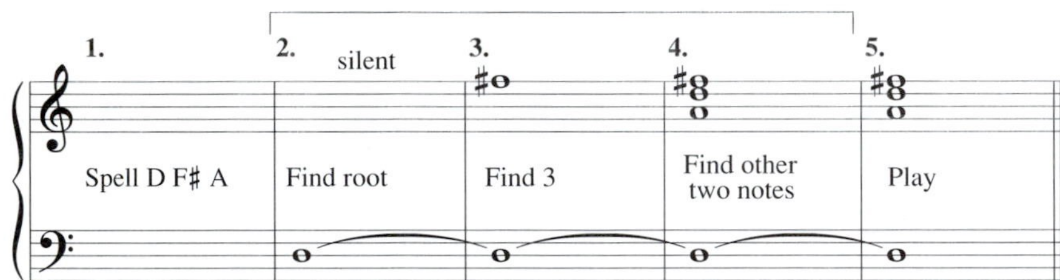

ASSIGNMENT 4.11 *Playing triads at the keyboard.*

(a) Using the five steps of Figure 4.17, play these triads ("C major-5" means the C major triad with its fifth in the soprano):

C major-5	E major-1
F major-1	D♭ major-5
E♭ major-3	B major-3

(b) Play any other triad in any soprano position, as chosen or assigned.

(c) Play successively a given triad in each of its three soprano positions, illustrated on the next page with the A major triad.

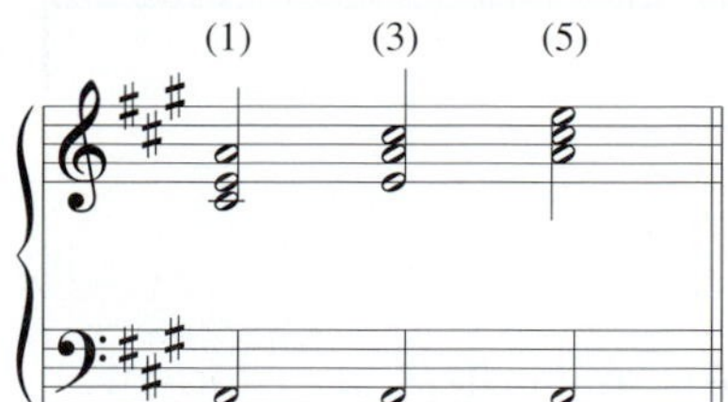

Summary

A *cadence* marks the close of a musical idea, temporary or final.

Cadences using the progression V–I or V–i are called *authentic* and may be *perfect* or *imperfect,* depending on their soprano and bass lines. A cadence ending on V (or any other chord) is a *half* cadence.

Form in music is determined by the location and types of cadences.

Cadences may include triads only, or they may contain additional nonharmonic tones.

In the Baroque era, cadences in a minor key often concluded with either a major triad (*Picardy third*) or a triad without a third.

Melody lines often outline triads or seventh chords, especially those chords on the dominant and the tonic.

The relationship of root movement by fifth in the authentic cadence represents the most important and frequent root movement in the period of music under study.

ARTICLE #5

The Universality of the Cadence

The use of cadences is a typical feature of all music, regardless of historical period or geographical area. There must always be places in any piece of music where the melody or the ensemble reaches a temporary or concluding resting point. How this is accomplished varies widely in differing times and places, as is demonstrated in the few but diverse examples that follow.

In contrast to these examples, most of the cadences of the common practice period reflect some type of tonic–dominant relationship, with V–I as a final cadence used almost exclusively.

South African Folk Song

Guillaume de Machaut (ca. 1300–ca. 1370), *La Messe de Notre Dame*

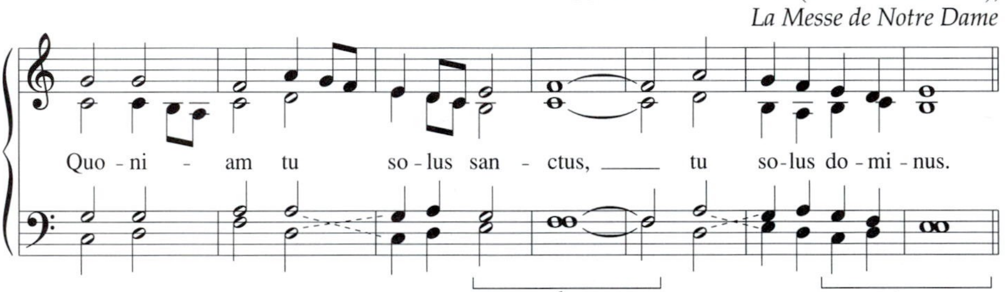

Igor Stravinsky (1882–1971), Mass (1948)

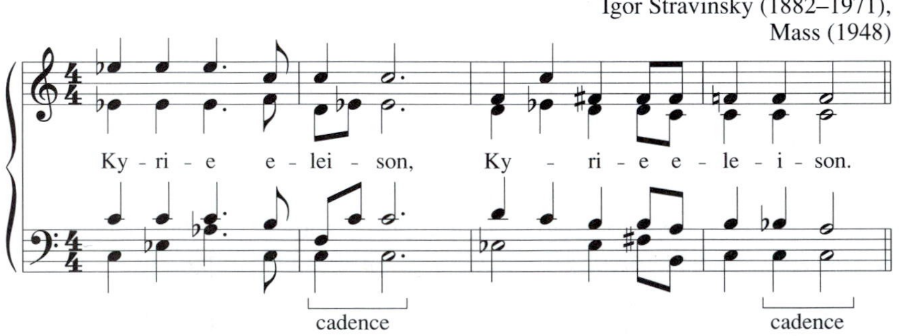

5

Tonic and Dominant II

part-writing

Part-writing, the procedure for connecting a series of chords, requires the skill of thinking in two musical directions at once. You might compare it to the art of weaving, in which the finished fabric is the result of combining vertical and horizontal threads ("warp" and "woof").

FIGURE 5.1

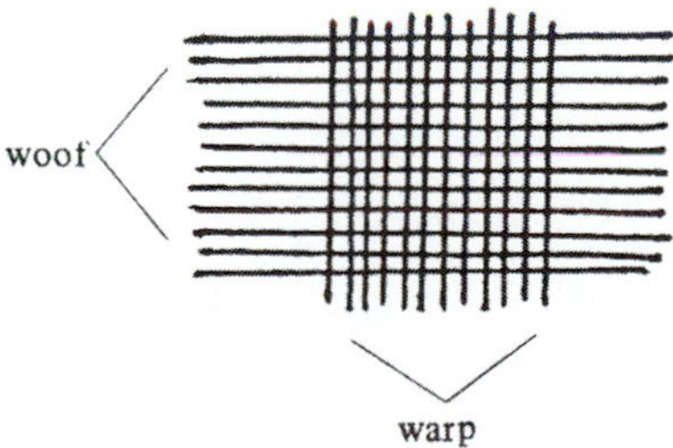

Looking at the simple hymn in Figure 5.2, we see the same type of interaction: The music is both a series of triads *and* a sounding of four melodic lines (voice lines)—soprano, alto, tenor, and bass. Each triad is identified by its spelling, describing the *vertical* structure of the hymn. At the same time, the four voice lines describe the music's *horizontal* structure. The tune in the soprano (highest voice) is obviously a melody, but the alto, tenor, and bass lines are also melody lines. If you sing the notes of the alto line (treble clef with stems downward), you are singing a melodic line. The same is true of the tenor and bass lines.

FIGURE 5.2

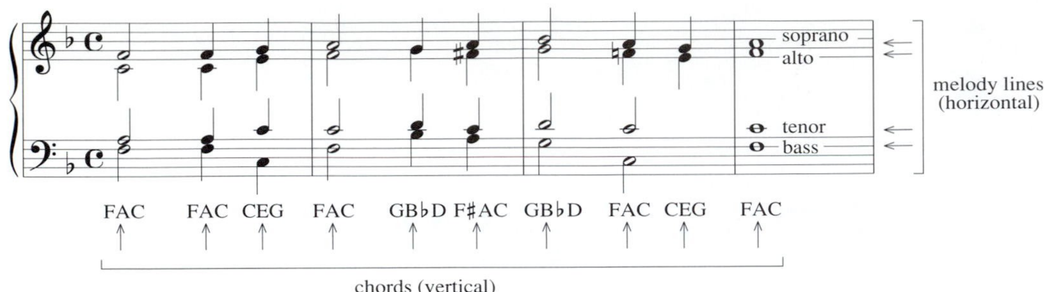

Achieving a good melodic line in each voice line[1] during a succession of chords is the goal of part-writing. Part-writing principles describe

1. how to distribute the various members of the chord among the number of voices in the composition (four voices in Figure 5.2, three in Figure 4.9); and
2. how to move each note in a given voice from chord to chord.

Placing individual notes of a given chord in one voice part or another at random can hardly be expected to produce good voice lines. If we were to rewrite Figure 5.2 using the same melody, bass line, and chords but filling in the alto and tenor voices at random, a version of the hymn such as that in Figure 5.3 might result.

FIGURE 5.3

As this "arrangement" is played at the piano, try to sing the alto line. It is difficult because it is a poor melodic line, with numerous skips and with the leading tone and the altered tone resolving awkwardly. In Figure 5.4, compare the alto line of the arrangement with that of the original, noting how much easier it is to sing the original. The same comparison can be made with the two tenor lines.

[1]The term *voice line* commonly refers to a melodic line in either vocal or instrumental music.

FIGURE 5.4

Conventional Procedures

This and succeeding chapters will present procedures for part-writing. There are many ways to progress from one chord to the next while achieving the goal of good melodic lines. A number of these procedures have been used so consistently by composers that they can be considered conventional. But other procedures are also useful, especially when they produce more interesting musical results. Conventional procedures will be presented first, but study of alternative procedures and the advantages of their use will be considered as your writing skill develops.

In most cases, conventional procedures are introduced by examples in four-part chorale style. Students may wonder why such a restriction is employed, especially those whose major interest is other than vocal music. Actually, the same basic principles of harmonic writing exist in both the vocal and the instrumental music of the common practice period, but four-part vocal writing provides the easiest introduction to harmonic writing. Other applications will be introduced as harmonic studies become more advanced.

All the conventional procedures presented in this and the following chapters will be found together in Appendix A. You will find this appendix a convenient reference point to locate quickly the conventional procedure for any part-writing situation. We recommend that you take advantage of this compilation to review old procedures as you are learning new ones.

Writing a Single Triad

For the first part-writing project, we will place on the staff a single triad with its root in the bass. Although this is an easy project, it serves to introduce several procedures useful in future part-writing activities.

Our triad will be written in four voices: soprano, alto, tenor, and bass, conforming to the four ranges of the human voice. When the treble and bass staves are used, the soprano and alto voices appear on the treble staff, and the tenor and bass voices appear on the bass staff. Observe the stem directions: soprano, stem up; alto, stem down; tenor, stem up; bass, stem down (Figure 5.5*a*). When two voices on the same staff are the same note, the note carries both stem up and stem down (Figure 5.5*b*), or if the note is a whole note, the two whole notes are interlocked (Figure 5.5*c*).

FIGURE 5.5

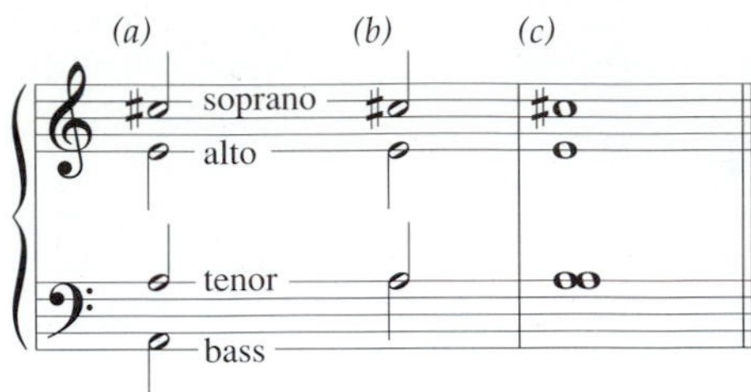

However, when the two identical pitches are the alto and tenor voices, each must remain on its own staff (Figure 5.6).

FIGURE 5.6

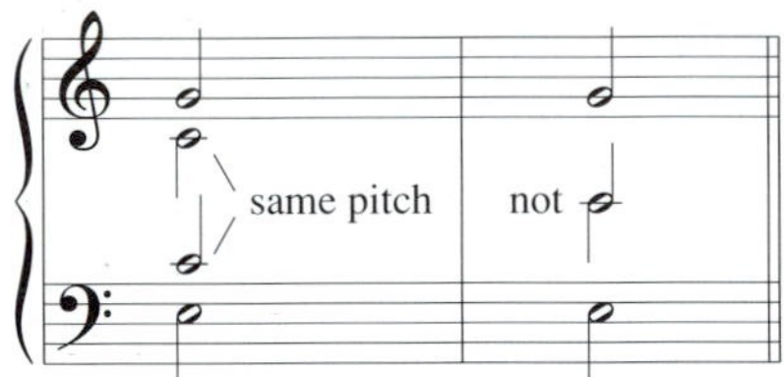

When part-writing a single triad, you must take four factors into consideration: voice range, doubling, triad position, and distance between voices.

Voice Range Each of the four voices should, as a rule, be written in the normal singing range of that voice.

FIGURE 5.7

Voices ordinarily should be kept within the ranges outlined by the whole notes in Figure 5.7. Pitches outside these ranges are possible but should be used only sparingly and within the limits of the black notes.

Doubling Since four notes will be used, one note of the triad must be doubled; that is, two voices will have to use the same letter name, either in unison or in an octave relationship. A general rule for doubling in most triads is to double that tone which is strongest and most stable in the key. These tones are the scale steps tonic, dominant, and subdominant. In tonic and dominant triads, the root is ordinarily doubled (Figure 5.8).

FIGURE 5.8

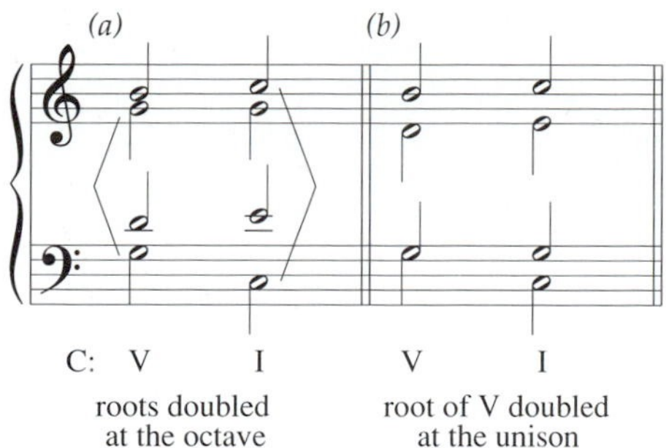

Other doublings are not necessarily wrong. There are circumstances, usually melodic, in which doubling the third or the fifth of the triad is desirable, as will be shown later. However, doublings should not be chosen haphazardly. If there is no particular reason to double the third or the fifth in a major triad, doubling the root is preferable.

Triad Position Triads may appear in either of two positions, *open* or *close*. In open position,[2] the distance between the soprano and the tenor is an octave or more; in close position, the distance between the soprano and the tenor is less than an octave. In either position, any interval may appear between tenor and bass.

FIGURE 5.9

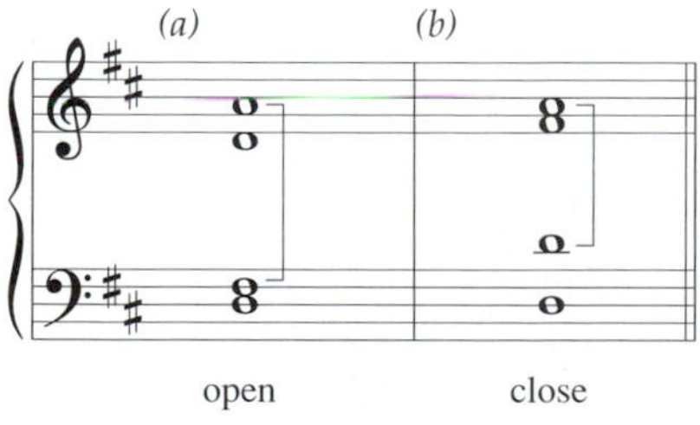

Note also that in open position, another note of the triad could be inserted between the tenor and the alto or the alto and the soprano, whereas in close position, the three upper voices are as close together as possible.

Distance between Voices The distance between any two adjacent voices (for example, soprano and alto) usually does not exceed an octave, except that an interval larger than an octave may appear between the bass and tenor voices (Figure 5.10).

[2]The terms *open structure* and *close structure* are commonly used synonymously with *open position* and *close position.*

FIGURE 5.10

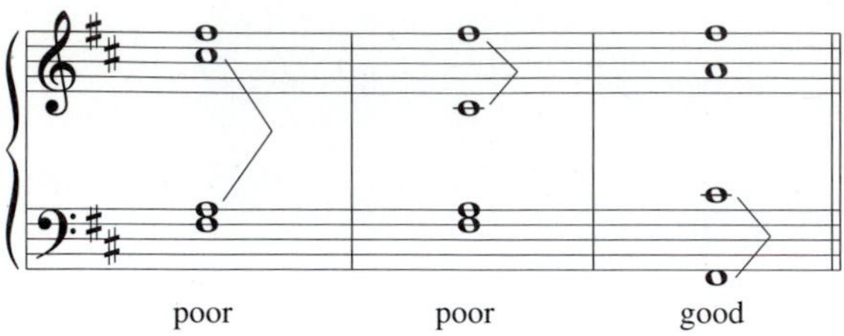

Crossed voices should be avoided at present. The tenor should not be placed above the alto, the alto above the soprano, and so forth.

ASSIGNMENT 5.1 Fill in the inner voices of each triad in both close and open position, in that order. At present, use two roots, one third, and one fifth, and observe instructions for range and distance between voices. Assume each triad to be tonic and name the key, indicating M or m. Here is an example:

In the Workbook: Do Assignment 5.1a. Answers are given.

The Connection of Repeated Triads

When you are writing repeated triads with a change in the soprano tone, the only decision you must make is whether to write the two triads in the same position or to change position in the second chord.

Maintaining the same position is accomplished by moving the three upper voices in similar motion.

FIGURE 5.11

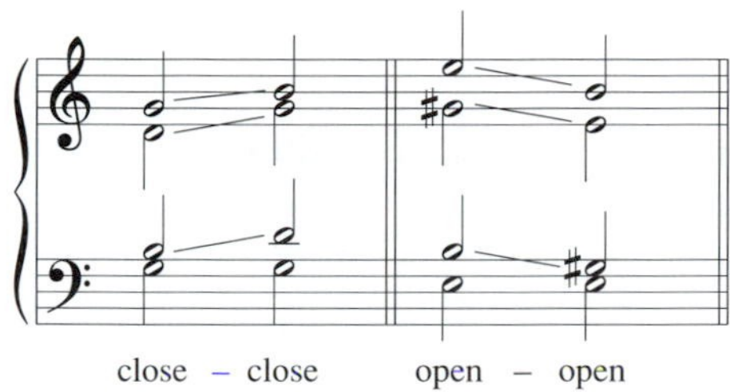

When the second chord changes position, two voices, the bass and one other, remain stationary while the other two voices exchange tones.

FIGURE 5.12

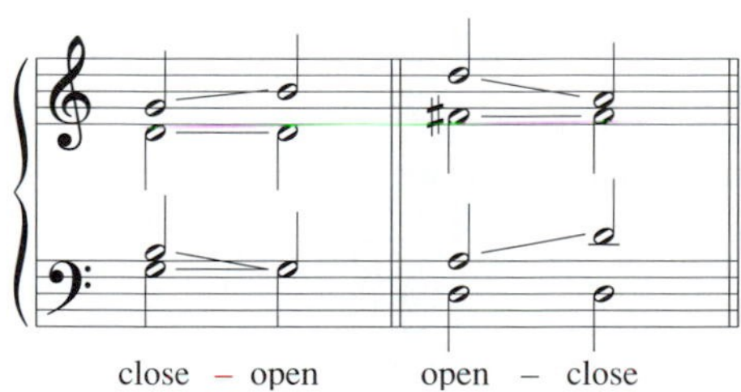

Change of position is usually necessary in three situations:

1. When an upper voice moves out of its usual range. In Figure 5.13, the notes are too high for the alto and tenor voices. Changing position puts these voices in a better range.

FIGURE 5.13

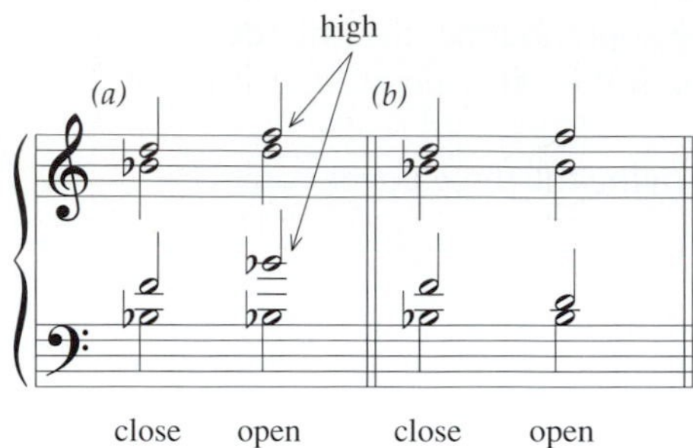

2. When there are large intervals in inner voices (Figure 5.14). Change of position produces more desirable small intervals or held notes.

FIGURE 5.14

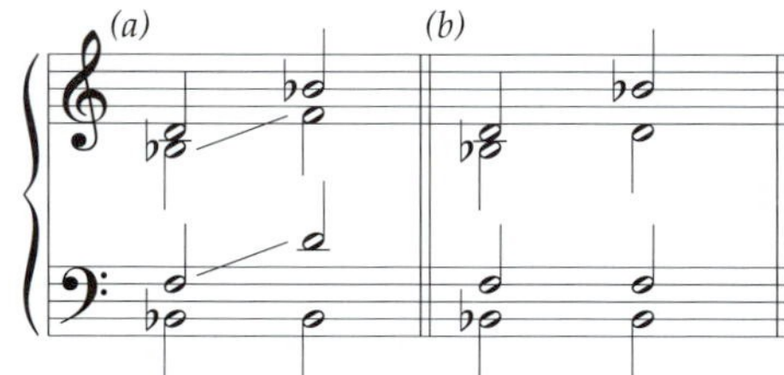

3. When the second triad contains no fifth, as in Figure 5.15. Changing from open to close position restores the usual distribution of voices. However, we will encounter acceptable exceptions later in our studies.

FIGURE 5.15

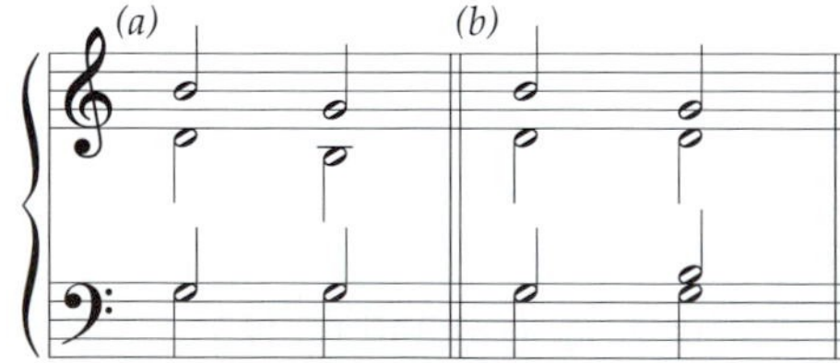

In the Workbook: Do Assignment 5A a, c, *and* d. *Answers are given.*
Do Assignment 5B. Answers are given.

ASSIGNMENT 5.2 *Writing repeated triads.* The first triad of each pair is complete. For each, decide whether the position of the first triad needs to be changed or whether the same position may be maintained. Place the name of the key below each example. In some examples, either way will be satisfactory.

In Appendix E: Answers to (1)–(3) are given.
*In the Workbook: Do Assignment 5.2*a. *Answers are given.*

ASSIGNMENT 5.3 *Writing repeated triads.* Only the soprano and the bass of the two triads are given. Fill in the alto and tenor voices. Name the key of each, indicating M or m.

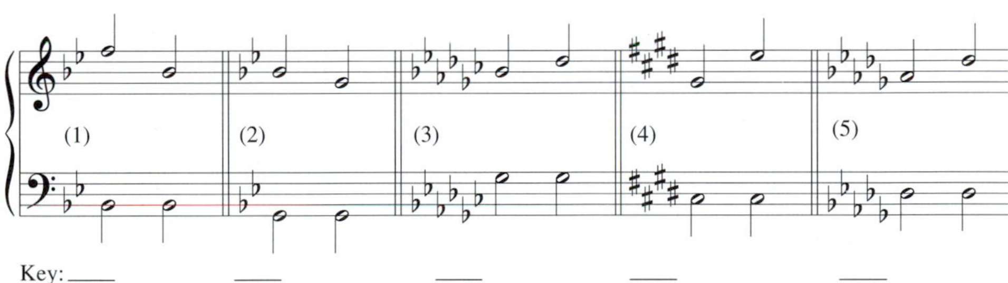

Writing the Authentic Cadence

In the various forms of the authentic cadence, the roots of the dominant and tonic chords are always separated by the interval of a fifth, or its inversion, the fourth. Because root movement by fourth is always implied in speaking of root movement by fifth, only the term *root movement by fifth* is necessary to convey both meanings. The following procedures are useful in connecting any two triads whose roots *in the bass* are a fifth apart; here they are applied to the writing of the authentic cadence.

Of the several ways of connecting the dominant and tonic triads, two are so commonly used that we will term them conventional. They can be applied in both major and minor keys.

First Procedure The first procedure is based on the assumption that if any two chords have a note (or notes) in common, it is best to carry that tone in the same voice into the next chord. G B D and C E G have a common tone, G. Holding G in the same voice allows the other two voices to move by step, the smoothest possible movement.

FIGURE 5.16

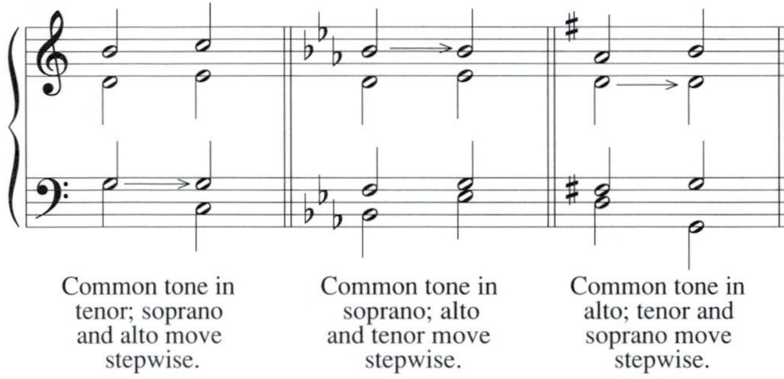

In a minor key, the third of V is ♯$\hat{7}$ (g: V = D F♯ A). To indicate this in a part-writing exercise, we use a figured bass symbol (review page 31), a ♯, ♮, or × below the staff, indicating that the third above the bass note is to be raised one half step (Figure 5.17*a–c*).

The Picardy third can be indicated in the same way (Figure 5.17*d*).

FIGURE 5.17

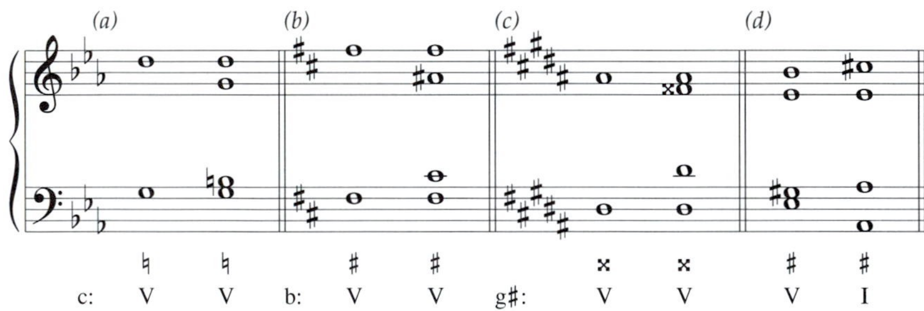

Examples of this first procedure from music compositions can be seen in cadences from earlier examples: the perfect authentic cadence in Assignment 4.3 (1), page 68; the imperfect authentic cadence in Figure 4.8*a,* page 67); and the half cadence in Figure 4.3, measure 2, page 62.

Second Procedure What if the common tone cannot be held? This predicament, as illustrated in Figure 5.18*a* in which I is left without a third, calls for another procedure: Move the three upper voices in the same direction (similar motion) to the nearest tones of the next triad. Note that when the soprano descends, the leading tone also descends to make the following triad complete (Figure 5.18*b* and *d* and Figure 5.19).

FIGURE 5.18

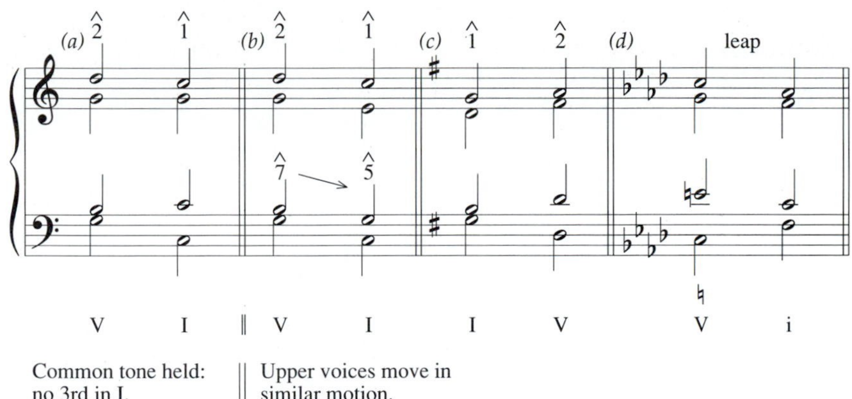

FIGURE 5.19

Martin Luther, "Ein' feste Burg"

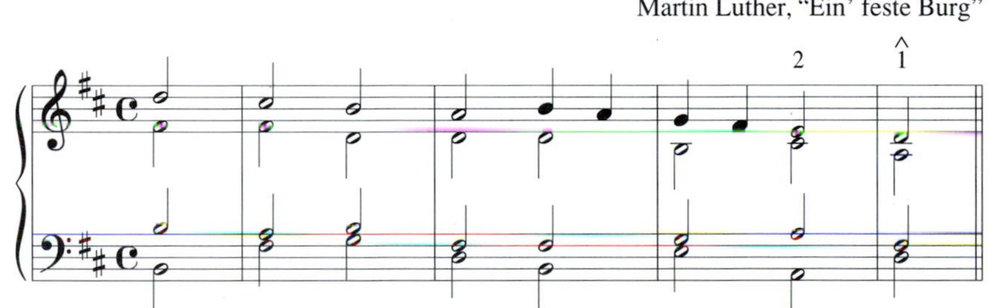

ASSIGNMENT 5.4 *Writing authentic cadences.* Fill in alto and tenor voices, using open or close position as appropriate (some can be written either way). Examples of both procedures are included. Use the first procedure unless the soprano line moves 1̂–2̂, 2̂–1̂, or by leap. In the three lines under each example, write the name of the key (M or m) and the roman numeral for each triad.

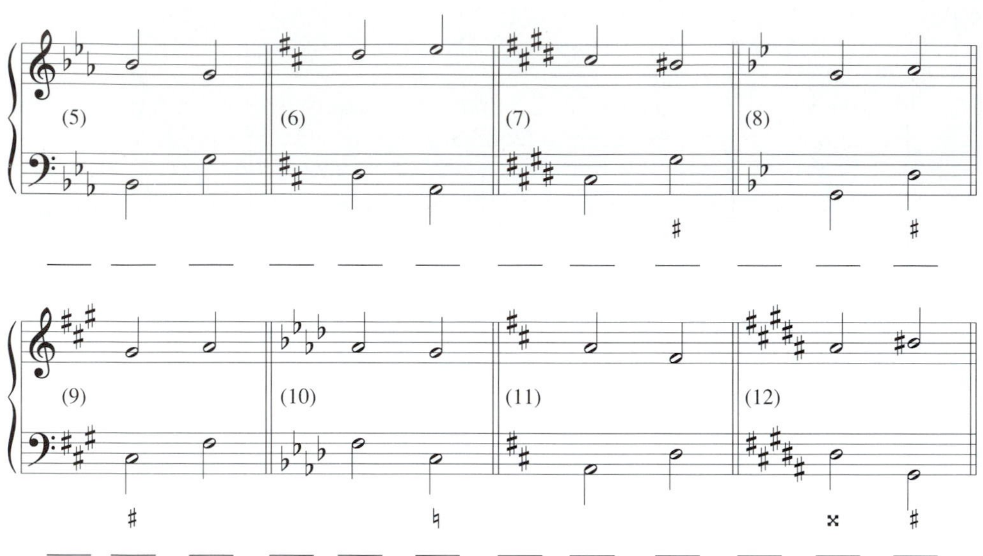

In Appendix E: Answers to (1)–(3) are given.
In the Workbook: Do Assignment 5.4a. Answers are given.

ASSIGNMENT 5.5 *Writing authentic cadences with only the soprano given.* Follow these steps:

1. Identify the key.
2. Write the scale-step numbers above each soprano line—for example, $\hat{2}$–$\hat{3}$.
3. In the three lines under each example, write the name of the key and the roman numeral for each triad.
4. Write first the bass line, then the inner voices.

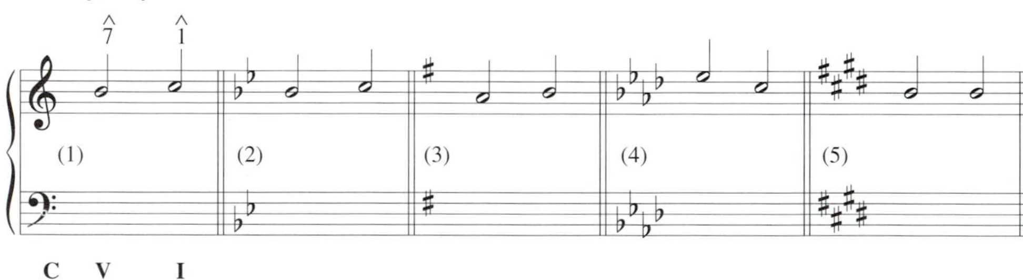

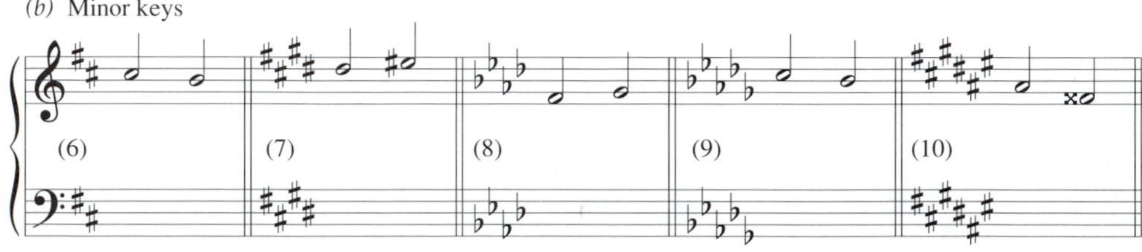

Alternative Procedures (1) In a final cadence, the leading tone in V may rise in any circumstance. The result is often an incomplete triad, three roots and one third (Figures 5.20 and 5.21).

(2) In any place in a phrase, the third of V may skip by the interval P4 to the third of I, or the reverse; the remaining voice is stationary. This skip usually appears in the soprano or tenor voice. Each triad includes all notes of the triad. The procedure is an effective way to change from open to close position or vice versa (Figure 5.22).

FIGURE 5.20

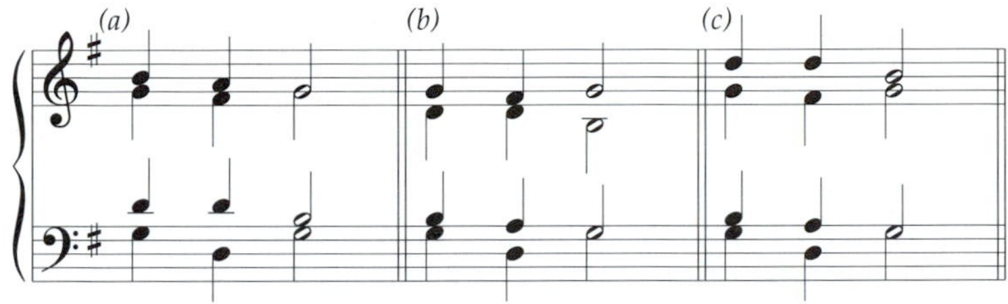

FIGURE 5.21

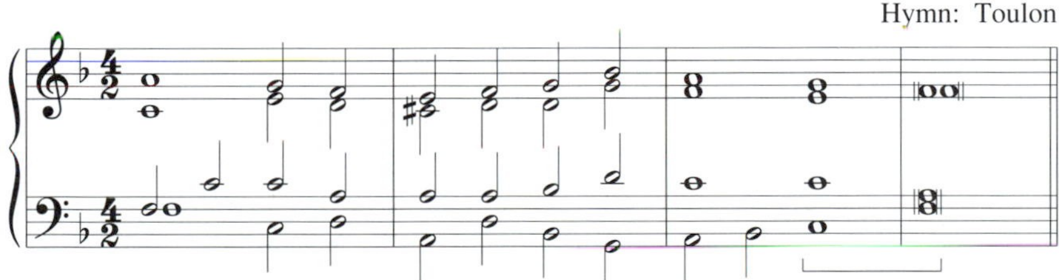

FIGURE 5.22

ASSIGNMENT 5.6 *Writing authentic cadences using the two alternative procedures just described.* In the examples indicated by an asterisk(*), use the "third-to-third" skip as in Figure 5.22. In all others, triple the root in the final tonic triad. Add a passing seventh in the V triad if you wish. (Review Figure 4.13 and preceding comment.)

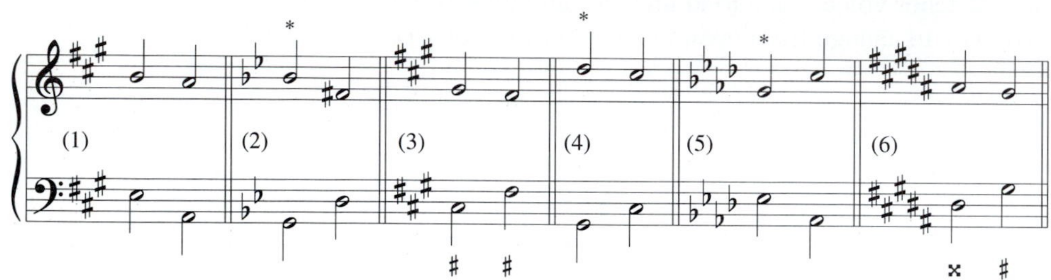

In the Workbook: Answers to the entire assignment are given.

ASSIGNMENT 5.7 *Writing the cadence, bass line only given.* Your choice of a soprano note will determine which part-writing procedure to follow. Demonstrate at least one each of these:

1. The common tone
2. Similar motion in the three upper voices
3. The tripled root in I (i)
4. The "third-to-third" cadence of Figure 5.22

In the Workbook: Answers to the entire assignment are given.

Writing in Phrase Lengths

The part-writing procedures for cadences can be used just as effectively in a phrase-length series of tonic and dominant triads. Figure 5.23 shows such a phrase; Figure 5.24 shows the solution.

FIGURE 5.23 *Extended Part-Writing Problem*

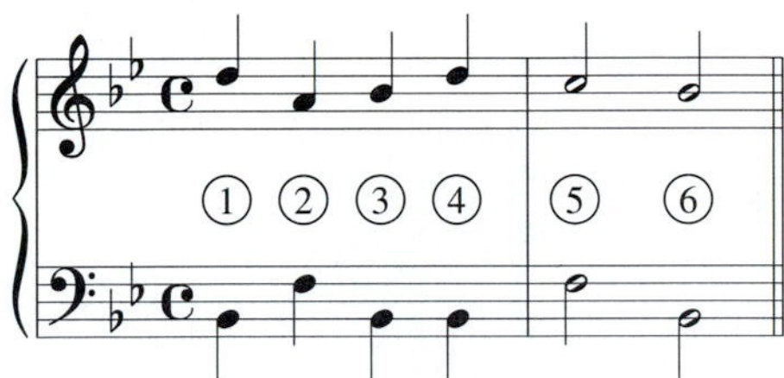

Here is how it can be done:

First triad: Better to start in open position to avoid high tenor note.

Triads 1–2: Here is the "third-to-third" movement, this time in the soprano. Part-writing is the same as in the cadence of Figure 5.22.

Triads 2–3: Easy common-tone progression.

Triads 3–4: Close to open, or open to close? The range of the tenor voice is the main consideration.

Triads 4–5: Easy common-tone progression again.

Triads 5–6: Use any of three different cadences. All are shown in Figure 5.24.

FIGURE 5.24 *Solution of Figure 5.23*

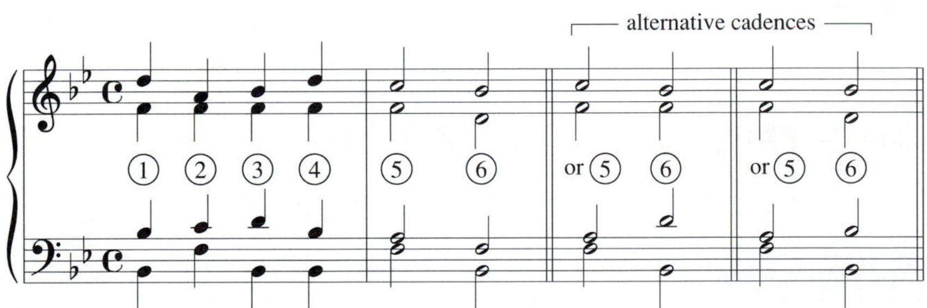

ASSIGNMENT 5.8 *Writing extended exercises.* Place triad numbers below the staff.

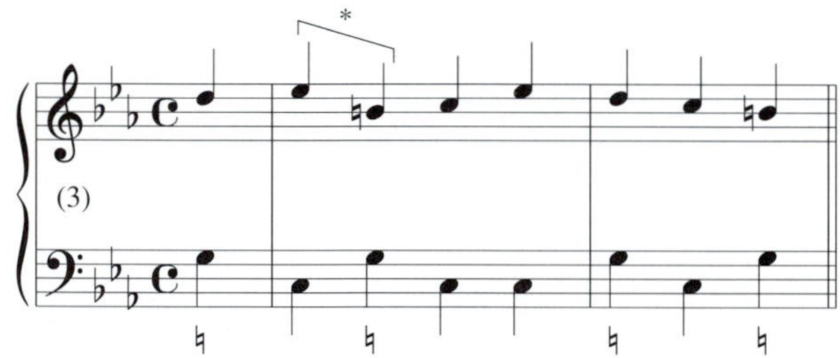

*What is this interval?

In Appendix E: The answer to (1) is given.

Harmonizing a Melody

Here are a few melodies, each note of which can be harmonized with a tonic or dominant triad. Any two successive notes will suggest either a repeated triad or one of the V–I or I–V progressions. (For example, $\hat{7}-\hat{1}$ anywhere in the melody is harmonized the same as the perfect authentic $\hat{7}-\hat{1}$ cadence.)

1. Determine the scale-step numbers. In Assignment 5.9 (1), the first two notes (C–B) are $\hat{1}$–$\hat{7}$ in C, the same as the half cadence $\hat{1}$–$\hat{7}$, harmonized as I–V.
2. Place the root of the triad in the bass clef exactly below the soprano note. In (1) of Assignment 5.9, the first two bass notes are C (for C E G) and G (for G B D).
3. Write triad numbers below the staff.
4. Fill in the inner voices, just as in previous exercises.

ASSIGNMENT 5.9 *Melody harmonization.*

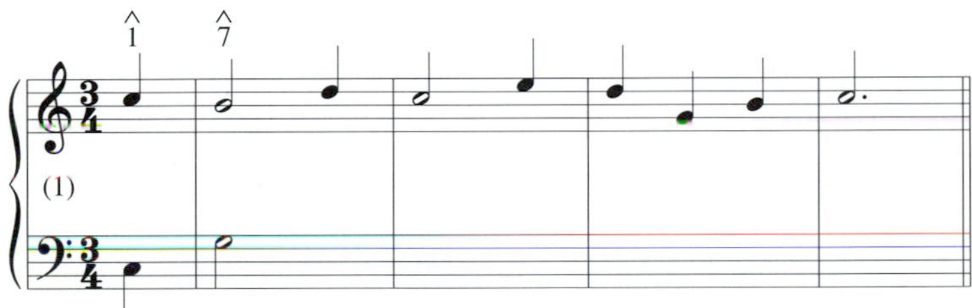

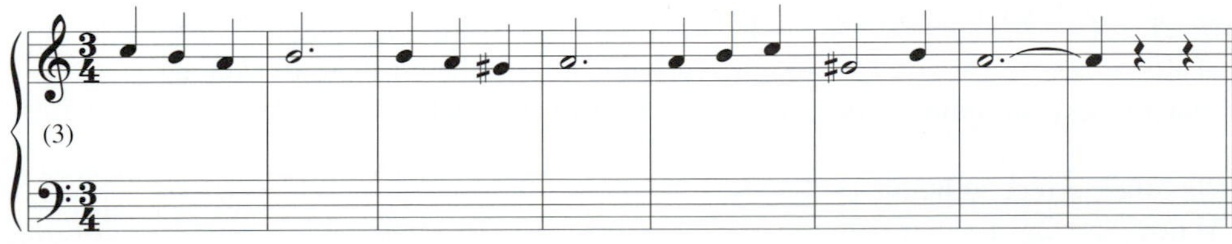

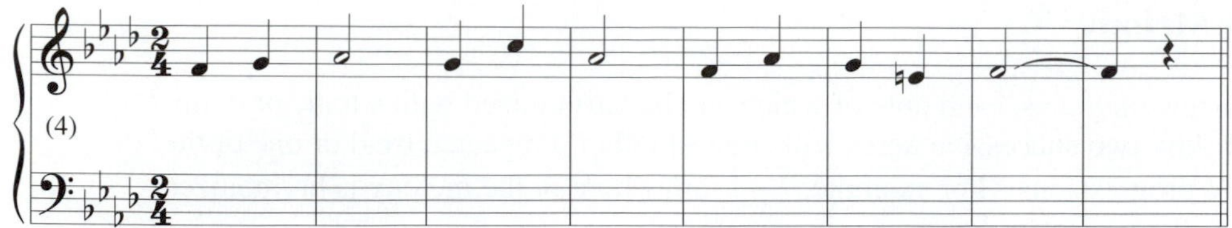

Keyboard Harmony

Authentic Cadences You have already played single triads at the keyboard. To play a cadence, simply play two triads in succession, the choice of triads and position determined by the type of cadence and the soprano line. For example, play a perfect authentic cadence in D major, soprano line $\hat{7}$–$\hat{1}$.

1. Spell the dominant and tonic triads.
2. Locate $\hat{7}$ of D major (C♯) on the piano; locate lower notes of the V triad (right hand, A, E; left hand, A). Play the triad.
3. Locate $\hat{1}$ of D major (D) on the piano; locate lower notes of the I triad. Play the triad.
4. Play the V–I progression.

FIGURE 5.25

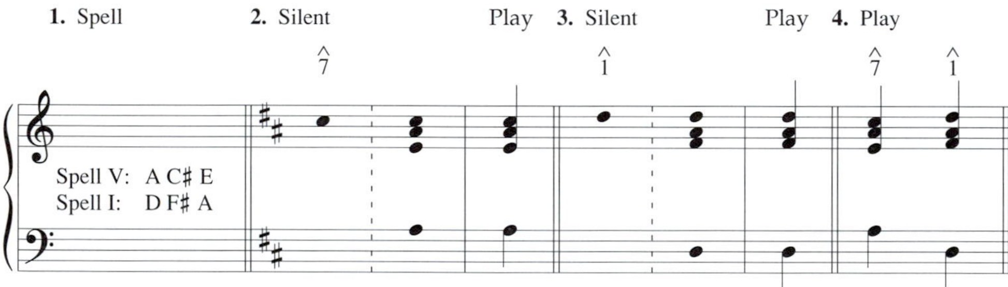

When close position is used in the right hand, part-writing procedures will always be acceptable, and at the same time the cadence can easily be played. Playing two notes in each hand, open position, is also acceptable but is slightly more difficult.

ASSIGNMENT 5.10 *Playing cadences.* In practicing the following cadences, use the circle of fifths, starting at any key and progressing around the circle until you arrive at the starting key. In minor keys, consider each I as i and each $\hat{7}$ as ♯$\hat{7}$.

(*a*) Play the perfect authentic cadences:
Major: $\hat{2}$ $\hat{1}$ $\quad$ $\hat{7}$ $\hat{1}$
V – I $\quad$ V – I

(*b*) Play the imperfect authentic cadences:

Major:	$\hat{2}$ $\hat{3}$	$\hat{5}$ $\hat{5}$	$\hat{5}$ $\hat{3}$
	V – I	V – I	V – I

(*c*) Play the half cadences:

Major:	$\hat{1}$ $\hat{7}$	$\hat{1}$ $\hat{2}$	$\hat{3}$ $\hat{2}$	$\hat{5}$ $\hat{5}$
	I – V	I – V	I – V	I – V

Harmonizing Melodic Cadences As a first step in learning to harmonize an entire melody, we will learn to harmonize melodic cadences with harmonic authentic cadences. In Figure 5.26, we see two motives from a folk song with the melodic cadences $\hat{2}$–$\hat{3}$ and $\hat{2}$–$\hat{1}$. These can be harmonized with an imperfect authentic cadence and a perfect authentic cadence, respectively.

FIGURE 5.26

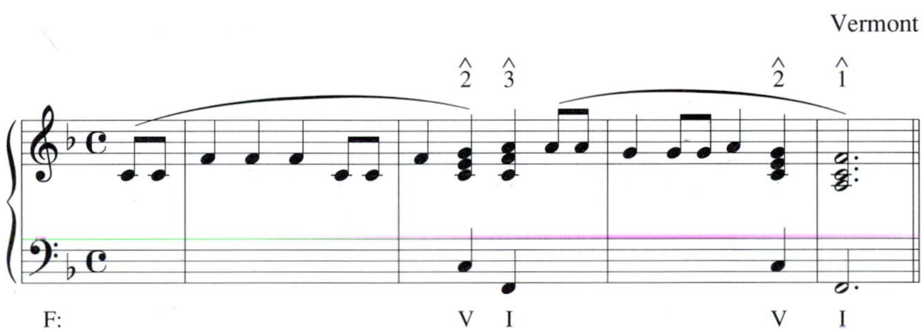

ASSIGNMENT 5.11 Play these tunes (phrases from chorales and from well-known melodies) and supply a harmonic cadence at the point of the melodic cadence, as in Figure 5.26.

(1)

(2)

(3)

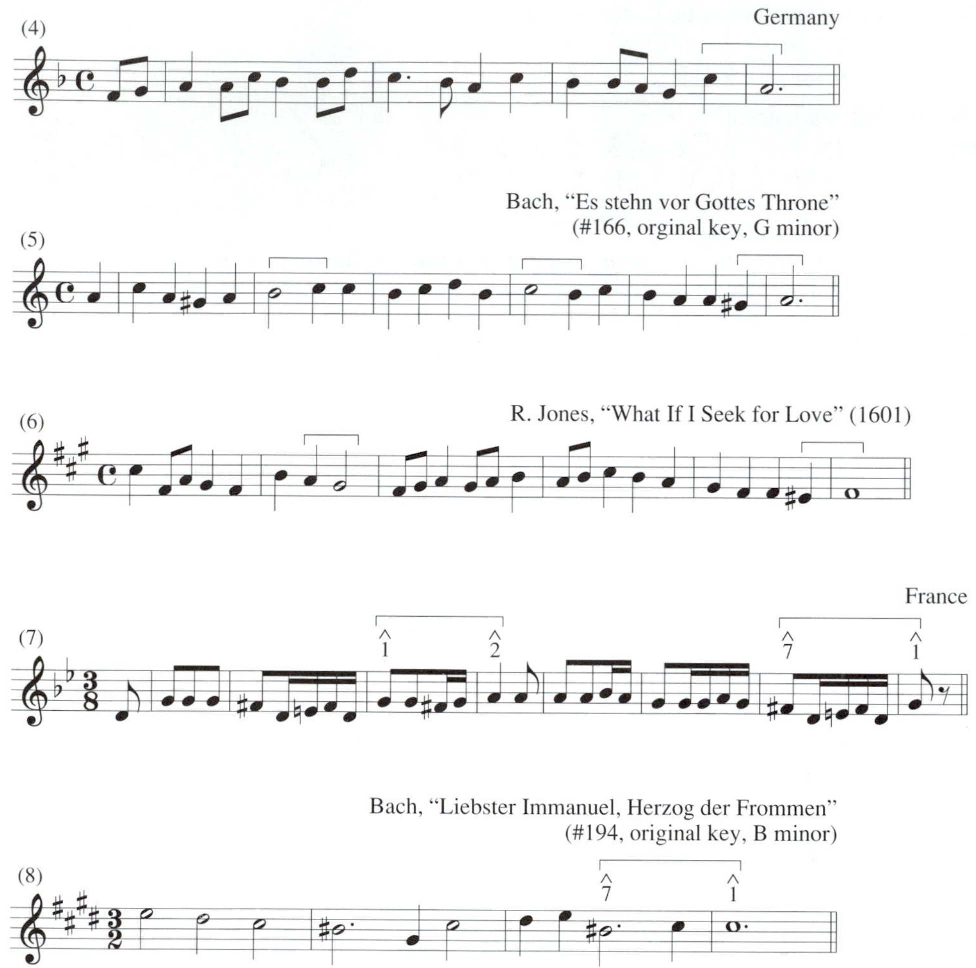

Melody Harmonization Using Lead Sheet Symbols

Music literature contains a vast amount of melodic material that can be harmonized using only I and V. Before asking you to choose *and* play a complete harmonization, we will ease you into this skill through the use of the *lead sheet* or *fake sheet.* This type of melodic presentation is found in most of the current series of public-school music textbooks. "Fake books" are well known in the popular music field; in these the performer improvises upon the given tune and its accompanying letter-name symbols.

In the simple nursery tune in Figure 5.27, the letter name of the root of each chord is used instead of the chord number. (You could have quickly figured out this harmonization, but the tune illustrates the point clearly.)

FIGURE 5.27 *Lead Sheet Symbols*

Of the many possible modes of performing a lead sheet, the following two are the simplest and at the same time yield musical results.

Playing an Accompaniment Only When someone else performs the tune, or when you sing or whistle the tune yourself, use a simple "oom-pah" style: Play the root in the left hand on the strong beat and play the triad in the right hand on the weak beat (on the second and third beats in triple meter).

FIGURE 5.28

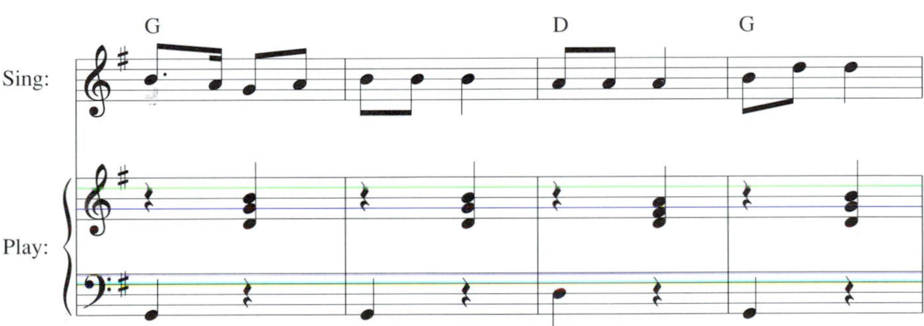

After the first triad is played, triads that follow should be connected by using the part-writing procedures already learned. Note that in going from measure 2 to measure 3 (I to V), the common tone was held.

Playing Melody and Accompaniment Together Play the given chord on the downbeat, three notes in the right hand and one in the left hand, with the melody note being the highest note in the chord. Play a chord again (1) after a bar line (measures 1–2) or (2) at the point a new chord is required (measure 3). See "Note" on page 105.

FIGURE 5.29

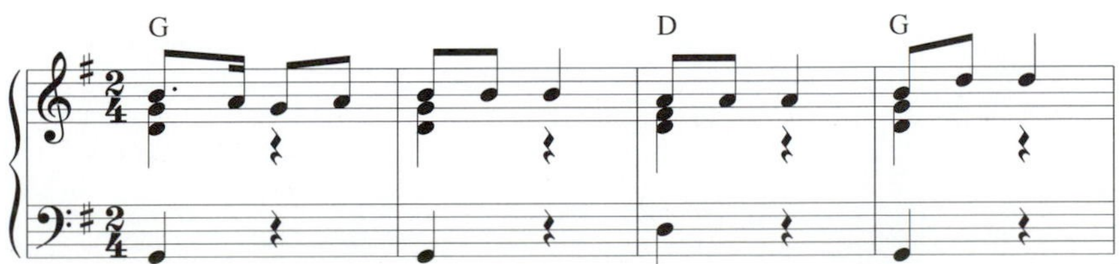

Practicing from lead sheets such as this will improve your keyboard facility, and careful observation of what you are doing will bring you insights into the reasons for harmonic choices and nonharmonic usages.

ASSIGNMENT 5.12 *Playing a harmonization from a lead sheet.* Circled notes are nonharmonic tones (review page 72).

For a minor triad, "m" is added. Fm = F A♭ C.

Note: Playing chord progressions in melody harmonization is often taught the "easy" way, playing block triads with a minimum of finger movement in the left hand, leaving the right hand free to play the melody. This method works well enough in the study of tonic, dominant, and subdominant chords but becomes awkward and difficult in using the remaining harmonies. In addition, the left-hand sound is inferior and unprofessional: Musical voice leading is impossible, parallel octaves are frequent, and the sound of a cluster of notes in the bass range is usually harsh and unpleasant, as in this example.

FIGURE 5.30

Students needing instruction in playing chords only for nonprofessional purposes are referred to *Rudiments of Music,* third edition (Prentice Hall, 1995), Chapters 21 and 23, for a complete presentation of this method.

Summary

Part-writing is the art of achieving good melodic lines when connecting a series of chords.

Procedures used consistently by composers are said to be conventional, though these do not restrict the use of other ways of connecting chords.

These factors must be considered when writing a single triad: *voice range, doubling, triad position,* and *distance between voices.*

In *close position,* the three upper notes of a triad are as close together as possible. In *open position,* there is more than an octave between the soprano and tenor voices.

When a triad is repeated with a different soprano note, the position of the triad may change or remain the same, depending upon the musical context.

Conventional procedures for connecting the tonic and dominant triads are (1) hold the common tone and move the other voices stepwise, and (2) when the common tone cannot be held, move the three upper voices in similar motion.

Other procedures to connect these two triads apply in special situations.

6

The Subdominant Triad

Upon completion of Chapter 5, either of Chapters 7 and 8, or both, may, if desired, be studied before or concurrently with this chapter.

FIGURE 6.1

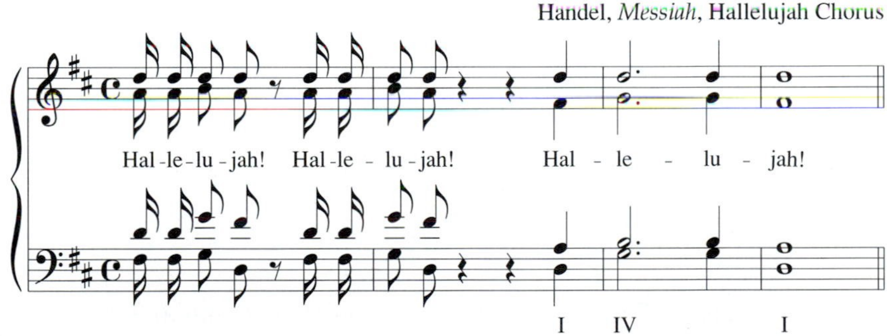

Who with any interest in music at all is not acquainted with this glorious conclusion to the Hallelujah Chorus? Most of the work's many "hallelujahs" are set to the progression I–IV–I, ending with the stately plagal (IV–I) cadence above.

Spelling the Subdominant Triad

The subdominant triad has its root on the fourth (subdominant) scale step of the key. In a major key, the triad is a major triad. In a minor key, the subdominant triad is usually minor, but when melodic considerations require the use of the raised sixth scale step, it is major. (Use of the major subdominant triad in a minor key will be studied in Chapter 10.)

FIGURE 6.2

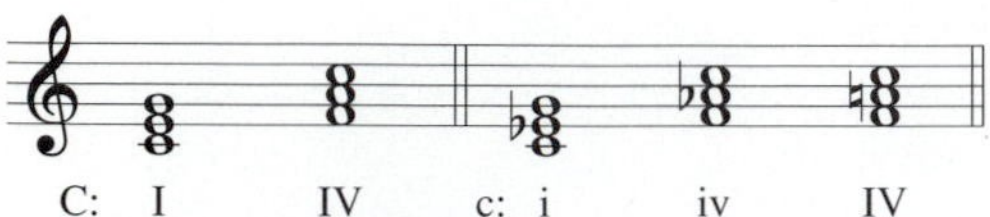

ASSIGNMENT 6.1 Spell the subdominant triad in each major key.

In the Workbook: Answers to the entire assignment are given.

ASSIGNMENT 6.2 *(a)* Spell the minor subdominant triad in each minor key.
(b) Spell the major subdominant triad in each minor key.

In the Workbook: Answers to the entire assignment are given.

Plagal Cadences

Like the dominant triad, the subdominant triad can occur during the course of the phrase and also as part of a cadential progression. Cadences using the subdominant and the tonic triads are known as *plagal cadences* and may be found in the same forms as authentic cadences. The plagal cadences are these:

Perfect Plagal (PP) The progression IV–I or iv–i in which the subdominant triad has its root in the bass and the final tonic triad has its root in both bass and soprano (Figure 6.3*a;* see also Figures 6.1 and 6.4).

Imperfect Plagal (IP) The progression IV–I or iv–i in which the final tonic triad is found with its third or its fifth in the soprano. The commonly used soprano lines are $\hat{6}$–$\hat{5}$, $\hat{4}$–$\hat{3}$, and $\hat{1}$ up to $\hat{3}$ (Figure 6.3*b–d*).

Half Cadence (H) A little-used cadence, the progression I–IV or i–iv (Figure 6.3*e–g;* see also Figure 6.5).

If we replace the key signature of F major, one flat, with four flats, Figure 6.3 displays the same cadences in F minor.

FIGURE 6.3 *Plagal Cadences*

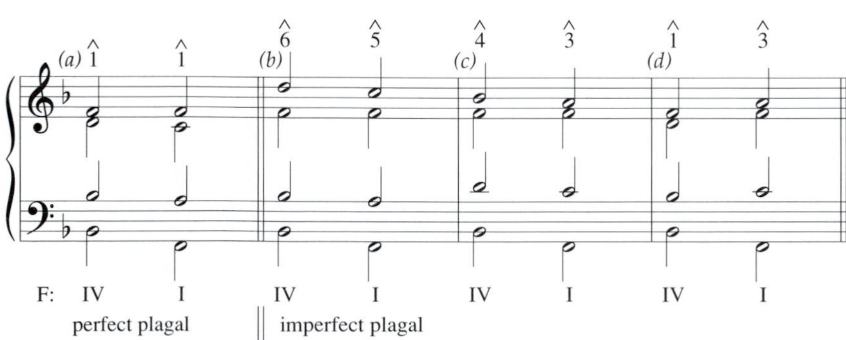

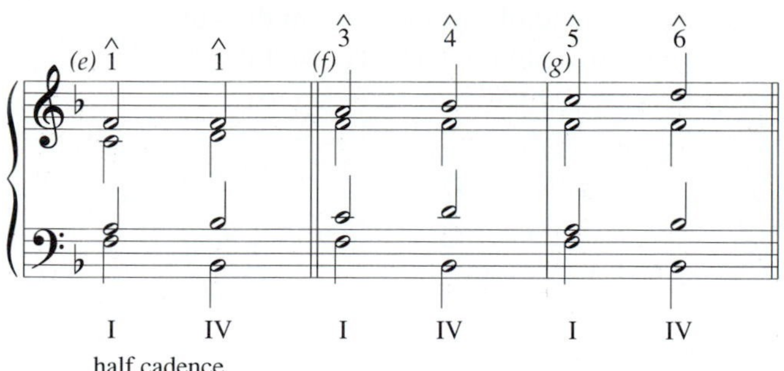

Actually, plagal cadences are infrequent in music composition, usually following a V–I progression.[1] Figure 6.4 shows an extended perfect plagal cadence (soprano $\hat{6}$–$\hat{5}$) following V–I at the close of a *lied* (song) by Brahms.

FIGURE 6.4

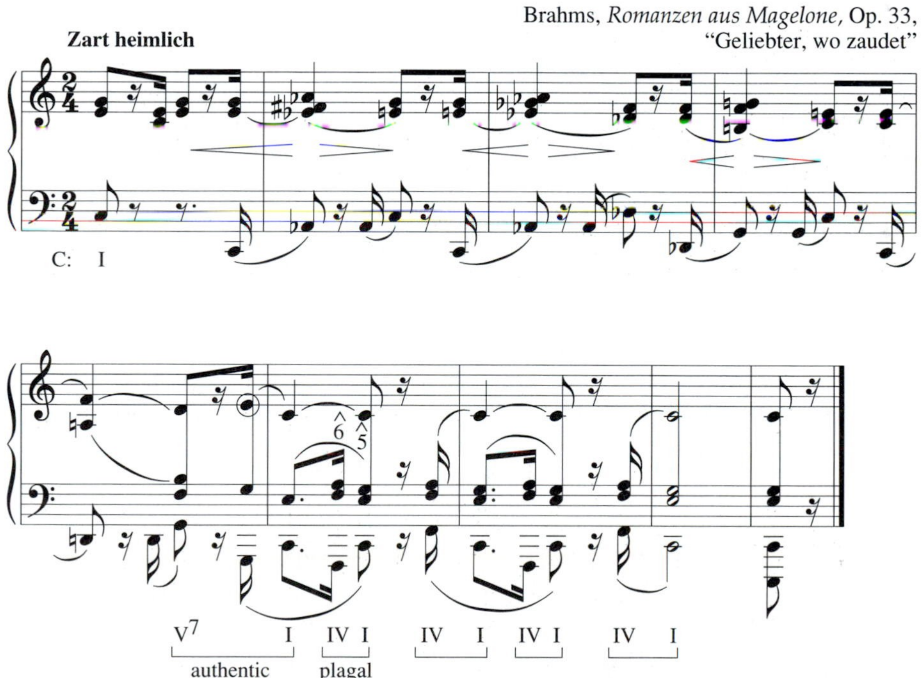

[1]A plagal cadence to the text "Amen" frequently concludes a hymn tune in the music of many religious denominations.

The uncommon half cadence may occur at the end of a phrase within the composition, as shown in Figure 6.5. You may also recall a similar cadence from the first phrase of "Auld Lang Syne" (". . . and never brought to mind?").

FIGURE 6.5 *Half Cadence, I–IV*

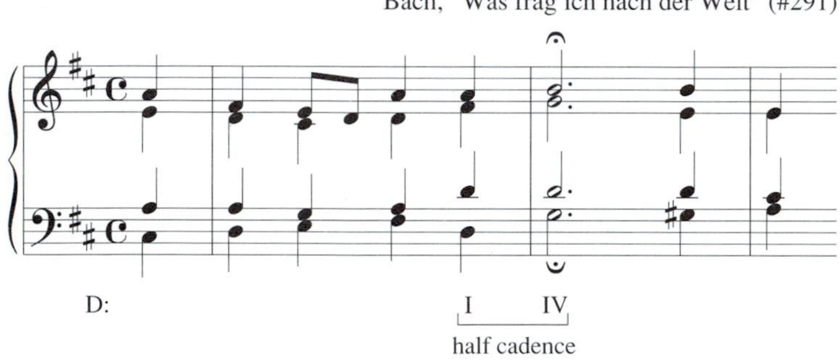

ASSIGNMENT 6.3 *Identifying plagal cadences.* For each cadence, name (1) the key (major or minor), (2) the cadence (PP, IP, or H), and (3) the scale steps in the soprano. For the cadence of Figure 6.1, the answers would be D, PP, $\hat{1}$–$\hat{1}$

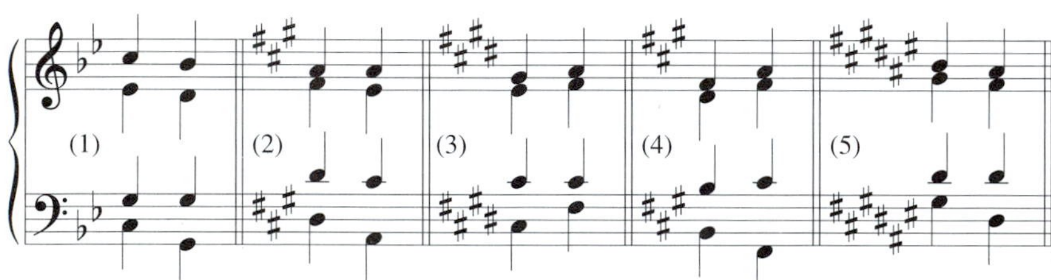

In Appendix E: Answers to the entire assignment are given.

IV or iv in Other Progressions

The subdominant triad may progress freely to or from the tonic or the dominant, with the exception of V–IV, which is infrequently used. When the authentic cadence is preceded by IV or iv, the progression IV–V–I or iv–V–i is often known as a *full cadence,* shown in major in Figure 6.6 and in minor in Figure 6.7. (Do you remember the special name for the major cadential tonic triad in a minor key?)

FIGURE 6.6

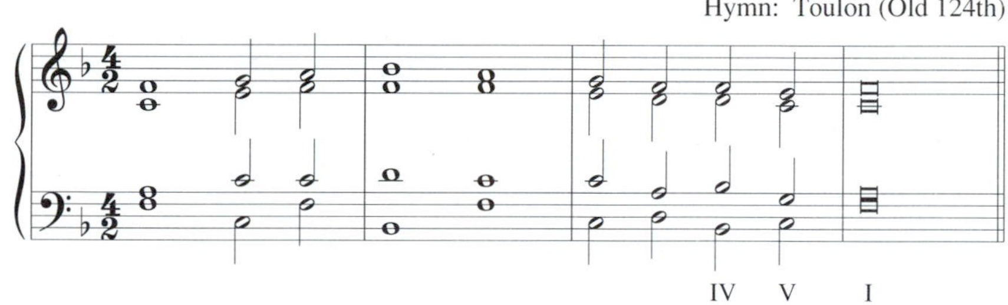

FIGURE 6.7

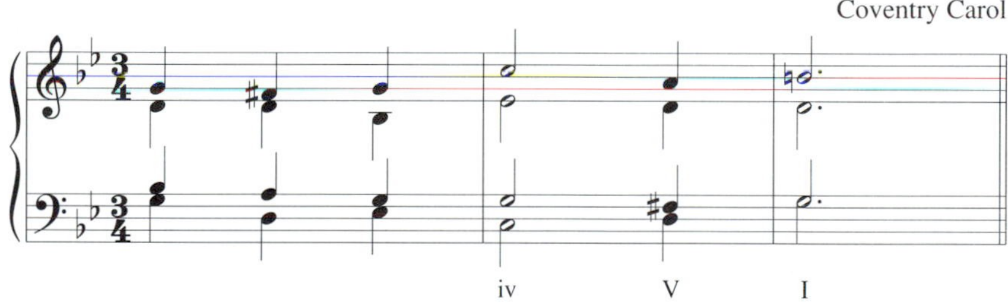

Any progression involving the subdominant triad can be used within the phrase, as in Figure 6.8, IV–I.

FIGURE 6.8

The tonic, dominant, and subdominant chords are widely used as the principal "guitar chords," especially for strumming along with a simple folk tune or with many of the country and western tunes of popular music.

FIGURE 6.9

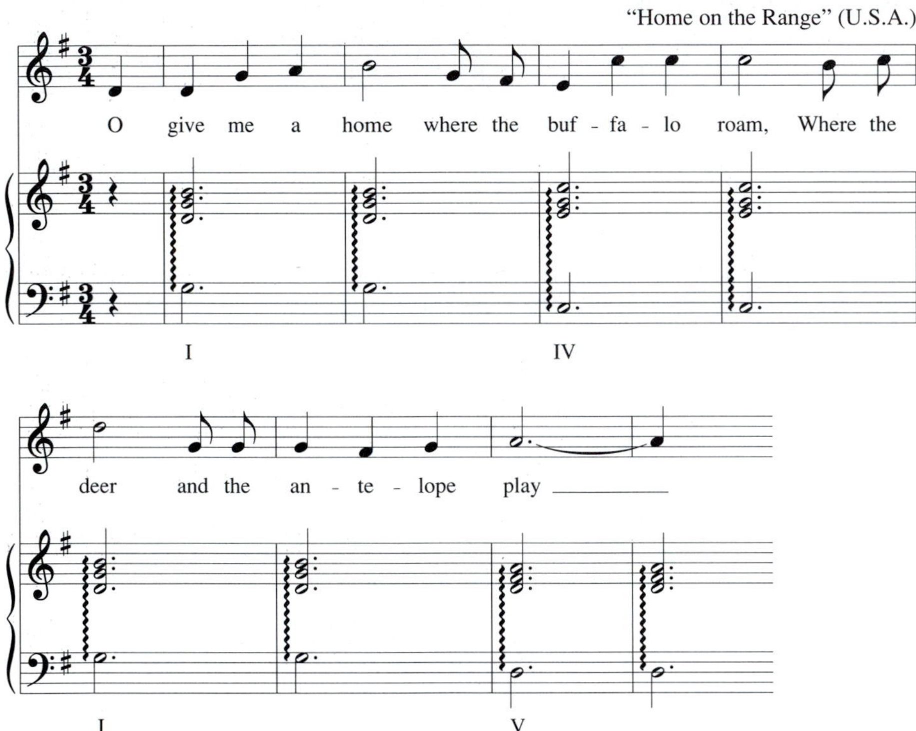

ASSIGNMENT 6.4 *Harmonic analysis.* Analyze these excerpts using roman numeral symbols. Circle all nonharmonic tones.

Wagner, *Das Rheingold,* Prelude to Scene 2

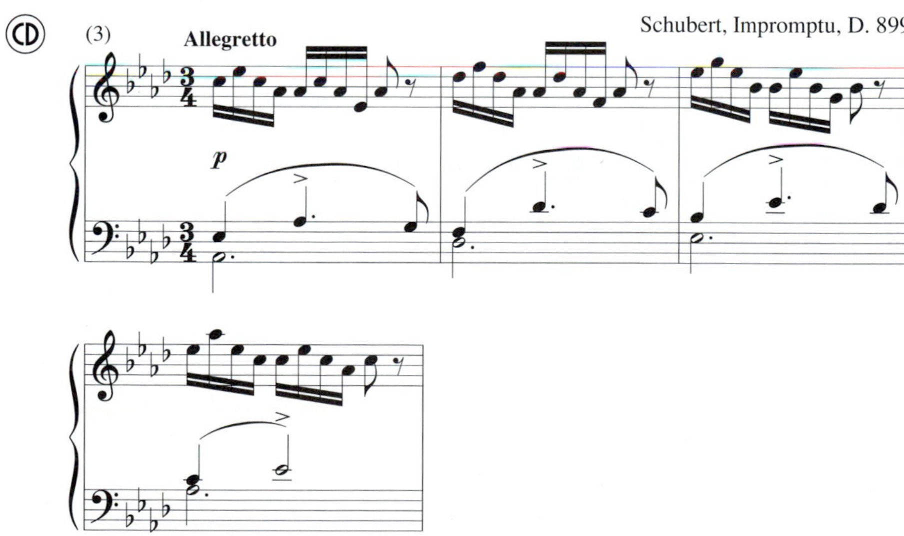

(4)
Adagio molto
Beethoven, Sonata for Piano, Op. 10, No. 1
p
cresc.
f
p

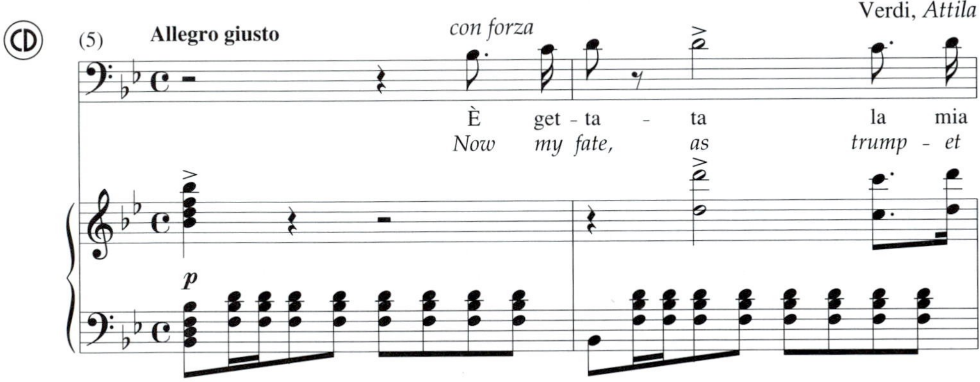
(5)
Allegro giusto
Verdi, Attila
con forza
È get - ta - ta la mia
Now my fate, as trump - et
p

In Appendix E: The answer to (1) is given.

The Subdominant Triad in Melodic Writing

Intervals from the subdominant triad can be used effectively in melodic writing, although they are used less frequently than intervals from tonic and dominant triads.

FIGURE 6.10

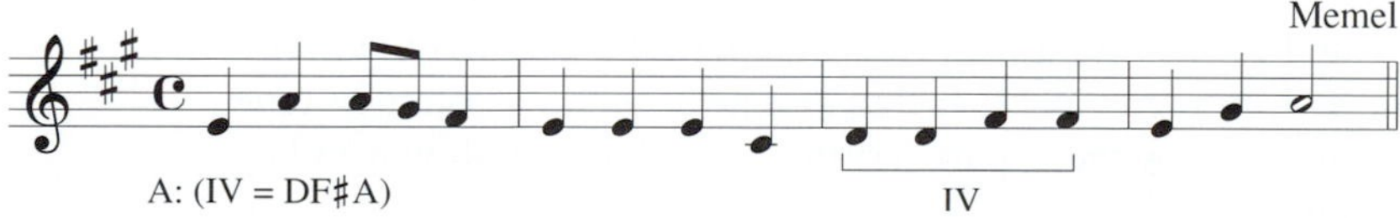

ASSIGNMENT 6.5 Locate and bracket intervals from the subdominant triad in these melodies, as in Figure 6.10.

Writing the Progression IV–I or iv–i

Since the roots of the IV and I triads are a fifth (fourth) apart, the part-writing procedures are the same as for V–I. In Figure 6.11, each pair marked *a* has a common tone; the pair marked *b* has none. Review these part-writing procedures as shown in Figure 6.3 and in Assignment 6.3.

FIGURE 6.11

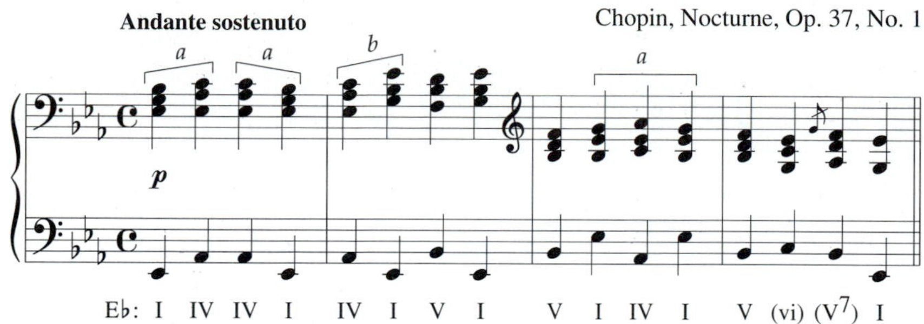

The "third-to-third" skip is not infrequent. Note the change of position in each I–IV progression when the skip is used: close to open in *a* and open to close in *b*.

FIGURE 6.12

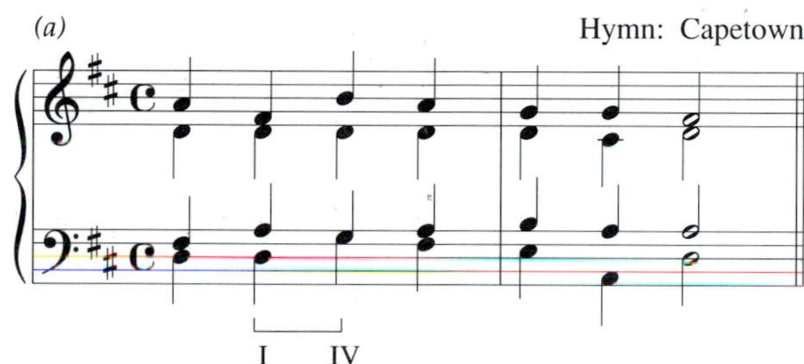

ASSIGNMENT 6.6 Write plagal cadences, (1)–(7), and progressions using the "third-to-third" skip, (8)–(10). Identify the cadences as PP, IP, or H. Place chord numbers below the staff.

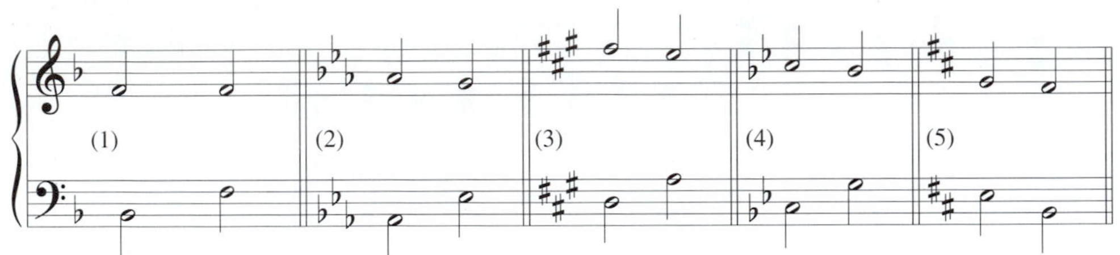

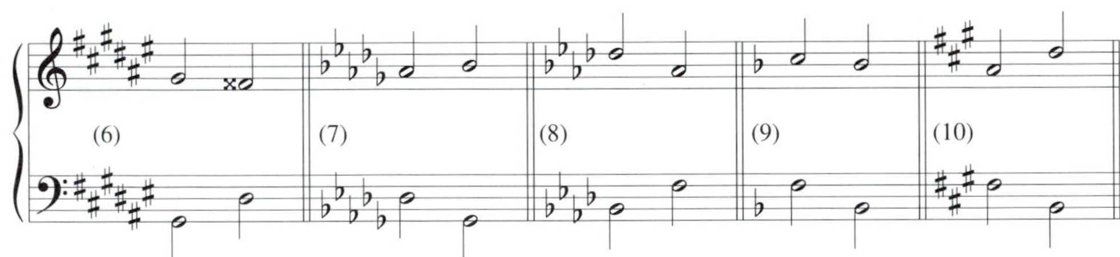

ASSIGNMENT 6.7 Write plagal cadences when

(a) only the bass line is given. Include two PP cadences and one each of the IP cadences shown in Figure 6.3.

(b) only the soprano line is given. Be sure that each bass note is the root of a triad.

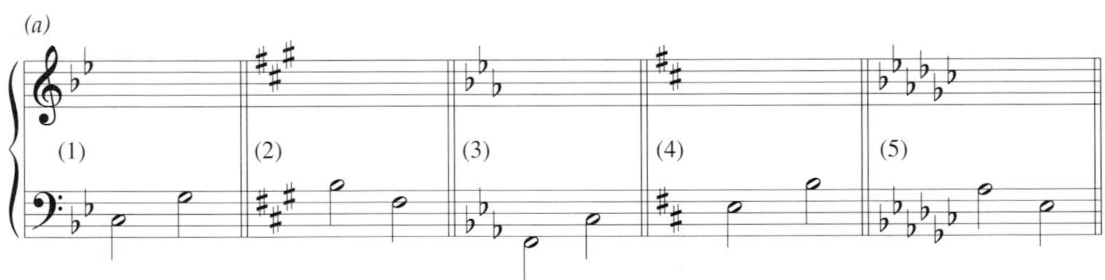

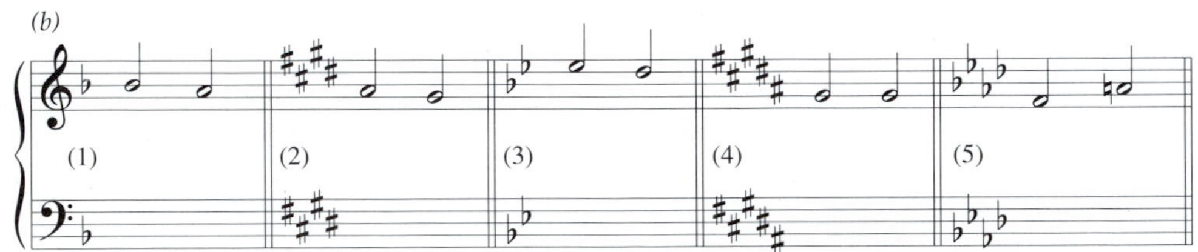

Writing the Progression IV–V (iv–V)

When the roots of two triads are a second apart, as in IV–V, no common tone is available. In the conventional procedure, each of the three upper voices moves to its nearest triad tone in contrary motion to the bass, as in Figure 6.13. Also review Figures 6.6 and 6.7

FIGURE 6.13

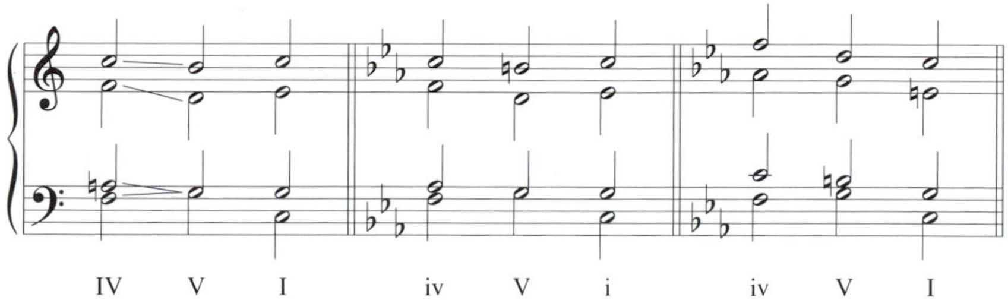

Did you notice in the preceding figures that the soprano note of IV (iv) always descends? The soprano may, of course, ascend; but in that case, the chord following is almost always vii°, a procedure to be studied in Chapter 10. There is one exception, very little used and available only for a IV (major) triad with its third in the soprano, as shown in Figure 6.14. The aural effect of parallel fifths is present, even though absent in the notation.

FIGURE 6.14

Parallel Fifths and Octaves; the Melodic Augmented Second

The heading of this section lists three weaknesses in part-writing that students almost always find frustrating. Since they can easily occur in the writing of triads with roots a second apart, they are first mentioned here, but they can occur in almost any part-writing problem. These are the three, shown in Figure 6.15:

1. Parallel perfect fifths
2. Parallel octaves
3. The melodic augmented second

FIGURE 6.15

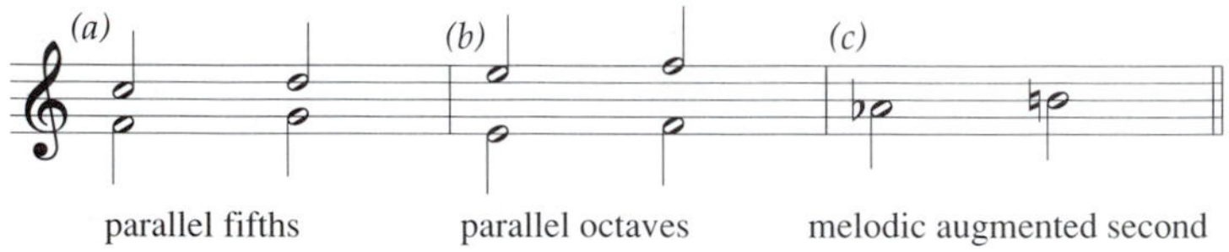

Figure 6.16 shows how easy it is to produce these errors when not using conventional procedures.

FIGURE 6.16

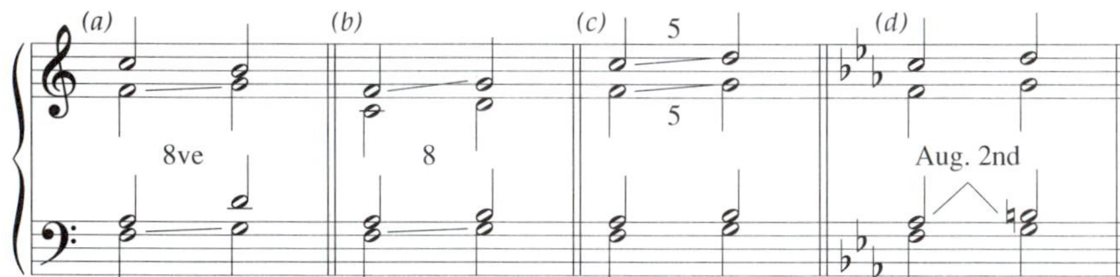

(Be sure to read Article #6, "The Three Demons of Part-Writing," in this chapter. Included is a discussion of why these procedures are objectionable.)

Any attempt to avoid parallel octaves by changing the direction of one of the two notes involved does not produce successful results. In Figure 6.17*a,* an attempt was made to avoid an octave by moving the bass down a minor seventh instead of up a major second. These are still parallel octaves, but they are called, in seemingly contradictory language, *parallel octaves by contrary motion.* There are, in our illustration, two F's going to two G's in the same pair of voices.

FIGURE 6.17

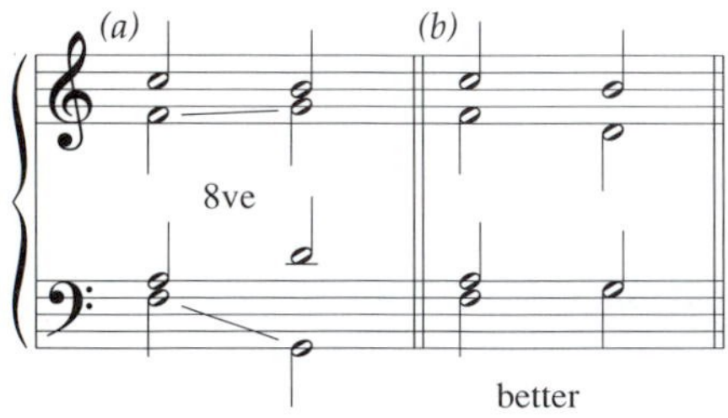

But there is an exception, as there usually is in part-writing! At the final cadence of a composition or at the end of one of its major sections, the soprano and bass commonly display the octave by contrary motion.

FIGURE 6.18

FIGURE 6.19

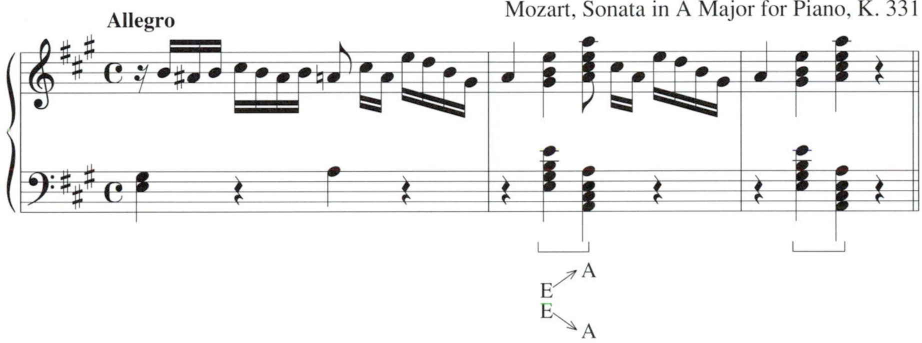

Parallel fifths by contrary motion are likewise to be avoided.

FIGURE 6.20

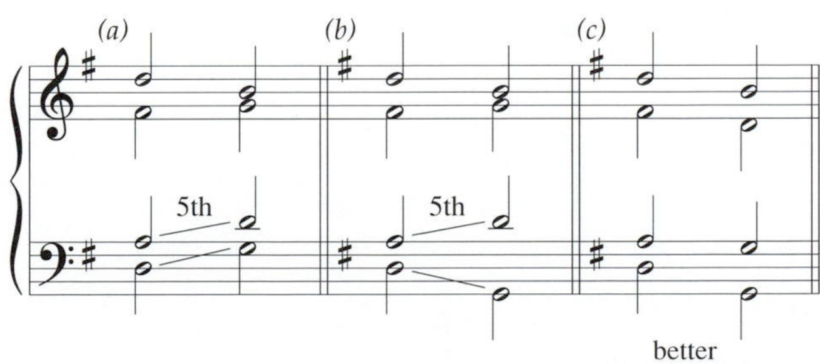

Note, however, that octaves or fifths repeated on the same pitches are *not* considered parallel; the use of these *stationary* octaves or fifths is acceptable.

FIGURE 6.21

The melodic augmented second occurs in a minor key when one voice line progresses from ♭$\hat{6}$ to ♯$\hat{7}$, as in the tenor line of Figure 6.22. Notice also that the movement of the tenor has produced an unwanted doubled leading tone.

FIGURE 6.22

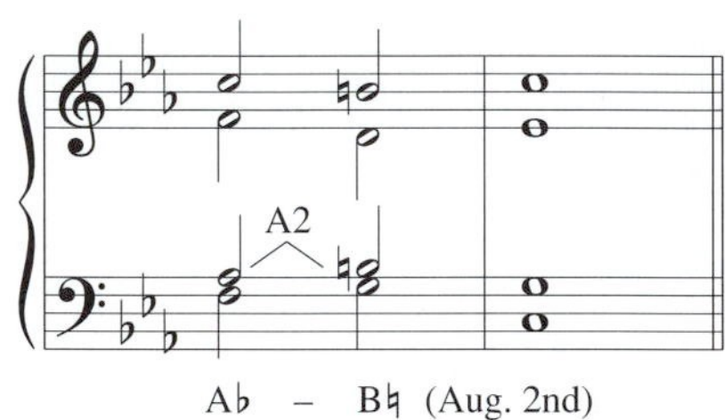

ASSIGNMENT 6.8 The following harmonization is full of these offending practices. How many can you find? Compare your answers with the list below.

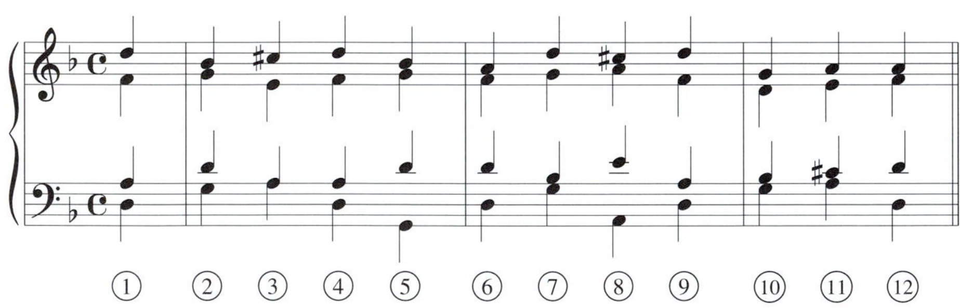

1–2	Fifths, tenor and bass
2–3	Augmented second, soprano
4–5	Fifths by contrary motion, tenor and bass
6–7	Fifths, soprano and bass
7–8	Octaves by contrary motion, alto and bass

8–9 Fifths by contrary motion, tenor and bass

9–10 Octaves by contrary motion, soprano and bass

10–11 Three! Octaves, fifths, and augmented second

Use of conventional procedures will usually avoid such errors. This is not to say that only conventional procedures should be used. With the study of inversions and nonharmonic tones, we will have the opportunity for much more freedom in part-writing. But still, it is always best to try the conventional ways first.

ASSIGNMENT 6.9 Write cadences as found below. Write chord numbers below the staff.

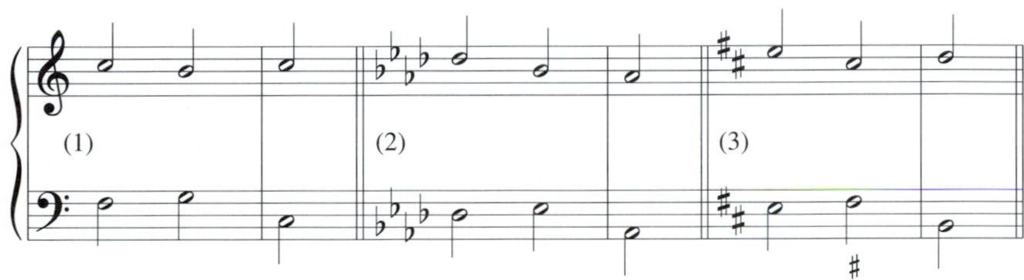

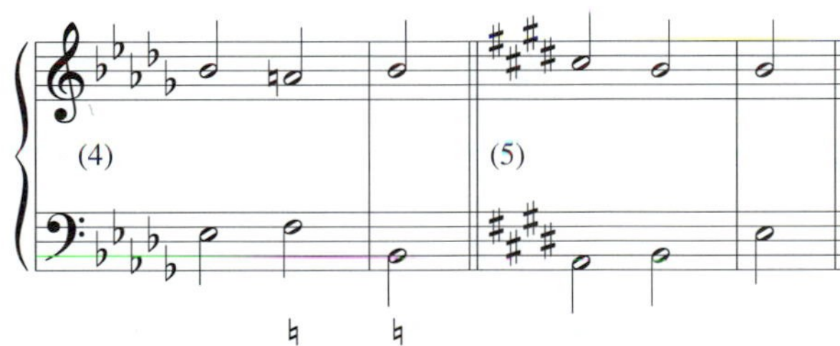

In the Workbook: Answers to the entire assignment are given.

ASSIGNMENT 6.10 Fill in alto and tenor voices using part-writing procedures studied thus far. Make harmonic analysis by placing the correct roman numeral below each bass note.

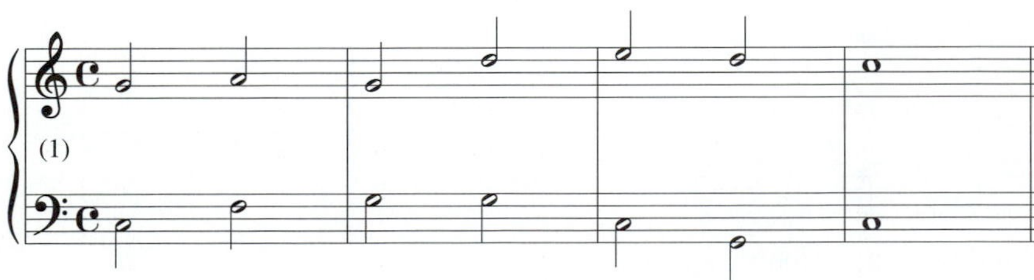

In Appendix E: The answer to (2) is given.

ASSIGNMENT 6.11 Harmonize melodies, supplying the alto, tenor, and bass parts. Follow this procedure:

1. Determine the key. Do not only check the key signature, but also sing the melody through, observing the nature of the cadence to determine whether the melody is major or minor.
2. Write in the chord numbers for the cadence below the bass staff.
3. Write in chord numbers leading up to the cadence.
4. Write in the bass line, each note being the root of the chosen chord.
5. Fill in the inner parts.

Melody 1 can be harmonized in both a major key and a minor key. The subdominant triad will not appear in one of these keys.

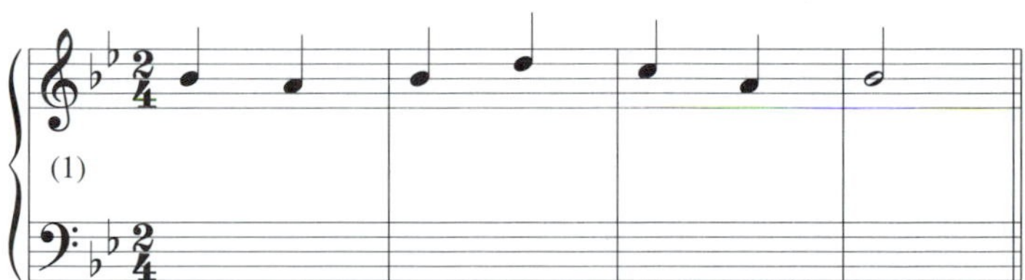

Keyboard Harmony

ASSIGNMENT 6.12 Play plagal cadences at the keyboard. Play them in each major or minor key.

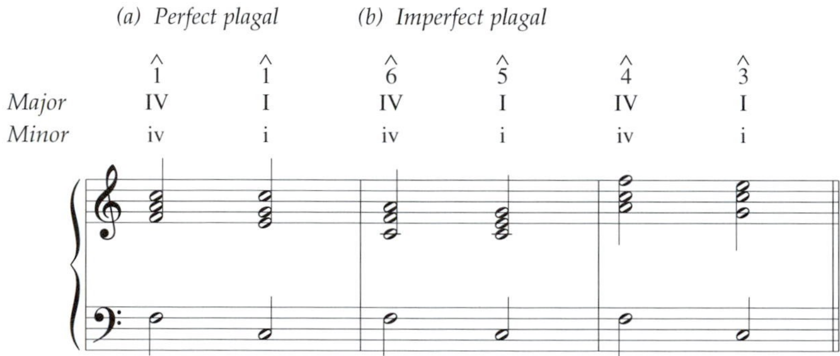

ASSIGNMENT 6.13 *Harmonizing cadences at the piano.* Play these melodies. When you reach a cadence (marked with a bracket), play an authentic or a plagal cadence as appropriate.

(1)

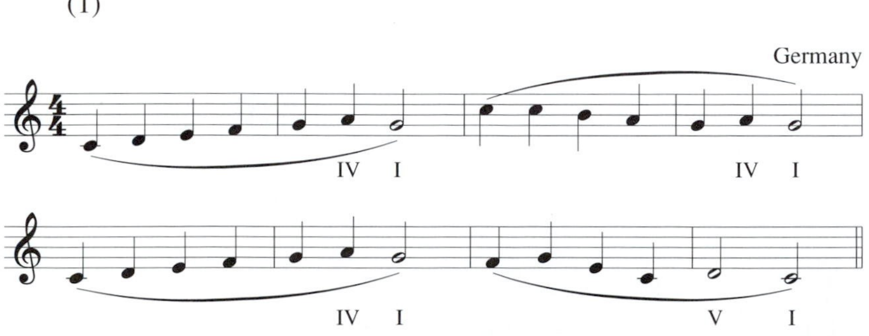

(5) The half cadence iv–V is included here.

The Progression I–IV–V–I

ASSIGNMENT 6.14 Play the progression I–IV–V–I and i–iv–V–i at the keyboard in each of its three soprano positions.

Melodic Harmonization

ASSIGNMENT 6.15 *Harmonizing a melody with lead sheet symbols.* The procedure is the same as that for I and V triads (review "Melody Harmonization Using Lead Sheet Symbols" in Chapter 5, page 102).

(3)

(4) Note the progression V–IV

(5)

Summary

The *plagal cadence* consists of a progression from the subdominant to the tonic triad.

The plagal cadence is found in the same forms as the authentic cadence, although the half cadence is uncommon.

In a minor key, the subdominant triad may be iv or IV, depending upon the use of $\hat{6}$.

More common is the use of the progression IV–V. The IV–V–I progression at the cadence is sometimes called a *full cadence.*

In part-writing from IV to V, the three upper voices generally move down in contrary motion to the ascending bass. An ascending soprano usually requires that IV be followed by vii°.

Certain part-writing difficulties may appear from this point on: the *parallel octave,* the *parallel fifth,* and the *melodic augmented second.*

ARTICLE #6

The Three Demons of Part-Writing

Well, not really demons. But many students, exasperated by their frequent and unwanted appearances, are ready to believe in some evil force at work!

There is nothing inherently wrong with parallel fifths, parallel octaves, and melodic augmented seconds. Any sound one can conceive is right if it pleases him or her, just as any sound is right for a particular era or a particular geographical area if it pleases the listeners of that time or place. However, during the period in Western music from about A.D. 1000 to A.D. 1900, these three sounds have generally *not* pleased composers or listeners; consequently, they have not been characteristic elements in the music of the West.

Ironically, the earliest known music for more than one voice line—the simultaneous sounding of a chant melody and the same melody a perfect fifth lower—produced, of course, a series of perfect parallel fifths.

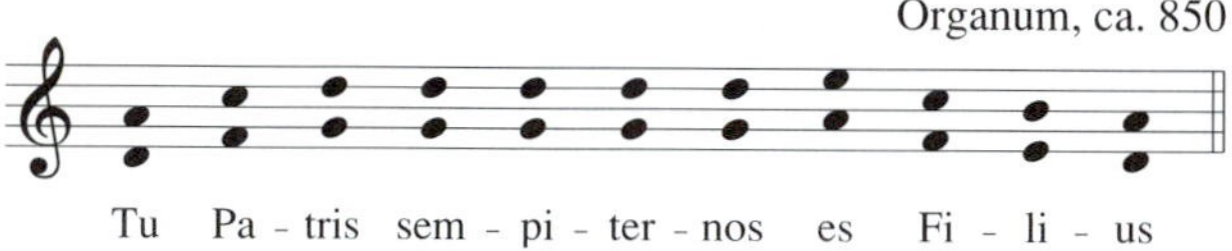

However, the monotony of this harmonic sound was replaced by the more interesting sounds of contrary motion about A.D. 1000, and from that time right up to our own, parallel fifths have been almost nonexistent in Western musical culture. They can be found occasionally, however, as in this excerpt from a Mozart sonata.

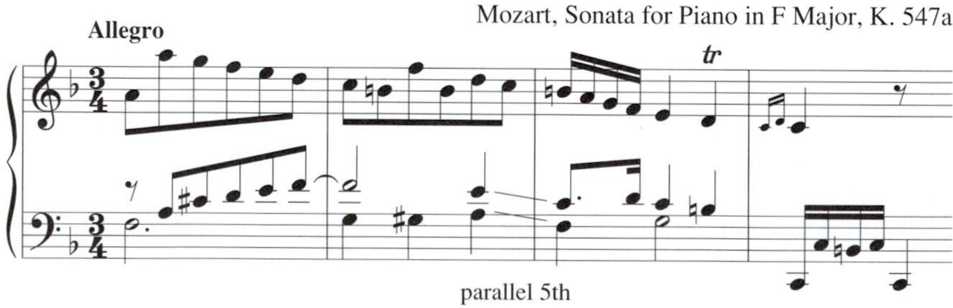

They have also been used to achieve special effects, as in the opening of the second act of *La Bohème,* in which they accompany a scene of general confusion.

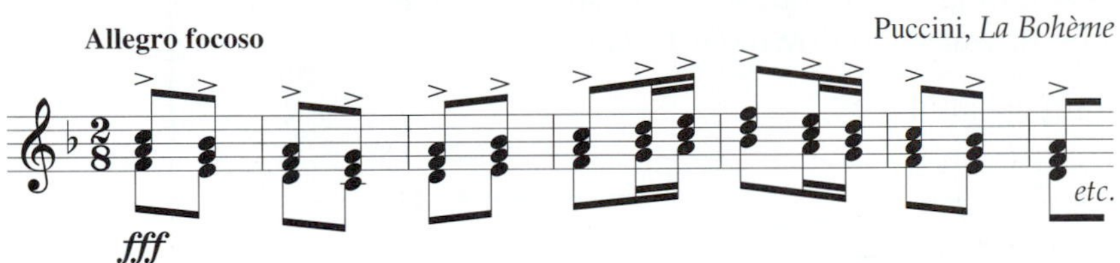

But in the twentieth century, and probably beginning with the music of Debussy (1862–1918), parallel fifths have regained their respectability after nearly a thousand years of neglect and are universally acceptable in contemporary music practice (see the following excerpt from a piece by Ravel).

Parallel octaves are of two varieties, one acceptable, the other not. An octave is merely the repetition of a given pitch at another level, higher or lower. When the two notes sound simultaneously, the two sounds represent the same note. When two *different* voice lines move in octaves, then these octaves represent only one moving sound, and the effect is the loss of one voice line. In the example below, the four-voice structure is reduced to three by this parallelism.

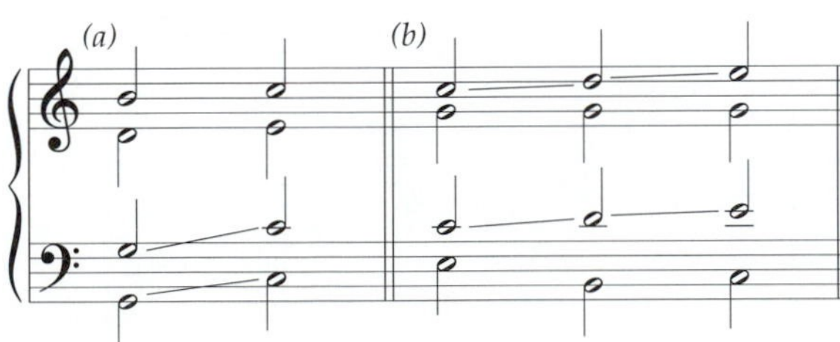

Parallel octaves are acceptable when they represent a doubling of a single voice line, called *sonority doubling,* as is common in instrumental and keyboard music. In the following example, the octaves in measures 2–4 are merely a reinforcement of a single melodic line. Beethoven emphasizes this by the single stem on each octave in contrast to measure 1, where tenor and bass are differentiated by upward and downward stems.

The melodic augmented second is a characteristic element in many Near Eastern and oriental scales (review the article "Some Varieties of Melodic Expression," on page 157). The interval is sometimes used in Western music to give a flavor of orientalism.

This interval also has its place in certain limited passages in Western music. These will be discussed later, since they have little relation to the elementary concepts now under discussion.

7

The Melodic Line I

This text is entitled *Harmony,* yet there is very little music that is only harmonic. Melody, on the other hand, can stand alone, as you know from your own experience when you whistle or sing a tune.

The earliest known music is exclusively melodic, and melody's importance in music composition continues to the present in spite of the many and diverse changes in musical styles over the years. Article #7, "Some Varieties of Melodic Expression," at the end of this chapter illustrates a few of the widely different concepts of melodic writing found during the course of the history of music.

Melodies associated with traditional harmony sound as they do because they represent the interaction of four musical elements: *form, pitch, harmonic implication,* and *rhythm and meter.*

Form

Most music is written in some orderly arrangement. In the music of the West, certain patterns of musical construction have come to be commonly (though not exclusively) used. These patterns are known as musical *forms.*

The term *form* refers to the shape or structure of the object or concept being described. In music, a form usually ends at a cadence point; a form begins either at the beginning of the piece or immediately after a cadence. Since a musical composition usually has more than one cadence, it usually contains a series of forms. These smaller forms, in turn, will often combine to make up a larger kind of form, the nature and description of which is determined by the number of cadences and the nature of the material between cadences.

The Phrase From this general description, we can turn our attention to the smallest of the forms, the *phrase.* In melodic writing, the phrase is a group of notes leading to a cadence. The distance from the first note of a phrase to the cadence may be any number of measures, though usually not more than eight. The four-measure phrase is so commonly used that it may be considered a standard length with which phrases of other lengths may be compared. Figure 7.1 shows such a phrase, ending with a perfect authentic cadence in measure 4. The phrase is marked off with a *phrase mark,* a curved line extending from the first note to the last note of the phrase.

FIGURE 7.1 *Phrase*

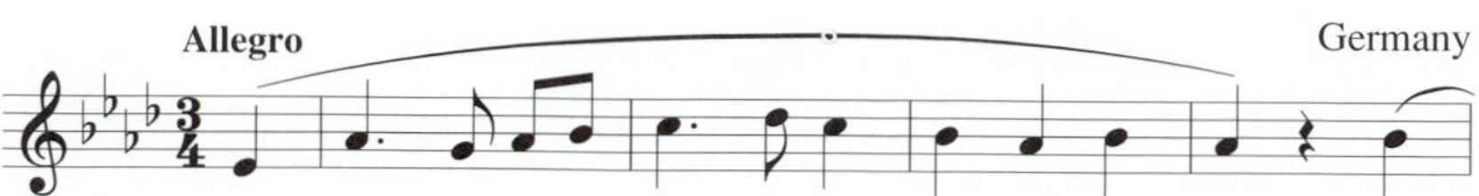

A phrase may also consist of two or more distinct units, called *motives.* In Figure 7.2, two two-measure motives combine to make the phrase. The motive is a unit of melody smaller than a phrase, usually identifiable by a pause in the melody, the rhythm, or both. The phrase mark is used to indicate the length of the motive.

FIGURE 7.2 *Phrase Composed of Two Motives*

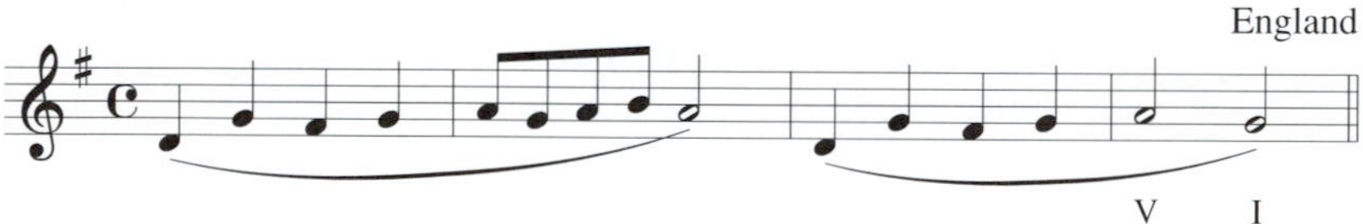

The Period Two phrases may combine to form a *period.* In the period, the first phrase, called the *antecedent phrase,* usually ends with a half cadence or an imperfect cadence. The second phrase, called the *consequent phrase,* then ends usually with a perfect cadence, though again an imperfect cadence is possible.

Periods may be *parallel* or *contrasting.* A period is parallel when the two phrases are similar in some respect. Often the two phrases are identical except at the cadence points, as in Figure 7.3, but any marked similarity in the two phrases will justify analysis as a parallel period. In Figure 7.4, measure 1, note that the skip of a sixth down is answered in measure 5 by a skip of a sixth up. Other melodic features are similar in the two phrases, and the rhythmic pattern is identical.

When the two phrases lack any specific or general melodic similarity, the period is contrasting, as in Figure 7.5.

FIGURE 7.3 *Parallel Period: Nearly Identical Phrases*

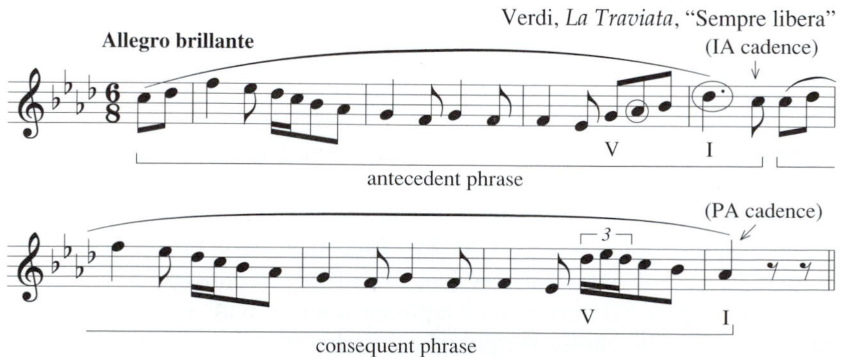

FIGURE 7.4 *Parallel Period: Phrases with Features in Common*

FIGURE 7.5 *Contrasting Period*

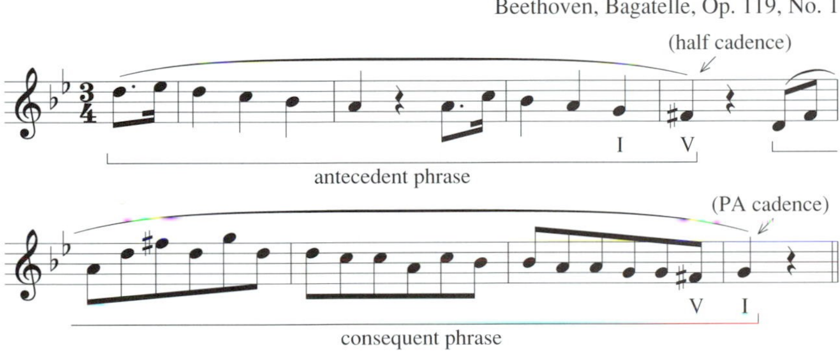

Often the close of the antecedent phrase of a period will be connected to the opening of the consequent phrase by one or more decorative pitches. Locating the cadence will help to identify the last note of the antecedent phrase.

FIGURE 7.6

At times, successive phrases will each end with the tonic note. Since the perfect cadence marks the *end* of a formal pattern, these phrases cannot be combined into a larger form. Figure 7.7 contains two four-measure phrases, each ending on the tonic note; therefore, this excerpt is not a period, but simply two phrases.

FIGURE 7.7 *Successive Phrases*

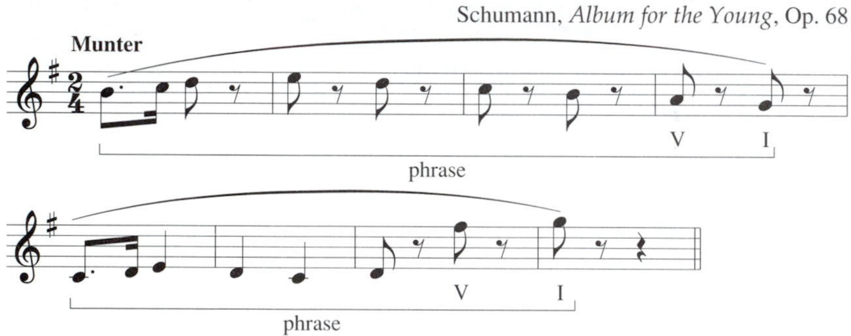

Phrases are also classified according to the rhythmic placement of their first and last notes, that is, whether these notes occur on a strong beat or on a weak beat of the measure. There are, of course, four such combinations, the most common of which are those with strong final tones.

First note	*Final note*	*Example*
strong	strong	Figure 7.7 (second phrase)
weak	strong	Figure 7.1
strong	weak	Figure 7.7 (first phrase)
weak	weak	Figure 7.3 (first phrase)

When two phrases combine to form a period, they commonly display the same beginning and ending characteristics; however, other combinations are not infrequent, as in Figures 7.3 and 7.7

ASSIGNMENT 7.1 *Analyzing form in melodies.* Each of these melodies will be a parallel period, a contrasting period, or two successive phrases. Copy out the melody and indicate *(a)* the location and name of the cadence, using roman numerals V–I or I–V; *(b)* the phrase lengths, by a bracket from the first to the last note of the phrase; *(c)* the nature (strong or weak) of the first and final notes of each phrase; and *(d)* the name of the entire form.

Example

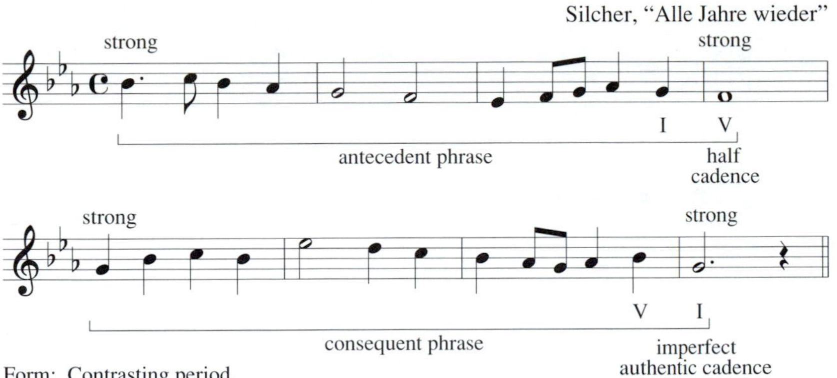
Silcher, "Alle Jahre wieder"
strong
strong
I V
antecedent phrase
half cadence
strong
strong
V I
consequent phrase
imperfect authentic cadence
Form: Contrasting period.

(1)

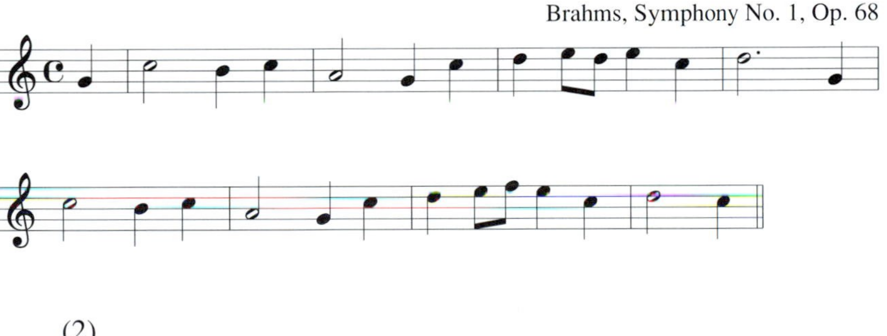
Brahms, Symphony No. 1, Op. 68

(2)

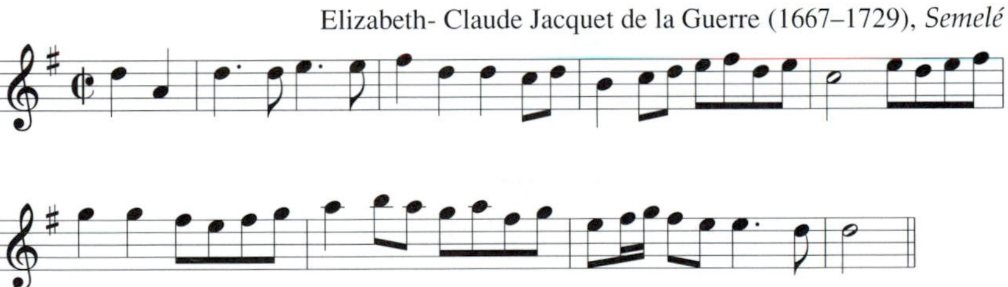
Elizabeth- Claude Jacquet de la Guerre (1667–1729), *Semelé*

(3)

(4)

(5)

(6)

In Appendix E: Answers to (1), (2), and (5) are given.
In the Workbook: Answers to (1) and (2) are given.

Repetition and Sequence In the parallel period, we have seen the second phrase act in some ways as a representation of the first. This repetition is often almost exact except for the last note or last few notes, as in Figure 7.3.

Repetition within the phrase is just as valuable as within the period, both for preventing too many ideas from being included in the short space of four measures and for emphasizing a good idea once it has been stated. Exact repetition can be effective if not done to the point of monotony. In Figure 7.8*a,* the repetition of measures 1–2 in measures 3–4 is exact, and in *b,* the sense of repetition is not disturbed by the final three notes.

FIGURE 7.8 *Repetition within the Phrase*

Chopin, *Valse*, Op. 69, No. 2
(b) Moderato

Repetition may be modified by *inversion.* In this process, each note in the repetition of the given melodic figure progresses to the next note by the same interval, but in the opposite direction. Measures 7–8 of Figure 7.9 are the inversion of measures 5–6. (The quality of the interval, whether major or minor, is not considered, only the interval number. Measure 5 shows a major second down, answered in measure 7 by a minor second up.)

FIGURE 7.9 *Melodic Inversion*

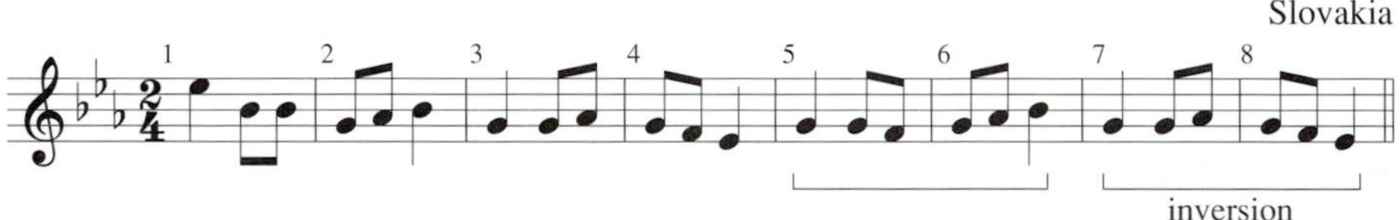

Sequence is similar to repetition, except that the repeated material appears at a new pitch level. This device thus allows similarity and variety simultaneously. Consequently, it is one of the most successful and widely used devices in music composition—not only in melody but in rhythm and harmony as well. In Figure 7.10, look first at measure 5. The melodic and rhythmic elements (the two usually go together) of this three-note figure are repeated in each of measures 6–8 as a sequence.

FIGURE 7.10 *Melodic Sequence*

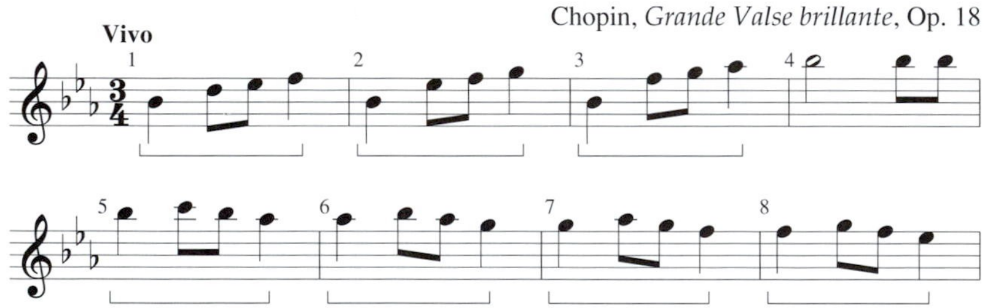

Are measures 1–3 modified repetition or sequence? Either analysis can be justified, since sequence need not be exact. It may be modified to some extent, as long as the aural impression of repetition is clear. In Figure 7.11, the last two measures are a sequence of the previous two measures, although they differ by one note.

FIGURE 7.11 *Modified Sequence*

Figure 7.12 contains the following uses of sequence:

1. There is a three-note sequence in measure 1.
2. Measures 3–4 are a sequence of measures 1–2.
3. Measure 6 is the inversion of measure 5.
4. To conclude this melody, measure 7 features, for contrast, the rhythmic figure in reverse, and measure 8 shows the inversion of the three-note figure located at the end of the antecedent phrase.

FIGURE 7.12

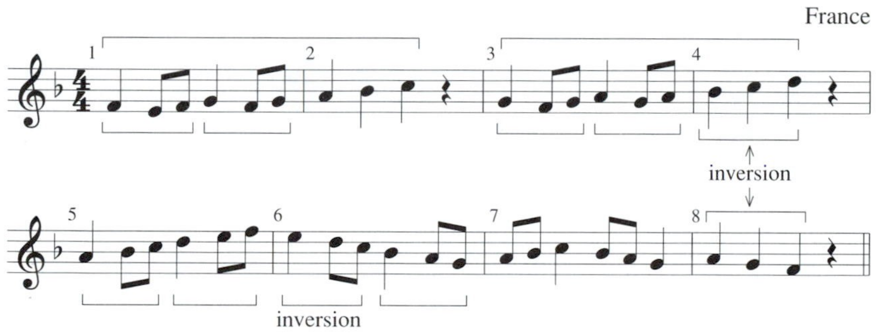

ASSIGNMENT 7.2 Locate and describe examples of repetition and sequence in these melodies, and also in (3) and (4) from Assignment 7.1.

(1)

In Appendix E: The answer to (1) is given.
In the Workbook: The answer to (1) is given.

Pitch

Intervals and Scale Passages How complex need a melody be to be considered a "good" melody? Not complex at all if one considers the well-known passage from Beethoven's Ninth Symphony, shown in Figure 7.13, a "good" melody! It consists entirely of scale steps and uses only quarter notes in the first three measures of each phrase. Also, look back at Figure 4.1 ("Jesu, Joy of Man's Desiring"), which includes only one interval other than a scale step.

FIGURE 7.13

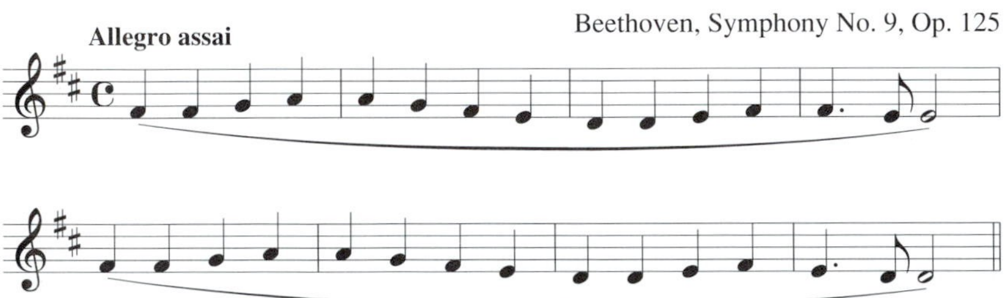

At the other extreme, the melody of Figure 7.14 uses in its first eight measures only intervals of a third and larger.

FIGURE 7.14

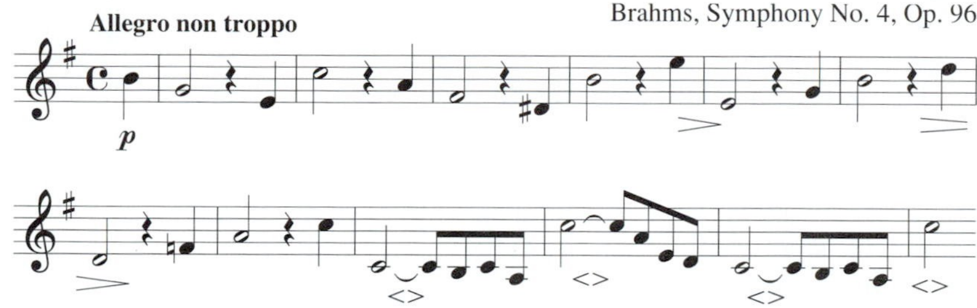

But we will find that most melodies lie somewhere between these two extremes, using a judicious combination of scale steps and larger intervals. The study of simple melodies should include these considerations:

a. Intervals. Intervals of a third or larger can be used freely when resulting in the arpeggiation of a chord, though the number of successive skips is usually not more than three.

FIGURE 7.15

The last of three successive skips at the beginning of Figure 7.16 is to a nonharmonic tone, the harmony remaining tonic.

FIGURE 7.16

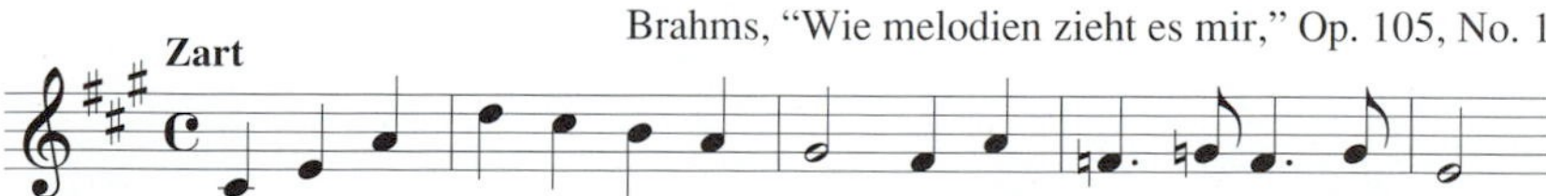

A large leap (a fifth or larger) is usually approached from the direction opposite the skip and left in the direction opposite the skip, as in Figure 7.17.

FIGURE 7.17

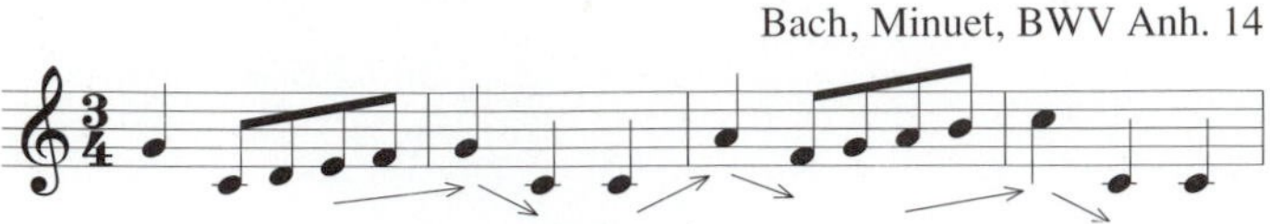

b. Scale passages. The usual scale-line passage does not exceed six tones, though longer passages are not uncommon. Looking at number 6 of Assignment 7.1 (page 136), we see that, with but one exception, each scalar passage is limited to four, five, or six notes. The exception, in measure 4, is a run of eight tones, but encompassing only the interval of a sixth because of the chromatic tones.

c. Range. The range of the melody (lowest note to highest note) must not exceed the range of the voice or instrument for which the melody is written. The ranges shown for part-writing voice lines on page 86 also apply here. Note the limited range of the folk songs included in this chapter. Instruments have a much wider range than the human voice. Their outer limits are included in Appendix B.

In most melodies, the highest tone, sometimes called the *climax note,* is not repeated within the phrase, and often not within the period. Its effectiveness is usually lost upon repetition. The same is true of the lowest note *(anticlimax note),* though in its case the rule is not so strictly observed.

ASSIGNMENT 7.3 Analyze the melodies on page 145, looking for the following features:

1. Scale lines. How many notes go in the same direction? How is the run in one direction approached and left?
2. Chord outline. Which chords are outlined in a series of two or more skips?
3. Large leaps. Is the leap approached and left by similar or contrary motion, and is it approached and left by scale step or by skip?
4. High and low notes. Check for the highest note and the lowest note in each phrase. Is either found twice or more?
5. Note any exceptional practices and try to determine why they were used.

Explanations for the melodic features indicated by the bracketed and circled notes are listed after the following example.

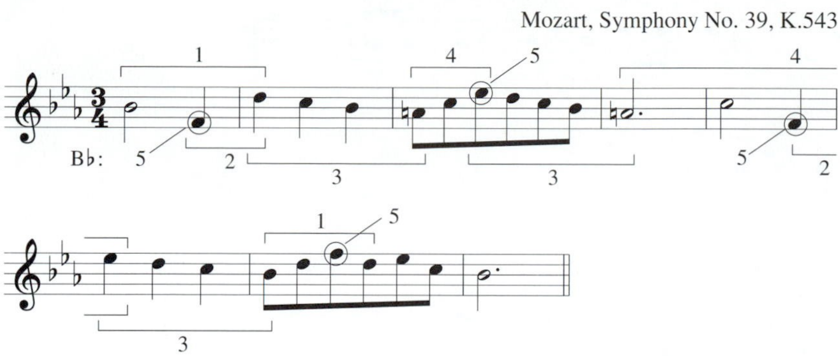

1. These skips outline the tonic triad. In measure 1, the last note is left in contrary motion. In measure 7, the first note is left in a motion contrary to its approach.
2. The large skip is approached and left by contrary motion.
3. In the scale line of four or five notes, each group is approached and left by contrary motion.
4. These skips outline the dominant seventh (V^7) chord, and each group is approached and left by contrary motion.
5. The low notes and the high notes of each phrase are circled. Each phrase displays one of each.

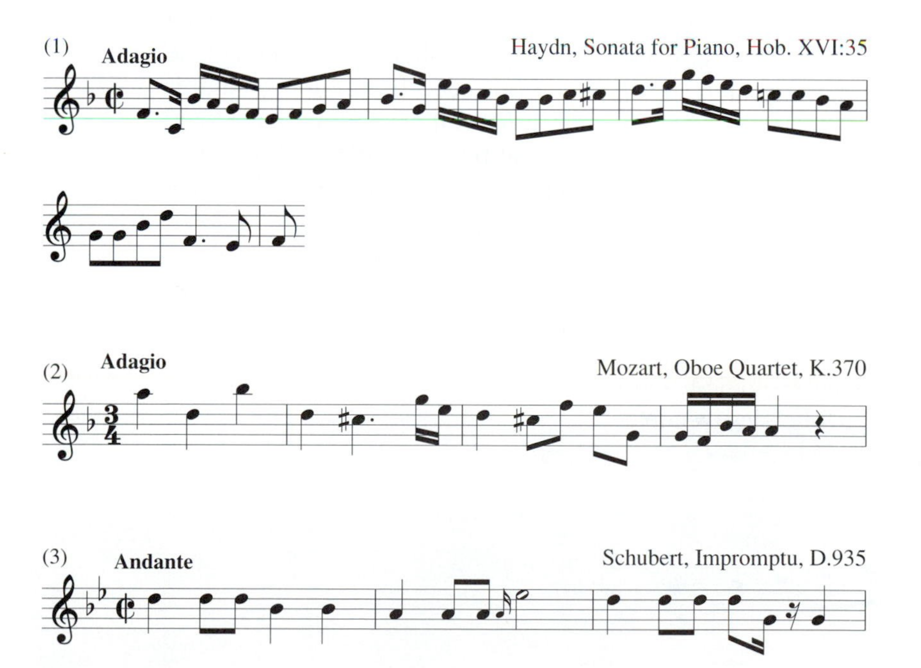

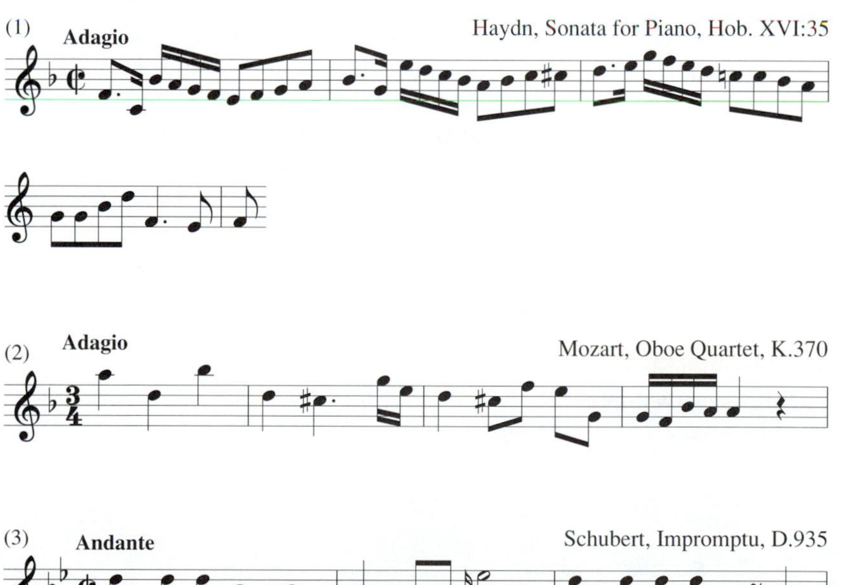

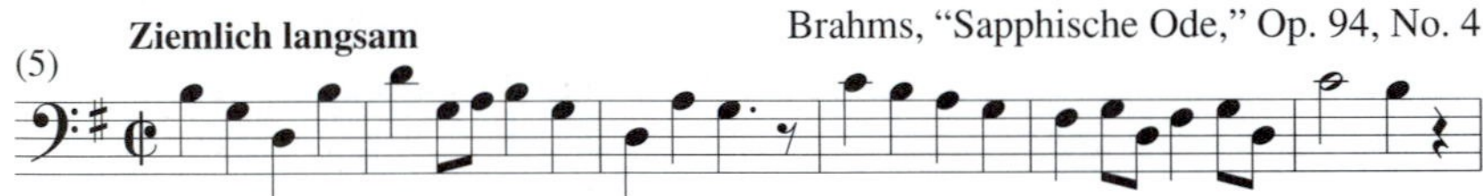

The Leading Tone The leading tone, $\hat{7}$, must be treated with care. As its name implies, it *leads* to the tonic. When approached by step from below, the leading tone must progress to the tonic (Figure 7.18*a*). When preceded by the tonic note, it may progress down by step, as in a scale (Figure 7.18*b*), or it may return to the tonic (Figure 7.18*c*). When it is part of an arpeggiated triad figure, its direction is determined by the direction of the arpeggio (except when it is found as the final note of the arpeggio, in which case it returns to tonic—Figure 7.18*d*).

FIGURE 7.18

Minor Keys: The Sixth and Seventh Scale Steps In a minor key, $\hat{6}$ and $\hat{7}$ require particular attention. If the harmonic form of the scale is used, the interval of the augmented second results. Although this interval does have limited uses, it is generally avoided, especially in less sophisticated styles.

FIGURE 7.19

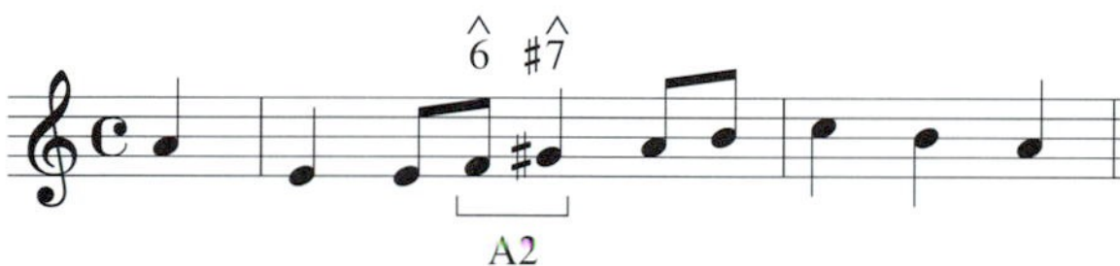

As its name implies, the melodic form of the minor scale is generally used in melodic writing. When a melody ascends through a scale line from the dominant tone to the tonic tone, $\hat{6}$ and $\hat{7}$ are usually raised.

FIGURE 7.20

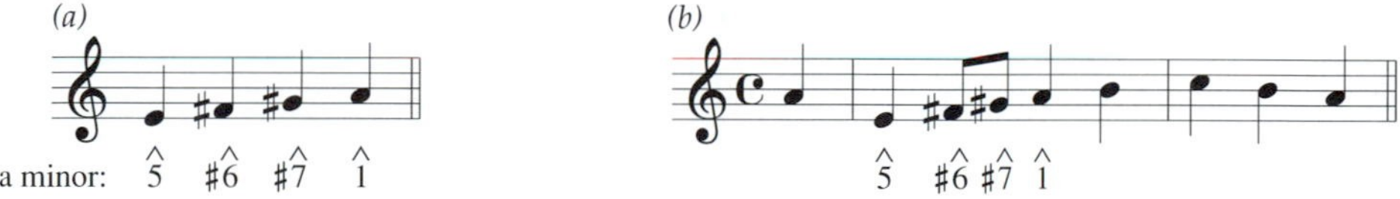

When the V triad is written as an arpeggio (either direction), ♯$\hat{7}$ is used. When this pattern is filled in with passing tones, it appears as though the ascending form of the scale were used in a descending passage (Figure 7.21).

FIGURE 7.21

Otherwise, when descending, $\hat{1}$ $\hat{7}$ $\hat{6}$ $\hat{5}$, $\hat{7}$ and $\hat{6}$ are generally lowered.

FIGURE 7.22

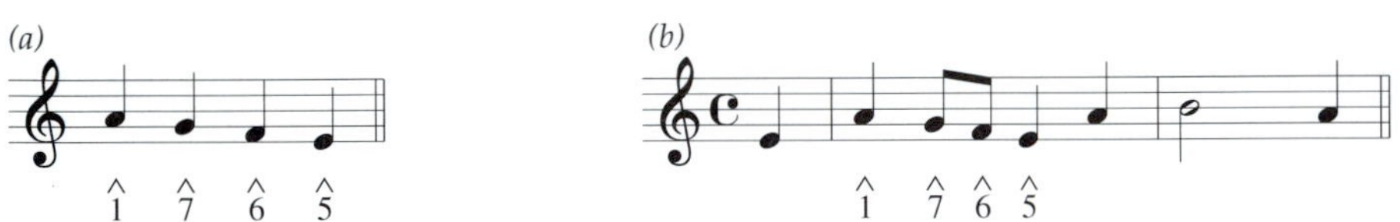

When $\hat{7}$ is used without $\hat{6}$ in a stepwise passage, it is raised and proceeds up (Figure 7.23*a*); when $\hat{6}$ is used without $\hat{7}$, it is lowered and proceeds down (Figure 7.23*b*).

FIGURE 7.23

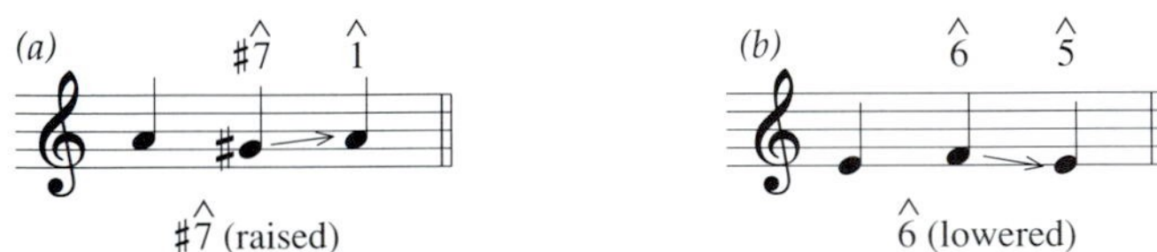

Occasionally, both $\hat{6}$ and $\hat{7}$ are found in a stepwise passage, but not between the tonic and dominant tones. In this case, each $\hat{6}$ and $\hat{7}$ of the group is treated alike. If the last note of the group is $\hat{7}$, all notes of the group are raised (Figure 7.24*a*). If the last note of the group is $\hat{6}$, all notes of the group are lowered (Figure 7.24*b*).

FIGURE 7.24

Last note of group ($\hat{7}$) proceeds up.
Use ascending melodic minor.

Last note of group ($\hat{6}$) proceeds down.
Use natural minor (descending melodic minor).

The G♯ of Figure 7.24*a* implies V in I–V–I, and the F♮ of Figure 7.24*b* implies iv in i–iv–i. The decorative (nonharmonic) tones, between G♯ and G♯ and between F and F, are so written to avoid the melodic augmented second.

ASSIGNMENT 7.4 Above each sixth scale step, write ♯6 or ♭6, and above each seventh scale step, write ♯7 or ♭7. Place the correct accidental before each of these tones. Remember that (1) a natural sign will be used in some instances and (2) an added chromatic sign applies to all notes on that line or space in a given measure.

In Appendix E: Answers to the entire assignment are given.

Harmonic Implication

It should take not much longer than a glance to figure out the obvious harmony that Mozart intended for this tune:

FIGURE 7.25

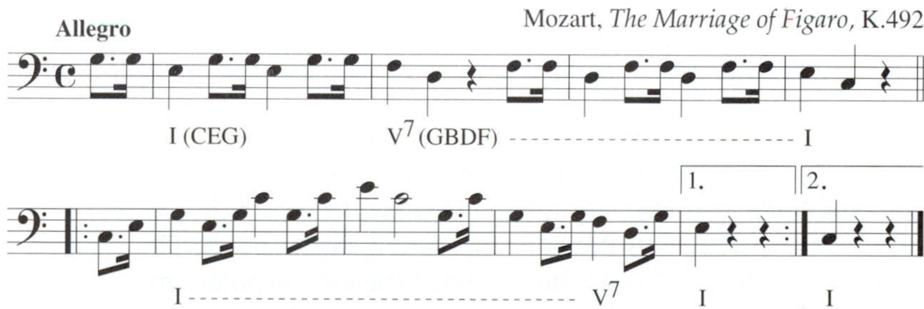

The implication of such simple harmonic structures is inherent in many folk songs and composed melodies in Western culture. That is not to say that a given tune can be harmonized in only one way, however. The folk song of Figure 7.26*a* shows lead sheet symbols of I and V only, but in *b* the same tune is shown with one of the many possibilities using a wider variety of harmonies..

FIGURE 7.26

But for now, we will study harmonic implication with tunes that can be harmonized using I, i, IV, iv, V, and V^7 only. Here is what to look for:

1. A chord is actually outlined in the melody, or suggested by an interval.
   Figure 7.25: Every tone is part of a chord—an interval from the chord or a complete chord.
   Figure 7.26: The first interval, G up to C, suggests C E♭ G.
   Figure 7.27: The interval C♯ up to E in E major obviously implies IV (A C♯ E).
   Figure 7.28: The entire V^7 chord is outlined in measure 3.

FIGURE 7.27

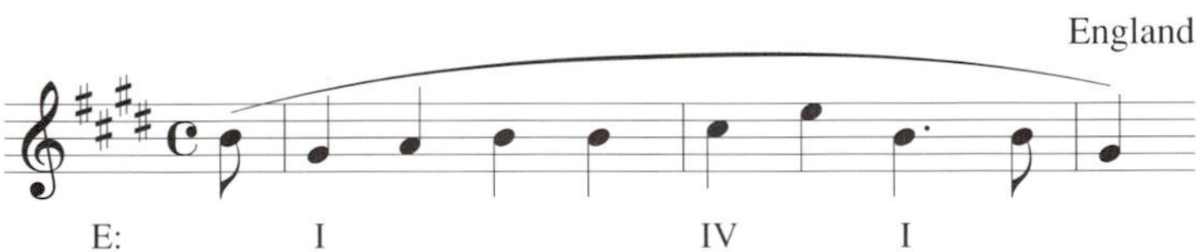

2. When there is no chord outline, the strong beat, or beats, of the measure may suggest the harmony. In Figure 7.28, measure 1, the three repeated notes, G, plus the final B suggest a tonic triad, G B D, and in measure 2, the A and the F♯ on the principal beats suggest the dominant triad, D F♯ A. (The circled notes are nonharmonic tones, to be discussed shortly.)

FIGURE 7.28

Chord changes may, of course, occur within the measure, as the melodic line dictates.

FIGURE 7.29

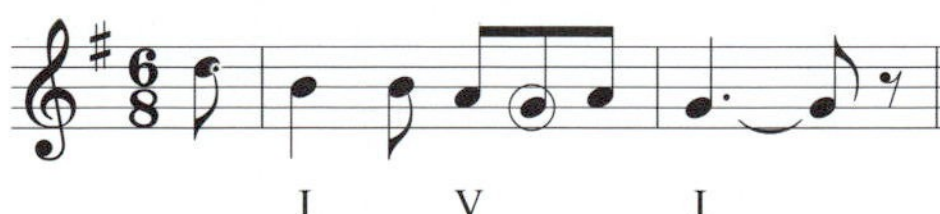

In some cases, $\hat{4}$ can be harmonized with *either* IV *or* V⁷. The arrow in Figure 7.30 points to $\hat{4}$ in F major, which in this context can be the B♭ of IV (B♭ D F), or the B♭ of V^7 (C E G B♭). Four harmonizations are therefore possible, though the last, V–IV, is neither conventional nor effective.

FIGURE 7.30

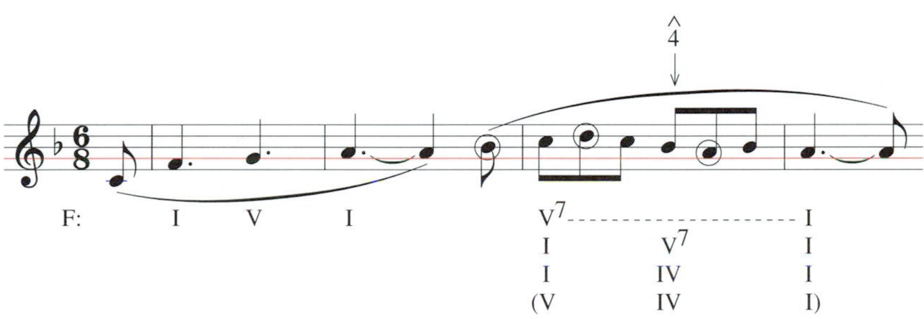

When 4 implies the seventh of a V^7 chord, it usually proceeds downward by step, but it may skip to another member of the V^7 chord (Figure 7.31).

FIGURE 7.31

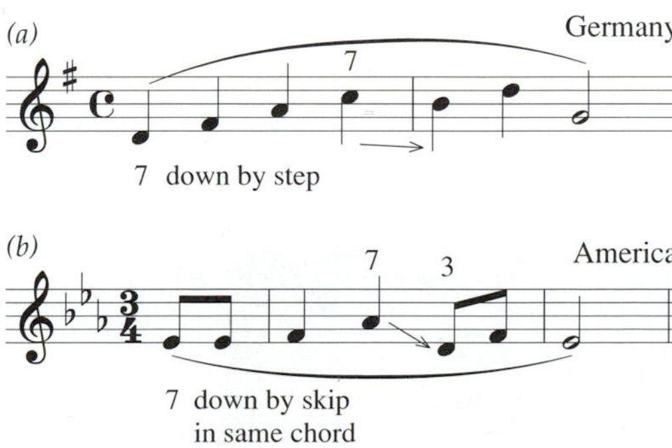

In rare cases in which the seventh is allowed to ascend, the melodic line usually descends immediately after to effect a normal resolution of the seventh.

FIGURE 7.32

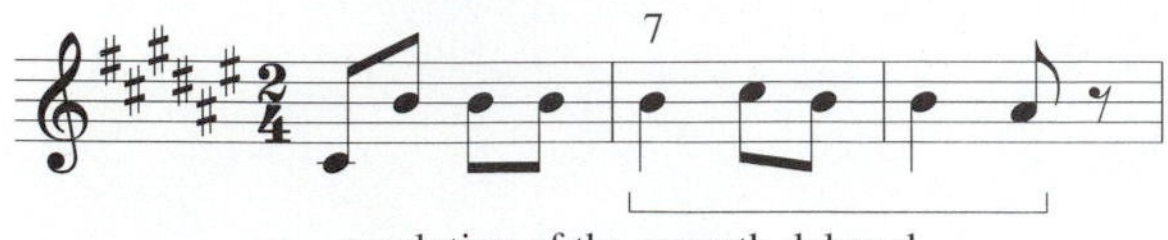

3. Most melodies will contain *nonharmonic tones* (review "Cadences Incorporating Dissonances," page 72). Most common and easiest to spot are those that occur stepwise between chord tones, as seen in Figure 7.33*a,* though nonharmonic tones approached otherwise are not uncommon (Figure 7.33*b*).

FIGURE 7.33

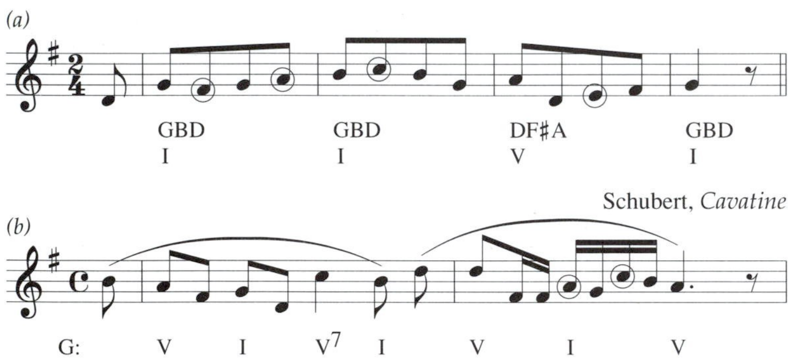

ASSIGNMENT 7.5 Analyze the harmony implied in these melodies, using the example as a guide.

1. Place the chord numbers I, i, IV, iv, V, and V^7 below the staff, as appropriate.
2. Place the chord spellings below the staff.
3. Circle the nonharmonic tones.

Upon completion, play the melody with its harmonization.

Rhythm and Meter

The simplest kind of rhythmic pattern in a melody would be the use of a single note value. Such melodies are rare. Melodic interest is heightened by contrast in the duration of the pitches. This contrast can be very simple, as demonstrated in the melody of Figure 7.13, which consists of only quarter notes except for the cadence at the end of each phrase.

Although more rhythmic variety can be expected in most melodies, the variety of rhythmic patterns is usually limited, and repetition of those chosen is frequent. The Schubert melody, number 3, from Assignment 7.3 (page 145) is a good example. Only the pattern ♩ ♫ ♩ ♩ or ♩ ♫ 𝅗𝅥 is found in five of its eight measures, with each phrase concluding with rhythmic patterns differing from each other.

A melodic sequence is, of course, almost invariably coupled with a rhythmic sequence, although rhythmic sequence is possible without its melodic counterpart; in Figure 7.7, the rhythmic pattern of the two phrases is basically the same (the second phrase uses ♩ instead of ♪𝄾), but the melodies differ.

Rhythmic patterns in recurring measures of equal lengths with accents implied on the strong beat(s) of the measure are typical of the music of the tonal era. Concepts of rhythm in the music of both the pre-seventeenth-century era and the twentieth century are described in the article "Another Metrical Concept" on page 343.

Melodic Composition

To the noncomposer, the composition of a piece of music often appears to come about when a special musical gift is aided by an unexplainable source of inspiration. Although the presence of both of these factors is certainly helpful, more important to a composer's accomplishments is a thorough knowledge of the materials with which he is working.

The well-known melody from Beethoven's Ninth Symphony (Figure 7.13) is a case in point, showing how a fine melody can be constructed from the simplest materials. In this melody

1. the scale line is used throughout;
2. the harmony implied is I and V only;
3. the rhythmic pattern of repeated quarter notes is varied only at each cadence;
4. the form is a simple eight-measure period.

The following assignments will give you the opportunity to write original melodies. The test of a good melody is its "singability." Playing a melody on the piano will not necessarily reveal a defect, since almost any melody can easily be played. If when you are singing, you find the melody contains an awkward interval or section, try to determine the cause of the defect. Then rewrite the melody as much as necessary until it is easily singable.

ASSIGNMENT 7.6 *Melody writing.* Continue each of these melodic beginnings to complete a four-measure phrase. Indicate the implied harmony using roman numeral symbols. Circle all nonharmonic tones. Upon completion, play your melody and harmonization at the keyboard.

(1) End with a perfect cadence.

(2) Use sequence and end with a perfect cadence.

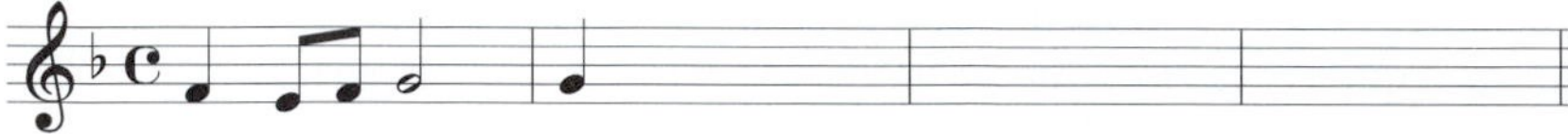

(3) Use sequence and end with a half cadence.

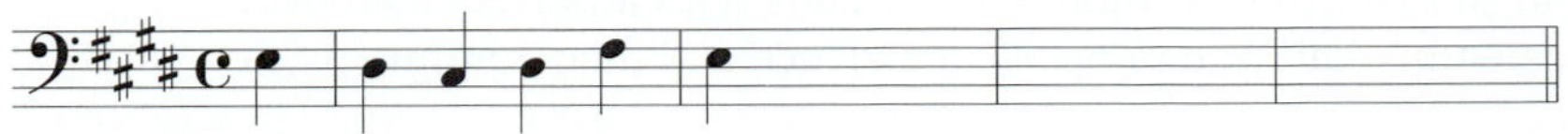

(4) Choose a cadence.

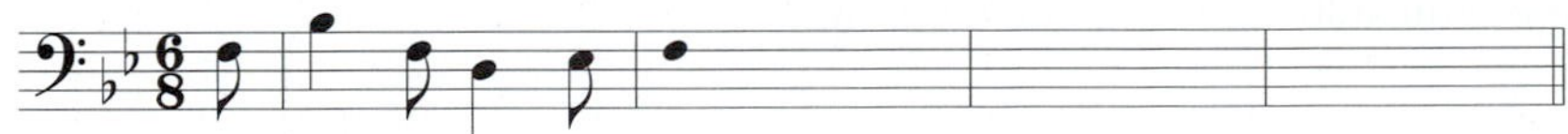

(5) Use sequence.

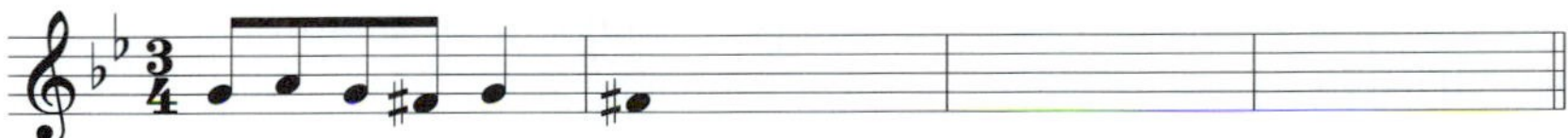

(6) Use sequence.

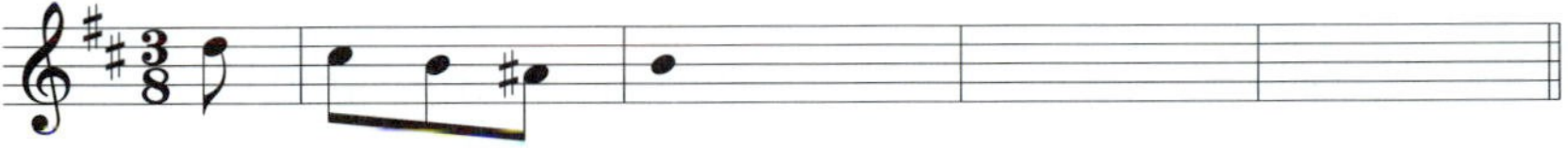

(7)

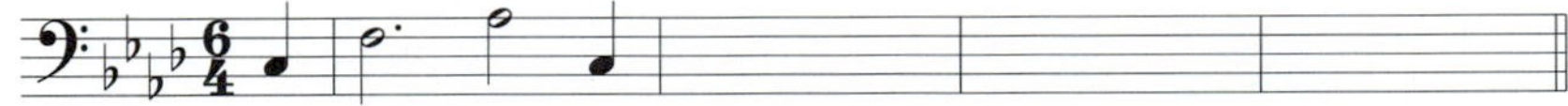

(8)

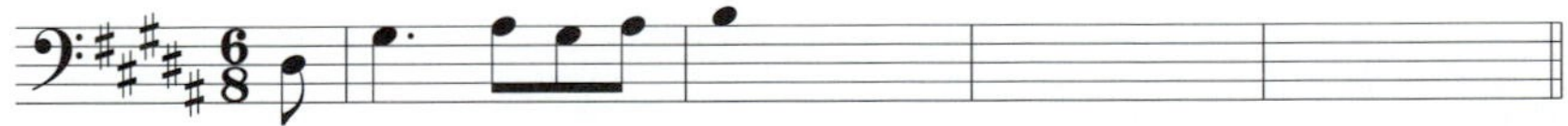

ASSIGNMENT 7.7 *Melody writing.* Using any of the phrases from the examples in Assignment 7.6 as the first phrase of a period, experiment with both parallel and contrasting periods. If your phrase from Assignment 7.6 ends with a perfect cadence, rewrite it so that it ends with a half or an imperfect cadence and then continue with the consequent phrase.

ASSIGNMENT 7.8 *Melody writing.* Write completely original periods, following your instructor's directions for such factors as clef, key signature, time signature, and use of sequence. Edit each melody by indicating motives or phrases with phrase marks and by including a tempo indication and dynamic markings.

Summary

Form is a term describing the structure of a composition.

A *phrase* is a group of notes leading to a cadence.

Two phrases may combine to form a *period.* The first phrase ends with a half or an imperfect cadence, and the second usually with a perfect cadence.

In a *parallel period,* the two phrases are similar melodically and/or rhythmically. In a *contrasting period,* the phrases lack such similarity.

A phrase may include *repetition* of musical ideas. A *sequence* is similar to repetition but at a different pitch level.

Melodies are commonly made up of scalar passages and chord outlines. Larger intervals are usually approached and left by contrary motion.

Some scale steps must be handled with care. The leading tone "leads" to the tonic. In a minor key, the sixth and seventh scale steps are raised or lowered according to the direction in which they move.

Many melodic lines imply a harmonic background, though an actual harmonization is not limited to the most obvious implication.

ARTICLE #7

Some Varieties of Melodic Expression

Since melody exists in all parts of the world and has existed presumably from prehistoric times to the present, we can assume that it has displayed many forms and characteristics. A few examples will show the contrast between these other forms and the characteristic melodies of the period of Western music (ca. 1600 through ca. 1900) being discussed in this text.

The following chantlike aboriginal melody, which has been placed in notation by researchers, certainly shows no harmonic implication, no regular metric system, and too few notes to establish a feeling for scale or key. However, a rudimentary form is established when the passage of repeated D's followed by repeated B's is started over again in measure 5.

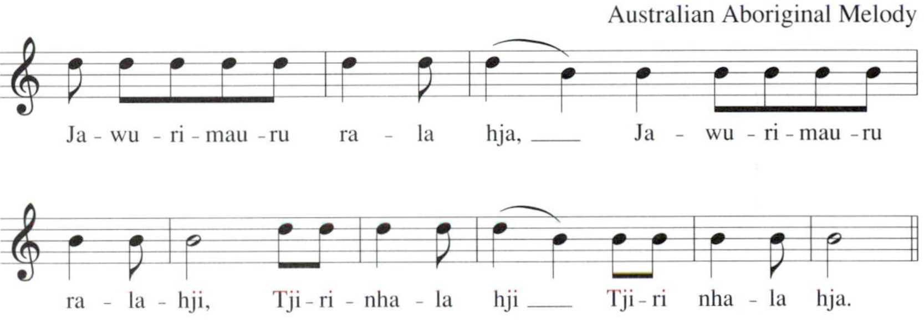

(Let us hurry, the wind is fierce and keen.)

The next example is taken from the earliest known body of Western music, the Gregorian chant of medieval times (ca. A.D. 800). It displays a scale pattern of E F G A B C D E, with tonic on E. This scale is known as the Phrygian mode and is one of several scales, known as *modes,* that were in use before 1600. Since that approximate date, this system has been reduced to two scales, now called major and minor.

Both the medieval modes and the present major and minor modes are based on half steps and whole steps only. In Eastern Europe, the Near East, and the Arab countries of Asia and Africa, scales containing one or two augmented seconds (three half steps, or a step and a half) are a major part of their melodic resources. In the next example, the augmented seconds are E♭–F♯ and B♭–C♯, and the entire scale is D E♭ F♯ G A B♭ C♯ D. In Eastern Europe, this scale is often known as the *Hungarian minor scale* or the *Gypsy minor scale.**

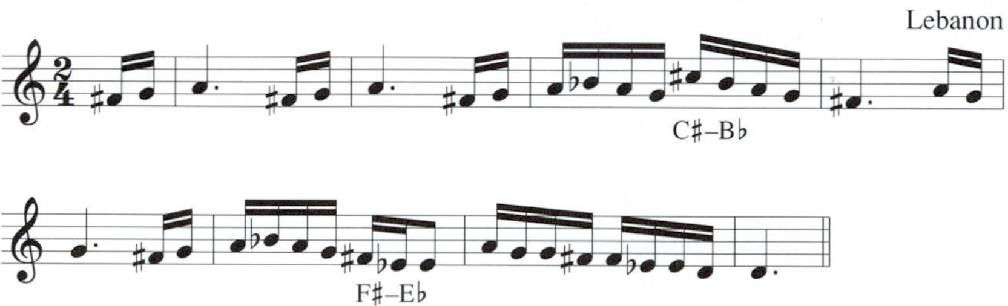

Folk music of Western European cultures has consistently made use of scale patterns that are the same as the medieval modes. This tune is based on the Mixolydian mode (G A B C D E F G).

(Further comment on modal writing in composed music is included in the article "Another Metrical Concept," on page 343.)

Since the common practice period, melody has often abandoned the tonal concept and proceeded in many directions. The most dramatic of these is called the twelve-tone system of music, in reference to the twelve tones of the chromatic scale. Its basic premises are that no note may be repeated until the other eleven have been sounded and that the so-called *row* of twelve tones, which is established before the composition is begun, will be used consistently throughout.

*Further examples of medieval modes can be found in Chapter 19 of the author's *Music for Sight Singing,* 4th ed. (Prentice Hall, 1996).

Characteristic of this melody is its angularity—the predominance of wide skips (also seen in the Brahms example, Figure 7.14)—and the inadmissibility of any harmonic implication.

Although these few illustrations can serve as only small samples of the wide variety of melodic practices found in different regions and eras, they should serve to point out several characteristics that differentiate melodies of the common practice period from those of other cultures and other times.

8

C Clefs; Transposing Instruments

Here is an excerpt from an orchestral score,[1] the opening of the third movement of Brahms's First Symphony. Can you read this score, or does its use of C clefs and transposing instruments baffle you? We will decipher this score one step at a time and reassemble it near the end of the chapter.

FIGURE 8.1

[1]A score in which each instrumental or vocal line is on a separate staff, such as the one in Figure 8.1, is known as an *open score.*

C Clefs

The C clef[2] is universally used in music, though not as commonly as the treble and bass clefs. The C clef sign 𝄡 or 𝄡 indicates the location of *middle C* on the staff. It is particularly useful for those instruments whose range extends from the middle part of the bass clef to the middle of the treble clef because it avoids excessive ledger lines.

When the C clef is found on the third line of the staff, it is known as the *alto clef,* used almost exclusively by the viola and occasionally by the trombone. When the C clef is found on the fourth line of the staff, it is known as the *tenor clef;* it is often used by the cello, the bassoon, and the trombone, and occasionally by the double bass.

FIGURE 8.2

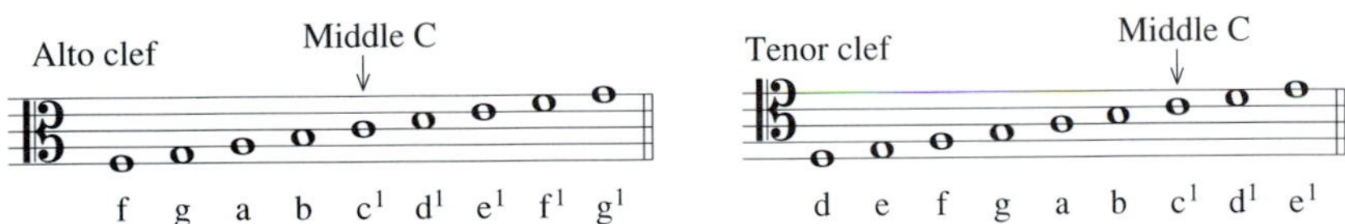

The viola part of Figure 8.1 uses the alto clef (Figure 8.3*a;* shown in *b* in the bass clef).

FIGURE 8.3

The bassoon in Figure 8.1 uses the tenor clef. Figure 8.4 shows its notes:

[2]Early versions of various clefs, including C clefs, can be seen on page 39.

FIGURE 8.4

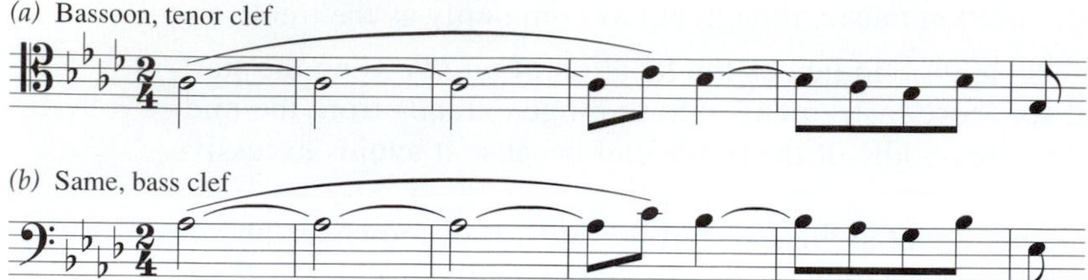

The alto, tenor, treble, and bass clefs are the only ones in common use today from a system of ten clef signs used in music before about 1750. The other six clefs are shown in Figure 8.5.

FIGURE 8.5

These clefs can be found in very old editions of music and in many modern publications of pre-nineteenth-century music.

ASSIGNMENT 8.1 Learn the names of the lines and spaces of the alto clef. Check your ability in the following two ways:

(a) Name the pitch when the line or space is given. Example: fourth line; answer, E.

(b) Name the line or space when the pitch name is given. Example: F; answer, first line or fourth space.

In the Workbook: Answers to the entire assignment are given.

ASSIGNMENT 8.2 Learn the names of the lines and spaces of the tenor clef. Follow the procedures of the previous exercise.

In the Workbook: Answers to the entire assignment are given.

Figure 8.6 shows how sharps and flats for the key signatures are placed for the alto and tenor clefs. Observe that the patterns are the same as for the treble and bass clefs, except for the sharp keys in the tenor clef. Starting with the first sharp on F (second line), succeeding sharps are in a pattern, up a fifth, down a fourth.

FIGURE 8.6

ASSIGNMENT 8.3 Write the key signature for each major and minor key in both the alto and the tenor clefs.

ASSIGNMENT 8.4 *Writing intervals in the C clefs.* Write the second note of the given interval *(a)* in the alto clef and *(b)* in the tenor clef.

In Appendix E: Answers to Assignment 8.4 a (1)–(5); and b (1)–(5) are given.
In the Workbook: Answers to the entire assignment are given.

ASSIGNMENT 8.5 Rewrite both lines of each example, replacing the C clef with a treble or bass clef as appropriate and using the correct notation for that clef. Remember that the C clef indicates *middle C.*

In Appendix E: The viola line in (1) is given.

ASSIGNMENT 8.6 *Writing cadences in open score.* Write each cadence in four parts, one part to a staff, using clefs as shown below. Example: E♭ major, $\frac{\hat{2}\text{–}\hat{1}}{\text{V–I}}$ ($\hat{2}$–$\hat{1}$ indicates scale-step progression; in E♭ major, F–E♭).

Observe:

1. Brace connecting the staves in open score.
2. Use of stem direction for a single melodic line on each staff.

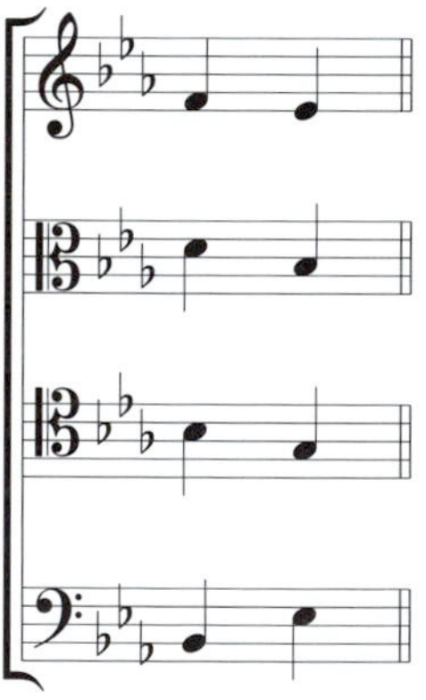

Write these cadences in the same manner:

(1) G major	$\hat{2}$ V	$\hat{1}$ I	(5) B♭ major	$\hat{3}$ I	$\hat{2}$ V
(2) D minor	$\hat{1}$ i	$\hat{7}$ V	(6) F♯ minor	$\hat{5}$ V	$\hat{5}$ i
(3) E major	$\hat{7}$ V	$\hat{1}$ I	(7) D♭ major	$\hat{5}$ V	$\hat{3}$ I
(4) F minor	$\hat{2}$ V	$\hat{3}$ i	(8) G♯ minor	$\hat{1}$ i	$\hat{2}$ V

In Appendix E: Answers to (1) and (2) are given.
In the Workbook: Answers to the entire assignment are given.

A Clef for the Tenor Voice

The tenor clef is ideal for the tenor voice, since use of either the treble or the bass clef results in a large number of ledger lines. Though the tenor clef was once used for the tenor voice, it has been replaced by the treble clef, but with its notation an octave higher than it sounds (Figure 8.7). The clef is sometimes written as 𝄞𝄞 or 𝄠, the latter now becoming commonly used.

FIGURE 8.7

Transposing Instruments

The clarinet part of Figure 8.1 is marked "Clarinet in B♭." Such a description indicates a transposing instrument, that is, one whose written notation is different from its actual pitch. In this case, "in B♭" means that when the clarinet plays C on its staff, the sound produced is a major second lower, "concert B♭," the B♭ of the piano or other nontransposing instruments. Thus the general rule: A transposing instrument sounds its name when it plays C. The B♭ clarinet sounds B♭ when it plays C.

There are two transposing parts in the Brahms score, Figure 8.1; they are shown separately in Figure 8.8. Note that the composition is written in the key of A♭ major.

1. In Figure 8.8*a,* the part for the B♭ clarinet is written in B♭ major, a major second *above* the concert key of A♭ major. Therefore, each note of the clarinet part sounds a major second *lower* than written. The first note, F, sounds E♭, and so forth.
2. In Figure 8.8*b,* the part for the horn in E♭ is written in F major, a major sixth *above* the concert key of A♭ major. Traditionally, horn parts have been written without key signatures, with accidentals placed in the music as needed. In the example, the second note requires a flat, since B♭ is $\hat{4}$ of the F major scale. In reading the E♭ horn part, each note sounds a major sixth *lower* than written. The first note, A, sounds C, and so forth.

Since about the mid–twentieth century, many composers have been writing horn parts *with* key signatures. Figure 8.8*b* so written would have a key signature of one flat.

FIGURE 8.8

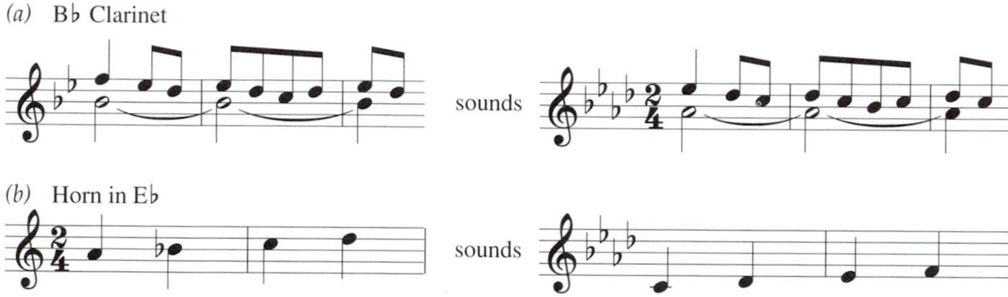

Putting these together with the C-clef parts (Figures 8.3 and 8.4) and the remaining nontransposing instruments, the opening five measures of Figure 8.1 look like this in piano score.

FIGURE 8.9 *Figure 8.1 in Piano Score*

Regardless of your preferred performance medium, your ability to read various notations as presented here should greatly increase your musical horizons and music literacy by making available to you the means for comprehending music scores more complex than those for solo performance.

Writing for Transposing Instruments. When the instrument name includes a pitch name, find the interval between that pitch name and the C above. For the clarinet in A, the pitch A up to C is a minor third. Therefore, the part for clarinet in A will be written a minor third above concert pitch. For example, for a piece in G major for clarinet in A and piano, the piano part will be in G major (signature, 1 sharp) and the clarinet part in B♭ major (signature, 2 flats).

Horns may be in D, E♭, E and F, the last the most common. The part for a horn in F is written a perfect fifth above concert pitch.

ASSIGNMENT 8.7 *(a)* Write or name the concert pitch in each of these examples.

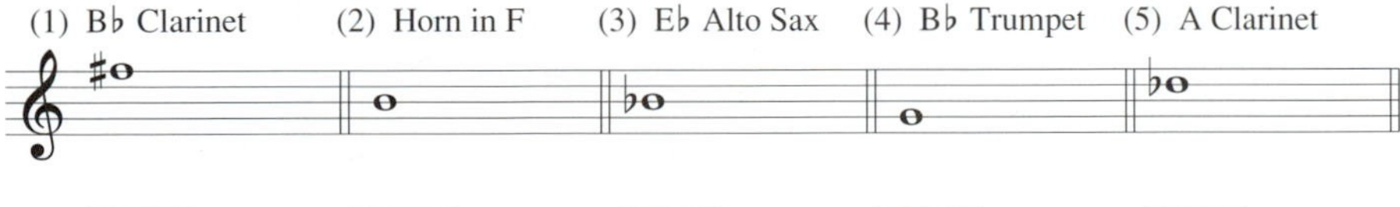

(b) Write the note on the staff that will sound the given concert pitch.

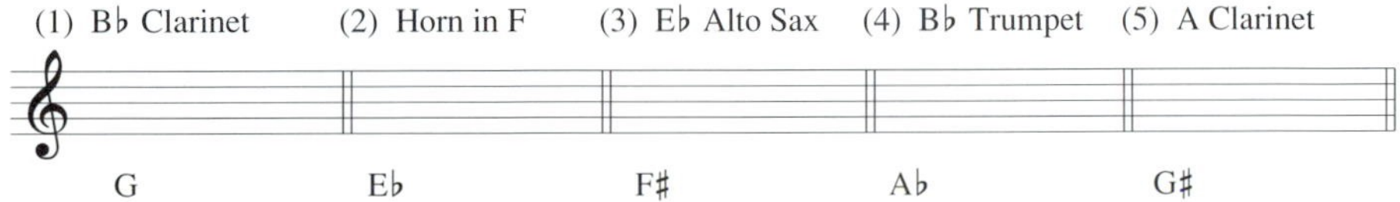

In Appendix E: Answers to the entire assignment are given.
In the Workbook: Answers to the entire assignment are given.

ASSIGNMENT 8.8 Rewrite previous part-writing examples for various instruments.
(a) From Assignment 5.8 (1), fill in the two inner voices.

(b) Using (2) from Assignment 5.8, make a staff such as the one above and use the following instruments, starting with the top staff: flute, viola, bassoon (tenor clef), and contrabass.

(c) Continue with (3) and (4), using instrumentation as chosen or assigned. Examples from Assignment 6.10 may also be used.

Summary

C clefs locate middle C on the staff.

The C clef on the third line is called the *alto clef;* the C clef on the fourth line is called the *tenor clef.*

C clefs are used by a number of orchestral instruments, including the viola, the bassoon, and the trombone.

The tenor voice, written in the treble clef, sounds an octave lower than written, often indicated by 𝄠.

Some instruments are *transposing instruments,* such as the clarinet in B♭. Each transposing instrument sounds its name when it plays its C.

9

The Triad in Inversion

Review "Inversion" and "Figured Bass" in Chapter 2.
See the article "The Theory of Inversion" at the end of this chapter.

Inverting a chord means simply placing a chord member other than the root as the lowest sounding voice. Except for certain types of music in a popular vein, the exclusive use of roots as bass notes is rare. One such example is a well-known prelude by Chopin, a sixteen-measure composition without a single inversion. The first four measures are shown as Figure 9.1

FIGURE 9.1

The Triad in First Inversion

Use of inversions has two advantages, one harmonic and the other melodic.

1. *Harmonic:* A triad and its inversions provide three different sonorities while using the same letter names (four for seventh chords). Thus, the easiest way to introduce an inversion is by arpeggiating the bass line. In Figure 9.2, Schubert uses mostly roots in the bass but makes three welcome changes in sonority where he places the third in the bass.

FIGURE 9.2

2. *Melodic:* Without the inversions, the lowest voice lacks any sense of being a melodic line. With inversions, the bass can become truly melodic. The bass line of Figure 9.3 consists only of scale steps, made possible by the use of two triads in first inversion. Of particular interest is Handel's determination to maintain a scale line even though in measure 3 the bass note C♯ is held throughout the duration of the E G♯ B triad.[1]

FIGURE 9.3

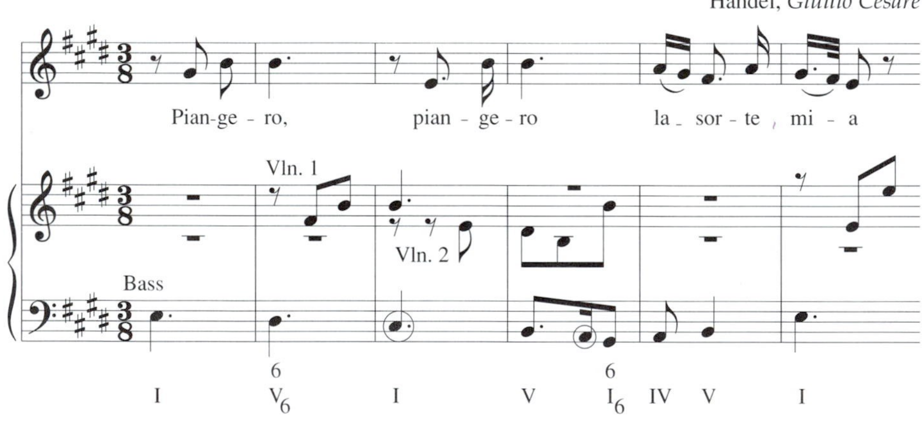

Listen to Figure 9.4, a lead sheet version of Figure 9.3 using a minimal harmonization (roots in the bass); now there should be no question about the heightening of musical interest through the use of inversions.

[1]The C♯ in the bass might be considered the root of C♯ E (G♯) B, a seventh chord, vi^7. However, the treatment of the seventh (B) is atypical (Chapter 13). On the other hand, the long duration of C♯ as a nonharmonic tone is also uncommon. Ambiguous situations such as this are not infrequent in music. In these cases, specific analyses may not be possible.

FIGURE 9.4

In one of Mozart's most popular works, first inversions are used to create a melodic sequence in the bass line, measures 1–2. Also notice the initial interval in the first measure, the leap of a fourth from "third to third." Written in only two voices, the harmonic movement is implied and should be quite clear. We have added middle voices (for analysis only—not for performance!) in stemless notation.

FIGURE 9.5

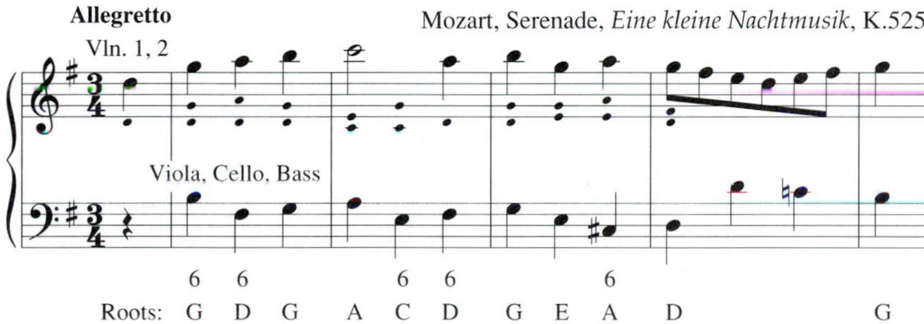

Also effective is the use of first inversions to create parallel thirds and sixths between the bass and an upper voice. Figure 9.6 shows thirds in measures 1–2 and sixths in measure 3. The triad marked I^6_4 will be discussed shortly.

FIGURE 9.6

Like the bass line of Figure 9.3, the bass line of Figure 9.7 is mostly stepwise. Of interest here is the V_6–IV_6 progression.[2] In a series of first inversions in which the bass moves stepwise, any chord progression may appear, even those that are otherwise uncommon or rare. In Chapter 6, we noted that the use of V–IV is limited, but as a succession of first inversions its use is common.

FIGURE 9.7

Bach, "Du Friedefürst, Herr Jesu Christ" (#42)

In another pair of first inversions (Figure 9.8), the bass line in minor passes through ♯6 and ♯7, requiring the subdominant triad to be major, IV_6, as it progresses to V_6. Also note that IV_6 is preceded by V to begin the stepwise motion in the bass.

FIGURE 9.8

Anon. (ca. 1670) "Nun sicht der Tag"

In summary, inversions can create more musical inter

1. arpeggiating a triad (Figure 9.2);
2. progressing by leap from triad root to inversion (or re rom inversion to inversion (Figure 9.5);
3. using a scale line in the bass, where the inversion is fo mittently (Figure 9.3), or when inversions are in succession (Figures 9 d 9.8);
4. moving the bass line in thirds or sixths with an upper voice (Figure 9.6).

[2] v_6–iv_6 can be used in a minor key. The minor dominant triad will be studied in Chapter 16.

The Triad in Second Inversion

In contrast to the liberal use of first inversions, the second inversion is restricted to a limited number of specific devices. This is because the triad in second inversion contains a perfect fourth between the bass and one of the upper voices. From very early times in the history of Western music, the perfect fourth above the bass has been considered a dissonance, requiring specific resolution and therefore limiting the ways in which the inversion can be used.

The Cadential Six-Four Chord This chord is so named because of its frequency of use at a cadence point, though it is used commonly in other locations. Harmonic movement culminating in a I^6_4–V–I cadence is so common that the progression is virtually a "trademark" of tonal harmony, and for that reason it was virtually abandoned in the new concepts of music composition developing in the early years of the twentieth century.

Look at the triad marked I^6_4 in Figure 9.6. You can clearly see the spelling G B D in G major; yet, if asked to sing the root of this triad, most people respond by singing (not incorrectly) the bass note D. There must be an explanation for this contradictory interpretation.

Figure 9.9 demonstrates these interpretations.

1. In *a,* the "dissonant" fourth above the bass is clearly marked.
2. In *b,* the progression to V is analyzed the way it *looks*—two triads, I and V.
3. In *c,* the progression is analyzed the way it *sounds*—a V triad with nonharmonic tones above its root in the bass.

Try playing (or listening to) Figure 9.9, stopping at the six-four chord. The necessity for resolution should be obvious. Note that the sixth (B) above the bass tone, though consonant with the bass note (D), is at the same time dissonant with the implied harmony, D F♯ A.

FIGURE 9.9

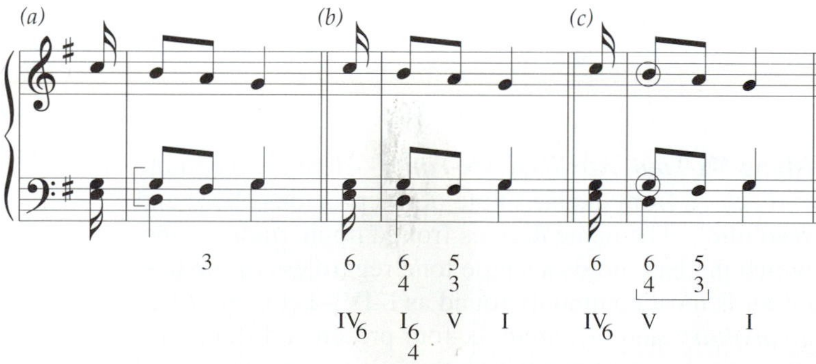

For purposes of analysis, we will consider the six-four sonority as a triad built above its fifth, as in Figure 9.9*b,* but in writing and listening, the dissonant function of the perfect fourth above the bass should always be kept in mind.

Even though the fourth usually resolves down, it is occasionally seen moving in the opposite direction (Figure 9.10).

FIGURE 9.10

In duple and quadruple time, the cadential six-four almost invariably occurs in a strong rhythmic position, allowing the ensuing tonic, root in bass, also to occur in a strong rhythmic position, as in Figure 9.10. In triple time, the six-four may also appear on the second beat of the measure, followed by V on the third beat leading to I on the next strong beat (Figure 9.11).

FIGURE 9.11

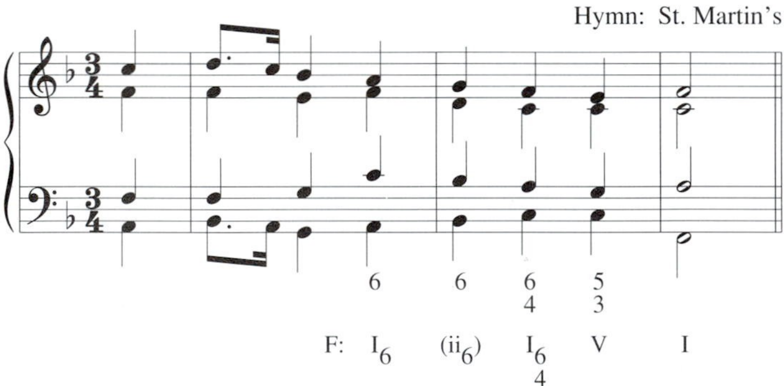

The Pedal Six-Four (Embellishing Six-Four, Auxiliary Six-Four) Here the bass note of the six-four is held over or repeated from the bass note of the previous chord and continued into the chord of resolution. The name derives from a nonharmonic tone, the *pedal point* or *pedal,* in which the bass holds a single tone regardless of the harmony above it. The pedal six-four is most commonly found as I–IV$^6_4$–I (Figure 9.12).

The terms *embellishing, auxiliary,* and *neighbor* six-four present a different interpretation: The bass note is a chord tone above which there is movement to and from a nonharmonic tone (neighbor tones, Figure 9.12*b* and 9.13).

FIGURE 9.12

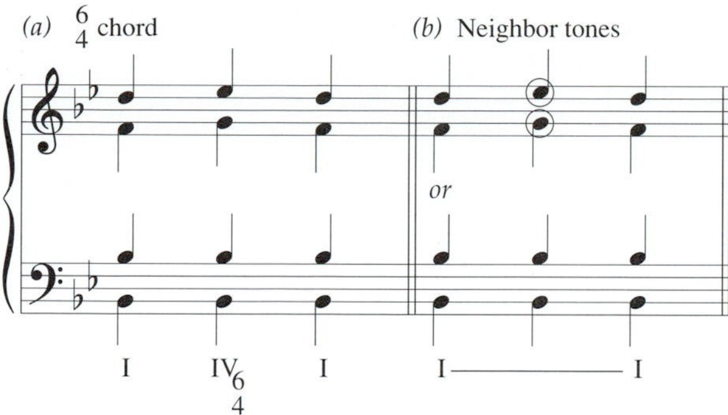

FIGURE 9.13

The Passing Six-Four This six-four is found between a triad in root position and its first inversion, or the reverse, and differs from the others in that there is no resolution of the perfect fourth. Rather, the root of the six-four sonority (G in Figure 9.14) functions as a chord tone sustained from the previous chord, the remaining tones acting as nonharmonic tones.

FIGURE 9.14

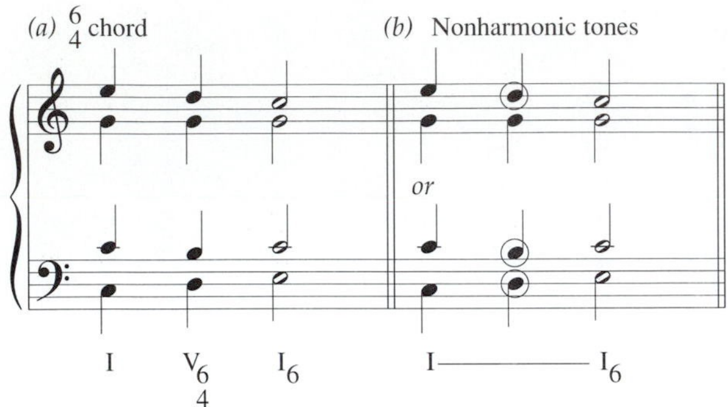

FIGURE 9.15

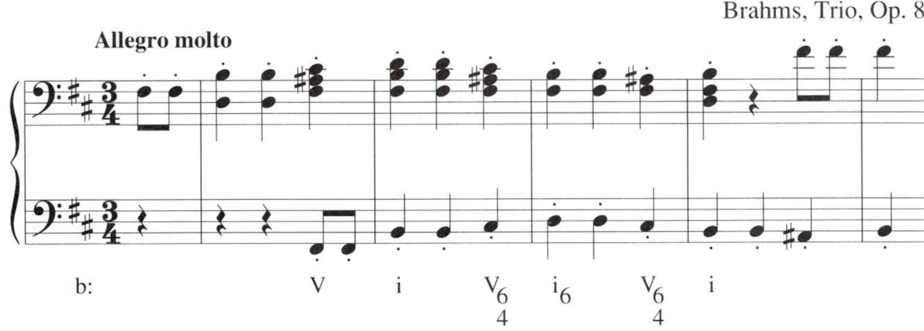

The most commonly used passing six-fours are (1) the I-V_4^6–I_6 or reverse, (2) the IV_6–I_4^6–ii_5^6, to be studied in Chapter 13, and (3) occasionally the iv–i_4^6–iv_6, shown in Figure 9.16. Note the lack of a G in the first i_4^6, allowing the two B's to function as nonharmonic tones in the iv triad.

FIGURE 9.16

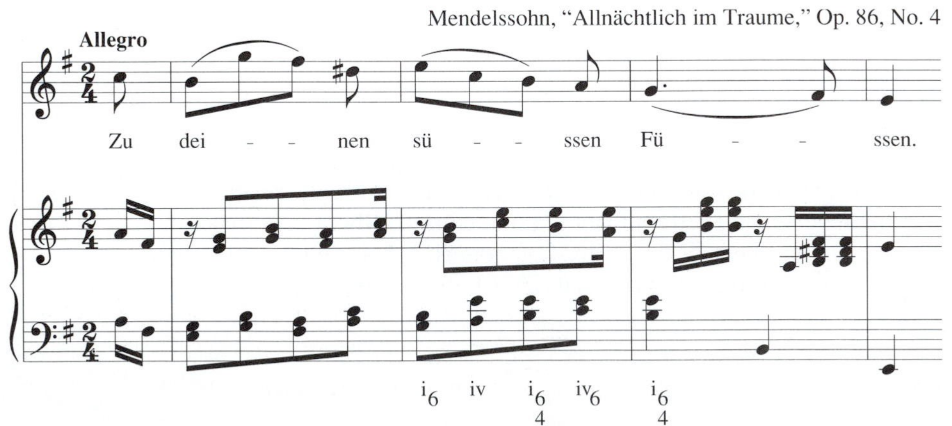

You are not likely to see any other variety of a passing six-four, although there is always a possibility, such as this unusual passing vi$^6_4$ from a Bach chorale.

FIGURE 9.17

ASSIGNMENT 9.1 *Identifying triads in inversion.* Each of these music excerpts includes one or more triads in first and/or second inversion. Locate each inversion and describe its use. For first inversions, check the summary on page 172, and for second inversions, name each as described on the pages immediately preceding this assigment.

(1)

(2)

(3)

Andante
Handel, Samson

(4)

Adagio
Mozart, Sonata in F Major for Piano, K. 332

(5)

Berlioz, Nuits d'été, "La Spectre de la rose," Op. 7
Plus d'un au-rait don-né sa vi - e; Car sur ton
poco sf
V7
sein j'ai mon tom-beau,
pp

(6)

(7)

In Appendix E: The answer to (1) is given.

Writing a Triad in First Inversion

Any doubling is possible in a first inversion (even the leading tone under the right circumstances, see page 252), but we will start with the conventional doublings, that is, those which are most frequently used.

Major Triads The soprano note is doubled, with one each of the remaining triad tones.

FIGURE 9.18

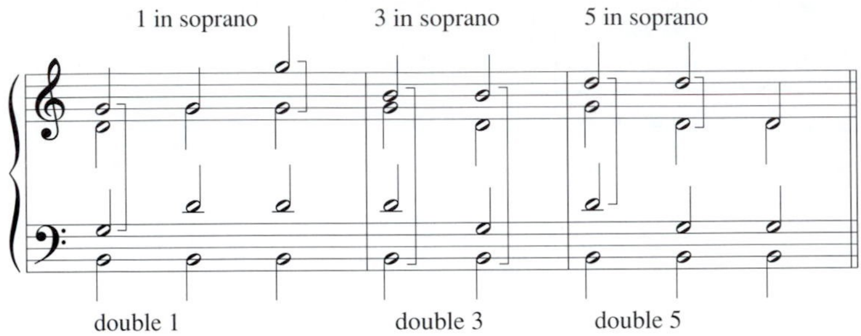

Minor Triads Although the same doubling applies to minor triads, it is also common procedure to double the third.

FIGURE 9.19

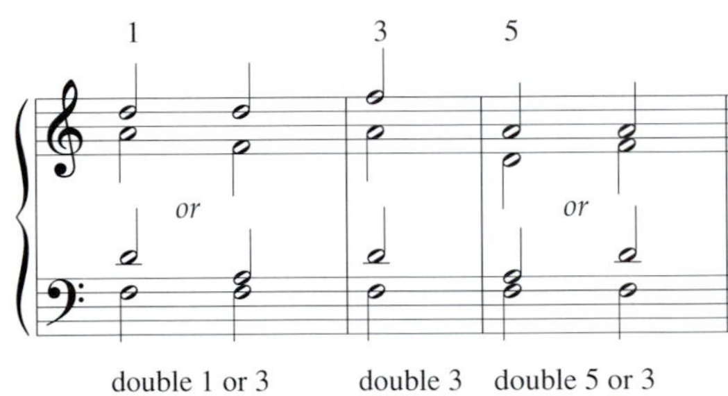

ASSIGNMENT 9.2 Add alto and tenor voices in these first-inversion triads. Write each in both open and close position, except where vocal range will not allow.

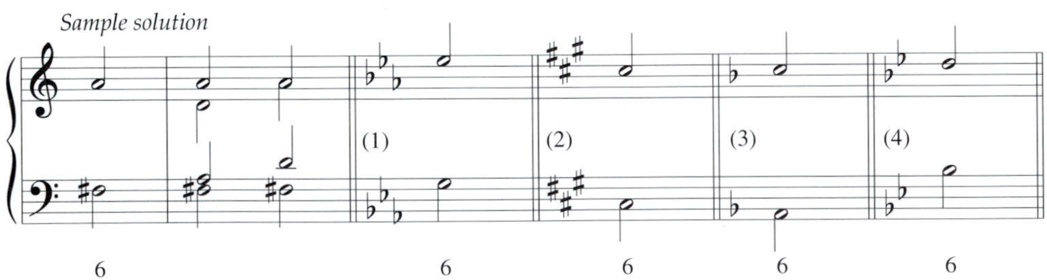

In Appendix E: Answers to (1)–(3) and (6)–(7) are given.
In the Workbook: Answers to the entire assignment are given.

Writing to or from a Triad in First Inversion

When progressing from a triad in first inversion to a triad in root position (such as V_6–I), or the reverse (I–V_6), you are most likely to avoid parallels and other problems by first writing the two voices that lead to and from the doubled note. These two voices can move in three different ways in relation to each other.

1. *Contrary motion:* The two voices move in opposite directions (Figures 9.20*a* and 9.21*a*).
2. *Oblique motion:* One voice remains stationary while the other moves (Figures 9.20*b* and 9.21*b*).
3. *Similar motion:* The two voices move in the same direction (Figures 9.20*c* and 9.21*c*).

FIGURE 9.20

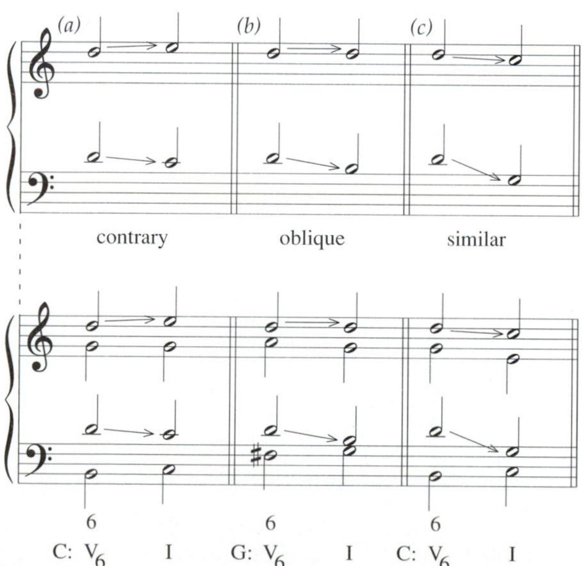

FIGURE 9.21

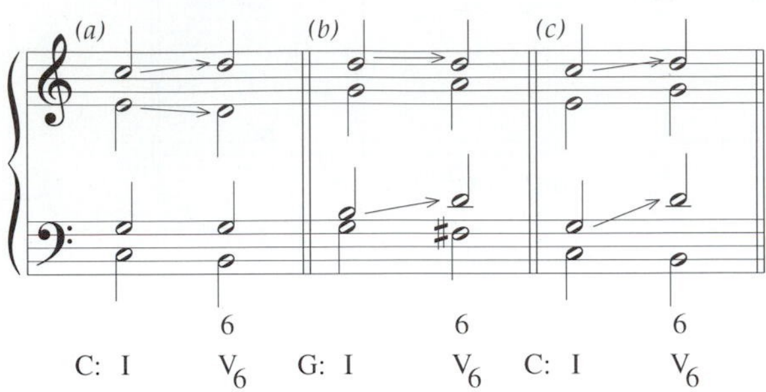

It is always best to use contrary or oblique motion in approaching and leaving the doubled note. In Figure 9.22, contrary motion is used exclusively at every occurrence of a triad in first inversion.

FIGURE 9.22

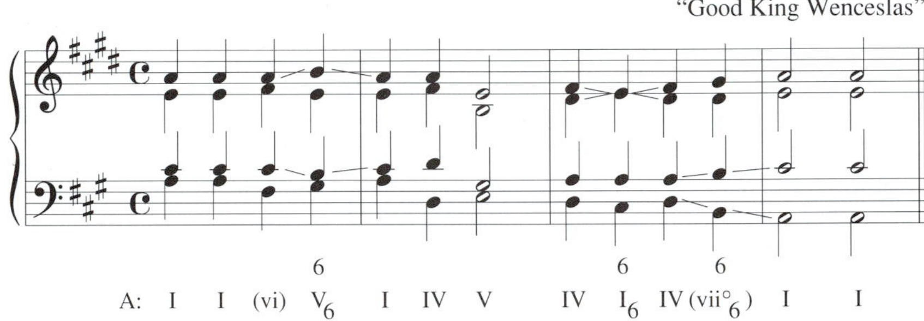

Similar motion is ordinarily necessary only in unusual cases when one voice must be brought into a better range or to effect a change of position.

FIGURE 9.23

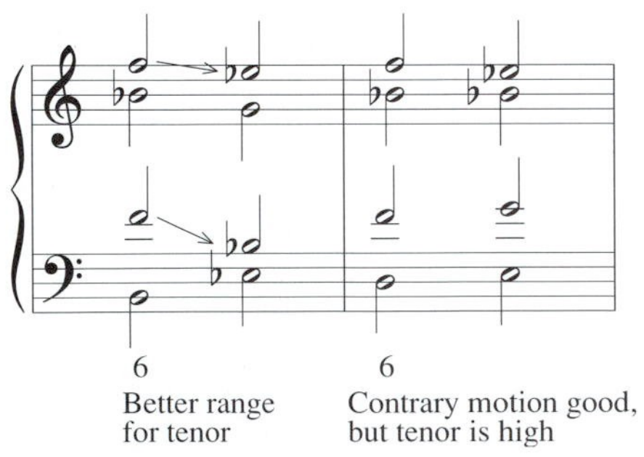

The most efficient procedure for part-writing to or from a triad in first inversion is as follows (Figure 9.24):

Step 1. Complete the first of the two triads.

Step 2. Approach or resolve the doubled note by contrary or oblique motion if possible.

Step 3. Fill in the remaining voice with the note necessary to produce normal doubling. When the doubled note moves by contrary or oblique motion, the remaining voice usually moves by step or remains stationary, rarely moving by leap.

FIGURE 9.24

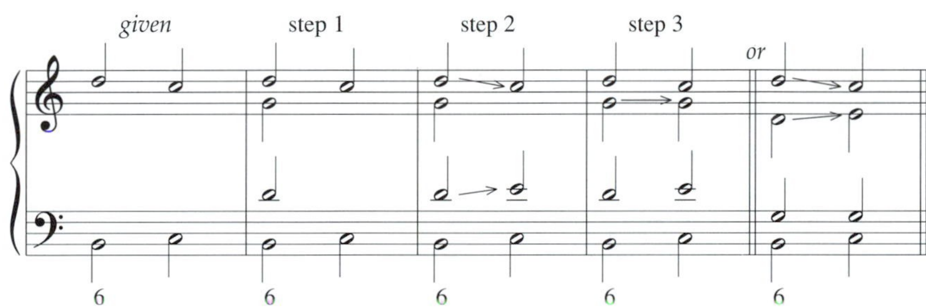

ASSIGNMENT 9.3 Write pairs of triads. Where possible, write the example in both voicings, as shown in Figure 9.24. Place the chord number below each bass note.

In Appendix E: Answers to (1), (5), and (7) are given.
In the Workbook: Answers to the entire assignment are given.

Writing Successive Triads in First Inversion

When triads in first inversion are used in succession, it is impossible for each of these triads to be found with the usual doubling in the same pair of voices, since parallel octaves and fifths will result.

FIGURE 9.25

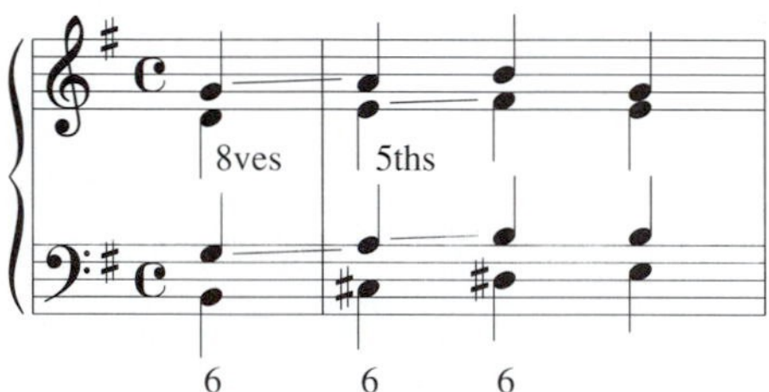

To avoid these, use a different doubling for each triad in inversion, if necessary.

In a most instructive example, Figure 9.26, Bach has successfully handled three successive first inversions, including ♯$\hat{6}$ and ♯$\hat{7}$ in the bass. He has avoided all the "booby traps" by carefully choosing his doubled notes, a different one in each triad. As a result, each doubled note is both approached and left by contrary motion. Study this example carefully, because in your work in inversions, you are unlikely to encounter any problem more difficult.

FIGURE 9.26

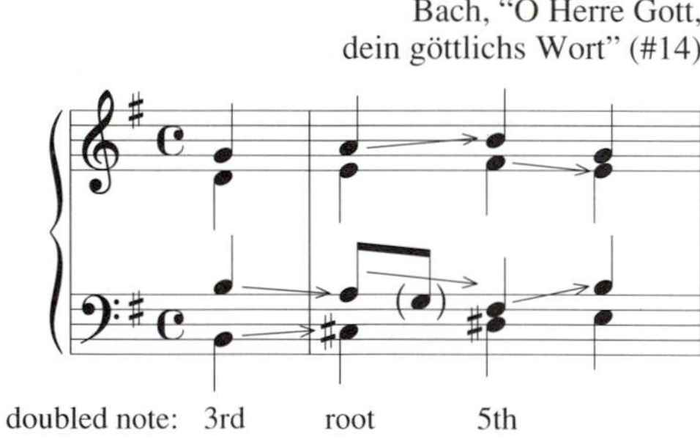

When selecting doublings, be sure not to double the leading tone or any altered tone. Notice the ♯$\hat{6}$ and ♯$\hat{7}$ in Figure 9.26. Neither is doubled.

ASSIGNMENT 9.4 Write examples of successive first inversions.

In Appendix E: Answers to (1)–(3) are given.
In the Workbook: Answers to the entire assignment are given.

Writing a Triad in Second Inversion

The ambiguity of the six-four triad, a sonority that appears to be a triad with tones that function as nonharmonic tones, places limitations on its doubling and its part-writing in a progression.

Doubling The fifth (bass note) is ordinarily doubled.

Approach and Resolution

1. *Cadential:* The bass note is *not* approached from the same tone or from the leading tone. In resolution, $\hat{6}$ moves to $\hat{5}$ above the bass, and $\hat{4}$ moves to $\hat{3}$ (Figure 9.27*a*).
2. *Pedal:* Motion above the bass is usually stepwise. (Figure 9.27*b*).
3. *Passing:* The "dissonant" fourth remains stationary (Figure 9.27*c*).

FIGURE 9.27

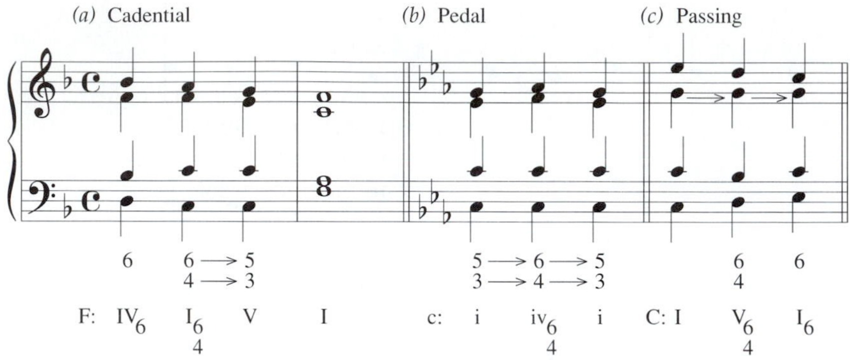

ASSIGNMENT 9.5 *Writing six-four chords.* Numbers 1–3 are cadential, number 4 is passing, and number 5 is pedal. In number 6, bass line only, supply three upper parts and include one example each of the three types of six-four chords.

In Appendix E: Answers to (1) and (5) are given.
In the Workbook: Answers to the entire assignment are given.

Other Part-Writing Considerations

Before we continue with phrase-length exercises, three additional observations applicable to any part-writing procedures will make your efforts easier.

The Melodic Augmented Fourth This interval is usually avoided in melodic writing and, therefore, should not appear in any voice line. Both tones of the interval have strong resolution tendencies, the upper resolving up and the lower resolving down. In a melodic leap, both resolutions cannot be accommodated, and the undesirable large leap must continue in the same direction (Figure 9.28*a*).

The problem is easily solved by using the augmented fourth's inversion, the diminished fifth, thus allowing the melodic change of direction (Figure 9.28*b*). How it works in a practical application, IV–V_6, is seen in Figure 9.29.

FIGURE 9.28

FIGURE 9.29

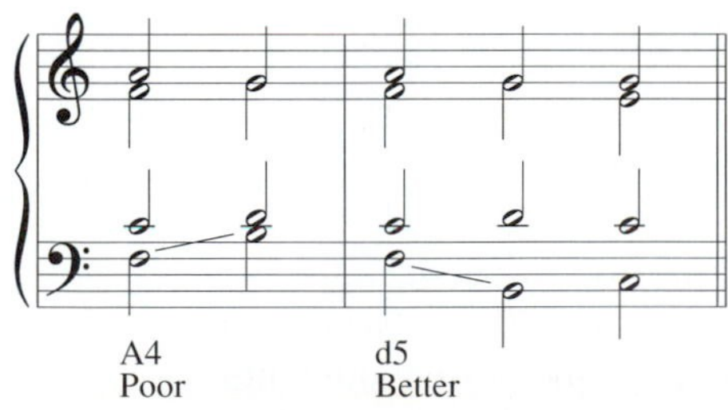

Overlapping Voices These can be illustrated better than described. In Figure 9.30*a,* measure 1, the bass note D moves to G, but the G is higher than the previous tenor note. These are overlapping voices, and they can occur between any pair of adjacent voices, ascending or descending. Correction is sometimes as simple as changing the direction of one voice (Figure 9.30*a*). Otherwise, change the triad position at some point before the overlapping pair. A good place to change position is at a repeated triad, as in Figure 9.30*b*.

FIGURE 9.30

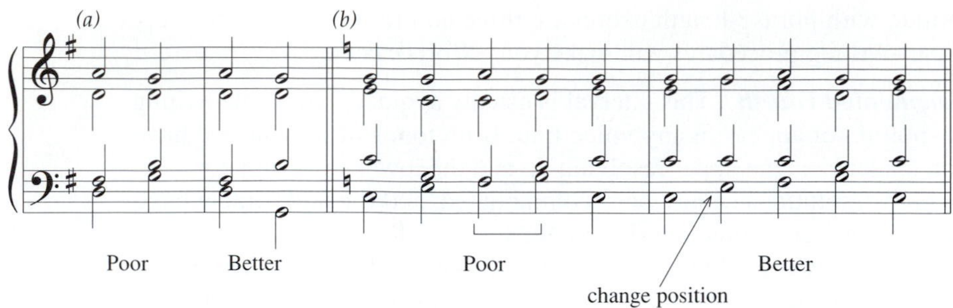

Unlike parallel fifths, overlapping voices are not to be considered completely unusable. They, along with crossed voices (page 88), are often useful when creating melodic lines using inversions and nonharmonic tones, as will be shown later.

Hidden Octaves and Hidden Fifths (Direct Octaves and Fifths) A hidden octave occurs when two voices progress in similar motion to a perfect octave. A hidden fifth occurs when two voices move in similar motion to a perfect fifth. Although not parallel, they often produce the aural effect of parallel movement.

FIGURE 9.31

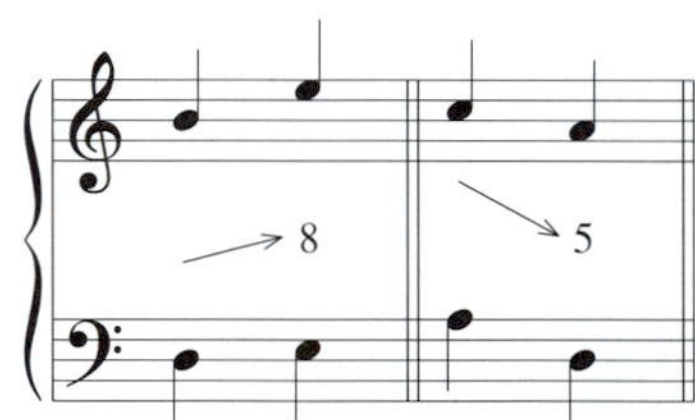

Hidden octaves and fifths are a problem *only* when they occur between the two outside voices of a composition (soprano and bass in four-part writing). Even then, they are acceptable when (1) the soprano moves by step, as in the perfect authentic cadence, soprano $\hat{2}$–$\hat{1}$ with bass descending (Figure 9.32*a*), and (2) when the bass moves by the interval of an octave, considered the same as a repeated tone (Figure 9.32*b*).

FIGURE 9.32

In other circumstances, a hidden fifth or octave between outside voices is not necessarily entirely unusable but should be chosen only after careful consideration of its aural effect.

ASSIGNMENT 9.6

(a) Write extended exercises (the soprano and bass lines are given). Make a harmonic analysis.

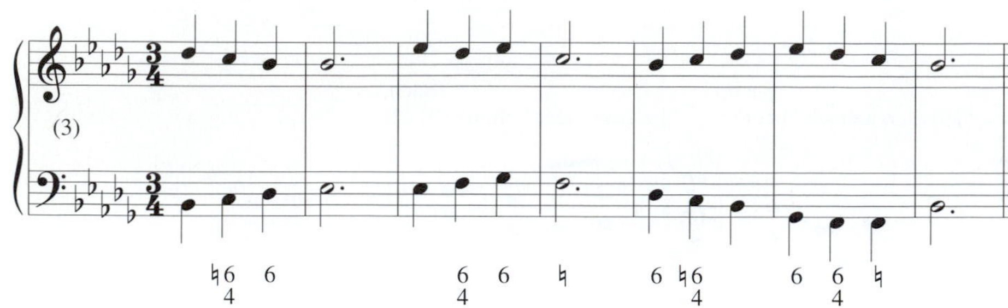

(Review Figure 9.26.)

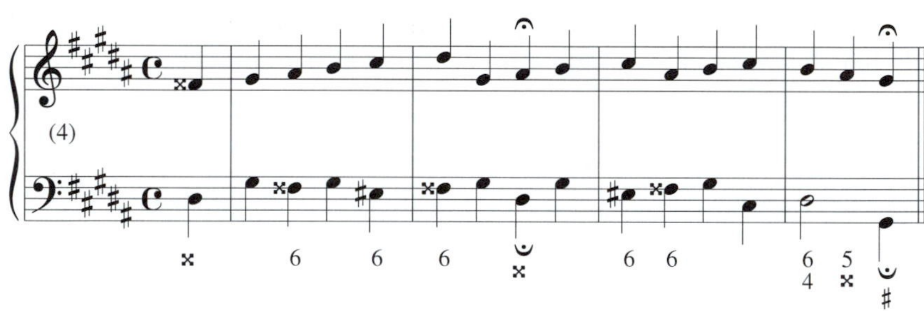

(b) The bass only is given. Write the soprano line and fill in the alto and tenor voices. Make a harmonic analysis. When you write the melodic line, be sure to follow the procedures of good melodic writing as described in Chapter 7. Choosing a soprano note at random simply because it fits the designated chord rarely produces worthwhile results.

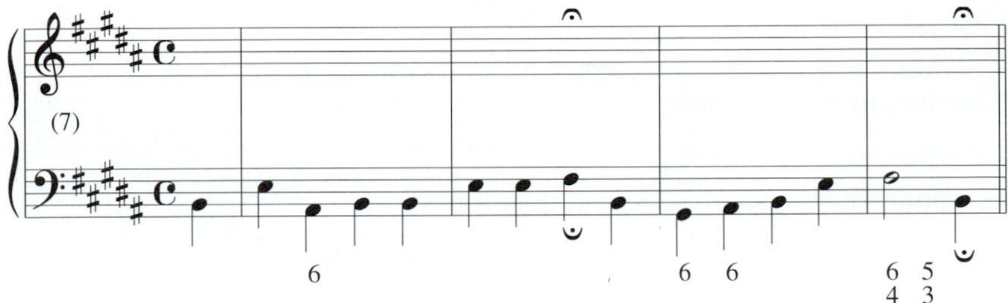

Alternative methods of solution

1. Write any exercise on four staves (open score), using correct transposition for the tenor voice. Don't forget to use correct stem directions when writing a single voice line on the staff.
2. Write any exercise in open score, using treble, alto, tenor, and bass clefs, reading from the top staff down.

ASSIGNMENT 9.7 *Part-writing for instrumental ensemble.* Add inner voices to the following example. For additional experience, rewrite exercises from Assignment 9.6 for instruments of your choice or as assigned.

Melody Harmonization

When harmonizing a melody using inversions, you must decide which triads will be in inversion and which will have the root in the bass. Therefore, write the complete bass line first, *before* the inner voices.

When the bass moves with the soprano, their related movements can be in any one of four directions:

1. *Contrary motion* to each other
2. *Oblique motion*—soprano stays on the same tone while bass moves, or soprano moves while bass maintains the same tone
3. *Similar motion* to each other
4. *Stationary motion*—both soprano and bass repeat their tones

FIGURE 9.33

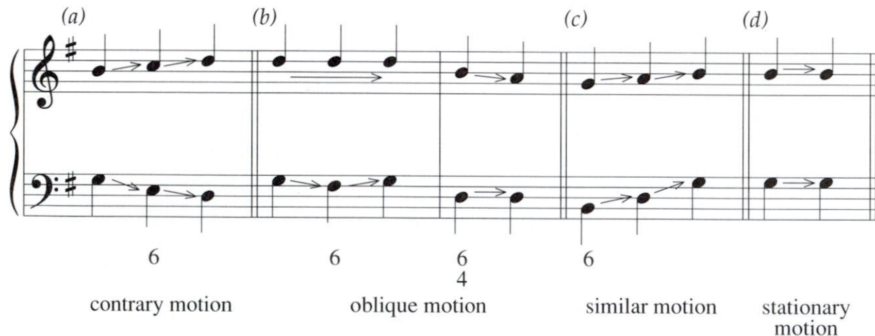

Of the four types of motion, contrary and oblique are the most frequently used. Similar motion is very effective for intervals of thirds or sixths between soprano and bass (see Figure 9.6, bracketed voices) but otherwise should be used with care, avoiding parallel or hidden octaves and fifths. Stationary motion, having no melodic or harmonic motion, is little used.

The chorale in Figure 9.34 uses I, IV, and V only. Here is the count of the motions between outside voices: contrary, 3; similar, 3; oblique, 1. Note that the similar motions occur during a repeated triad, as thirds between soprano and bass, and in the V–I cadence.

FIGURE 9.34 *Motion between Outside Voices*

As a final test of the chosen bass line, play or sing (two persons) your soprano and bass lines only. The sound of the two-voice composition should be musically effective, even without the inner voices, as already demonstrated in the Mozart example, Figure 9.5. Try this on Figure 9.34, or on any other Bach chorale.

ASSIGNMENT 9.8 *Analysis of motion between outside voices.* Using music examples from this chapter, indicate each motion by C (contrary), S (similar), or O (oblique), as in Figure 9.34. Count the total number of each motion. Also count the number of similar motions involving parallel thirds or sixths. Be able to discuss the significance of these statistics.

		C	S	O	S: 3rds or 6ths
Example:	Figure 9.34	3	3	1	1
	Figure 9.5	___	___	___	___
	Figure 9.7	___	___	___	___
	Figure 9.11	___	___	___	___
	Figure 9.17	___	___	___	___

In Appendix E: Answers to the entire assignment are given.

ASSIGNMENT 9.9 *Melody harmonization.* Following directions from Assignment 6.11 (page 125), first write the bass line using roots only, then decide where use of inversions will be effective, with special attention to the motion between the outside voices. Each exercise asks you to use certain inversions, but you are not limited to these.

(1) Use two different six-four chords.

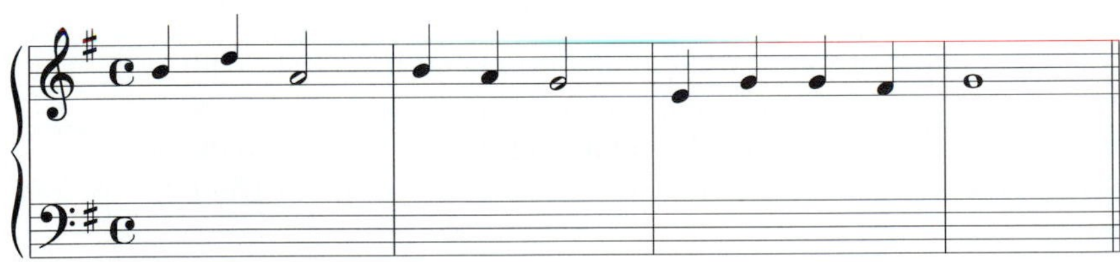

(2) Use $\sharp\hat{6}$–$\sharp\hat{7}$ in the bass.

(3) Use a pedal six-four and a measure similar to measure 1 of Figure 9.5 (page 171).

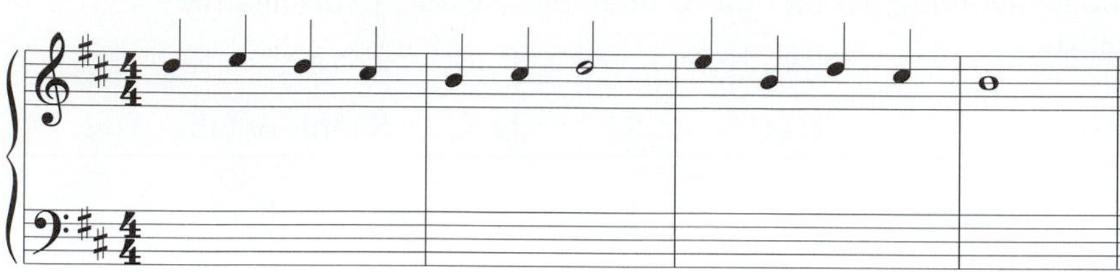

(4) Use a V_6–IV_6 progression and a cadential six-four chord on a weak beat.

Keyboard Harmony

ASSIGNMENT 9.10 Play any major or minor triad in first or second inversion, with any member of the triad in the soprano. As in previous keyboard performances of single triads, play each triad in inversion with three notes in the right hand and one in the left, using correct doubling. Example: Play the first inversion of the D major triad, with its fifth in the soprano.

FIGURE 9.35

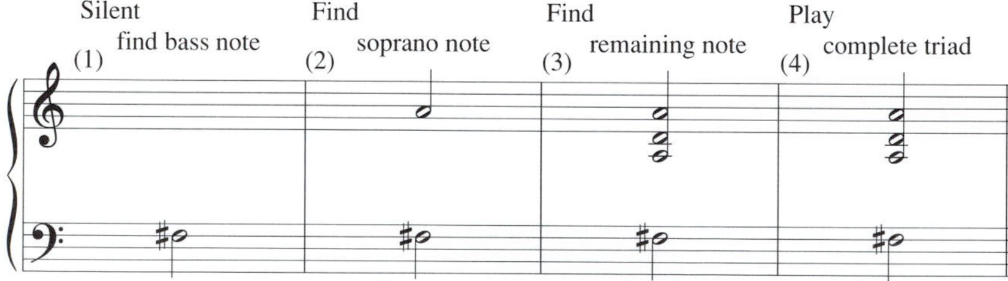

Play these triads or others as assigned. Soprano note is indicated in parentheses.

First Inversion: Major—C(1), E♭(5), A(3), B(1), D♭(5)
Minor—D(1), G(5), F♯(3), B♭(1), D♯(5)

Second Inversion: Major—A(3), F(1), G♭(5), E(1), C♯(3)
Minor—A(1), F♯(5), B(3), G♯(1), E♭(1)

ASSIGNMENT 9.11 Play these progressions in each major and minor key. The first three are written out. Also, try each exercise beginning with one of the two other soprano positions of the opening tonic triad.

(1)

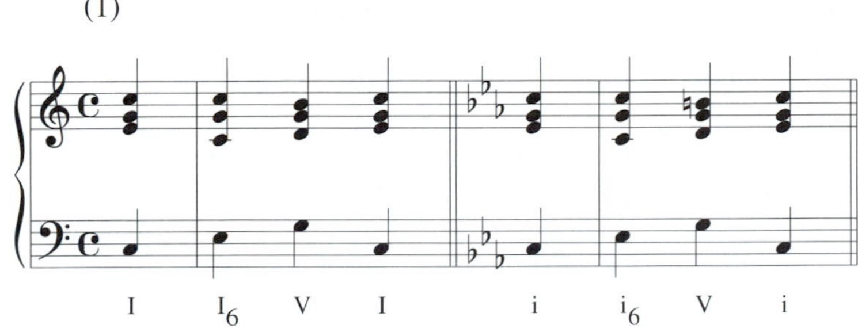

(2)

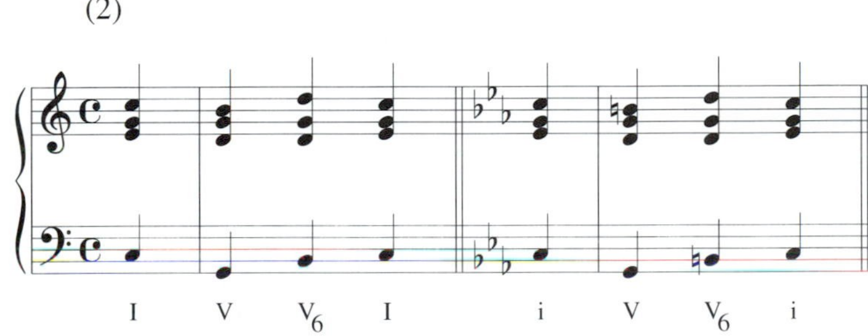

(3)

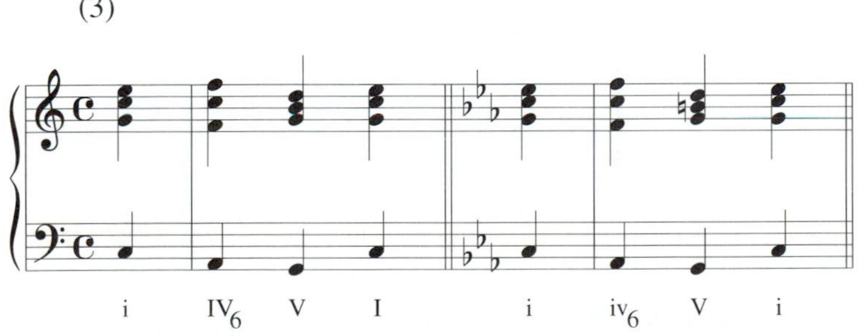

(4) I I_6 IV V I; i i_6 iv V i
(5) I IV_6 V_6 I; i IV_6 V_6 i
(6) I IV I^6_4 V I; i iv i^6_4 V i
(7) I IV_6 I^6_4 V I; i iv_6 i^6_4 V i

Summary

A chord in inversion is one in which some tone other than the root is the lowest tone: in first inversion, the third; in second inversion, the fifth.

Inversions are valuable for creating bass lines with melodic interest greater than that possible with chord roots alone. Specific devices made possible are melodic sequences in the bass and parallel thirds or sixths between the bass and an upper voice.

When first inversions are used in succession, any resulting chord progression is usable, including V–IV, not ordinarily found with roots in the bass.

In a minor key, the bass line ascending through ♯$\hat{6}$ requires the use of the major subdominant triad, IV.

The use of second inversion is limited because the interval of the perfect fourth above the bass is considered a dissonance, requiring resolution to a third above the bass.

The second inversion is used principally as a *cadential* chord, resolving to V at a cadence. Other uses are the *pedal* six-four and the *passing* six-four.

Conventional doubling in first inversion is the soprano note; in second inversion, the bass note. Successive first inversions require differing doublings as needed to avoid parallels.

Part-writing inversions is best accomplished by writing to and from the doubled note first.

When inversions are used to harmonize a melody, contrary and oblique motion between the outside voices should be the most frequent. Similar motion is effective when soprano and bass move in parallel thirds or sixths.

ARTICLE #8

The Theory of Inversion

The fact that a chord can be inverted—that, for example, E G C is the same chord as C E G, only inverted—appears so obvious to us now that we assume the concept must have been known to the very earliest composers. In reality, however, the seemingly "simple" fact of harmonic invertibility became formally established only in the year 1722 by Jean-Philippe Rameau (1683–1764) in his *Traité de l'harmonie reduite à ses principes naturels (Treatise on Harmony Reduced to Its Natural Principles).*

To understand why the concept of the chord and its inversion came so late, we must once again look back to the beginnings of composition in Western music. The earliest known music is melodic, that of the chants of the medieval church.

Music in two voices, two melodic lines together, appeared in the ninth century, with the chant also stated a perfect fifth higher than the original melody and with the two lines sung simultaneously.

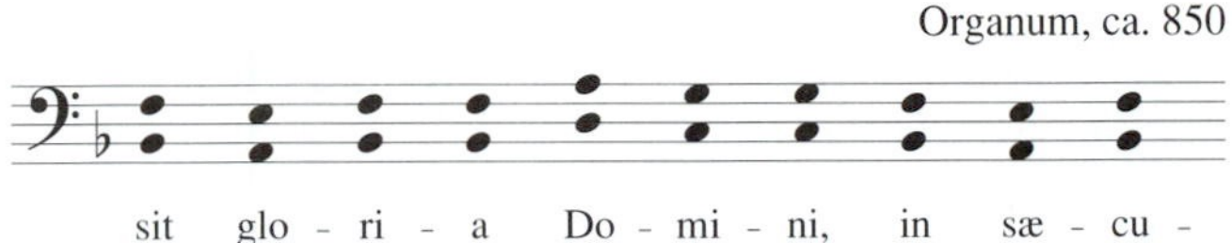

This simple device of sounding two melodies simultaneously, known as *counterpoint,* evolved first through independence of direction in the two lines,

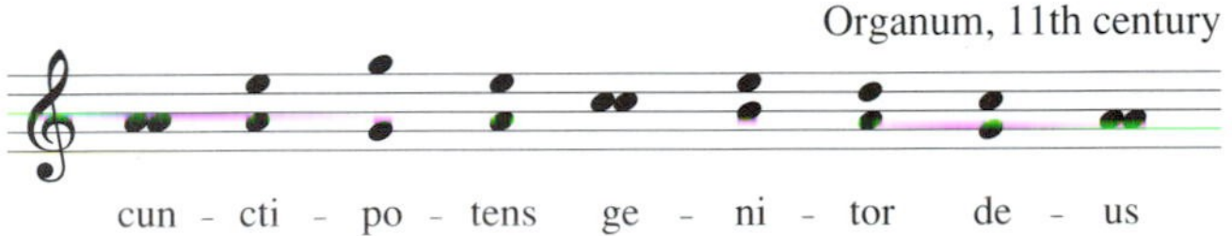

then with independence of rhythm,

followed by the addition of more and more melodic lines,

*These first five excerpts are reprinted by permission of Harvard University Press, Cambridge, Mass., from Davison and Apel, *Historical Anthology of Music,* Vol. I (1949).

and reaching its culmination in the *polyphonic* (many-voiced) contrapuntal writing found in the masterworks of the late sixteenth century.

Palestrina (1525–1594), *In Dominicus Quadragesima*

In all these developments, the primary compositional concern was the setting of voice lines against each other. The harmonic aspect was controlled exclusively by making sure that intervals above the lowest sounding notes were consonant with these notes (though specific dissonances in well-defined situations were allowed). Hence, the first vertical sonority in measure 4 of the Palestrina example we would call a D minor triad, but in the sixteenth century it would have been described simply as a minor third and a perfect fifth above the D in the bass. On the fourth beat of the measure, we see from the bass up the notes C E A, to us the first inversion of an A minor triad, but at that time a major third and a major sixth above the C in the bass. Only the major triad occurring at the end of a composition was given an identity, and called the *trias harmonica* (harmonic triad).

The impetus of performance and composition through the use of figured bass (see the article "Figured Bass" in this chapter) heightened awareness of the harmonic aspect of music. Many theorists during this time attempted a rational explanation of this new concept, but none was successful until the theories of Rameau appeared, approximately 125 years after the introduction of the figured bass. Rameau's proof of the invertibility of a chord or of an interval was arrived at through the principle of the "identity of the octave." In the interval of the octave, the two notes sound identically; therefore, the octave actually represents a single pitch of the same name. It should follow that any interval of a chord that is changed only by an octave transposition of one or more of its notes has not really been changed at all.

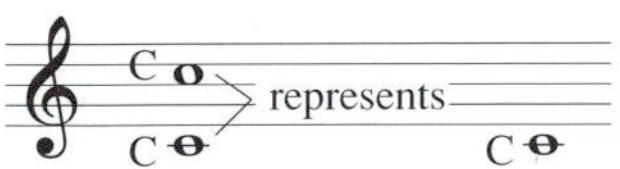

Thus, E G C is C E G, the same triad but in a different form, the first inversion; and G C E is C E G, but in second inversion.

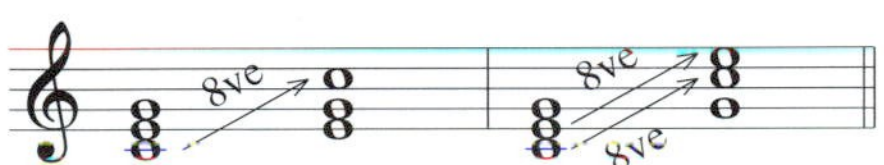

But why is C the fundamental note of this triad, rather than E or G? The answer to Rameau was based on an acoustical phenomenon well known as far back as early Greek times and said to have been discovered by Pythagoras (sixth century B.C.). We take a string that when played sounds C. If we press a finger at the halfway point on the string and play on one half of the string, the note produced is another C an octave higher. If we place the finger to divide the string in thirds and play on one third of the string, we get the pitch G an octave and a fifth above the original note. Here are the pitches derived from the first six divisions of a string sounding C.

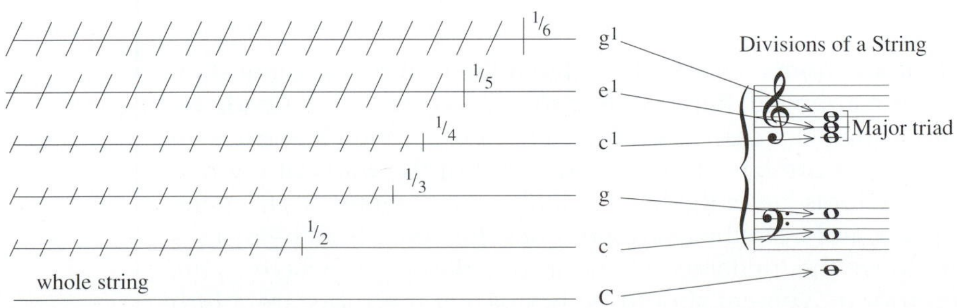

Rameau observed that each note created by dividing the string was directly related thereby to the entire string, the source from which the upper tones are derived. In our illustration, the triad c^1 e^1 g^1 is derived from the division of an original string sounding C. c^1 is in an octave relationship to the original C; it therefore represents the fundamental or generating tone and becomes the root or fundamental of the triad, no matter in what order the triad notes are arranged.

Another acoustical phenomenon, the *overtone series* (described in Appendix C), displays the same relationship of intervals as that found in the division of a string. Although it was discovered by Joseph Sauver, a blind and deaf music theorist, twenty years before Rameau's theories, Rameau, once he had become acquainted with it, pointed to the overtone series as further confirmation of his work. In the following overtone series on C, the C E G triad appears as partials numbered 4, 5, and 6, comparable to the fourth, fifth, and sixth divisions of the string.

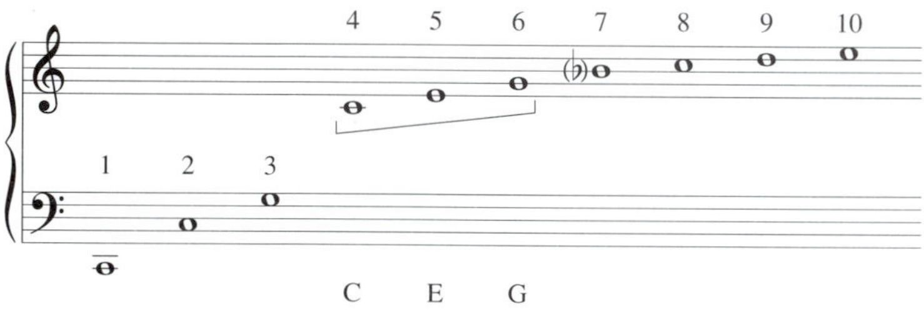

Intervals are invertible in the same manner. Moving the lower note up an octave or the upper note down an octave changes the interval only by the ratio of 1:2. Since this ratio indicates the octave, which in turn represents the fundamental, the two intervals are inversions of each other. Perfect fifths and perfect fourths are inversions of each other; minor thirds and major sixths are inversions of each other.

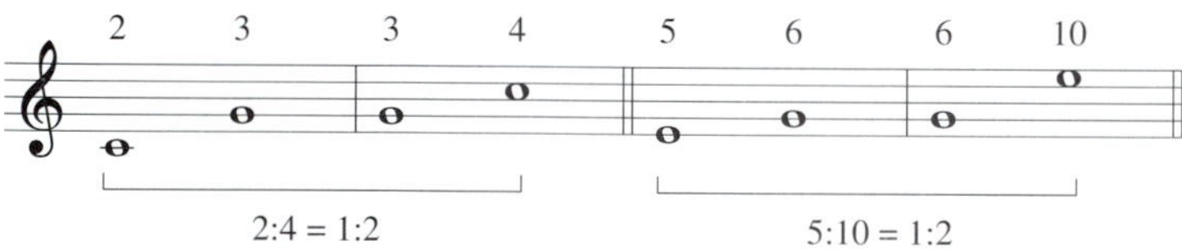

Having found that all chords have roots and that the root remains constant when the notes are rearranged, Rameau next sought to discover the underlying principle governing the progression of one chord to another. Rameau said that these progressions are based upon movement of the roots of chords, whether or not those roots are in the bass. In looking at the intervals from the division of the string and from the overtone series, he noted that the first interval to appear above the fundamental and its repetition, the octave, is the fifth. Therefore, root movement should be best when the roots are a fifth apart. This can be shown by taking a piece of music and extracting the roots, placing these on a third staff, as in the following example. It should be kept in mind that there are three possible root movements: by fifth, by third, and by second. According to the theory of inversion, the effect of the fourth is the same as that of the fifth (C up to F is the same as C down to F), the sixth is the same as the third (C up to A is the same as C down to A), and the seventh is the same as the second (C up to B is the same as C down to B).

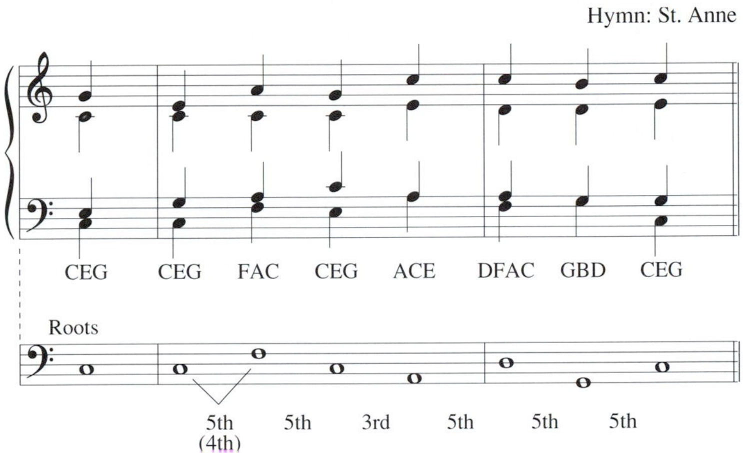

In this part of his theory, Rameau was correct; subsequent analysis has shown that in the music of almost every composer during the years 1600–1900, the majority of root movements were by the interval of the fifth. Rameau's reasoning that root movement by thirds should be next best and root movements by seconds least best has been reversed by the practice of composers.

But on the whole, Rameau was eminently successful in discovering satisfactory principles of chord construction and chord progression. Chords have roots that may or may not be in the lowest sounding voice, and chord succession is a function of the movement of these roots, movement by the fifth being the best. These principles allow us to identify a chord by numbering the chord according to the location of its root in the scale and to study the relationship of chords through the movements of their roots.

Music written after the time of Rameau and up to about 1900 can, for the most part, be studied and analyzed by the principles first outlined by Rameau. It is because of this fact, and in spite of the large number of composers and diverse styles in this three-century span, that we can study the music of this period under the single subject heading of harmony.

ARTICLE #9

Figured Bass

In its four-hundred-year history, figured bass has functioned in three distinct areas of musical endeavor. It began as a solution to a performance problem; then, during the Baroque era, it became an important compositional device; and, finally today, it serves as a widely used aid in the learning of harmony and part-writing.

Its history dates from the late sixteenth century. You will read in the article "Another Metrical Concept," in Chapter 15, that vocal music of the time was written on separate pages for each of the voices. And although much of this music was written without accompaniment *(a cappella),* it was the custom of the time to include instrumentalists informally, playing any or all of the vocal parts or even playing them without singers. The performance problem we have spoken of arose when the keyboard player tried to read all the separate parts of a work simultaneously when performing it with the ensemble. The problem was compounded by the fact that in this pre-seventeenth-century music, each line was a melodic line, and all the lines were superimposed on each other to create a contrapuntal composition (as we will see in the Palestrina excerpt in the article "Another Metrical Concept," previously mentioned).

A solution to the keyboard player's dilemma came when someone thought of using the bass part only and writing numbers under or over certain bass notes to indicate the intervals above those notes. The performer quickly calculated the intervals above the bass and played these notes as a group—as a *chord.* As the music evolved, the succession of chords harmonized with the contrapuntal composition, even though it was in direct contrast to the melodic intent of the composition.

Although a concept of harmony, as opposed to one of counterpoint, was stirring in the sixteenth century, this practice of playing from a figured bass—of preparing a solo line and a figured bass line—actually provided composers with the impetus to write chordally. The first such music in this style was written by Lodovico Viadanna, in or about the year 1596. The style was eagerly accepted and practiced by most composers, and thus harmony soon replaced counterpoint as the predominant characteristic of music.

The following example is taken from Caccini's *Le Nuove Musiche (The New Music),* published in 1601. Only the vocal solo line and the bass line with figuration, called *continuo* or *basso continuo,* were written by the composer. The rest of the notes represent one possible interpretation, called a *realization,* of the figured bass.

Early figured bass examples, such as that of Caccini, often used numbers higher than 8 to indicate compound intervals (10 = 8ve + 3rd). Except for 9 in certain circumstances, these large numbers were soon discarded. The player seeing 6, for example, could play the sixth above the bass in any convenient octave.

Composition using figured bass continued throughout the mid–eighteenth century and included many of the great vocal and instrumental works of Bach, Handel, and their contemporaries.

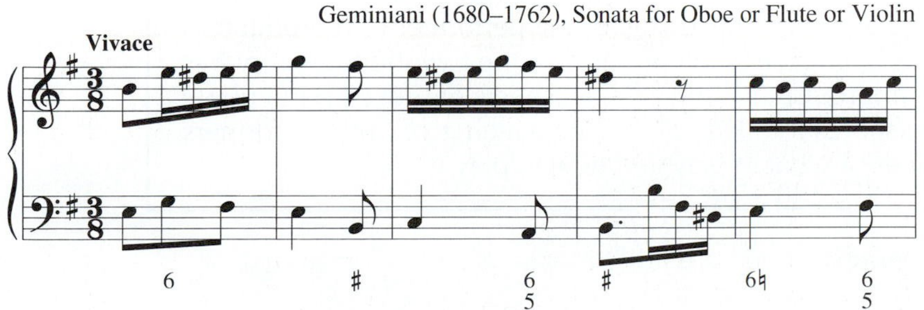

Whereas keyboard performers of this period improvised freely over the given figured bass lines, today's performers prefer to purchase a copy of the score with the keyboard part already written out. Thus, if one purchases the Handel violin sonatas in two different editions, one gets two different keyboard realizations. There is no reason, however, why any player cannot improvise or write out a keyboard part for any figured bass composition.

When looking at original figured bass lines, one notices that the method of writing for figured bass varied from composer to composer. For example, the markings ♯6, 6♯, 6+, and 6̸ all mean the same thing. Symbols are often missing when the composer thinks the harmony is obvious, but at times they are present when they seem unnecessary. The figured bass symbols shown in examples in this book are authentic to their historical period, but of necessity their style cannot be attributed to any one composer.

With the end of the eighteenth century, figured bass, together with improvisation and casual interpretation of the music score, became a thing of the past. Composers now wrote exactly what they wanted played, and since that time it has been considered an artistic necessity for the performer to reproduce as exactly as possible the composer's intentions. But the twentieth century has seen a revival of the improvisatory and casual aspects of music, particularly in jazz groups and in scores for aleatoric music, which give both performers and conductors choices of what to play and how to play it.

10

Harmonic Progression; the Leading-Tone Triad and the Supertonic Triad

By "harmonic progression" we mean the order in which chords follow one another. A harmony once sounded is, of course, followed by another, but which one should it be? Is there any particular order? Are some progressions favored over others? Does it really make any difference?

Root Movement

Progression of chords, one to another, is always described in terms of root movements—that is, the intervallic distance between the roots of the two successive chords in question, regardless of the actual bass notes (inversions) used. Intervallic distances between chord roots can be only three: the fifth, the third, and the second. The fourth, the sixth, and the seventh are merely inversions of these (a root movement C up to G, a fifth, is the same as a root movement C down to G, a fourth).

Root movement *down by a fifth* accounts for a large percentage and often a majority of the chord progressions in the music of most composers. This is the movement of the authentic cadence (V–I), which is so effective in establishing a sense of key. It has been surmised by many theorists that the basic quality of the downward fifth lies in its relationship to the first interval (other than the octave) in the overtone series:[1] a fifth, the third partial descending to the second.

In Figure 10.1, the pattern of root movement in an excerpt from Mozart is shown on the third staff. Note that when the roots move a fourth, the progression is labeled "5th," and when a chord is in inversion, the root, rather than the bass note, is shown.

[1]See Appendix C.

Counting the root movements (considering the root of the six-four to be F), we find

by fifth—6
by second—1
by third—1

FIGURE 10.1 *Root Movements*

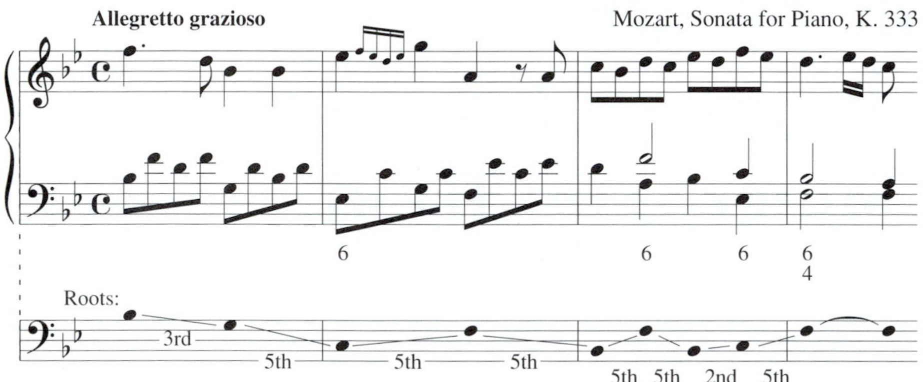

The preponderance of root movement by fifth in this example is typical of tonal harmony in general, though not always in this same proportion, of course. But it bears out our earlier statement that "root relationship by fifth . . . is probably the most significant element delineating the character of tonal harmony."

Harmonic Progression

Having established a system of root movements, we still need to know what specific chords are used and in what progression we would find them.

If we made an extensive survey of thousands of progressions in tonal music, probably any chord progression imaginable would show up. But in such a survey, we would notice that certain progressions occur over and over again, others less frequently, and still others rarely. It is obvious that composers have not chosen to utilize all chord progressions equally. We will discover these choices through analysis of root movements.

Root relationship by fifth has already been considered in the study of the authentic cadence, V–I, in which the root of V descends a fifth to the root of I. What root, then, descends a fifth to the root of V? It is, of course, ii. Counting back by descending fifths, we arrive at this succession, any pair of which is a commonly used progression.

FIGURE 10.2 *Harmonic Progression by Fifths in Major*

(IV → vii°) → iii → vi → ii → V → I
IV vii°

But you will note that IV and vii° seem to be misplaced. In movement by fifths, vii° should precede iii. However, vii° usually functions as a dominant, progressing to I. Why? The three tones of the vii° triad are the same as the upper three tones of V^7 (C: vii° = B D F; V^7 = G B D F). Because of its urgency to progress to I, and because its spelling is so similar to that of V^7, many theorists define vii° as an incomplete V^7 with root implied ($V^7_{\circ}$).[2] In this sense, the *implied* root is a fifth above the tonic. However, IV–vii°–iii is useful in a harmonic sequence (Chapter 17).

We have already studied the remaining triad, IV, in its movement to V and to I. As stated in Chapter 6, the IV–V progression is commonly implied in folk melodies, and this harmonization is common in amateur performance. It is interesting to note that in composed music, the progression ii–V is much more frequent than IV–V.

So we have a cluster preceding I; the arrows indicate these useful progessions.[3]

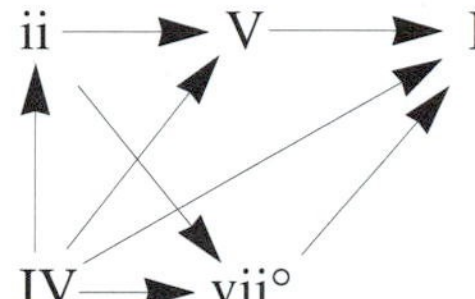

ii: to V or vii°

IV: to ii, V, or vii°

vii°: to I

In a minor key, ii and IV in the above list will be ii° and iv. But when $\hat{6}$ in either triad progresses to $\hat{7}$ in the following triad, ii (minor) and IV (major) will be used to avoid the interval of an augmented second.

The progression ii°–vii°, two successive diminished triads, is not useful.

These two additional common progressions remain:

1. When a triad skips in the direction of tonic (sometimes called *elision*): vi–V, iii–IV (actually more common than iii–vi), and iii–ii_6[4]
2. When a triad moves away from the tonic (sometimes called *retrogression*): V–vi, vi–iii–IV (vi–iii is uncommon except when followed by IV)
3. A common progression interrupted by a tonic triad: ii–I–V, for example

Harmonic Progressions in Minor Keys

In minor, iv and VII *are* included in the series of progressions by fifths. Since these two are minor and major triads respectively, they can progress by perfect fifth, iv to VII and VII to III, continuing as in Figure 10.3. The entire series can be seen in G minor in the Haydn example, Figure 10.6

[2]In this text, the designation vii° is used rather than $V^7_{\circ}$ because of significant differences in part-writing the two chords (page 224).

[3]For study of the common progression IV–ii (shown in the cluster), see page 310.

[4]Why ii_6 and not ii? See page 304.

FIGURE 10.3 *Harmonic Progression by Fifths in Minor*

iv → VII → III → VI → ii° → V → i
iv → vii° → i

Note that:

VII is built on $\flat\hat{7}$ (C minor: B♭ D F).[5]

vii° is built on $\sharp\hat{7}$ (C minor: B D F).

The triad on $\sharp\hat{6}$ is seldom seen (C minor: A C E♭).

iv appears twice, preceding VII as well as the dominant

Figure 10.4 consolidates all the information about common harmonic progressions and refers to both major and minor keys, except as noted. You should use this table for future reference.

FIGURE 10.4 *Table of Common Progressions*

I, i	(1) May progress to any other triad (2) May interrupt any progression, such as ii–I–V		
Major keys		*Minor keys*	
ii	ii–V, ii–vii$^{\circ}_{6}$	ii$^{\circ}_{6}$	ii$^{\circ}_{6}$–V
		ii*	ii–V, ii–vii$^{\circ}_{6}$
iii	iii-ii$_{6}$, iii–IV, iii-V, iii–vi	III	III–ii$^{\circ}_{6}$, III–iv, III–VI
IV	IV–I, IV–ii, IV–V, IV–vii$^{\circ}_{6}$	iv	iv–i, iv–ii$^{\circ}_{6}$, iv–V, iv–VII
		IV*	IV–V, IV–vii$^{\circ}_{6}$
V	V–I, V–vi	V	V–i, V–VI
		v*	v–VI
vi	vi–ii, vi–IV, vi–V, vi–iii–IV	VI	VI–ii$^{\circ}_{6}$, VI–iv, VI–V, VI–III–iv
vii$^{\circ}_{6}$	vii$^{\circ}_{6}$–I	vii$^{\circ}_{6}$	vii$^{\circ}_{6}$–i
		VII	VII–III

*ii and IV in minor used with ascending $\sharp\hat{6}$; v in minor used with a descending $\hat{7}$.

[5]Discussed on page 350.

ASSIGNMENT 10.1 After sufficient study of Figure 10.4, place an X before those of the following progressions that appear in the table. Do not refer to the table until you are finished.

(1)	______	ii–V	(6)	______	iii–I–IV
(2)	______	IV–vi	(7)	______	vii°–V
(3)	______	vi–iii–V	(8)	______	iii–vii°
(4)	______	V–vi	(9)	______	vi–iii–IV
(5)	______	I–iii	(10)	______	VII–III (minor)

Other Common Types of Progressions

There are three additional categories of harmonic progression. In these, the progression standing alone is infrequently used, but in special situations it can be considered equally deserving of use as any common progression.

1. *First inversions in succession.* When a bass line moves by step and each note is the third of a chord, any resulting succession of chords is acceptable.

CD FIGURE 10.5

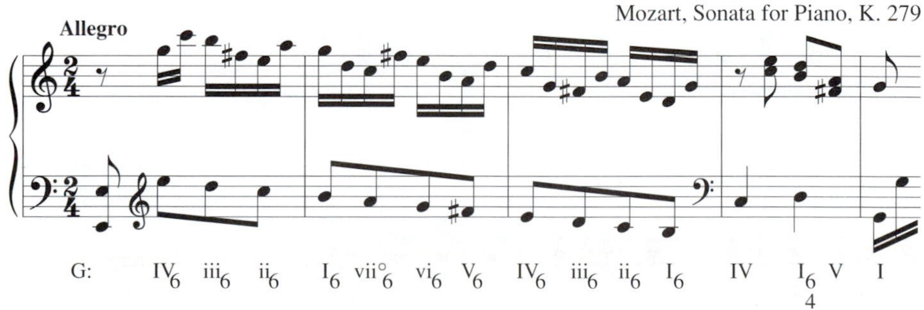

2. *Harmonic sequence.* A harmonic sequence is a series of chords, four or more, with a regularly recurring pattern of root movements, a series in which any resulting pair of triads is acceptable. In the most common harmonic sequence, the roots alternately descend a fifth and ascend a fourth, which, of course, is the same as the series in Figures 10.2 and 10.3. In Figure 10.6, which shows the complete series, first inversions and root positions alternate, but this does not affect root movement.

FIGURE 10.6 *Harmonic Sequence*

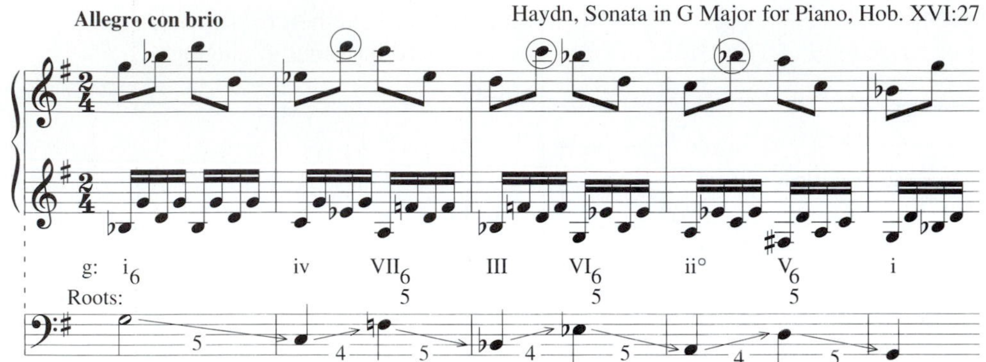

A harmonic sequence can display any other pattern of root movements. In Figure 10.7, roots descend a fourth and ascend a fifth, just the opposite of Figure 10.6. A major triad built on $\hat{6}$ is used here rather than the diatonic vi. The progressions V–ii and ii–VI are a result of the sequence, and otherwise they are not ordinarily encountered.

FIGURE 10.7

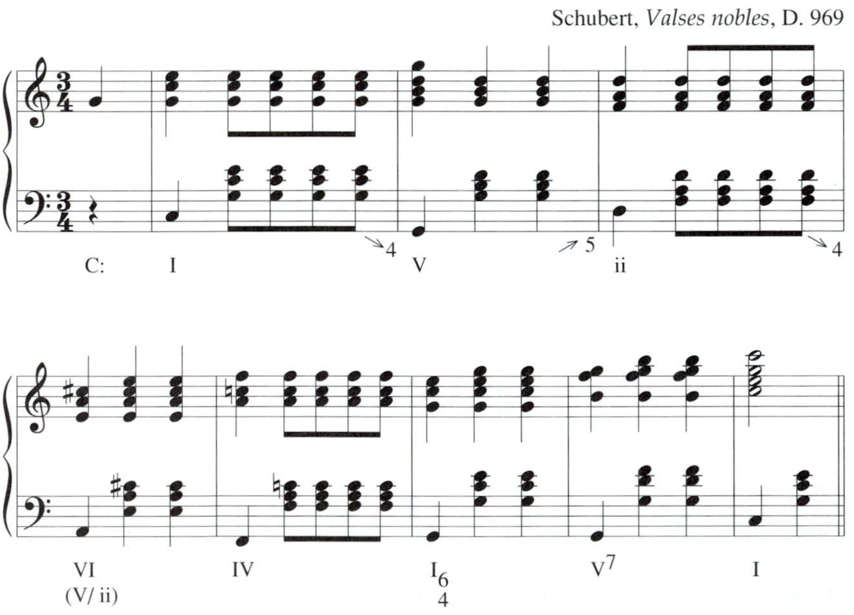

3. *Chromatic bass line.* When the bass line ascends or descends by a series of half steps, any resulting chord succession is usually satisfactory. Further discussion and illustration of this type of chord movement will be presented during the study of altered chords in *Advanced Harmony.*

The Diminished Triad

The diminished triad consists of two successive minor thirds. Together, these produce the interval of the diminished fifth (d5), which when inverted becomes an augmented fourth (A4).

FIGURE 10.8

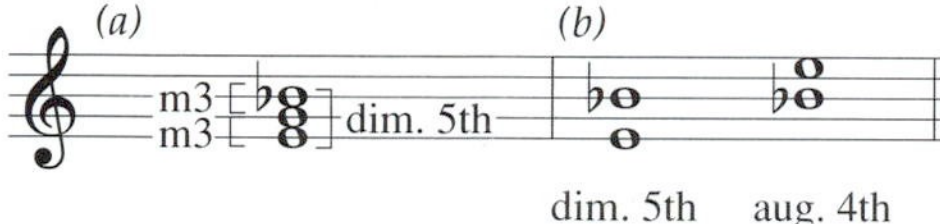

Because of the interval of the diminished fifth, the diminished triad is classified as one of the dissonant triads. Both the interval of the diminished fifth and its inversion, the augmented fourth, are known commonly as a tritone, referring to the fact that the interval is composed of three whole steps (six half steps). The interval under either name equally divides the octave.

FIGURE 10.9 *The Tritone*

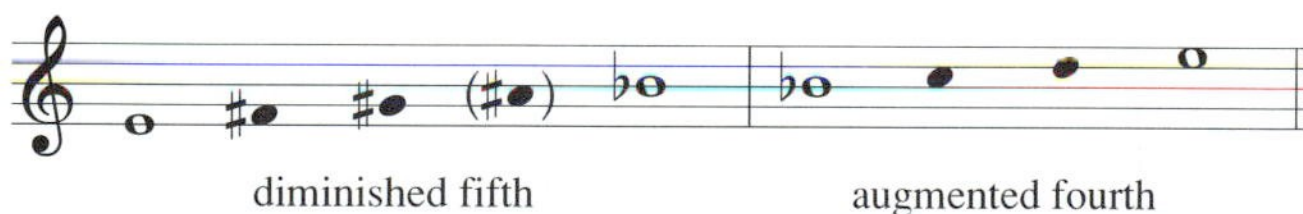

Only in the first inversion is there no tritone above the bass note. For this reason, the diminished triad is used almost exclusively in the first inversion. (See the article "The Devil in Music," in this chapter.)

FIGURE 10.10 *Tritones in the Diminished Triad*

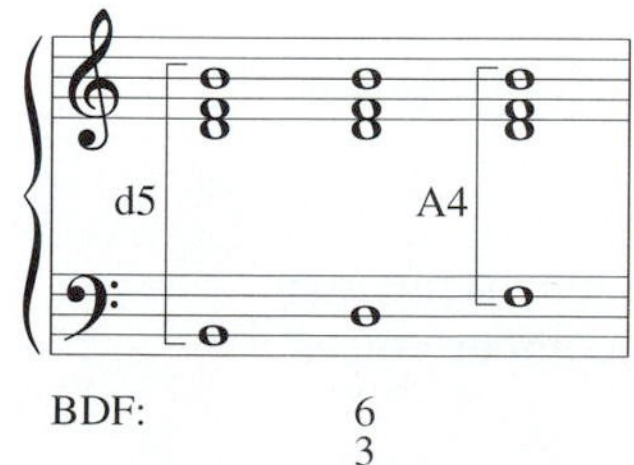

As a diatonic triad, the diminished triad is found on the leading tone (vii°) in both major and minor, and on the supertonic (ii°) in minor.

ASSIGNMENT 10.2 Spell these diminished triads by spelling two minor thirds.

(1) C ____ ____
(2) ____ B♭ ____
(3) F♯ ____ ____
(4) ____ ____ A
(5) E♯ ____ ____
(6) ____ ____ A♭

In Appendix E: Answers to the entire assignment are given.
In the Workbook: Answers to the entire assignment are given.

The Leading-Tone Triad

The leading-tone triad is diminished in both major and minor. For example, in either G major or G minor it is spelled F♯ A C. It functions as a dominant triad, since it almost invariably progresses to tonic.

The leading-tone triad, vii°, has two principal uses:

1. Between the tonic and its first inversion, or reverse.

FIGURE 10.11

The aural effect is similar to the passing six-four. The use of I–vii$^{\circ}_{6}$–I$_{6}$ is much more frequent and can be considered the preferred choice.

2. Following the subdominant triad when the melody ascends. You may remember that in the progression from IV to V, contrary motion between the upper voices

worked out best. But when the soprano ascends, parallel motion is almost inevitable, except for the infrequently used progression shown in Figure 6.14. Using IV–vii$^{\circ}_{6}$ instead of IV–V avoids any real or implied parallels and so is the usual choice in this circumstance.

FIGURE 10.12

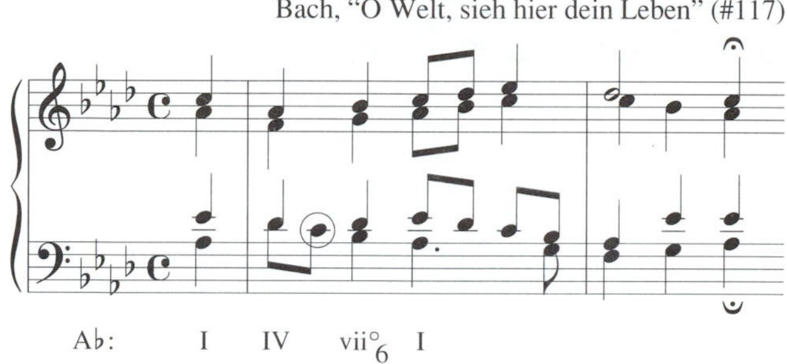

Should the progression be found in a minor key, the major IV triad is necessary to avoid the augumented second interval between ♭$\hat{6}$ and ♯$\hat{7}$.

FIGURE 10.13

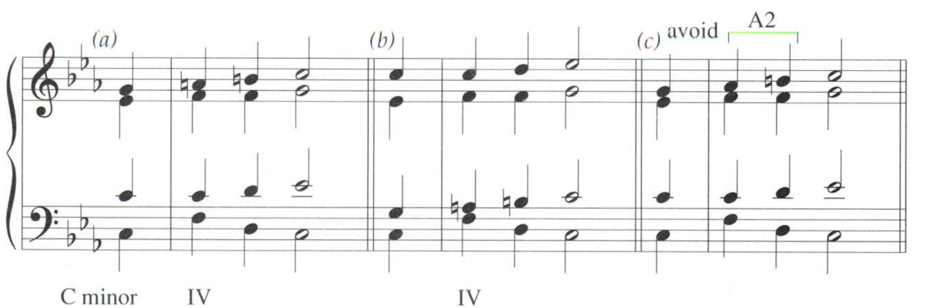

In the Table of Common Progressions (Figure 10.4), the progression vii°–V was not included. In our next example, Figure 10.14, there appears to be a clear-cut example of this progression, with the root of vii° in the bass. When the two chords vii° and V^7 are adjacent, as here, there is a better explanation. The entire measure, as in analysis *a,* is V^7, with all notes sounding, but not simultaneously. This is simpler than trying to account for every note change with a different chord number, as in *b.* As a general rule, when successive notes can be grouped together to make a single chord, that analysis is usually preferable.

CD FIGURE 10.14

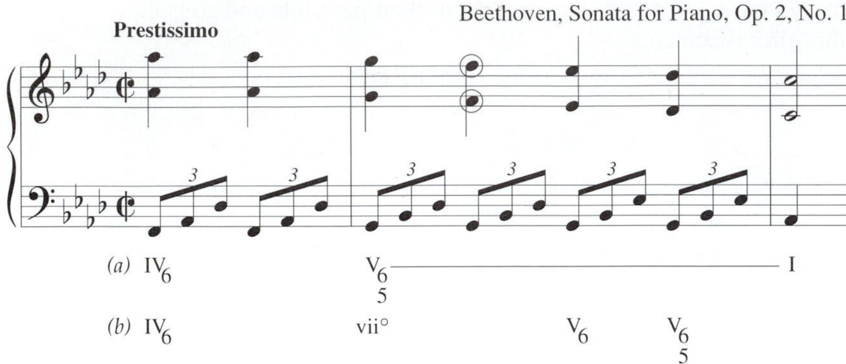

The Supertonic Triads

The supertonic triads (ii in major and ii° in minor) have much in common with the subdominant triad. Not only do ii and IV (ii° and iv) have two notes in common, but also, when ii and ii° are found in first inversion, which is most of the time, they have the same bass note as the root of IV. Figure 10.15*a* and *b* differ by only one note, the tenor note in the first triad.

FIGURE 10.15

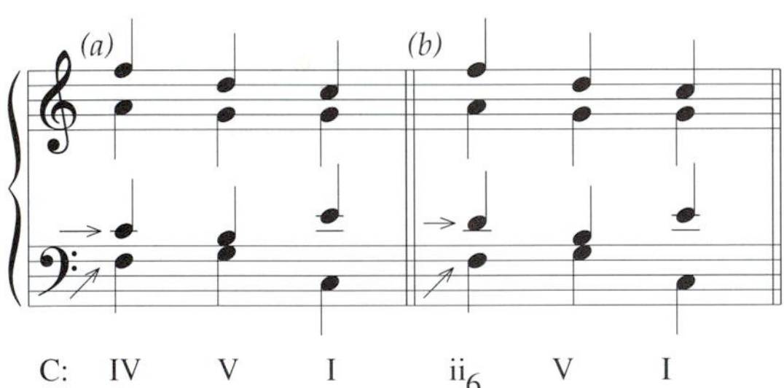

In addition, both triads commonly resolve to V or I, and consequently both are considered to be subdominant in function.

Like V as opposed to V^7, ii and ii° are used far less frequently than ii^7 and $ii^{ø7}$, but the basic principles stated here set the stage for the presentation of the seventh chords in Chapter 13.

ASSIGNMENT 10.3 *Spelling and identifying diminished triads built on the leading tone or the supertonic.* Each answer will be one of these: vii°, ii°, or a key name.

a. D♯ F♯ A is _____ in _____ major and ii° in _____ minor.

b. _____ _____ _____ is _____ in A♭ major and ii° in _____ minor.

c. _____ _____ _____ is _____ in _____ major and ii° in G♯ minor.

d. C E♭ G♭ is _____ in _____ major and _____ in _____ minor.

e. F♯ A C is ii° in _____ minor and _____ in _____ major.

f. _____ _____ _____ is _____ in _____ major and ii° in F♯ minor.

g. E♯ G♯ B is ii° in _____ minor and _____ in _____ major.

h. _____ _____ _____ is ii° in b minor and _____ in _____ major.

In Appendix E: Answers to the entire assignment are given.
In the Workbook: Answers to the entire assignment are given.

Here are typical uses of the supertonic triad.

1. In first inversion. This is the most common use of the supertonic triad. It usually leads to V–I or to I. As a preparation for the dominant, it is used much more frequently than IV (iv).

CD FIGURE 10.16 *ii*^{6}–*I*$^6_4$

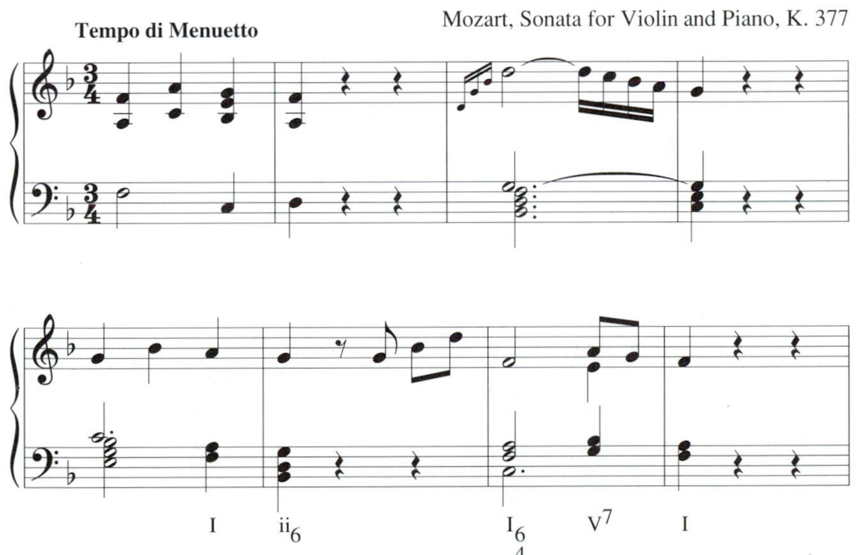

FIGURE 10.17 ii°_{6}–V

2. With root in bass. The supertonic triad with its root in the bass is useful only in major keys, but still much less so than in first inversion. Root position in minor is rarely used (except in harmonic sequence; see example in Figure 10.6), since it is a diminished triad. Figures 10.18 and 10.19 show root position movement to I^{6}_{4} and V, respectively. Observe in Figure 10.18 how easily Brahms could have used a IV triad simply by changing the bass note B to D.

CD FIGURE 10.18 ii–I^{6}_{4}

Brahms, Intermezzo, Op. 118, No. 2

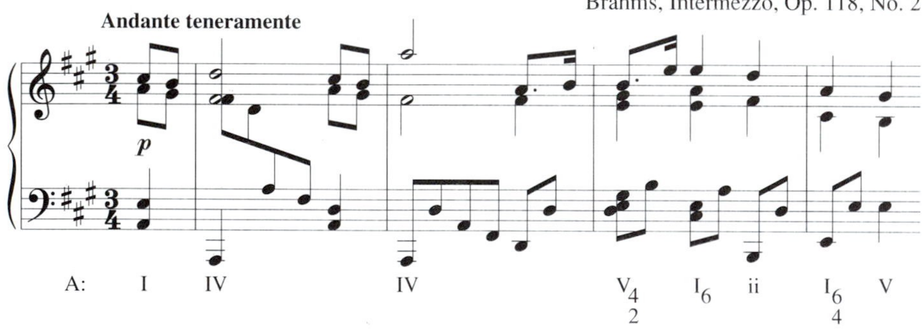

FIGURE 10.19 *ii–V*

Beethoven, Sonata in C Minor, for Violin and Piano, Op. 30, No. 2

3. The ii triad in a minor key. When a voice line ascends at the point where a supertonic triad is used, $\hat{6}$, the fifth of the triad, must be raised to ♯$\hat{6}$ to progress to ♯$\hat{7}$ without incurring an augmented second. In Figure 10.20*a,* the alto line is 5 ♯6 ♯7 8 (C♯ D♯ E♯ F♯) of the F♯ melodic minor scale. Note that three analyses are given.

In (1) is D♯ a passing tone in the vii° triad?
In (2) is E♯ a passing tone in the ii triad?
In (3) are there two triads, ii followed by vii°?

When ambiguous passages such as this are encountered, analysis depends upon the tempo of the composition and upon the aural effect on the listener.

In *b,* the use of ii (C minor: D F A) is clearer, even though it appears on the second half of the beat. Its appearance and sound indicate an independent sonority.

FIGURE 10.20

ASSIGNMENT 10.4 *Harmonic analysis.* These examples include leading-tone triads and supertonic triads. Write chord numbers below the staff and circle all nonharmonic tones. Included with the examples of vii° are the ♯$\hat{6}$–♯$\hat{7}$ scale line and the “vii°–V” (Figure 10.14). Indicate the location of these.

(1)

Anon., “Alle Menschen müssen sterben”

(2)

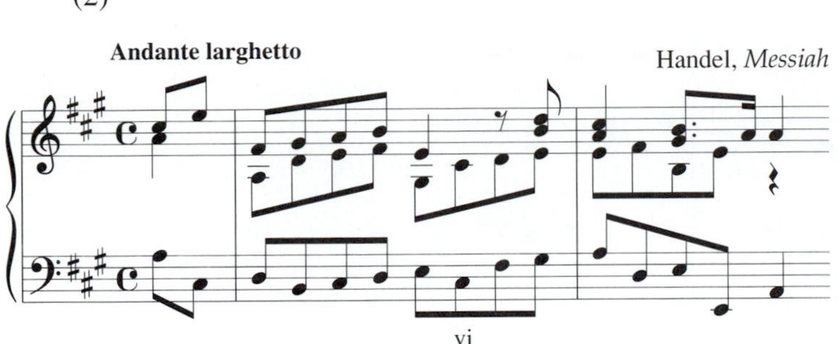
Andante larghetto
Handel, *Messiah*
vi

(3)

Schumann, *Myrten*, Op. 25, "Lied der Suleika"
Ziemlich langsam
Wie mit in - nig stem Be - ha - gen

(4)

Schumann, *Myrten*, Op. 25, "Rätsel"
Gut zu declamiren
Es flü - sterts der Him-mel, es murrt es die Höl-le, nur Schwach

(5)

Bach, "Herr Jesu Christ, du höchstes Gut" (#294)

(6) Could Beethoven have used a IV triad instead of ii?

Beethoven, Sonata for Piano, Op. 14, No. 2

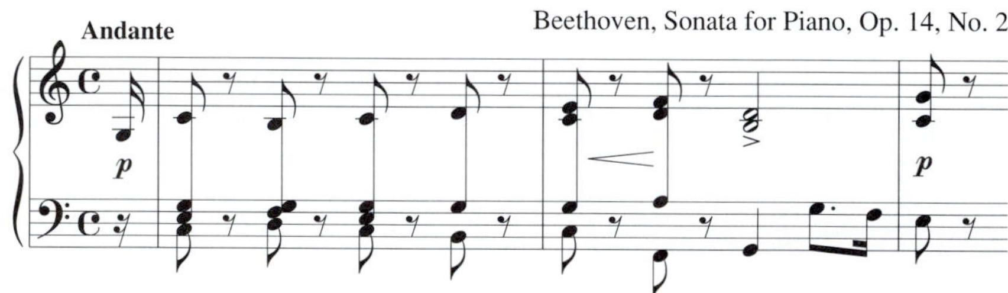

(7) The second triad of measure 2 appears diminished, but it could be a V^7. Can you explain why Haydn would omit the root?

Haydn, *L'Anima del Filosofo*, Hob. XXXVII:13

(8)

Mozart, Sonata in D Major for Piano, K. 284

(9) Only two notes of the supertonic are used. What is the complete spelling?

Haydn, Sonata for Piano, Hob. XVI:2

(10) The series of first inversions can easily be seen, but it is interrupted in measure 6. What chord interrupts the series, and what would its spelling have been had Beethoven continued the series through this measure?

In the cadence, the notes B♭ and D♭ imply E♭ G B♭ D♭, an implied V^7. Sounding simultaneously with an A♭ implying tonic, the dominant seventh chord functions as an *appoggiatura chord* (see page 272).

Beethoven, Sonata for Piano, Op. 2, No. 1

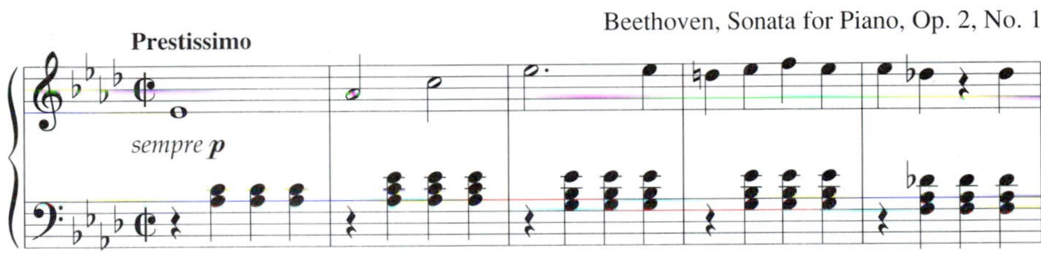

(11)

Bach, *French Suite III*, Courante, BWV 814

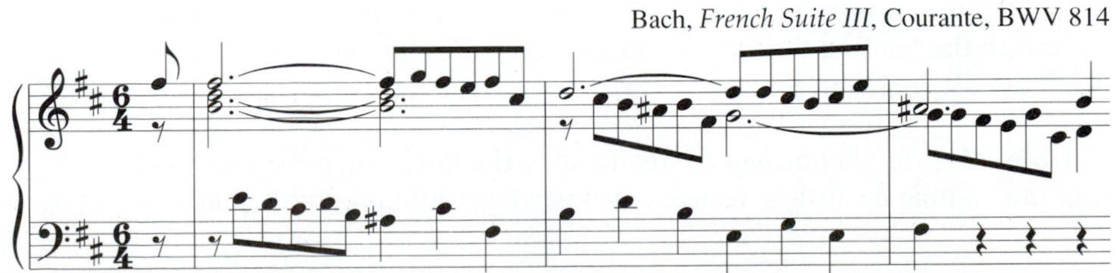

Writing the Diminished Triad

Only the use of the first inversion of the diminished triad will be considered at this time. Root position is used in harmonic sequence (see the ii° in Figure 10.6). Use of second inversion is very rare.

The common voice distribution for any diminished triad in first inversion is two thirds, one root and one fifth (bass note doubled), except that when the triad is found with the fifth in the soprano, the fifth is usually doubled (two fifths, one root, one third).

FIGURE 10.21 *Root (or Third) in Soprano*

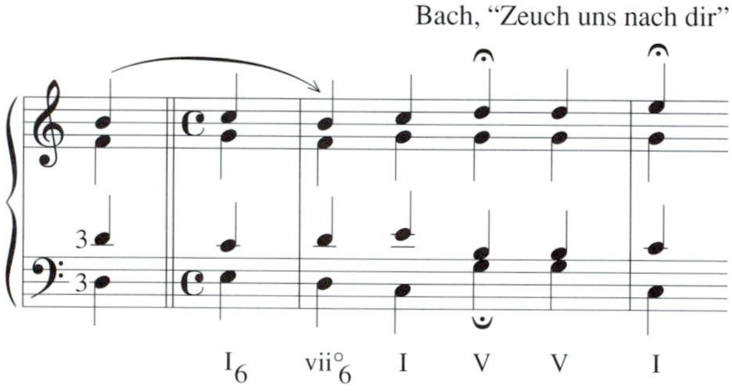

FIGURE 10.22 *Fifth in Soprano*

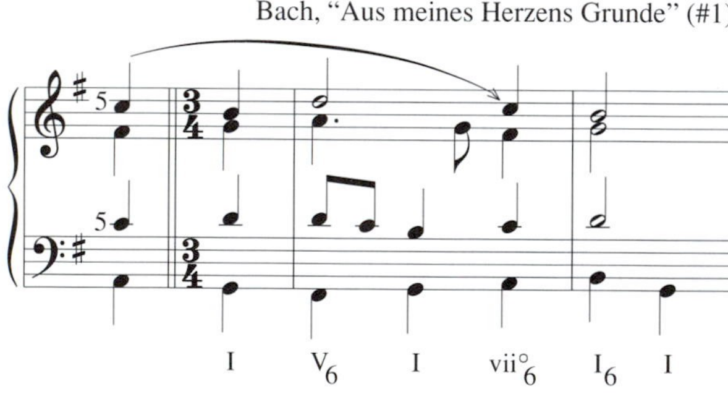

The fifth of ii° is infrequently used in the soprano. The doubled soprano is the lowered sixth scale degree; resolving both down by step results in octaves, and resolving one upward to the leading tone results in an augmented second. Any other doubling usually is aurally ineffective.

ASSIGNMENT 10.5 *Writing diminished triads.* Double the third when the root or the third is in soprano; double the fifth an octave lower when the fifth is in the soprano.

In Appendix E: Answers to (1)–(5) are given.
In the Workbook: Answers to the entire assignment are given.

Writing to and from the Diminished Triad

1. *Doubled notes.* Since the diminished triad is usually found in first inversion, the main part-writing consideration is the same as that for other triads in inversion: *Approach and resolve the doubled note whenever possible by contrary or oblique motion.*

FIGURE 10.23

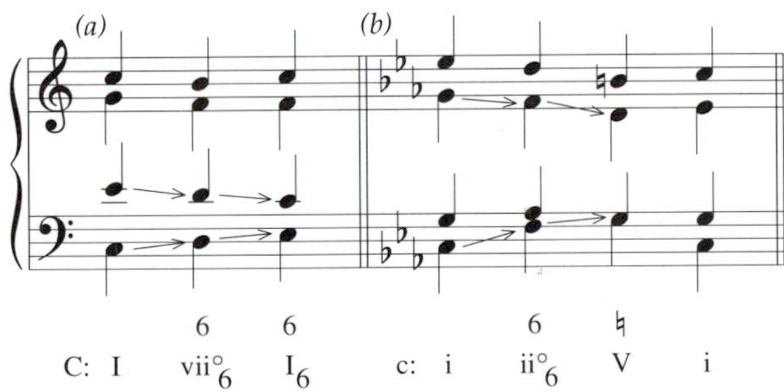

2. *Unequal fifths.* This term describes a diminished fifth preceded or followed by a perfect fifth in the same pair of voices. The visual effect is that of parallel fifths, but since they are unequal in size they are acceptable, except between the two outer voices.

FIGURE 10.24 *Unequal Fifths*

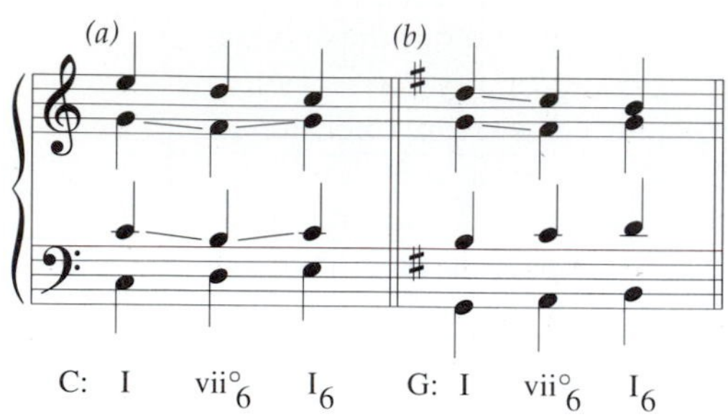

3. vii°6 with the fifth in the soprano. As a soprano tone, the fifth of the vii° triad (or any diminished triad) usually descends, as does the soprano line of Figure 10.22. But the fifth in the soprano may ascend when found in a melody line moving in similar motion with the bass at the interval of a tenth, as in Figure 10.25.

FIGURE 10.25

With this knowledge of the usual part-writing procedures for diminished triads, we can now explain why vii° should not be considered an incomplete V^7, even though it sounds and functions like a V^7. The difference is this: In progressing to the tonic, the seventh of the V^7 usually resolves down, whereas in the vii° triad, the fifth (the same note as the seventh of V^7) usually resolves up, allowing the doubled note to resolve by contrary motion (Figure 10.26).

FIGURE 10.26 *vii° and V^7*

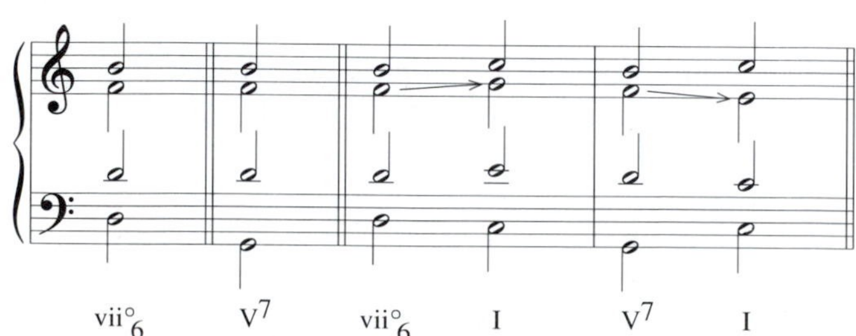

Writing the Supertonic Triad

In the commonly used ii and ii°, the third is usually doubled. This note is the subdominant scale step. Since this triad usually precedes dominant harmony and in first inversion uses the same bass tone as IV (in root position), the supertonic harmony is classified as having a subdominant function.

Progression to and from ii in root position (major only) uses conventional procedures already studied. Figure 10.27*a* is the basic part-writing of the Beethoven example, Figure 10.19.

FIGURE 10.27 *Part-Writing the ii Triad*

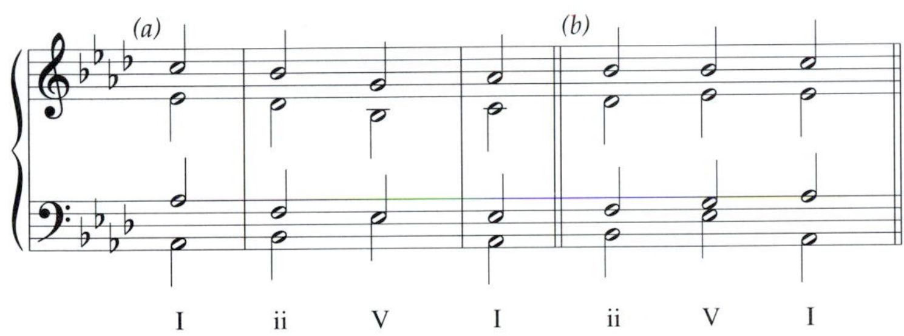

(a) I–ii and ii–V: Contrary motion between upper voices and bass.[6]

(b) ii–V: Hold common tone; other voices move stepwise.

ASSIGNMENT 10.6 *Part-writing leading-tone and supertonic triads.* These short examples illustrate most of the common uses of these triads. Add inner voices and harmonic analysis.

(a) Leading-tone triads

[6] I–ii (soprano and bass ascending) and IV–ii will be discussed in Chapter 14.

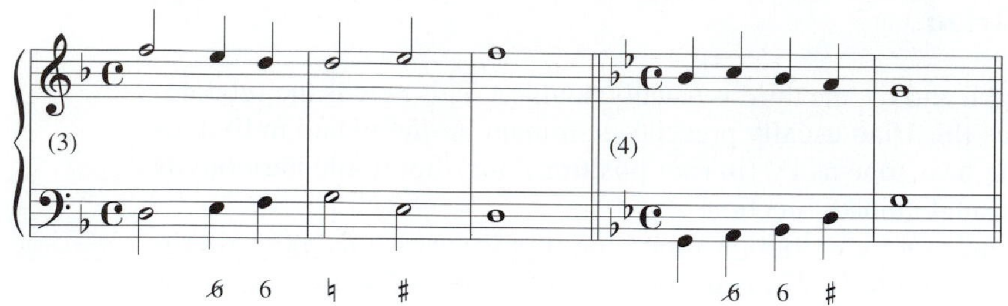

In Appendix E: Answers to (1) and (3) are given.
In the Workbook: Answers to Assignment 10.5a are given.

(b) Supertonic triads

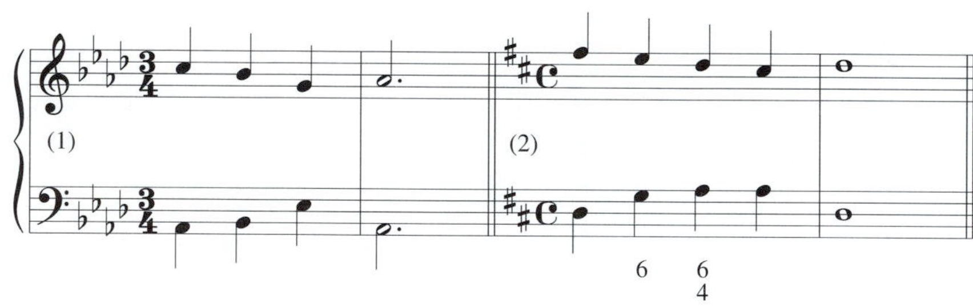

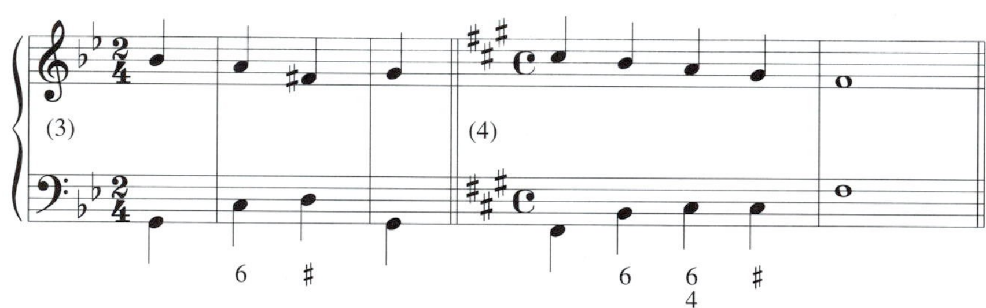

In Appendix E: Answers to (2) and (3) are given.
In the Workbook: Do Assignment 10.6b, c. Answers are given.

ASSIGNMENT 10.7 *Part-writing leading-tone and supertonic triads.*

(1)

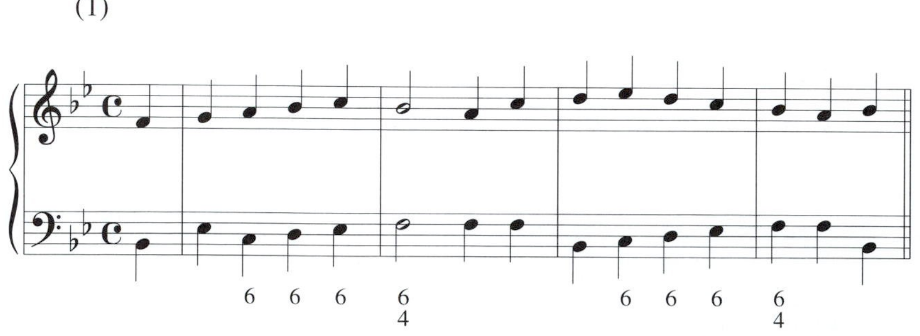

(2)

(3)

(4) See Figure 10.25 for help.

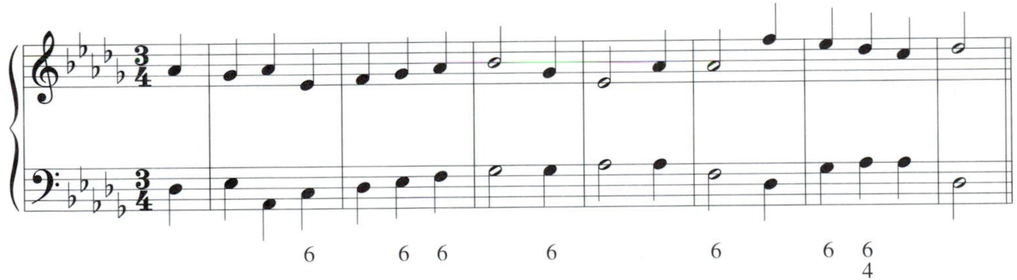

ASSIGNMENT 10.8 Add soprano, alto, and tenor voices when bass line only is given. Make a harmonic analysis.

(1)

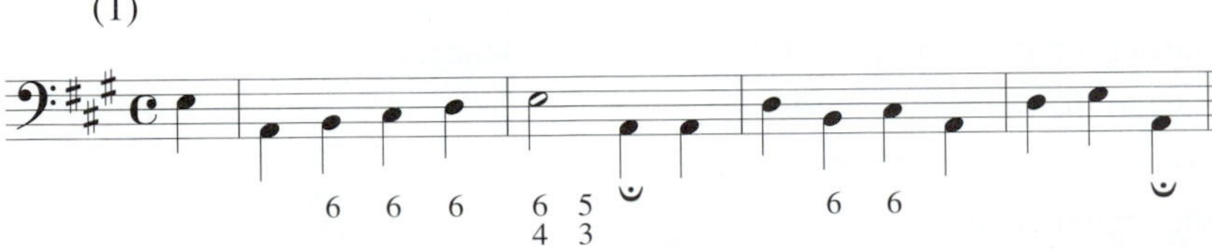

(2) See Figure 10.20 for help with 5̸ 6̸.

ASSIGNMENT 10.9 Write the following harmonic progressions in four parts. Choose a time signature and write a progression that is rhythmically interesting.

1. E♭ major	I ii_6 I_6 vii°_{6} I IV V I
2. F minor	V i i_6 vii°_{6} i ii°_{6} V i
3. B major	V I_6 V_6 I I ii_6 V I
4. A♭ major	I IV vii°_{6} I ii_6 I^{6}_{4} V I

In the following progressions, no inversions are indicated. Choose inversions that will make a good bass line.

5. A major	I I IV vii° I vii° I ii I V I
6. B minor	i iv V i vii° i i V V i ii° i V I
7. D♭ major	V V I IV vii° I ii vii° I ii I V I

Melody Harmonization

ASSIGNMENT 10.10 Harmonize these melodies, using supertonic and leading-tone triads where appropriate. Use either a two-stave score (piano score) or an open score with C clefs, as assigned. Look for places to use the progressions we have studied.

1. $\hat{2}$ and $\hat{4}$ can be harmonized with the supertonic triad, usually in first inversion, when the next chord is V or tonic six-four.
2. When a triad is repeated, one of them might be a good place for a first inversion.
3. Try V–I_6 or V_6–I rather than V–I at places other than the cadence.
4. After IV, use vii°_{6} when the melody ascends.
5. Use vii°_{6} between two positions of the tonic triad.
6. Use I^{6}_{4} at the cadence when possible.

Keyboard Harmony

ASSIGNMENT 10.11 Play these progressions in any major or minor key.

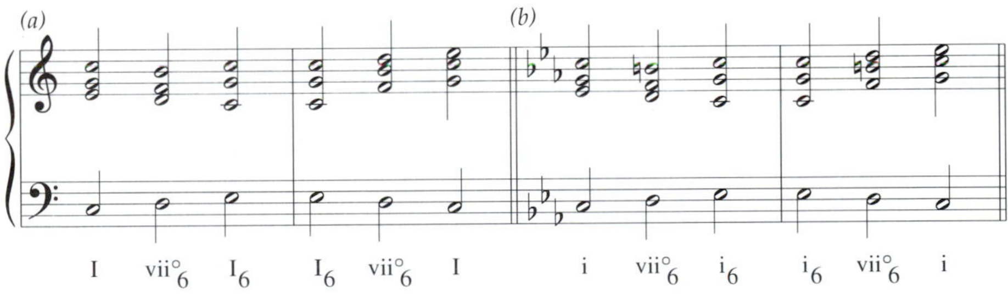

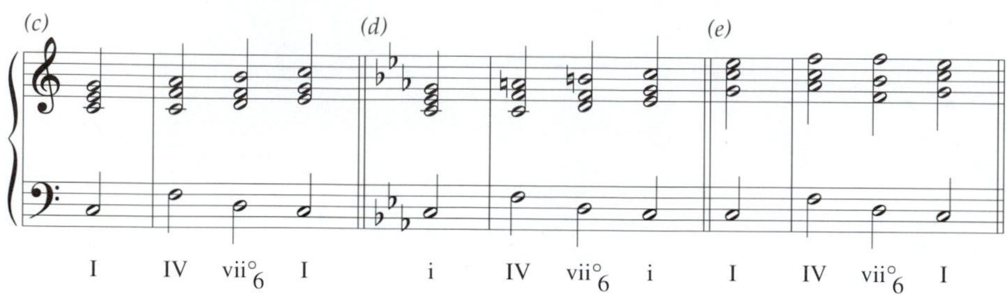

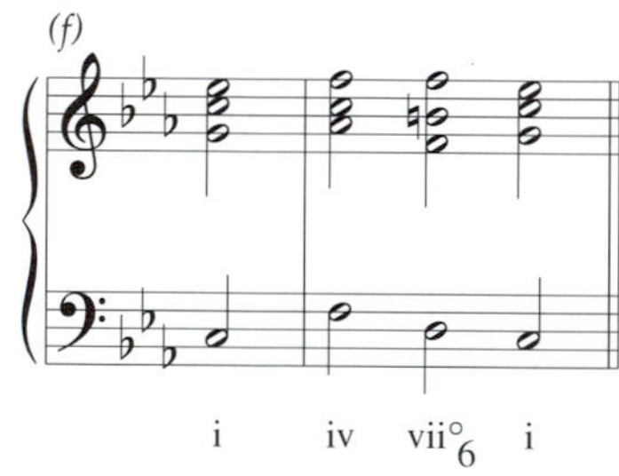

ASSIGNMENT 10.12 Play these progressions in any key. Play (3) in major as well, using ii_6 instead of ii°_6.

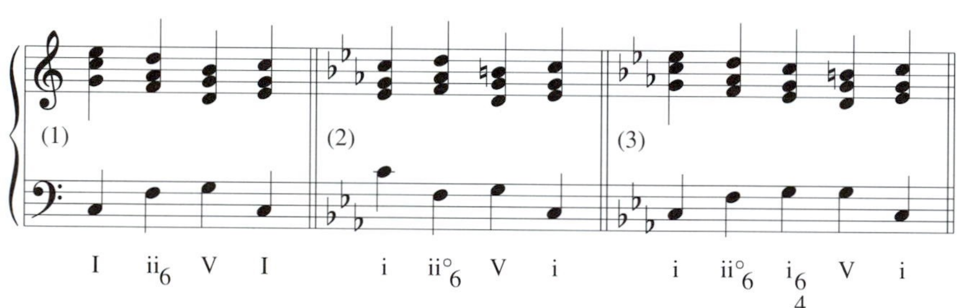

ASSIGNMENT 10.13 *Harmonizing a lead sheet melody.* The suggestions in Assignment 10.10 will be just as useful here. Triads marked with a °, such as g°, are diminished triads. Be sure to play these in first inversion. The symbol $^6_4$ indicates a place to use the tonic six-four.

Summary

Harmonic progression refers to the order in which chords follow one another. Considering the progressions possible, their use ranges from very frequent to rare. Progressions with their roots descending a fifth are the most common, and a few by other intervals are also common.

A progression not common by itself may be freely used in a series of first inversions or in a harmonic sequence.

The supertonic triads, ii and ii°, usually resolve to the dominant and, therefore, like IV are considered chords of subdominant function.

The leading-tone triad, vii° in major and minor, "leads" to the tonic and therefore functions as a dominant. Because of its similarity to V^7, it is considered by some to be V^7 with its root missing.

vii° is particularly useful between I and I_6, or reverse, and after IV when the melody ascends.

In part-writing, the third is commonly doubled in the ii, ii°, and vii° triads, except that the fifth of vii° in the soprano is usually doubled. The fifth as the soprano note of ii° is uncommon.

Part-writing these chords in a harmonic succession requires no procedures not previously studied.

ARTICLE #10

The Devil in Music

This uncomplimentary term (from the Latin *Diabolus in musica*) was applied in medieval times (ca. 1200) to the interval of the tritone. Composers and writers in music theory found it a difficult interval to understand or to use. Although it equally divides the octave (see Figure 10.9), in doing so it causes two different intervals to appear, each made up of the same number of scale steps (three whole steps). These intervals, the diminished fifth and the augmented fourth, lack the stability of the commonly used consonances: the octave, the fifth, and the thirds and sixths. As a consequence, their use in music was severely limited until the seventeenth century. Any melodic use was forbidden, either as a direct skip (*a*) or as the outward limit of a series of notes in one direction (*b*).

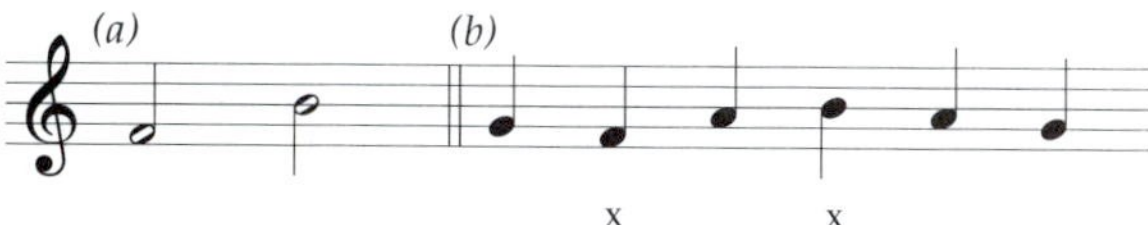

Harmonically, a tritone could appear between any two upper voices in music written for three or more voices. At that time, the consonance or dissonance of a vertical structure was determined by the consonance or dissonance of each upper note in relation to the lowest sounding note. At the asterisk in the following example, we find what looks like the first inversion of G♯ B D (diminished) triad. In pre-seventeenth-century terms, this sonority consists of a sixth above the bass (B up to G♯) and a third above the bass (B up to D). Both intervals are consonant, and therefore the vertical sonority is consonant. The resulting augmented fourth (D up to G♯) was not considered in this process.

Palestrina, Missa, *Spem in alium*

Restrictions against the tritone began to disappear in the seventeenth century, when the tritone emerged as a harmonic interval in its own right, even when found above the lowest sounding note.

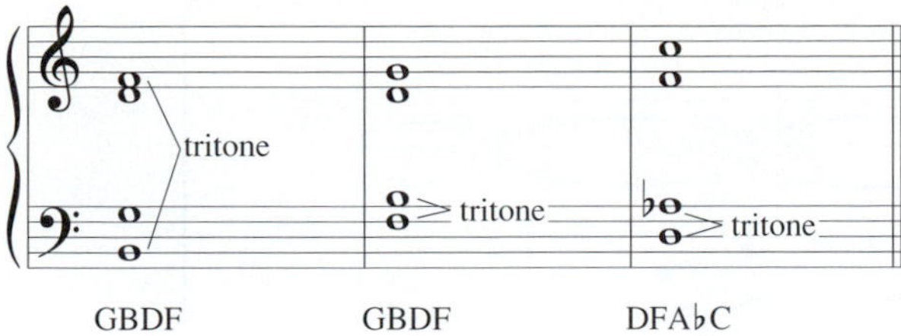

The tritone is particularly important in the dominant seventh chord because the resolution of the tritone positively establishes a feeling of key.

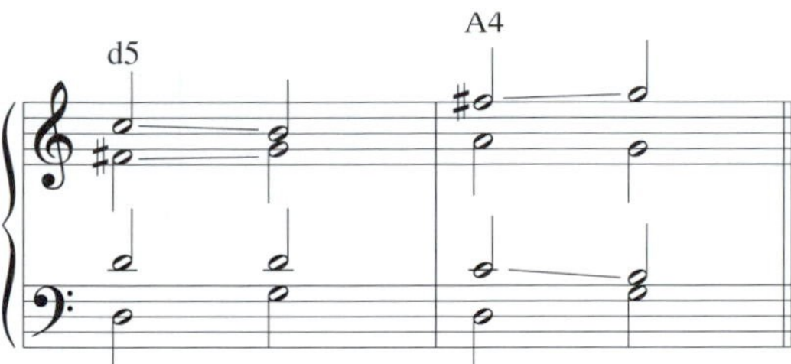

Made up of tritones, the diminished seventh chord became one of the most characteristic sounds of nineteenth-century music. When inverted, the chord continues to produce tritones, a property not exhibited by any other chord. The sound of these simultaneous tritones tends to destroy the feeling of tonality, especially when they are sounded at length or follow one another in succession.

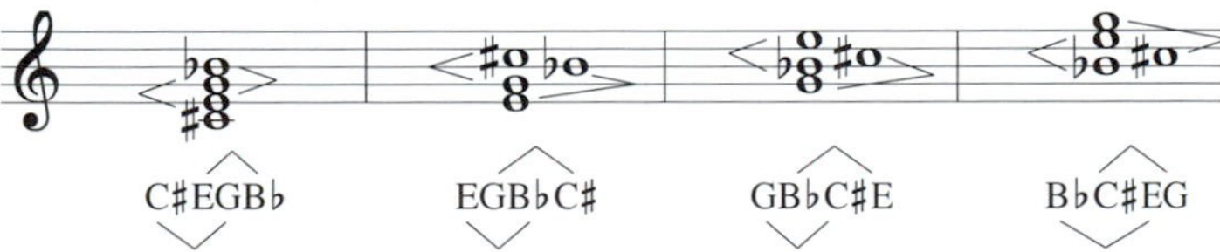

The ambiguity of the tritone in its diminished fifth–augmented fourth relationship (same sound, different spelling) was often capitalized upon by nineteenth-century composers. In the following example, the sustained tritone C–F♯ is first part of a D F♯ A C chord, then as an implied C–G♭, part of the A♭ C E♭ G♭ chord. (Since the tritone is tied throughout the passage, it is obvious that the composer, for performance reasons, has not changed the F♯ to G♭. The interval in parentheses shows the actual harmonic spelling.)

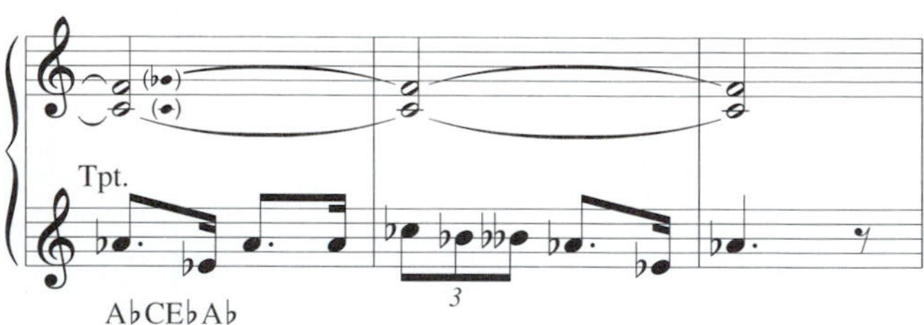

Twentieth-century music, in its quest for means to avoid the strong sense of tonic pervading music of previous eras, makes frequent use of the tritone. The opening of the following example shows the augmented fourth as the outer limits of the melody (C♯–G).

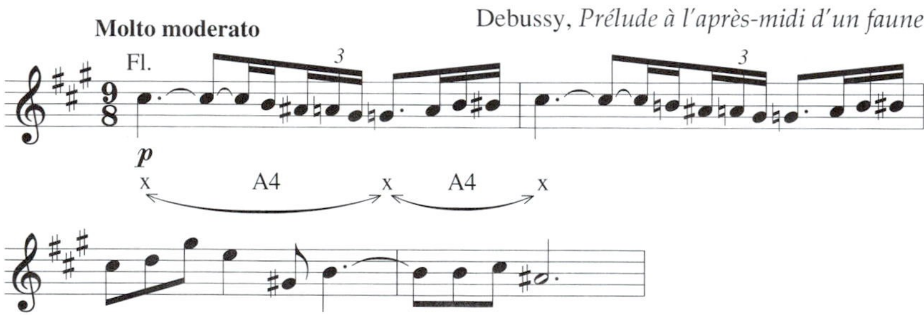

The ultimate application of the tritone is the whole-tone scale, new in the twentieth century. In this seven-note scale, all whole steps, the interval from any note to its fourth above is a tritone. In the first four measures of Bartók's whole-tone composition *Hagsorok egeszhangokbol,* there are four intervals of the tritone, plus two more when counting the first and last notes of the four-note scale lines.

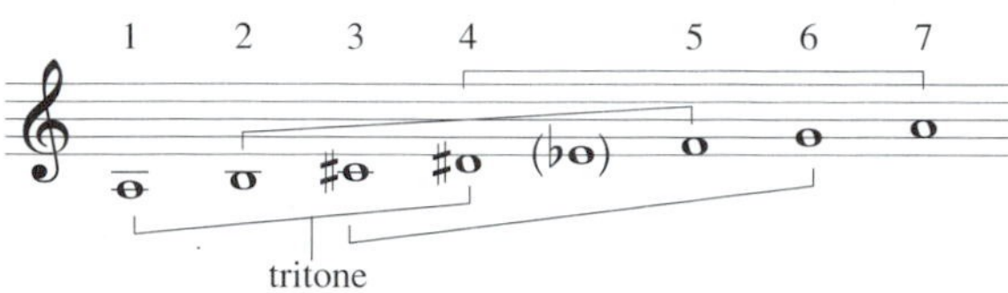

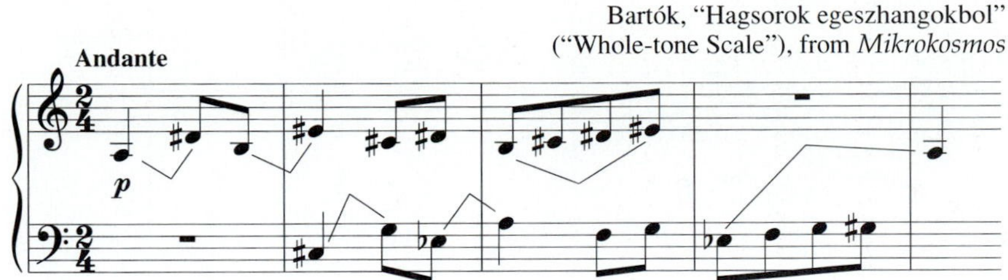

Bartók, "Hagsorok egeszhangokbol"
("Whole-tone Scale"), from *Mikrokosmos*

11

Nonharmonic Tones I

passing tones and neighbor tones

Previous chapters have provided you with considerable experience in locating nonharmonic tones in music examples. It is now time to define these and explore the many possibilities of their use, particularly as melodic elements in a harmonic context.

Defining Nonharmonic Tones

Recognizing that a tone is not part of a chord is the first step in identifying a nonharmonic tone. The several varieties of nonharmonic tones are differentiated by a *three-note melodic pattern:*

1. the harmonic tone preceding, called the *note of approach*
2. the dissonance
3. the harmonic tone following, called the *note of resolution*

As each nonharmonic tone is presented, you will find an example showing this three-note relationship.

The Passing Tone

A passing tone is found stepwise between harmonic tones of a different pitch. Passing tones may be either unaccented (UPT) or accented (APT).

FIGURE 11.1 *Passing Tones*

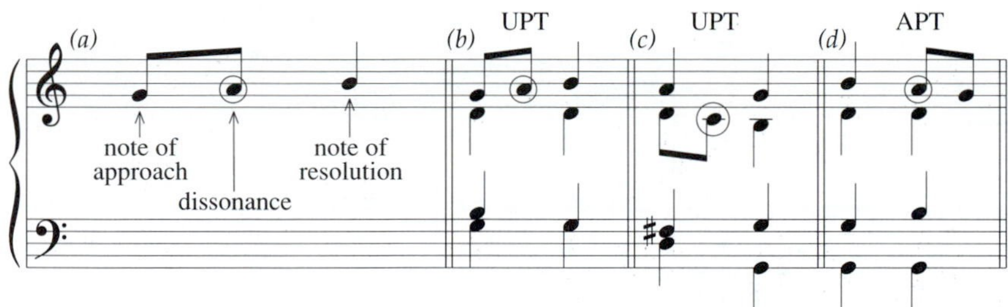

FIGURE 11.2 *Unaccented Passing Tones*

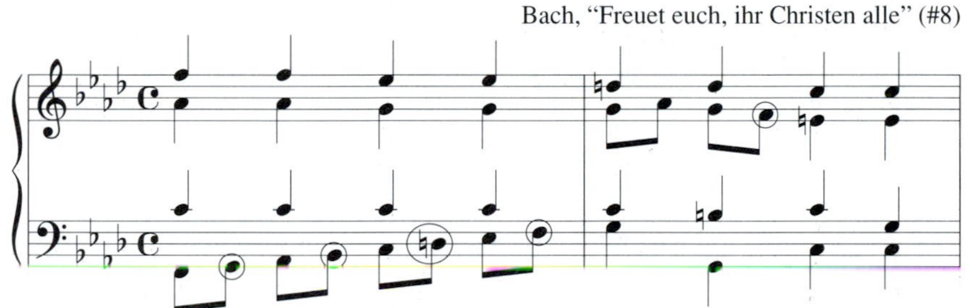

The term *accented* refers to any tone falling on a beat or that part of a beat in a stronger rhythmic position than the note following. These are indicated in Figure 11.3*a* as "S" and "W" (*strong* and *weak*). In S W S W (four sixteenth notes), the third sixteenth note is strong because it is stronger than the following note. In terms of the time signature, the complete first beat is still the strong beat, and the complete second beat is still the weak beat of the measure.

FIGURE 11.3 *Locations of Accented Tones*

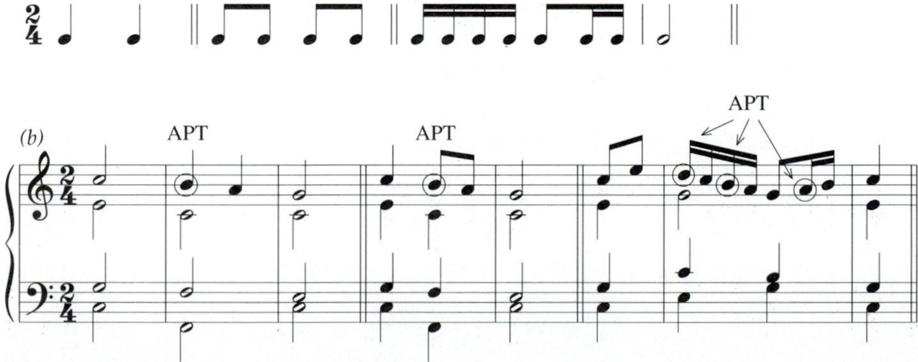

FIGURE 11.4 *Accented Passing Tones*

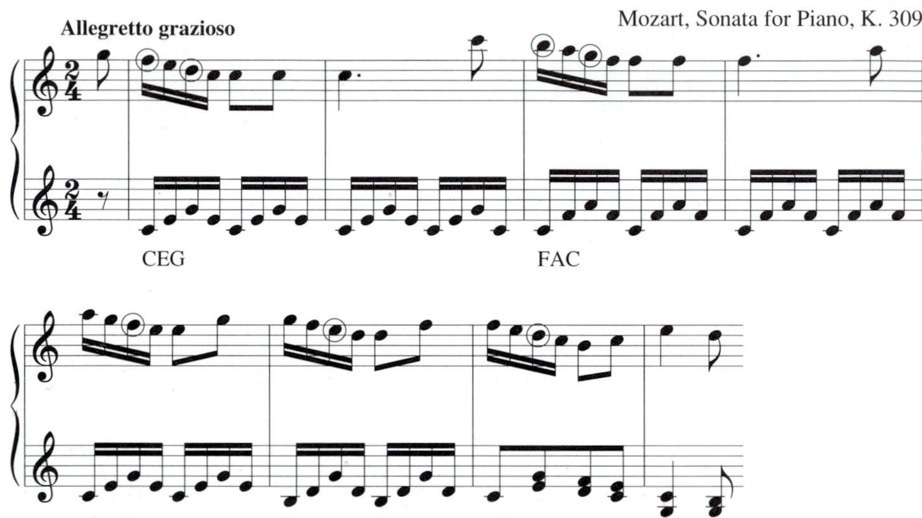

Passing tones are found most frequently between two chord tones a third apart, as in Figure 11.3. But if, for example, the harmonic tones are an interval of a fourth from the root down to the fifth of a triad, two passing tones are required to fill the gap.

FIGURE 11.5

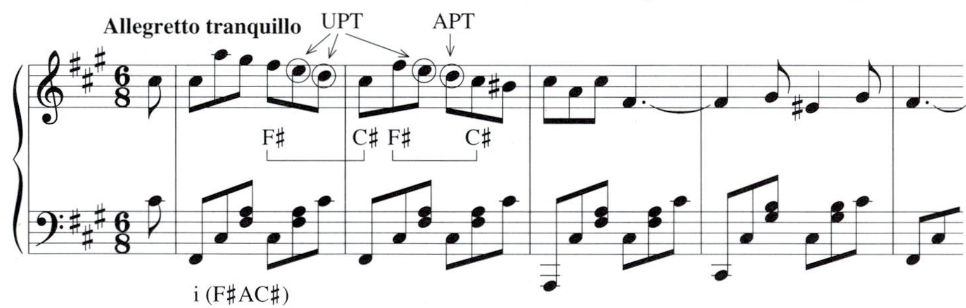

Two successive passing tones can also occur at the point of a change of chords, occurring twice in Figure 11.6.

FIGURE 11.6

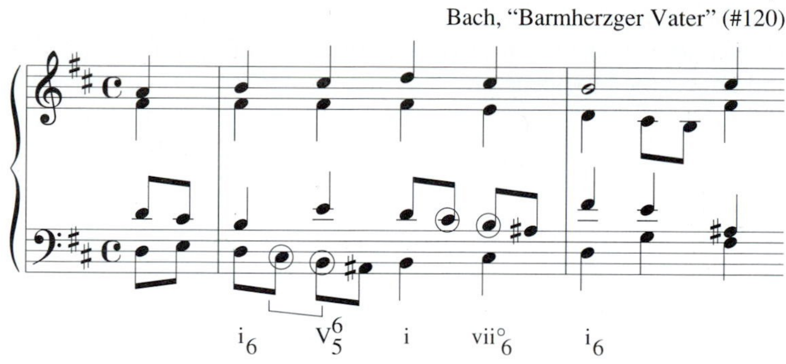

Chromatically altered nonharmonic tones are common. The chromatic scale in Figure 11.7 produces a maximum number of successive passing tones between members of both the A C E triad and the E G♯ B D chord.

FIGURE 11.7

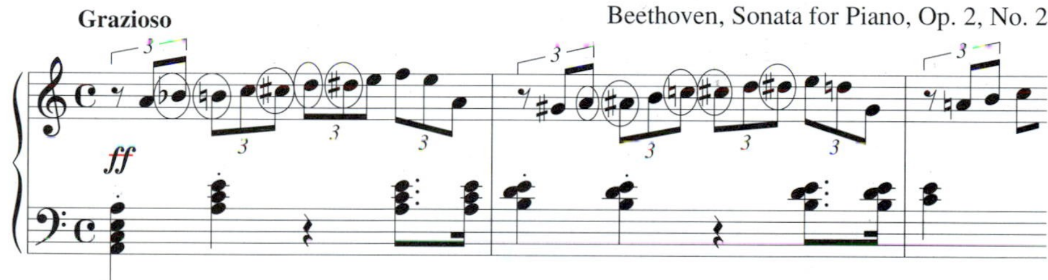

Double nonharmonic tones, two nonharmonic tones sounding simultaneously, are commonly found. The first and last phrases of this chorale show double passing tones in both similar and contrary motion. See also the upbeat in Figure 11.6

FIGURE 11.8

Bach, "O Haupt voll Blut und Wunden" (#89)

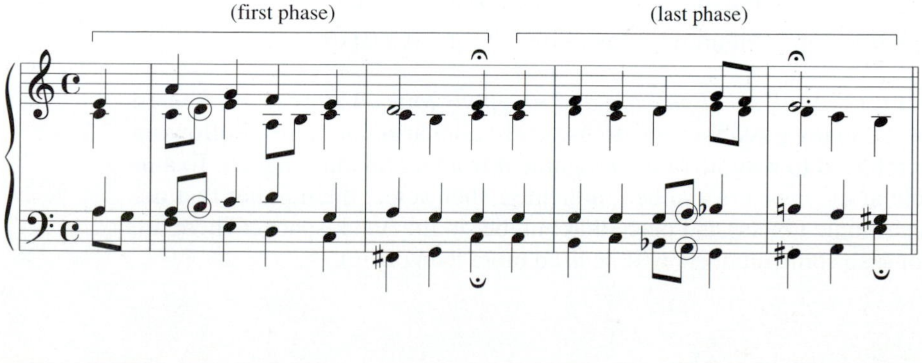

(first phase)

(last phase)

The Neighbor Tone

A neighbor tone is a nonharmonic tone found stepwise between two harmonic tones of the same pitch. The two varieties are upper neighbor (UN) and lower neighbor (LN), both of which may be found unaccented or accented.

FIGURE 11.9

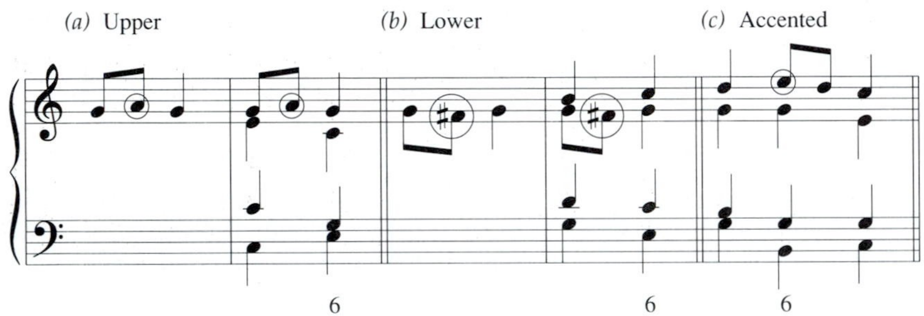

Figure 11.10 shows both the double lower neighbor and the double upper neighbor, and, in measure 3, a chromatic lower neighbor, C♯.

FIGURE 11.10

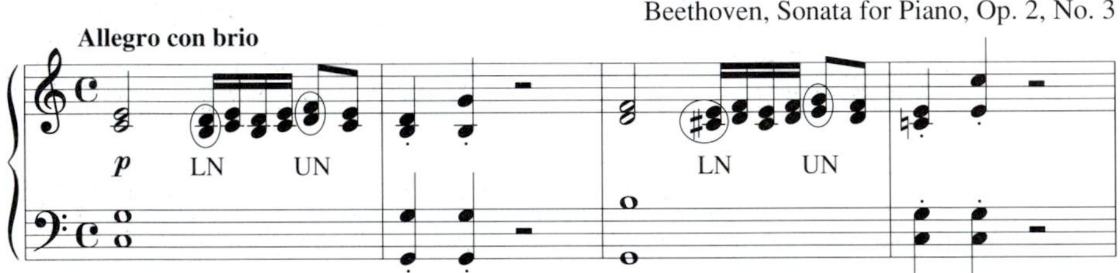

For the more common single neighbor tones, see the following examples. One of them is accented. Which one?

Upper neighbor:	Figure 11.2, measure 2, beat 1 (G A♭ G) Figure 11.7, measure 1, beat 4 (E F E)
Lower neighbor:	Figure 11.5, measure 2, beat 2 (C♯ B♯ C♯)

ASSIGNMENT 11.1 *Analysis of passing and neighbor tones.* Here is a numbered list of twelve of the many possible ways to use these nonharmonic tones. Following the list, you are referred to a figure or an assignment from a previous chapter. Examine each example at the measure and beat indicated, then select the number that describes the nonharmonic tone(s) and place that number in the blank space. (There are fourteen questions, so some numbers will be used more than once.)

1.	Single unaccented passing tone	**7.**	Lower neighbor, unaccented
2.	Single accented passing tone	**8.**	Upper neighbor, unaccented
3.	Consecutive passing tones	**9.**	Double lower neighbor
4.	Double passing tone, similar motion	**10.**	Double upper neighbor
5.	Double passing tone, contrary motion	**11.**	Lower neighbor, accented
6.	Chromatic passing tone	**12.**	Neighbor tone, chromatic

A. Figure 4.1 (page 60), measure 1, beat 2 _____

B. Figure 4.1, measure 7, beat 2 (alto) _____

C. Assignment 4.5 (3), (page 72), measure 1, beat 1 _____

D. Assignment 4.5 (3), measure 1, beat 2 _____

E. Assignment 4.6 (4), (page 76), measure 1, beat 3 _____

F. Figure 6.8 (page 111), measure 1, beat 2 _____

G. Assignment 6.4 (1), (page 113), measure 1, beats 2–3 _____

H. Assignment 6.4 (4), measure 2, beat 2 _____

I. Figure 9.11 (page 174), measure 1, beat 1 _____

J. Figure 10.19 (page 217), measure 1, beat 4 _____

K. Figure 10.19, measure 3, beat 3½ _____

L. Assignment 10.4 (7), (page 220), measure 2, beat 1 _____

M. Assignment 10.4 (9), measure 1, beat 2 _____

N. Assignment 10.4 (10), measure 4, beat 1 _____

In Appendix E: Answers to the entire assignment are given.
In the Workbook: Answers to the entire assignment are given.

Writing Passing Tones and Neighbor Tones

The writing of *any* nonharmonic tone, including those yet to be presented, follows these general principles:

Figured Bass Symbols A figured bass symbol does not indicate the type of nonharmonic tone above it. It simply indicates the intervals above the bass; the name of the dissonance is dependent upon its preceding and following notes. A given figured bass number can apply to any type of dissonance. Here is an explanation of some of those used in Figure 11.11.

4 3 = movement from a fourth to a third above G

3 2 = a doubled third above A, one moving to a second above A, the other
3 – (–) being held

8 7 = 8 moves to 7 above C; at the same time 6 moves to 5 above C.
6 5

Note that (1) when *two or more numbers* are found vertically below a given bass note, the numbers are usually placed in descending order, but this placement does *not* refer to order of notes above the bass; (2) when *horizontal successive numbers* appear under a single bass note, these refer to successive notes in one of the melodic lines above; and (3) when there is a *change of bass note,* the figures under the new note do *not* relate to the figures under the preceding note.

FIGURE 11.11 *Figured Bass Symbols*

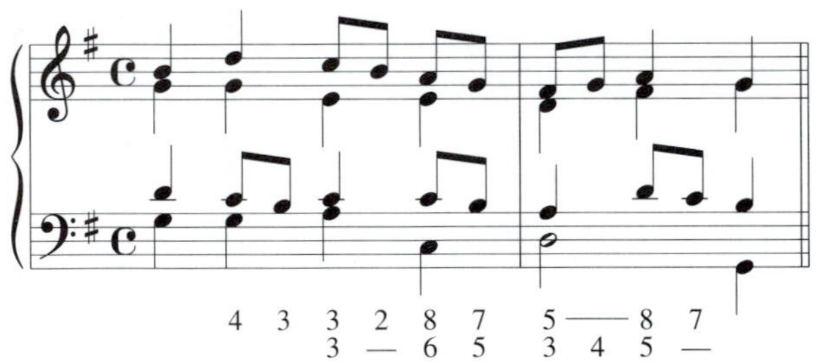

The Seventh above the Root When a nonharmonic tone is at the interval of a seventh above the root of a chord, even if the chord is inverted, that nonharmonic tone creates the aural impression of a seventh chord. As we will learn in the study of seventh chords, this notes proceeds downward, whether a nonharmonic tone or an actual seventh.

FIGURE 11.12 *The Nonharmonic Tone as a Seventh*

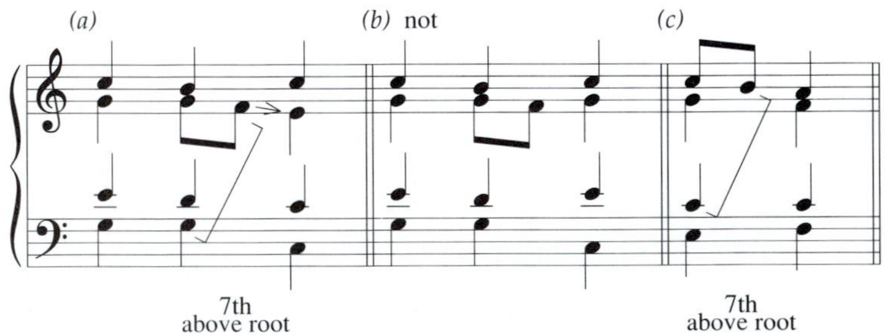

Avoiding Parallels It is very easy to create an unwanted parallel between a nonharmonic tone and a held tone in another voice. Always check each nonharmonic tone against any other voice moving in the same direction.

FIGURE 11.13 *Avoiding Parallels*

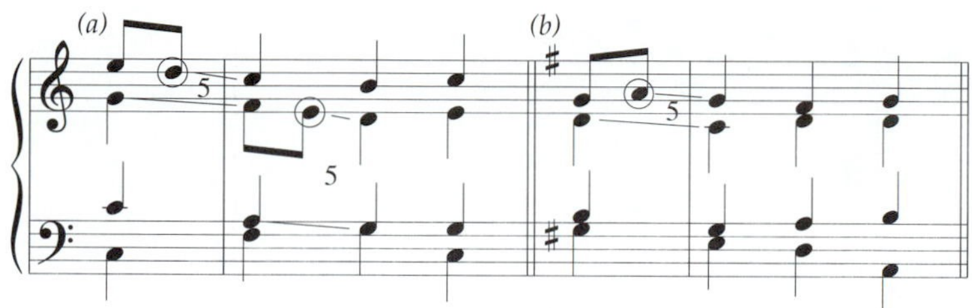

Accented Nonharmonic Tones An accented nonharmonic tone temporarily replaces a harmonic tone. To determine the doubling wanted, consider the accented nonharmonic tone the same chord member as the note to which it resolves. In Figure 11.14, triad G B D, the accented passing tone C resolves to B. Since C temporarily replaces B, it acts as the third of the triad, so the other voices are two roots and one fifth (in conventional doubling). At *c* in the same figure, A resolves to G in G B D. Since the conventional doubling for this triad is two roots, A and G sounding together is acceptable.

FIGURE 11.14 *Accented Nonharmonic Tones*

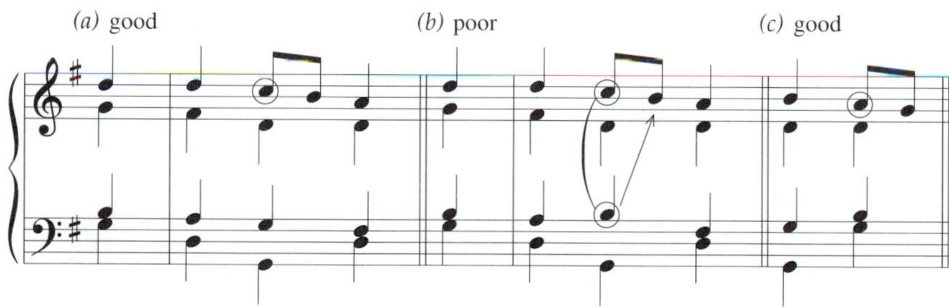

Simultaneous Nonharmonic Tones When any two nonharmonic tones sound simultaneously, the interval between the two should be consonant. In Figure 11.8, the passing tones of the pair in measure 1 are a third apart and those of the pair in measure 3 are an octave apart.

ASSIGNMENT 11.2 *Adding passing and neighbor tones to a score.* These chorale excerpts are just as Bach wrote them, except that the nonharmonic tones are omitted. Add passing and neighbor tones where effective. To accommodate an eighth-note dissonance, move the chord tone on the beat to the second half of the beat, as shown in Figure 11.14*a*.

Compare your results with Bach's version at the end of this chapter. Your version may be satisfactory even though different, since there are many good ways to harmonize a melody.

In the Workbook: Answers to the entire assignment are given.

ASSIGNMENT 11.3 *Part-writing.* Complete each example by filling in the inner voices. Make a harmonic analysis.

In the Workbook: Do Assignment 11A, two-measure exercises. Answers are given.

Relaxing Part-Writing Procedures to Heighten Melodic Interest

In your previous part-writing endeavors, you have been advised to follow certain conventional procedures. But as you have examined numerous examples from music literature, you must have observed the many deviations from these conventional procedures, deviations such as different doublings, wide spacing between upper voices, omitted tones, large leaps, overlapping voices, and even crossed voices.

Conventional procedures have been useful as an aid (in fact, almost a guarantee) in preventing awkward melodic lines and unwanted parallels. But often this improvement is only from "awkward" to "smooth but dull." (An alto line that stays on the same one or two notes for a measure or two is certainly dull.) But the use of inversions and nonharmonic tones, together with a relaxing of conventional part-writing procedures, makes possible even greater improvement in the melodic line. Figure 11.15 is a good example.

FIGURE 11.15

First notice that the harmony is limited to I, IV, and V. Next observe the unconventional doublings: at (a), a *doubled leading tone* (!) and at (b), doubled inner voices in an inverted triad. But look at what these two deviations, in combination with passing tones, have accomplished in the first measure. Not only has each voice line achieved maximum melodic movement, but more impressively, Bach has created three different passages of contrary or similar motion between pairs of voices (Figure 11.16): at *a,* contrary motion between soprano and bass; at *b,* contrary motion between soprano and tenor; and at *c,* parallel tenths between tenor and bass.

It is assumed that offending parallels and the melodic augmented second will still be avoided. Doubling the leading tone, as in Figure 11.16*b,* or any altered tone must be handled with great care, usually with stepwise motion and contrary movement between voices.

FIGURE 11.16

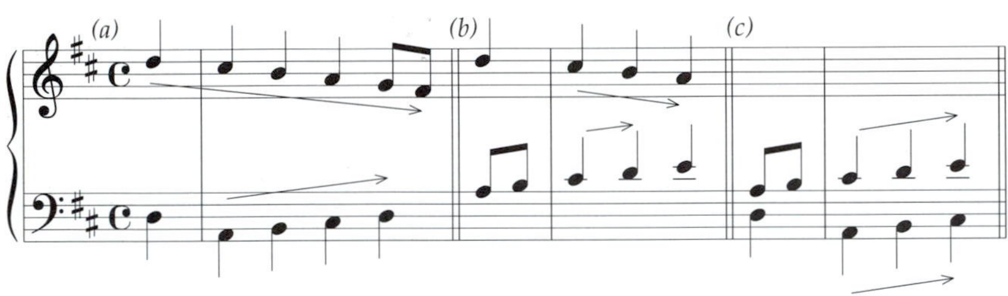

Thus, we can say that when an opportunity arises, you may consider relaxation of stated procedures to *improve* the harmonic texture. However, you should be able to explain *in writing* (just as we have done in Figures 11.15 and 11.16) exactly how you made your deviations and why they are an improvement over standard procedures. But it is still best to start with the conventional procedures and then look for opportunities for improvement.

ASSIGNMENT 11.4 *Analysis of less-conventional procedures.* In each example, explain why the indicated unconventional procedure was used. (Some chords not yet studied are included, but harmonic analysis is not required here.)

(1) Doubled thirds at each *. Also look at Figure 11.15 again and discuss the similarity between these two excerpts.

Bach, "O Welt, sieh hier dein Leben" (#50)

(2) Doubled thirds at *a* and *b;* crossed voices at *c.*

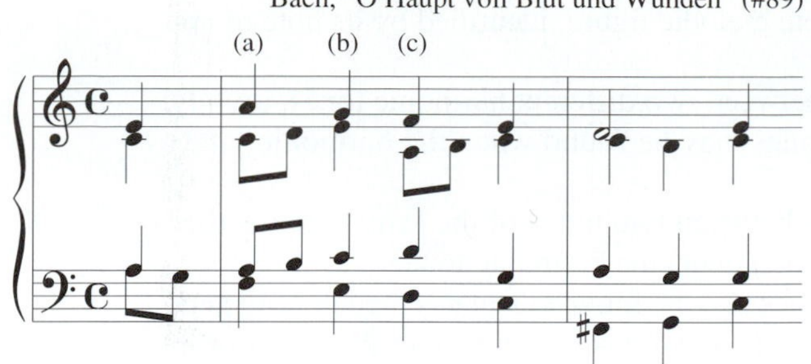

ASSIGNMENT 11.5 *Melody harmonization.* Three chorale melodies and the chords used by Bach are provided. Harmonize the melody with the given chords (root position or inversion) and experiment with passing tones and neighbor tones, using any conventional or new procedures that will enhance the melodic lines and/or the texture. But be sure that you can *justify* and *explain* how each departure from conventional practice has made improvement. For comparison, Bach's versions will be found at the end of this chapter. Since many satisfactory harmonizations of a given melody are possible, your harmonizations will undoubtedly differ but can still be satisfactory.[1]

[1]For a study of multiple harmonizations of a single melody, see Bach's nine harmonizations of "Herzlich tut mich verlangen," numbers 21, 74, 80, 89, 98, 270, 286, 345, and 367, or the nine of "O Welt, ich muss dich lassen," numbers 50, 63, 103, 117, 275, 289, 355, 363, and 366, all from *The 371 Chorales.* These are but two of many multiple harmonizations.

Summary

A *nonharmonic tone* is part of a three-note melodic figure, identified by its note of approach and its note of resolution.

A *passing tone* is found stepwise between two different harmonic tones, usually a third apart. Two successive passing tones may be found when the harmonic tones are a fourth apart.

A *neighbor tone* is found stepwise between two notes of the same pitch, either above (upper neighbor) or below (lower neighbor) the harmonic tone.

Both passing tones and neighbor tones may be found (1) unaccented or accented; (2) with chromatic alteration; and (3) in pairs, the tones moving either in similar or in contrary motion.

Figured bass symbols indicate the location of the dissonance above the bass note but do not identify the dissonance.

A dissonance located at the interval of a seventh above the root of a chord (even when the root is not in the bass) usually resolves downward.

An accented nonharmonic tone temporarily replaces the note to which it resolves and should be considered as that note when the doubling to be used is decided upon.

Nonharmonic tones sounding similtaneously should be consonant with each other.

Chorale Phrases for Previous Assignments

For *Assignment 11.2:*

(1) Bach, "Dies sind die Heiligen zehn Gebot" (#127)

(2) Bach, "Warum betrübst du mich" (#145)

For *Assignment 11.5:*

12

Nonharmonic Tones II

suspensions and other dissonances

The method of describing the remaining nonharmonic tones is the same as for those studied in the previous chapter. With one exception (the *pedal*), all are melodic figures consisting of note of approach, dissonance, and note of resolution. Figure 12.1 presents a complete list of these nonharmonic melodic figures. You will find it valuable for reference in present and future study.

FIGURE 12.1 *Nonharmonic Tones*

Name of non-harmonic tone	*Abbreviation*	*Example*	*Note of approach*	*Note of resolution*	*Direction of resolution*
Passing tone, unaccented	UPT		Stepwise	Stepwise	Same direction as approach
Passing tone accented	APT		Stepwise	Stepwise	Same direction as approach
Neighboring tone upper	UN		Stepwise	Stepwise	Opposite to approach
Neighboring tone lower	LN		Stepwise	Stepwise	Opposite to approach
Suspension	S		Same note	Stepwise	Down
Retardation	R		Same note	Stepwise	Up
Anticipation	A		Stepwise	Same note	Same note

Name of non-harmonic tone	*Abbreviation*	*Example*	*Note of approach*	*Note of resolution*	*Direction of resolution*
Appoggiatura	App		By leap	Stepwise	Opposite to leap
Escaped tone	ET		Stepwise	By leap	Opposite to approach
Successive neighbors	SN		Stepwise	Stepwise	Same note as note of approach
	or				
Pedal	P	Held note --			

In the Workbook: Do Assignment 12A. Answers are given.

The Suspension

The *suspension* (S) occurs when a nonharmonic tone is approached by a harmonic tone of the same pitch and resolved down by stepwise motion. The note of approach is often tied into the dissonance.

FIGURE 12.2

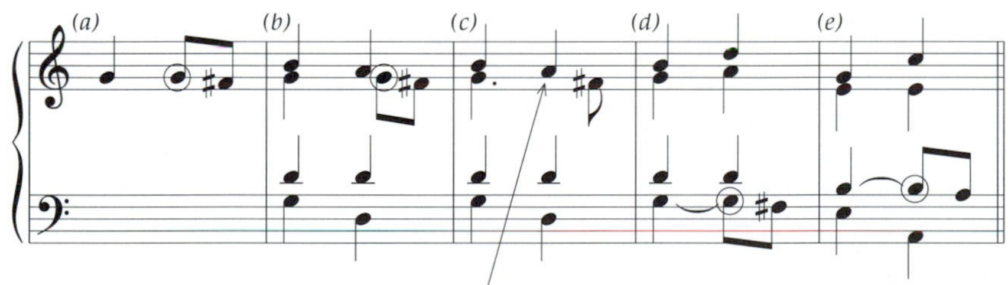

The suspension is always found in a strong rhythmic position, similar to that described for the accented passing tone (review page 243). The suspension functions in the vertical structure in a manner similar to the accented passing tone, as you can see in Figure 12.2*b,* in which the circled G temporarily replaces the F♯ of the D F♯ A triad. At the moment that the G sounds, the remaining tones are two roots and a fifth; when the G resolves, conventional doubling of two roots, one third, and one fifth results.

In chorale or vocal style, the duration of the note of approach is usually as long as or longer than the dissonant tone, as in each suspension in Figure 12.2. In instrumental style, such as writing for piano, this equal or greater length is often implied, and is discussed on page 260.

Unlike other nonharmonic tones, the suspension is described not only as a melodic device but also harmonically by the interval between it and the lowest sounding note. And if that were not enough variety, any suspension can be manipulated in a number of different ways in procedures not characteristic of other nonharmonic tones. Hence, it is a most versatile and useful nonharmonic device.

We will begin with the four basic suspensions in their simplest forms.

The 4 3 Suspension The suspension in Figure 12.3 is identical to that in Figure 12.2*b*. Here the A of A C E is suspended over the E G♯ B triad and then resolves into that triad. The suspended note, A, is a fourth above the bass, E.

FIGURE 12.3

Bach, Prelude and Fugue in A minor (organ), BMV 559

The 7 6 Suspension The "6" of "7 6" indicates that the suspension is found over a first inversion. In Figure 12.4, it is the first inversion of the vii° triad. Considering its soprano tone, is this the conventional doubling of vii°? The 7 6 can, of course, appear in any first-inversion triad.

FIGURE 12.4

Bach, "Auf meinen lieben Gott" (#304)

The 9 8 Suspension The "8" of "9 8" usually indicates that the suspension is found in a chord with its root in the bass. In Figure 12.5, measure 1, the dissonance, D, in the tenor sounds simultaneously with its resolution, C, in the bass. Remember that the usual doubling is two roots, so D simply substitutes for one of the two C's.

When this suspension is found in the tenor voice at an interval of a second above the bass voice, it is known as a 2 1 suspension. The 2 1 suspension is not commonly used.

FIGURE 12.5

FIGURE 12.6

The 2 3 Suspension This suspension is always found in the lowest voice. "2 3" is not a figured bass, but refers to the interval of a second above the bass, which becomes a third when the suspension resolves. In Figure 12.7*a*, G is a second below A, resolving to F♯, a third below A. Even when the compound intervals of a ninth and a tenth are used, as here, the suspension is still called 2 3 (Figure 12.7*b*).

The required figured bass is $^{5\,6}_{2}$.

FIGURE 12.7 *2 3 Suspension*

Less frequent is a suspension in the bass that resolves to a chord root. The suspended E at the asterisk in Figure 12.8 resolves to D of an incomplete D F A triad.

FIGURE 12.8

ASSIGNMENT 12.1 *Analysis.* Find the suspensions in these examples and indicate their location in the spaces on the next page.

Suspension	*In example (1) or (2)*	*Measure*	*Beat*
9 8	_____	_____	_____
7 6	_____	_____	_____
4 3	_____	_____	_____
2 1	_____	_____	_____
2 3	_____	_____	_____

In Appendix E: Answers to the entire assignment are given.
In the Workbook: Answers to the entire assignment are given.

ASSIGNMENT 12.2 *Writing suspensions.* In each example, one beat in one voice is missing. Supply the missing suspension by repeating the note from the previous voice and resolving it to a step below, in eighth notes.

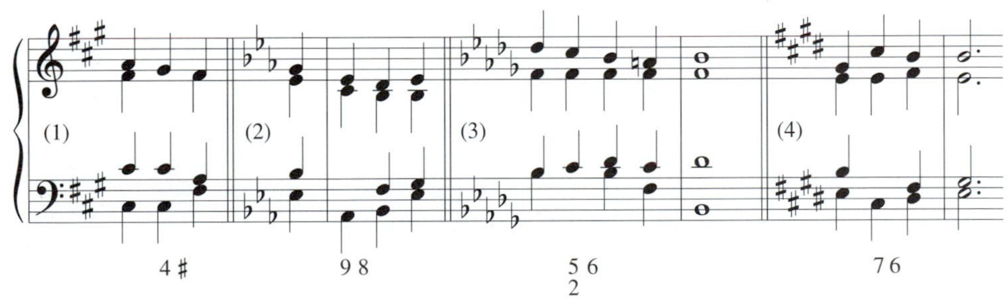

In the Workbook: Answers to the entire assignment are given.

ASSIGNMENT 12.3 *Writing suspensions.* Complete each exercise by filling in the alto and tenor voices. Make a harmonic analysis and circle each suspended note.

In Appendix E: Answers to (1), (4), and (7) are given.
In the Workbook: Answers to the entire assignment are given.

ASSIGNMENT 12.4 Add suspensions and passing tones to the examples given. Given notes may be changed rhythmically to make suspensions possible.

In Appendix E: An answer to (1) is given.
In the Workbook: Answers to the entire assignment are given.

Special Uses of the Suspension

Change of Bass Note As the suspension resolves, the chord may change to a different position (Figure 12.9), or the chord spelling may change altogether (Figure 12.10). This is a common occurrence in 9 8 suspensions. The note of resolution is still consonant, regardless of the change in context.

FIGURE 12.9 *Change in Triad Position*

FIGURE 12.10 *Change of Chord*

The Ornamental Resolution There is a wide variety of such resolutions, two of which are shown in Figure 12.11

FIGURE 12.11

Suspensions in the Six-Four Chord The ambiguity of the six-four chord, as described in Chapter 9, can at times cause further confusing harmonic interpretations, such as a six-four that includes a suspension.

In Figure 12.12, if we interpret the six-four as a V triad, the suspended A is a consonance resolving to the dissonant G, a perfect fourth above the bass. But the sound of the progression obviously indicates that the A is dissonant in G B D, a 9 8 suspension had the root G been the bass tone.

Similarly, in Figure 12.13, the 7 6 suspension, B♭ to A, resolves to the third of a six-four chord, F A C. But the sound is that of a 4 3 suspension above the root F, and not that of the usual 7 6 resolution to a first-inversion triad.

FIGURE 12.12

FIGURE 12.13

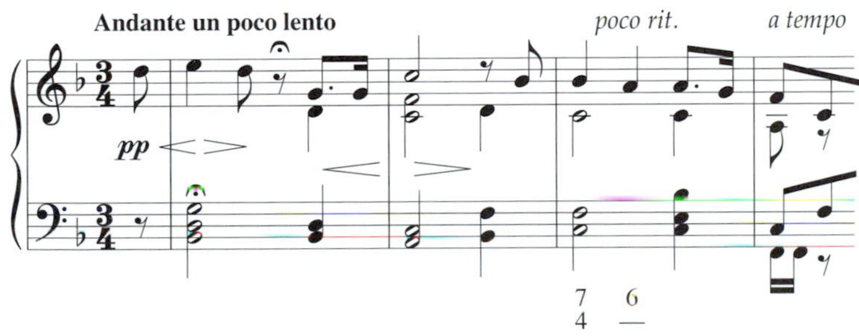

Chain Suspensions A chain suspension occurs when two or more suspensions follow each other in succession, the note of resolution of one suspension becoming the note of approach for the next suspension.

FIGURE 12.14 *Chain of 7 6 Suspensions*

FIGURE 12.15 *Chain of Alternating 4 3 and 9 8 Suspensions*

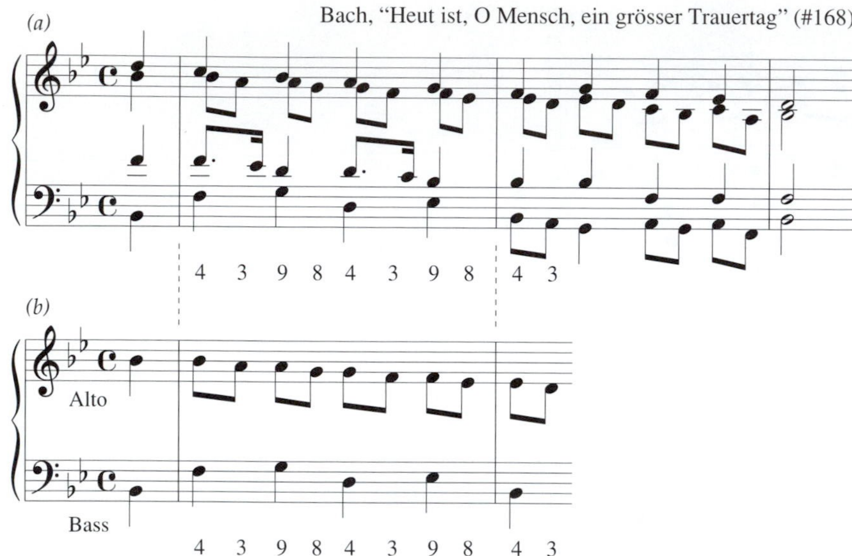

The Double Suspension This is infrequent but very effective because of the extra "bite" in the accented dissonance. Here are four measures with four double suspensions. You may say that the first and last of these are simple six-four chords, but remember that a note a fourth above the bass is a dissonance.

FIGURE 12.16

Bach, *Well-Tempered Clavier*, Vol. II, No. 12, BWV 881

6 5 / 4 ♮   9 8 / 4 3   9 8 / 7 6   6 5 / 4 ♮

Suspensions in Instrumental Writing In instrumental writing, the note of approach often is of shorter duration than the dissonance. Very often this is because the harmony preceding the dissonance is arpeggiated. Usually when the arpeggiation is reduced to a block chord, the conventional duration of the note of approach will be obvious.

FIGURE 12.17

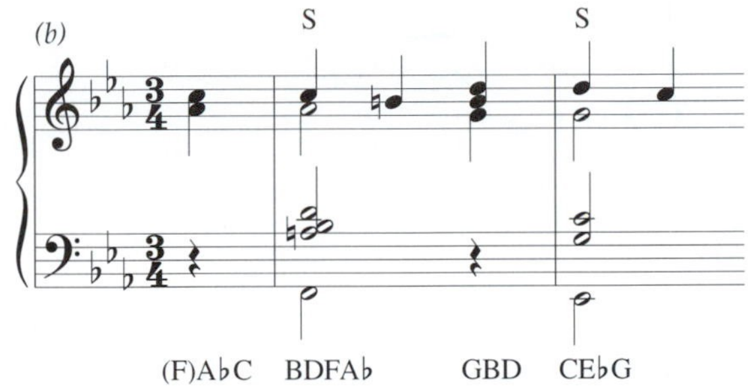

Note that the first suspension is in a diminished seventh chord, C against B D F A♭. As in Figure 12.12, the suspension is 5 4 above the bass F, but the dissonance is with the note D: C–B is 7 6 over D.

In the Workbook: Do Assignment 12B. Answers are given.

Other Nonharmonic Tones

Retardation The *retardation* (R) is like a suspension, except that the dissonance ascends. Retardations are not common.

FIGURE 12.18

Anticipation The *anticipation* (A) is the same pitch as its following harmonic tone, thus anticipating the note of resolution. In four-voice style, it is most common in the soprano voice as in Figure 12.19*a,* or in the tenor voice, where, in Figure 12.19*b,* it is part of a double anticipation.

FIGURE 12.19

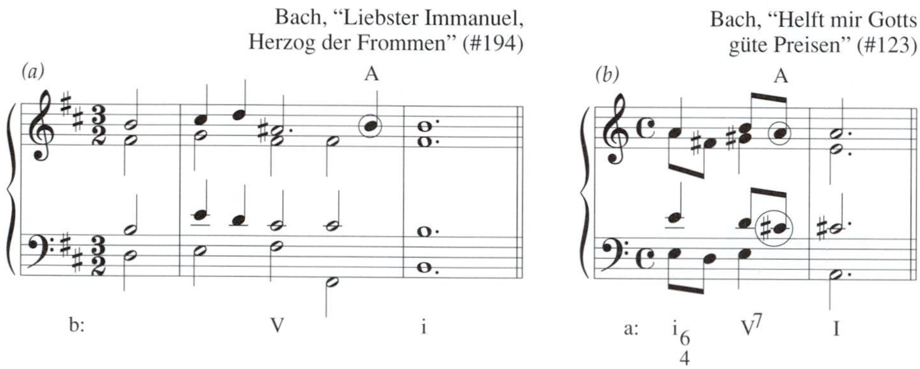

In a common melodic device, step down–repeat–step down, as in F–E, E–D, and so forth (measures 2–3 of Figure 12.20), most of the weak sixteenth notes are anticipations, as circled.

FIGURE 12.20

More unusual, but highly effective, is an anticipation used as a dissonant preparation to a suspension, occurring twice in Figure 12.21 and indicated by the circled notes. In the first instance, the suspended note E over the bass B♭ is anticipated by a dissonant E over the bass F. The second instance can be explained in the same way, but this time it is part of a double suspension.

FIGURE 12.21

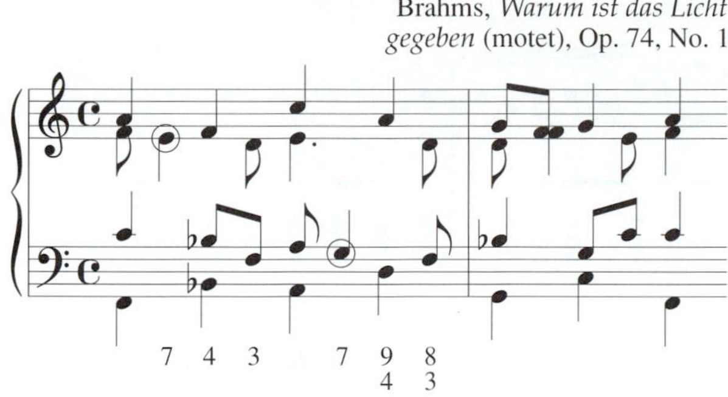

Appoggiatura The *appoggiatura* (App) is approached by leap and resolved by step. The resolution is usually opposite to that of the leap.

FIGURE 12.22 *The Appoggiatura*

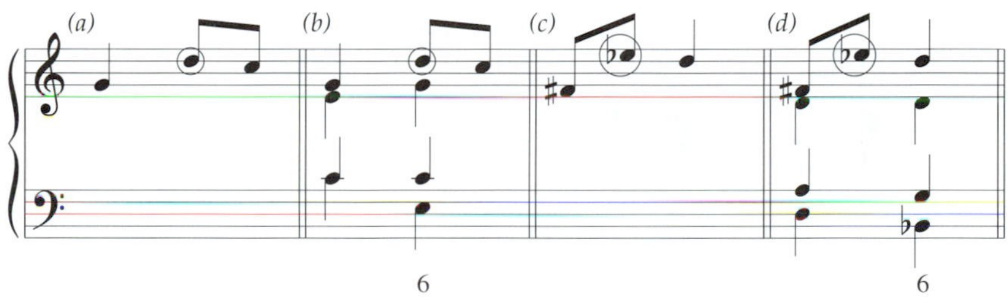

FIGURE 12.23 *Appoggiatura on a Strong Beat*

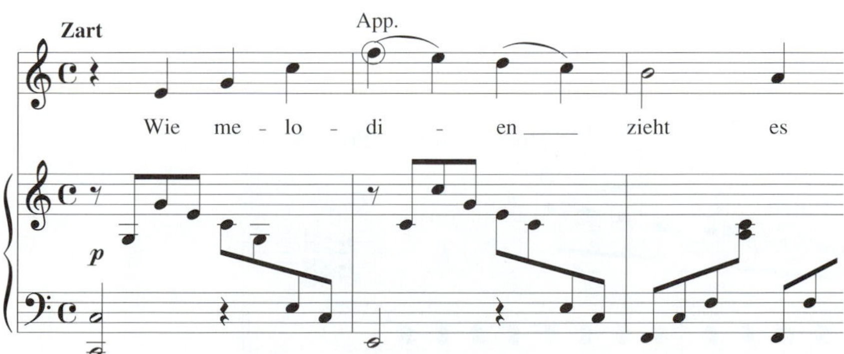

FIGURE 12.24 *Appoggiatura on a Weak Beat*

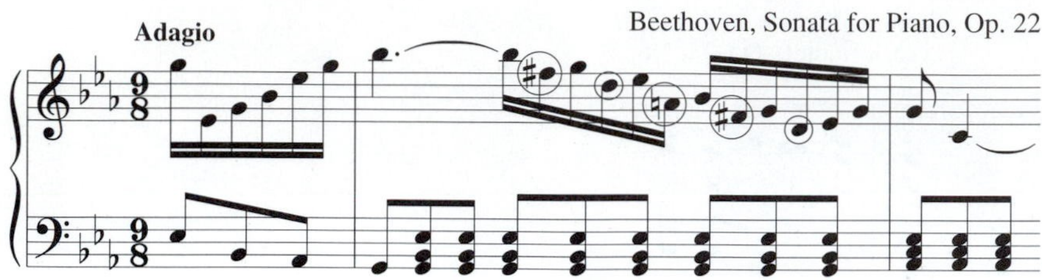

Occasionally, the appoggiatura continues in the same direction as the leap, making sense in Figure 12.25, where the leap is up to the leading tone.

FIGURE 12.25

In Figure 12.26, beginning at beat 3, Mozart approaches each member of the C major triad with a pitch a half step lower. One result is the three-note passage C–D♯–E, the C–D♯ being the usually unwanted augmented second. The aural effect is that of an appoggiatura, comparable to the G–B–C figure at the beginning of measure 2.

FIGURE 12.26

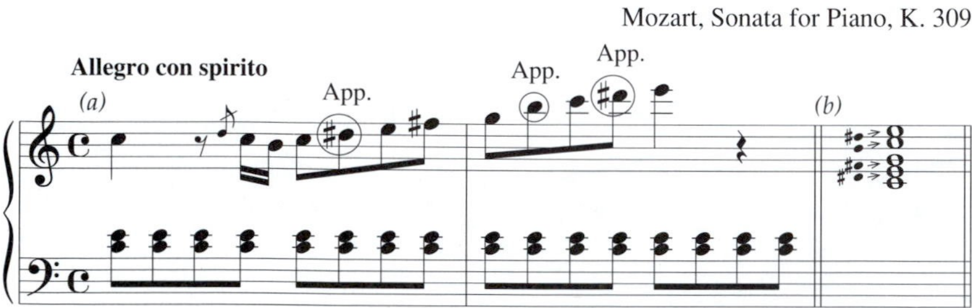

The term *appoggiatura* also has other meanings.

1. Many theorists apply the term to any nonharmonic tone in a strong rhythmic position, regardless of the note of approach. The suspension tied to its resolution is an exception.
2. The term is also given to a small note appearing before a principal note in a melody. This appoggiatura receives half the value of the following undotted note, or two thirds the value of the following dotted note value. This practice is found principally in music of the Baroque and early Classical eras.

FIGURE 12.27

This type of appoggiatura is not to be confused with the *grace note,* a note that looks like an appoggiatura but with a slash across the stem (♪̸). The grace note is performed without specific time value and as quickly as possible.

FIGURE 12.28

Escaped Tone (Escape Tone; Échappée) An *escaped tone* (ET) is a nonharmonic tone approached by step and left by leap. The resolution is usually in a direction opposite to that of the approach.

FIGURE 12.29

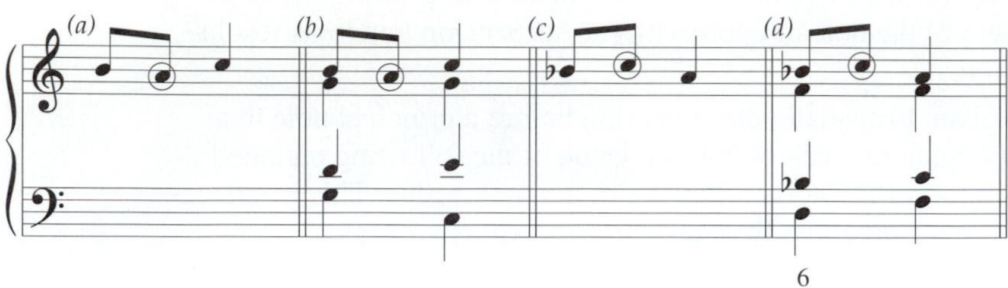

FIGURE 12.30

Mozart, Sonata for Piano, K. 283
(original an octave higher)

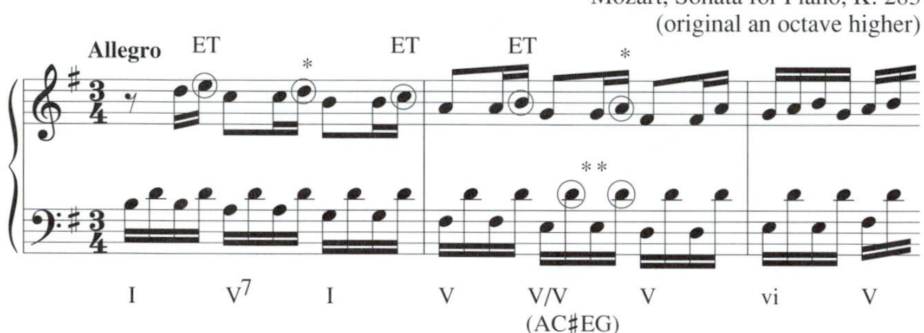

*When the three-note melodic figure is repeated in sequence, the circled note is sometimes dissonant and sometimes consonant, yet functions melodically the same each time. Some musicians would prefer to identify each occurance as a decorative pitch without a particular name or to call each an escaped tone, thereby assigning equal importance to each.

**The pitch d^1 that occurs throughout the bass clef is a *pedal tone* (see *Pedal*, page 267). At this point the pedal tone is dissonant.

Successive Neighbor Tones These are also known as "changing tones." Successive neighbor tones (SN) require four notes, the second and third of which act as successive upper and lower neighbors or vice versa. The first and fourth notes are usually the same, as in Figure 12.31, C–D–B–C, but occasionally there is a leap from the first note to the second note, as seen in Figure 12.25, measure 2, G♭–C–E♭–D♭.

FIGURE 12.31

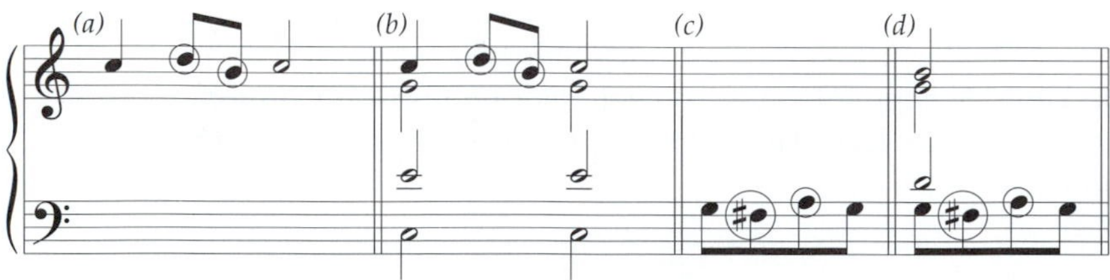

FIGURE 12.32

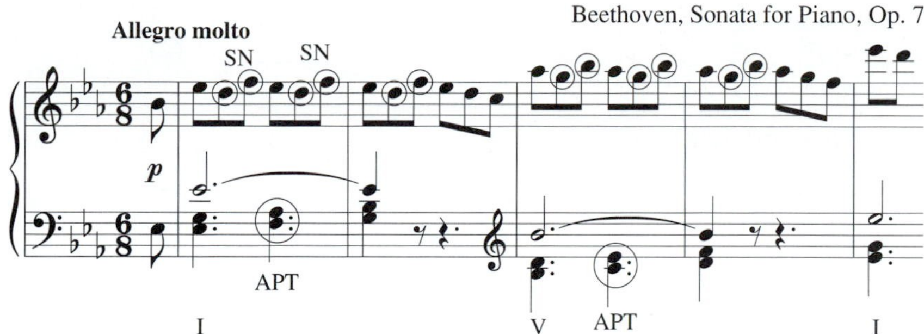

Pedal (Pedal Point, Organ Point) The *pedal* (P) is a note sustained in one voice while the harmonies are changing in the other voices. It often occurs in the bass voice, whence the name pedal, referring to the practice of holding down one note with the foot on the pedal of the organ. When the sustained tone is found as the highest voice, it is known as an *inverted pedal;* when the sustained tone is found in an inner voice, it is known as an *inner pedal* or an *internal pedal.* While being sustained, the pedal pitch may sometimes be consonant and sometimes dissonant. Figure 12.33 is an example of a common use of the pedal in the bass. The pedal of Figure 12.30 is in an inner voice; hence, it is an inner pedal. The keyboard figuration allows the pedal pitch to be sounded only on every other note, but the aural effect is that of a sustained note.

FIGURE 12.33

ASSIGNMENT 12.5 *Locating various nonharmonic tones and suspension devices.* Each excerpt includes one or more devices in the following list. Locate each by placing the example number and the cue number(s) (circled numbers below the staff) in the blank spaces. "(2)" means two or more cue numbers are required, such as "2–3."

Nonharmonic tone	*Example number*	*Cue numbers*	
Chain suspension	________	________	(2)
2 1 suspension	________	________	
Suspension with change in bass, different chord	________	________	
Successive neighbors	________	________	(2)
Ornamental resolution of suspension	________	________	
Anticipation	________	________	
Double suspension	________	________	
Appoggiatura	________	________	
Escaped tone	________	________	
Pedal	________	________	(2)
Double appoggiatura	________	________	
Retardation	________	________	

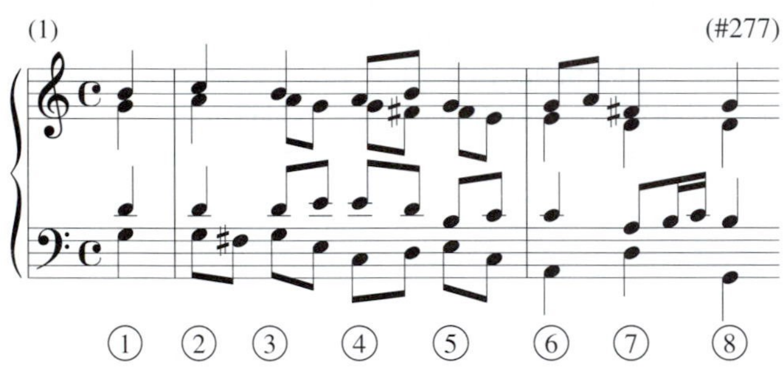

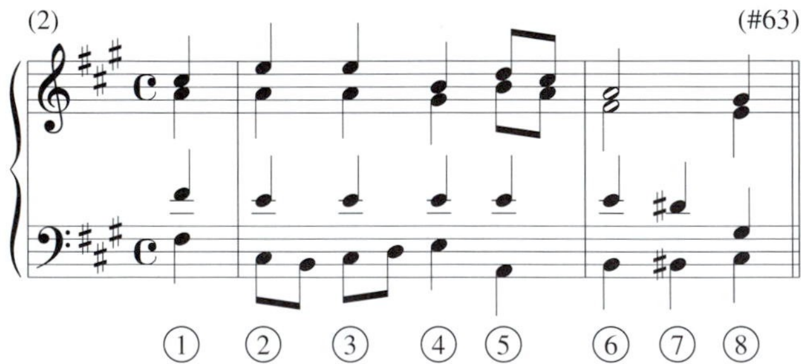

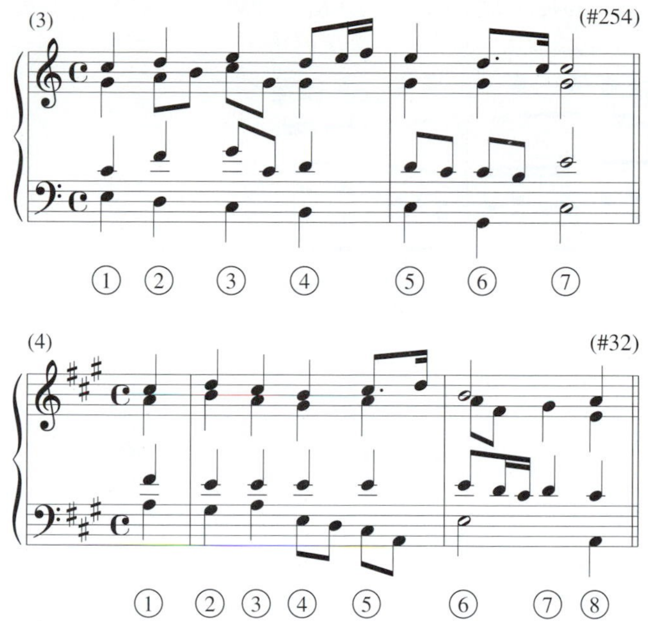
(3)
(#254)
① ② ③ ④ ⑤ ⑥ ⑦
(4)
(#32)
① ② ③ ④ ⑤ ⑥ ⑦ ⑧

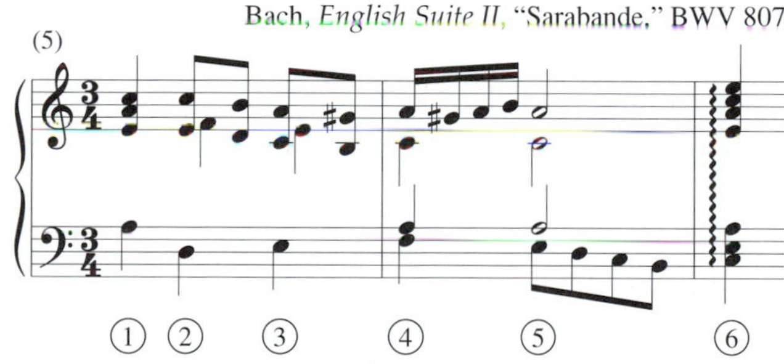
Bach, *English Suite II,* "Sarabande," BWV 807
(5)
① ② ③ ④ ⑤ ⑥

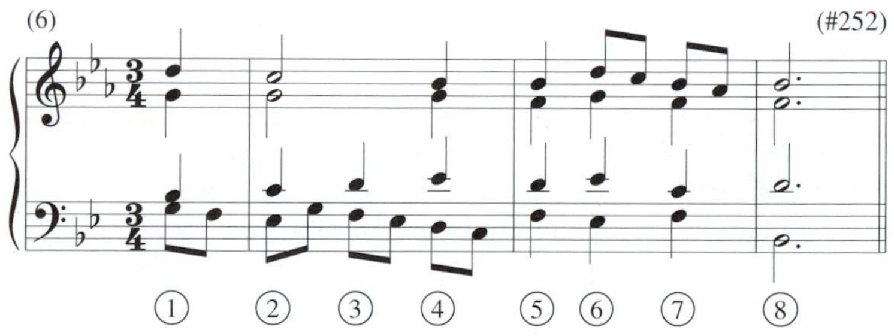
(6)
(#252)
① ② ③ ④ ⑤ ⑥ ⑦ ⑧

Bach, "Es spricht der unweisen Mund wohl" (#27)

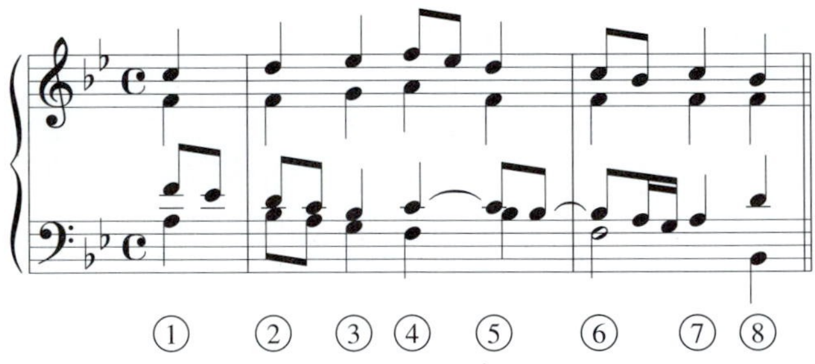

In Appendix E: Answers to the entire assignment are given.

Various Other Uses of Nonharmonic Tones

The versatility of nonharmonic tones knows no bounds. They can be found singly or in combination in so many different ways that it is virtually impossible to catalogue them. So the best we can do is to close this chapter with examples of a few of these ways, with the suggestion that you be on the watch for others in your particular musical endeavors.

Successive Different Nonharmonic Tones We have already discussed the use of successive passing tones. Successions of different nonharmonic tones are also possible. The circled tones in Figure 12.34 can be interpreted in two different ways, as shown in *a* and *b* of the figure.

FIGURE 12.34

Simultaneous Different Nonharmonic Tones Combinations of any two, and sometimes three, different nonharmonic tones are possible. The only limitation (also true of simultaneous similar nonharmonic tones) is that each nonharmonic tone must in itself be used correctly, and that each must be consonant with any other nonharmonic tone. In Figure 12.35, a lower neighbor and an escaped tone sound together, forming the consonant interval of a major sixth.

FIGURE 12.35

A more striking example (Figure 12.36) shows an anticipation and a passing tone together, each moving correctly but the pair resulting in parallel fifths.

FIGURE 12.36

The term *appoggiatura chord* is often applied to a group of tones forming a chord over a bass tone that implies a different harmony. In Figure 12.37, it is found twice, a V^7/ii over G of E G B, followed by a most common use as V^7 over the tonic tone at a cadence.

FIGURE 12.37

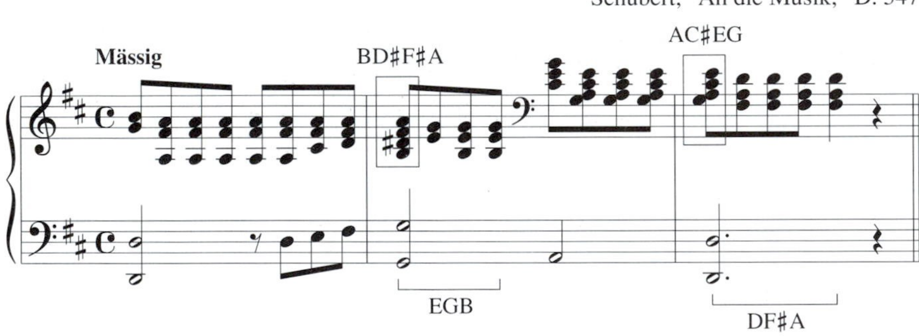

Unprepared Nonharmonic Tone This tone occurs when the first note of a melodic line or motive begins with a dissonance. It is usually termed an appoggiatura.

FIGURE 12.38

"Consonant" Nonharmonic Tones This contradictory designation refers to a tone that is consonant above the lowest tone but dissonant to the harmony implied in the chord progression. This happens frequently in music for fewer than four voices. In measure 2 of Figure 12.39, the D♯s obviously have no part in creating a G♯ B D♯ harmony. Even though D♯ is consonant with G♯ and B, it is dissonant against the E G♯ B (tonic) harmony of the measure.

FIGURE 12.39

In four voices, you will find this type of nonharmonic tone rather frequently, especially when it is a sixth going to a fifth above the bass. In Figure 12.40, measure 2, this "6 5" is a suspension over A C E (also look at measure 4, which is similar). In Figure 12.41, the "6 5" is an appoggiatura, A♭, over C E (G), making the sonority *look* like an augmented triad, A♭ C E. It is *most important* to remember that in analysis, you are analyzing *sound,* not necessarily the looks of the notes on paper. See also Figure 12.13 (page 259) at the V^7–I cadence.

FIGURE 12.40

FIGURE 12.41

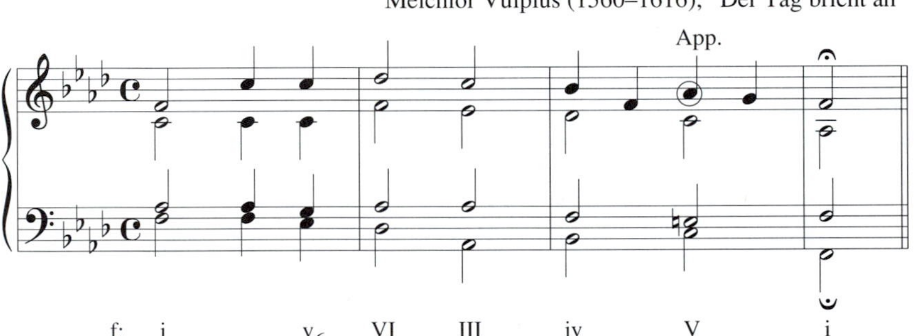

We conclude with this stunning seven-voice excerpt with its display of multiple nonharmonic tones, including a real retardation. First study measure 26, then see what you can do with measure 27. And note this interlocking of the iv–V–i progressions in these two measures.

iv	V	i		
D F A	E G♯ B	A C E		
		A C E	B D♯ F♯	E G B
		iv	V	i

The entire example includes several more melodic and harmonic "extravaganzas," well worth examining if only to be impressed once again with the genius of Bach.

FIGURE 12.42

ASSIGNMENT 12.6 *Part-writing.* These exercises include examples of the "special suspensions" and of the other types of nonharmonic tones described in this chapter. With each exercise, list by name the nonharmonic devices you have found.

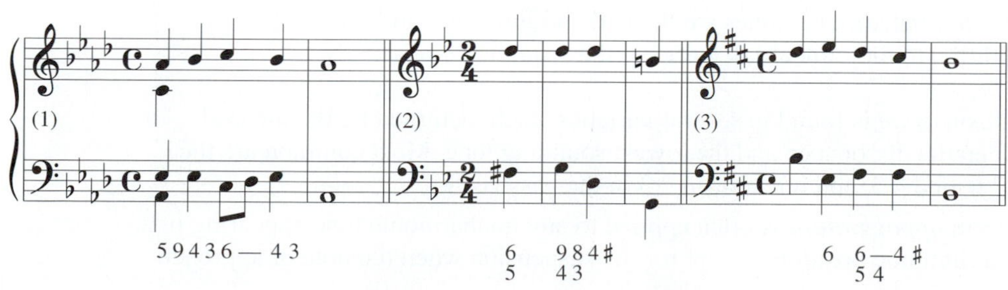

In Appendix E: Answers to (1)–(3) are given.
In the Workbook: Do Assignment 12D. Answers are given.

Summary

Any nonharmonic tone (except the *pedal*) is a part of a melodic figure consisting of the note of approach, the dissonance(s), and the note of resolution. Each variety of nonharmonic tone is defined by the melodic relationship of these notes to each other. All varieties of nonharmonic tones are defined and illustrated in Figure 12.1.

In addition to the standard definitions, these qualifications apply:

1. The *suspension* is found in several varieties, each identified by the interval between the dissonance and the lowest sounding tone. Most common are the 9 8, 7 6, and 4 3, and one termed 2 3 in the bass voice.
2. The term *appoggiatura* is often applied to any nonharmonic tone appearing in a strong rhythmic position, except for the suspension when the note of approach

is tied into it. The term also refers to a note small in size appearing before a principal note of a melody.

3. Nonharmonic tones, both singly and in groups, are so versatile that it is impractical to attempt to describe the many individual ways they can be used. A few are shown on pages 270–275.

13

The Dominant Seventh and Supertonic Seventh Chords

Review "Chords Larger Than a Triad," page 30, and "Inversion of Chords," page 31, both in Chapter 2, for the terminology of seventh chords and their figured bass symbols. Also review Chapter 4 for the spelling of dominant seventh chords.

Beginning with the first music examples in Chapter 4, we have seen many seventh chords and have learned to spell and to recognize them as such. Then why has it been necessary to delay the study of these important structures for so long?

As you know, a chord can be built in thirds and include a seventh above the root, such as the F in G B D F; and when so used, the seventh is considered a chord tone. On the other hand, the interval of a seventh above the root is a dissonance that must be handled with the same techniques and the same care as the nonharmonic tones we have just studied. So the seventh has a dual personality, as it were—a chord tone and a melodic dissonance simultaneously.

The Seventh as a Nonharmonic Tone

In pre-seventeenth-century music, a seventh above the lowest sounding voice was considered almost exclusively a rhythmically weak dissonance, like the passing seventh (V^{87}) in Figure 4.11. Not until early in the seventeenth century was the seventh combined with a triad in a strong rhythmic position to form what we now call a seventh chord. But even so, the seventh was treated as though it were a traditional dissonance, that is, requiring the same attention to the note of approach and to the note of resolution. This treatment continued up to the twentieth century and is still valid today when writing in traditional styles.

Having completed our study of nonharmonic tones, we can now see how four of these figures function in the use of the seventh chord. They are shown in Figure 13.1 for the V in G major, but the principles apply to all types of seventh chords in any inversion and in both major and minor keys. Note that the four nonharmonic figures are ones in which the dissonance resolves down. If you sing the soprano line while playing the harmony for any one of the four, it should be obvious that the circled note *must* descend.

FIGURE 13.1

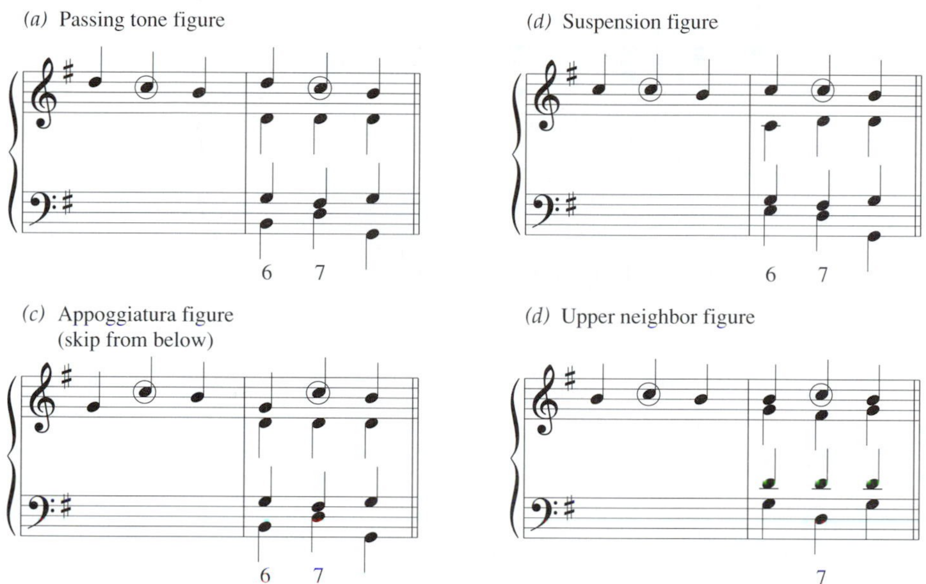

Passing Tone Figure In the soprano passing tone figure G–F–E (Figure 13.2), the alto leaps above the soprano to complete a full triad. Also note the suspension in the tenor at the same time as the seventh.

FIGURE 13.2 *Passing Tone Figure*

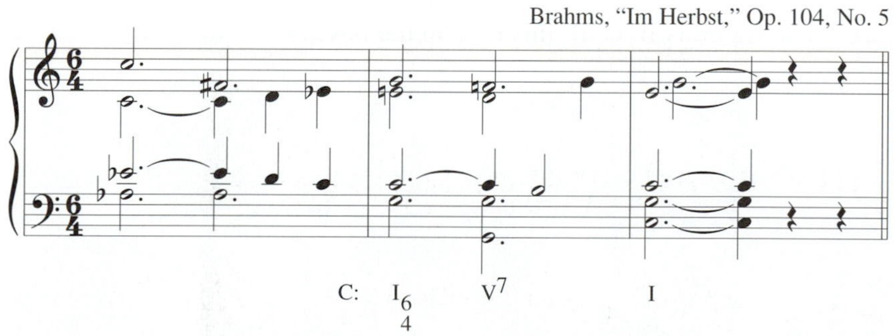

Suspension Figure This figure, F–F–E, is in the last three notes in the soprano (Figure 13.3). The V^7 is inverted, but that does not affect the dissonance treatment.

FIGURE 13.3 *Suspension Figure*

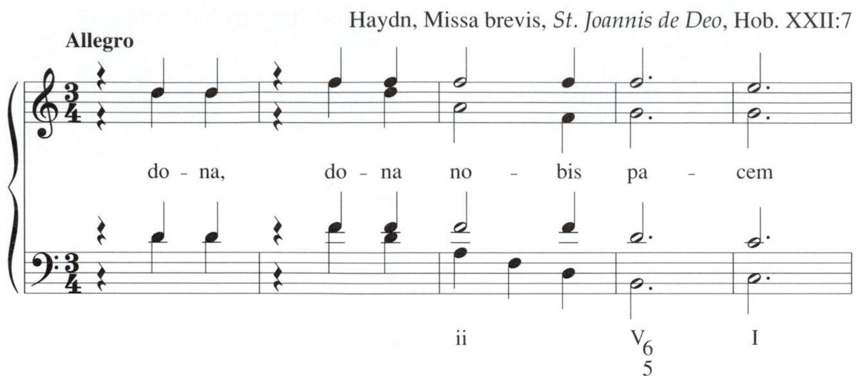

Appoggiatura Figure The figure C–F–E is again in the last three notes in the soprano.

FIGURE 13.4 *Appoggiatura Figure*

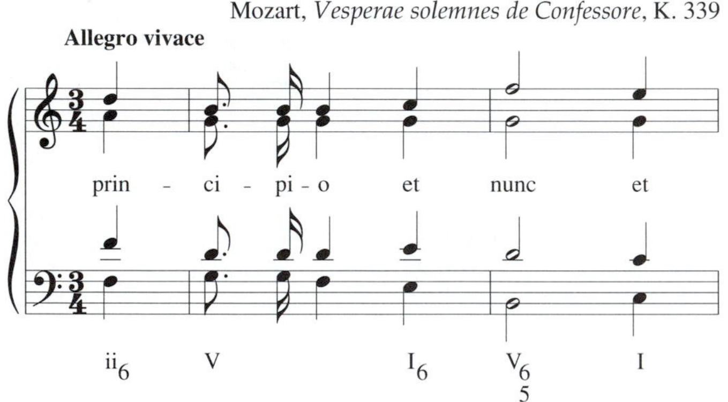

Upper Neighbor Figure The figure is B–C–B, this time in the bass, with the V^7 in the third inversion.

FIGURE 13.5 *Upper Neighbor Figure*

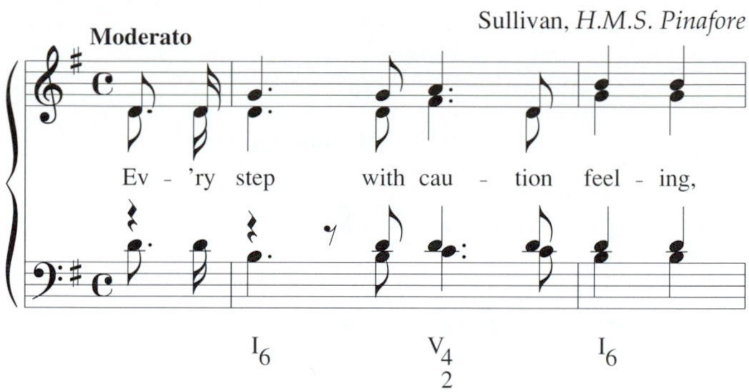

Characteristics of the Dominant Seventh Chord

1. The V^7 is freely used in any inversion, in both major and minor.
2. The V^7 can be complete or incomplete. If incomplete, the fifth is usually omitted. A complete V^7 is often followed by an incomplete tonic triad, or an incomplete V^7 by a complete tonic triad.

FIGURE 13.6

a. Incomplete V^7

b. Complete V^7

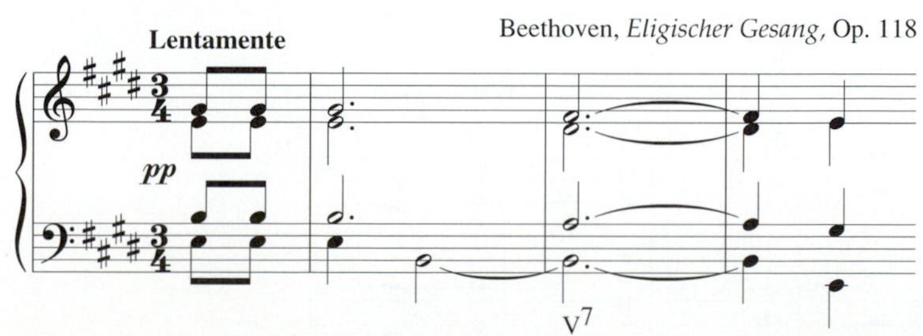

3. In inversion, all chord members are usually present, as demonstrated in Figure 13.7, where each of the three inversions shows all four tones present.

FIGURE 13.7

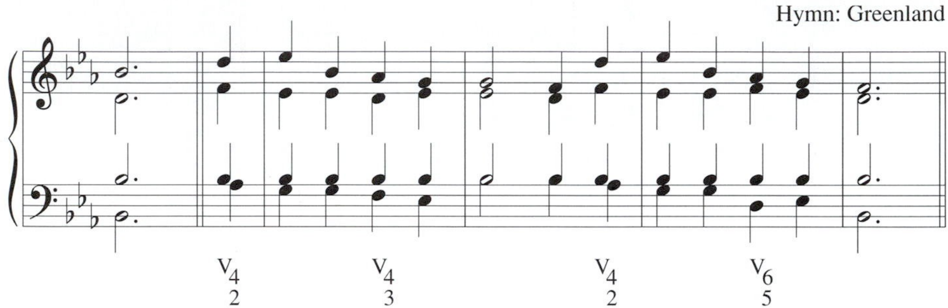

4. The *passing five-four-three* (V^4_3). When used as a passing chord, the V^7 is found between I and I_6 or the reverse, fulfilling the same function as vii° and the passing V^6_4. In its use between I_6 and I, shown in Figure 13.7, the seventh descends as expected. But between I and I_6, shown in Figure 13.8, the seventh ascends, moving in tenths with the bass line.

FIGURE 13.8

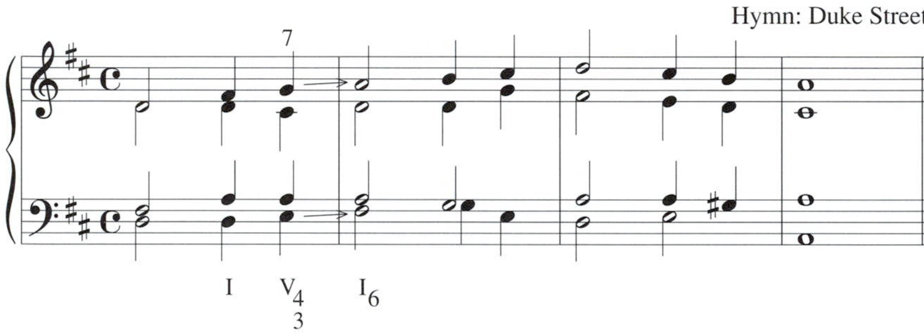

5. When the seventh chord is repeated, the seventh may appear in another voice; the last seventh in the series resolves conventionally.

FIGURE 13.9

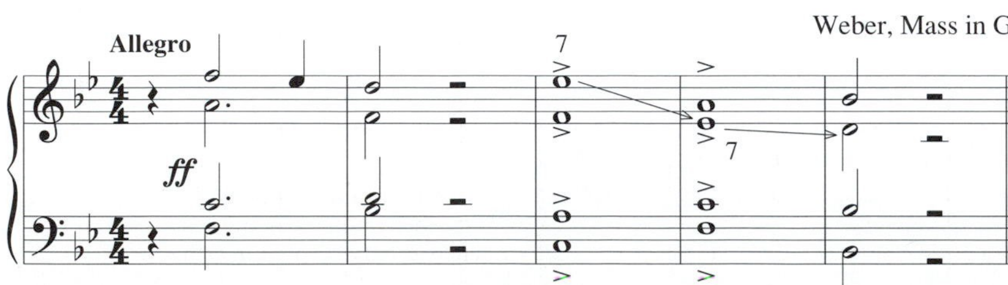

6. The seventh of the chord may display an ornamented resolution, similar to those described for the suspension. One possibility is shown in Figure 13.10.

FIGURE 13.10

7. When the seventh chord is arpeggiated, the resolution of the seventh may be delayed, or even implied.

FIGURE 13.11

The Supertonic Seventh Chord

Like the supertonic triad, the supertonic seventh chord is commonly used to precede the dominant. In fact, in the "full cadence" (page 111), the progression I–ii^7–V–I (most often ii$^6_5$—see below) is far more common than the I–IV–V–I or the I–ii–V–I progression.[1] In addition, the supertonic seventh is usually the preferred choice for a dominant preparation elsewhere in the phrase.

The supertonic seventh chord is a minor seventh chord in a major key, ii^7, and a half-diminished seventh chord in a minor key, ii^{ø7}.[2]

[1]It might seem logical that IV^7 could also be used, as in I–IV^7–V–I. Progressing from IV^7 to V presents several part-writing problems, including difficulty in avoiding parallel fifths, and consequently the use of IV^7 is much less common than might be expected.

[2]In minor, the supertonic chord with a raised fifth (♯$\hat{6}$) is rarely used and will not be considered here. Since ♯$\hat{6}$ resolves upward and the seventh of the chord resolves downward, the two meet on the same note, resulting in a doubled leading tone. This is not a problem in major, since $\hat{6}$ may resolve in either direction.

FIGURE 13.12

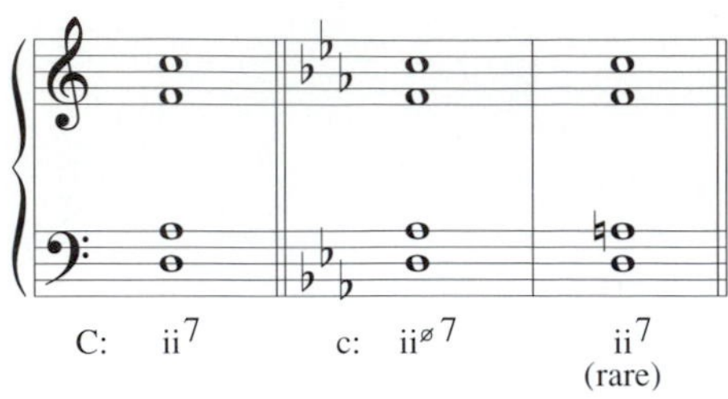

Characteristics of the Supertonic Seventh Chord

1. The approach to the seventh is commonly made by way of a suspension figure. Since the seventh is the tonic of the key, such an approach is very easy, as seen in the two instances in Figure 13.13. Also, the chords likely to precede ii^7 are vi and IV, both containing the tonic note of the key.

FIGURE 13.13

2. The first inversion of this chord[3] (Figure 13.13, measure 1) is used far more frequently than the other positions, though all are useful. Like the ii_6 and IV triads, the bass note of the ii^{6}_{5} is $\hat{4}$, providing an excellent preparation for the dominant tone ($\hat{5}$) in either V or I^{6}_{4}.

[3]The ii^{6}_{5} is often called an "added sixth" chord. In this inversion, there is no dissonant tone above the bass tone—only a M6, a P5, and a M3 (or in minor, a m3). The term is derived from pre-seventeenth-century practice when consonance and dissonance were determined by the intervals above the bass tone. In this case, all such intervals are consonant, yet there remains a dissonance, a second between the interval of the sixth and the fifth above the bass. This interval was treated as a 2 3 suspension (page 253) even though found in upper voices. The same procedure is used when treating the sonority as a ii^{6}_{5} or a $\mathrm{ii}^{\text{ø}6}_{5}$ chord.

3. ii^6_5 is found in the most common of the passing six-four chord progressions: IV_6–I^6_4–ii^6_5. Review the passing six-four on page 175.

FIGURE 13.14

Bach, "Du Friedefürst, Herr Jesu Christ" (#42)

IV_6 I^6_4 ii^6_5

4. The seventh is commonly held over to become the root of the tonic six-four. Since the root of I^6_4 is a dissonance (a fourth above the bass), the seventh of ii^7, simply by standing still, becomes another dissonance, which then resolves down by step, taking care of both dissonances.

FIGURE 13.15

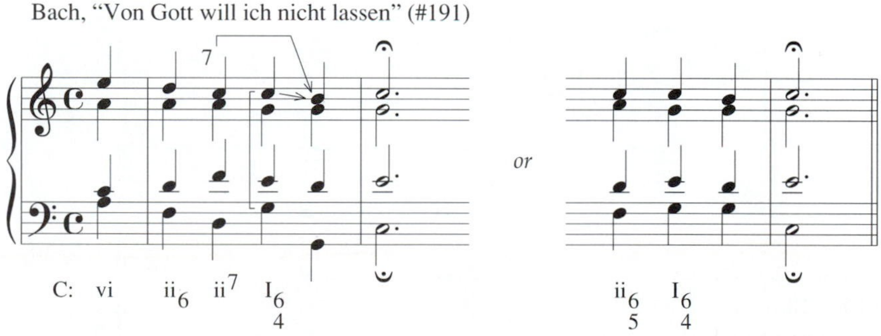

ASSIGNMENT 13.1 Spell the ii^7 in each major key and the $\text{ii}^{ø7}$ in each minor key. Simply spell the triad and add the tonic tone of the key. In D: ii = E G B; add tonic, D; ii^7 = E G B D.

In the Workbook: Do Assignment 13.1a. Answers are given.

ASSIGNMENT 13.2 *Harmonic analysis.* Locate each V^7, ii^7, and $\text{ii}^{ø7}$. Describe the approach and resolution of the seventh in each occurrence.

(1)

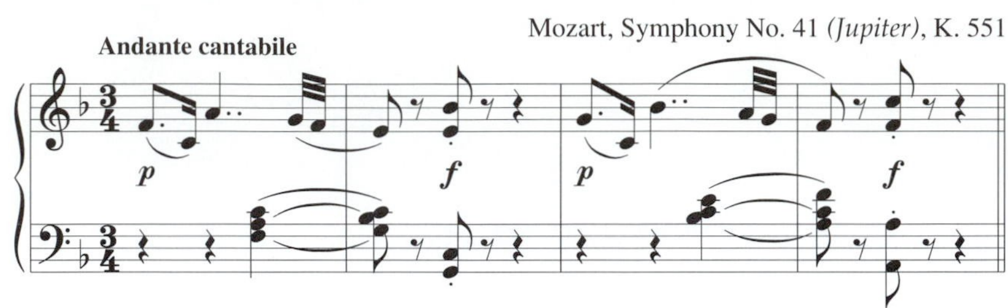
Mozart, Symphony No. 41 (Jupiter), K. 551
Andante cantabile
p
f
p
f

(2)

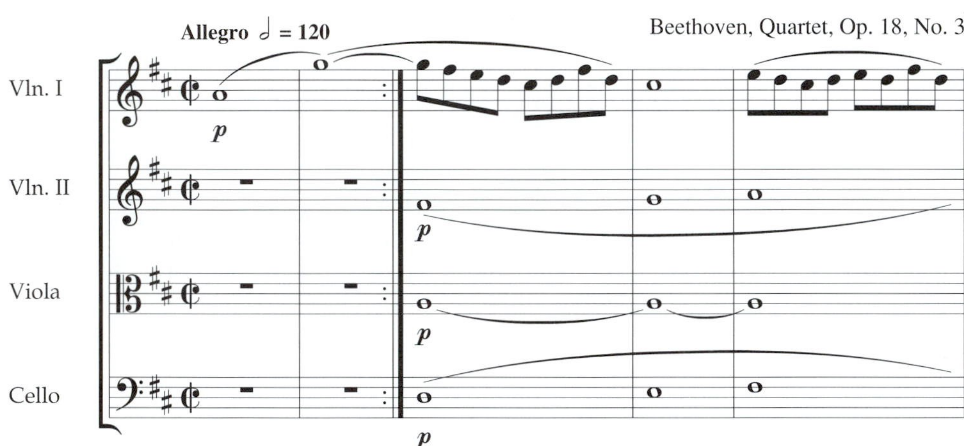
Allegro 𝅗𝅥 = 120
Beethoven, Quartet, Op. 18, No. 3
Vln. I
Vln. II
Viola
Cello
p
p
p
p

(3)

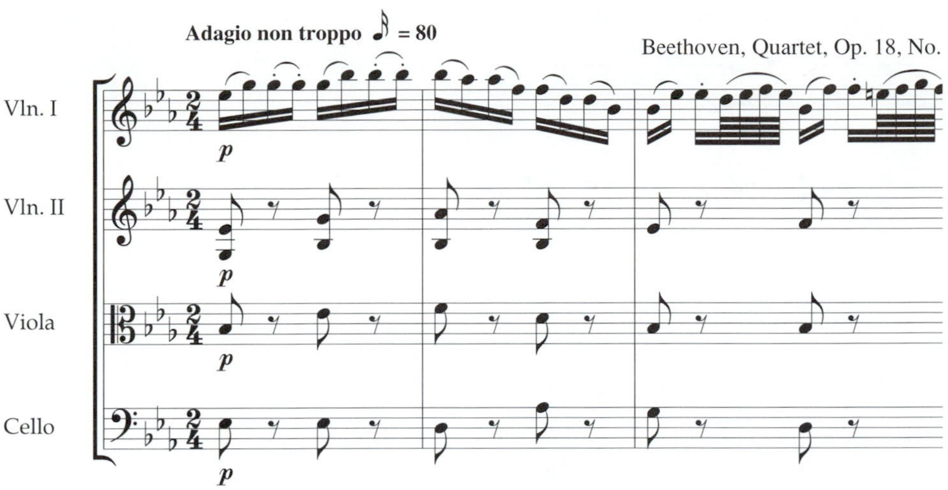

(4)

Bach, "O Mensch, bewein dein Sünde gross" (#201)

(5)

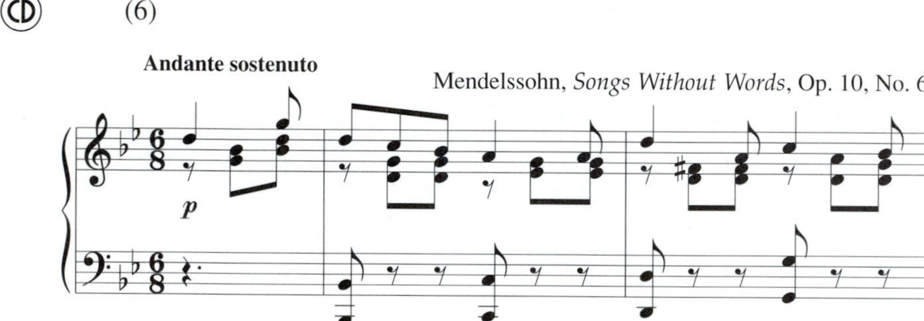

(6)

(7)

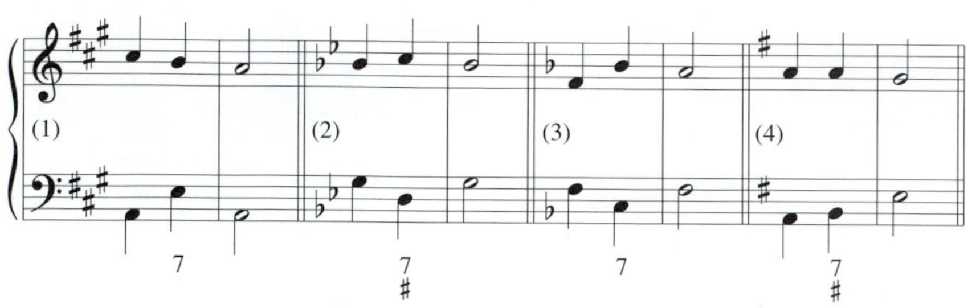

ASSIGNMENT 13.3 Write dominant seventh chords with the root in the bass. Numbers (1)–(4) demonstrate the nonharmonic figures shown in Figure 13.1. Indicate below each of these the figure used.

In Appendix E: Answers to (4)–(6) are given.
In the Workbook: Answers to the entire assignment are given.

ASSIGNMENT 13.4 Write dominant seventh chords in inversion. Indicate below each example the nonharmonic usage represented by the seventh of the chord.

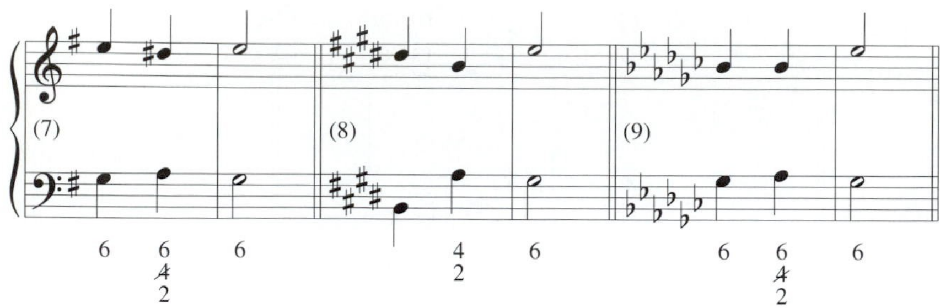

In Appendix E: Answers to (1), (5), and (6) are given.
In the Workbook: Answers to the entire assignment are given.

ASSIGNMENT 13.5 Write examples of the supertonic seventh chord. Write a harmonic analysis below each exercise. Solve some of the exercises in open score.

In Appendix E: Answers to (1), (3), (5), and (8) are given.
In the Workbook: Answers to the entire assignment are given.

ASSIGNMENT 13.6 Write extended exercises using both dominant seventh and supertonic seventh chords. For exercise (3), supply your own figuration. For exercises (4) and (5), the bass line only is given.

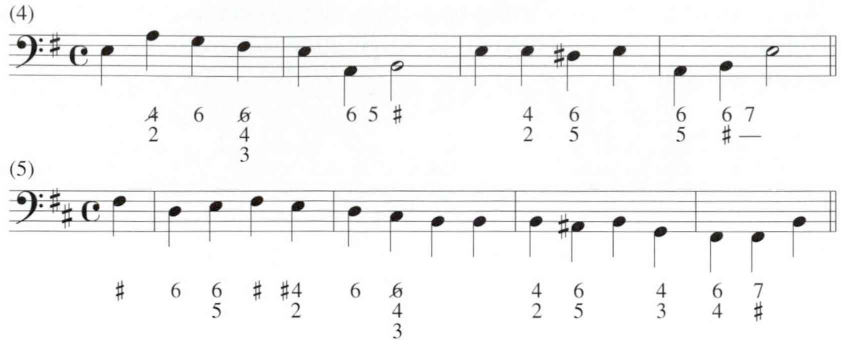

Intervals in the V⁷ Chord

Intervals in the V^7 chord are the same as those for the major triad except for those in which one of the tones is the seventh of the chord, as shown in Figure 13.16.

FIGURE 13.16

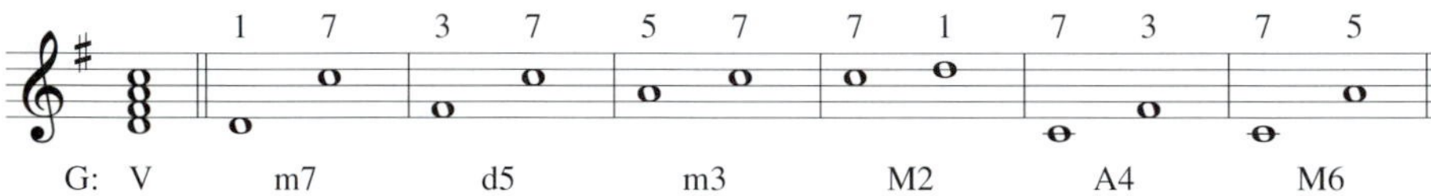

Of the intervals larger than the major second, all are useful, though m7, d5, and m3 are the most common.

ASSIGNMENT 13.7 Spell intervals from the V^7 chord. From any key, major or minor, spell the V^7 chord, then spell the minor seventh, the diminished fifth, and the minor third as in the preceding list.

In the Workbook: Answers to the entire assignment are given.
Do Assignment 13C. Answers are given.

The V⁷ Chord in the Melodic Line

Intervals from the V^7 chord are often incorporated in the melodic line. In Figure 13.17*a,* the entire V^7 is outlined; in *b* we see the interval from 7 down to 3.

FIGURE 13.17

ASSIGNMENT 13.8 *Melodic analysis.* One measure in each example contains an interval or intervals from a V^7 chord. Spell the V^7 for the given key and bracket the intervals from that chord, as in Figure 13.17.

ASSIGNMENT 13.9 *Melody harmonization.* Harmonize melodies using dominant and supertonic seventh chords where appropriate. Two suggestions are given for melody 1. Make a harmonic analysis of your work.

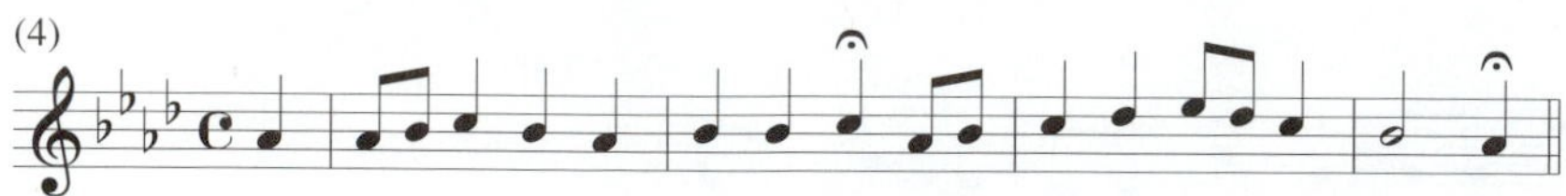

Keyboard Harmony

ASSIGNMENT 13.10 *Playing the I–V⁷–I progression.* Illustrated are but a few of the possibilities. The soprano of the opening triad may be any one of three triad members. In *a,* for example, the soprano line is $\hat{1}\ \hat{7}\ \hat{1}$, but it can also be $\hat{3}\ \hat{2}\ \hat{1}$ or $\hat{5}\ \hat{5}\ \hat{5}$. Experiment, using as many varieties as you can find.

Remember that when I and V^7 are both in root position, one of the chords is incomplete; but when V^7 is in inversion, both are complete.

These examples may be played in minor keys also. For the examples given, add three flats to the key signature and raise $\hat{7}$.

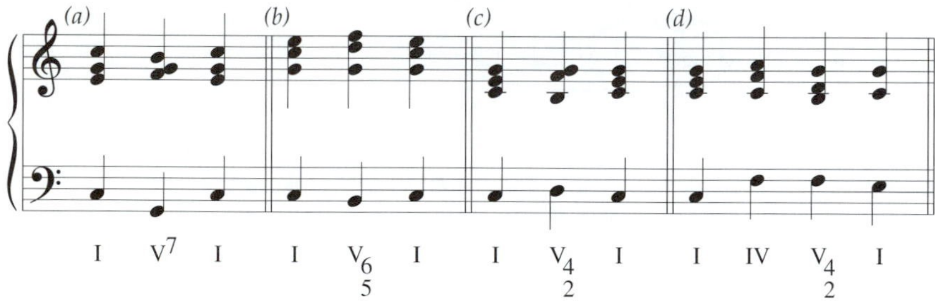

Harmonize at the keyboard the melodies from Assignment 13.8.

ASSIGNMENT 13.11 (*a*) Play the ii^6_5–V–I cadence. This common and effective cadence should be played in all keys.

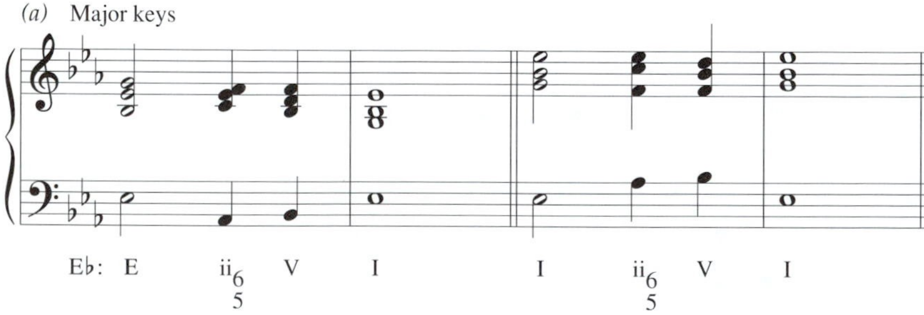

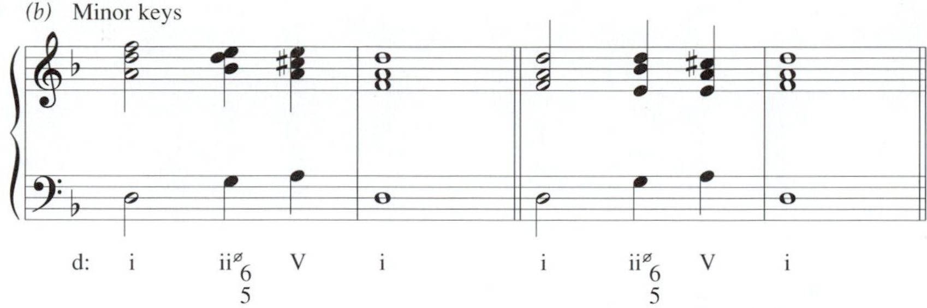

(b) Play the following progressions:

1. I–ii$^4_3$–V–I	**4.** i–ii$^{ø}{}^4_3$–V–i
2. I–ii$^4_2$–V$^6_5$–I	**5.** i–ii$^{ø}{}^4_2$–V$^6_5$–i
3. I–IV$_6$–I$^6_4$–ii$^6_5$–V–I	**6.** i–iv$_6$–i$^6_4$–ii$^{ø}{}^6_5$–V–i

Summary

The seventh of any seventh chord is a dissonance, and is therefore approached and resolved in the same manner as a nonharmonic tone. Four nonharmonic tone figures are used: the *passing tone* (descending), the *suspension,* the *appoggiatura* (skip from below only), and the *upper neighbor.*

The V^7 in root position may be complete or minus its fifth. In inversion, the chord is usually complete.

The passing V$^4_3$ is found between I and I$_6$, or the reverse. Between I and I$_6$, the seventh must ascend, the only such use of the seventh.

The seventh of the ii^7 (ii^{ø7}) is usually found as a suspension figure. The chord is most commonly used in first inversion, though all other positions are available.

The most common of the various passing six-four chord passages includes the supertonic seventh: IV$_6$–I$^6_4$–ii$^6_5$ (major or minor).

14

The Submediant and Mediant Triads

The *submediant triad* (vi or VI), though occurring less frequently than those previously studied, is the most versatile in terms of those triads to which it can relate.

1. In progressing toward the tonic, the submediant triad is commonly followed by the supertonic, subdominant, and dominant harmonies (in major, ii, IV, and V; in minor, ii°, iv, and V). A skip in the series of fifths toward tonic, as in vi–V, is often known as an *elision.*
2. The progression V–vi or V–VI is quite common. Because the expectation of V moving to I is so compelling, its progression to vi is commonly called *deceptive;* at a cadence the progression is called a *deceptive cadence.* The movement of any two harmonies away from tonic, including V–vi, is often known as *retrogression.*

The *mediant* triad (iii or III) is, in major, the furthest away from tonic in the progression of root movement by fifth (Figure 10.2). As you might expect, it is used considerably less than the other triads.

1. The mediant triad usually progresses to the submediant (iii–vi, III–VI) or to a subdominant function (iii–IV or ii_6, III–iv or ii°_6). Note that in both IV and ii_6, (iv and ii°_6), the bass is the subdominant note.
2. Probably the most frequent use of the mediant is in a progression of three triads vi–iii–IV (VI–III–iv). The progression vi–iii is infrequent without the following IV.

Figure 14.1 shows the two triads on the staff—in major and minor at *a* and *b,* and at *c,* the little-used triads in minor when $\sharp\hat{6}$ or $\sharp\hat{7}$ is required.[1]

[1]For vi°, See Figure 16.7; for III+, see Figure 17.9.

FIGURE 14.1

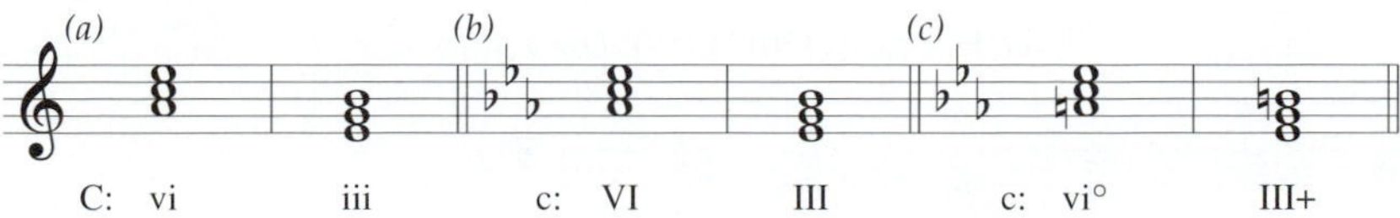

ASSIGNMENT 14.1 *Spelling the submediant and mediant triads.*

(*a*) Spell the submediant triad in each major and minor key.

(*b*) Spell the mediant triad in each major and minor key.

In the Workbook: Answers to the entire assignment are given.

Several additional conventional part-writing procedures are required in the use of these triads. The new procedures will be discussed in terms of root movements and will apply to both subdominant and mediant triads.

Root Movement by Downward Thirds

With the inclusion of the submediant triad, it is possible to construct a harmonic pattern based on root movement by thirds. Of all the possible root movements by thirds, the progression I–vi–IV–ii (in whole or in part) is of most common occurrence, as in Figure 14.2, roots G–E–C–A.

(CD) FIGURE 14.2 *I–vi–IV–ii*

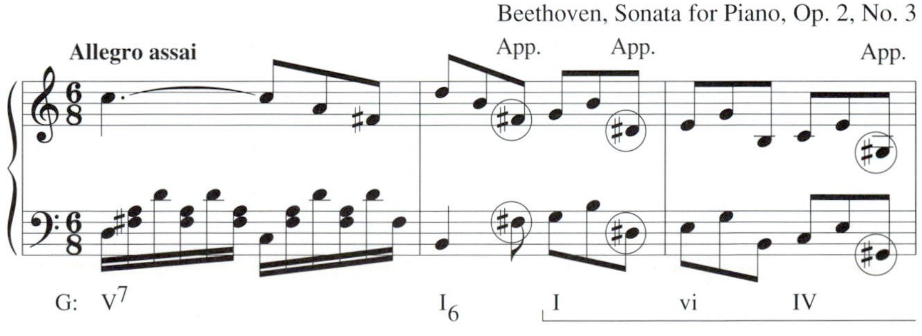

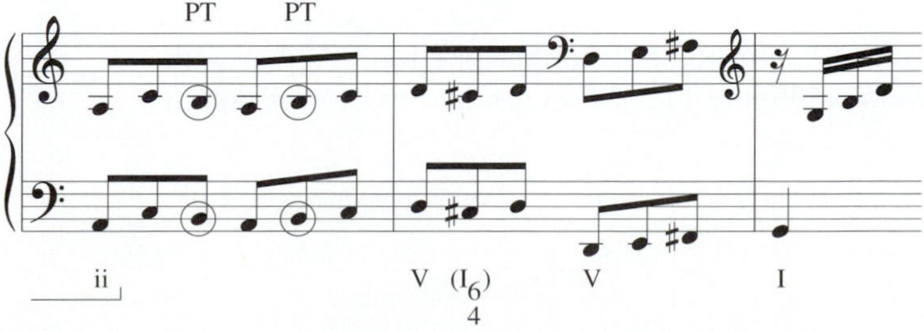

FIGURE 14.3 *i–VI–iv*

In vi–ii$_6$, the bass movement down a third produces an aural effect of root movement down a third, as though it were vi–IV.

FIGURE 14.4 *I–vi–ii$_6$*

Root Movement by Downward Fifths

The most useful progression from the submediant is to the supertonic, either with the root in the bass or in first inversion. Figure 14.5 shows resolutions of vi to both ii and ii$_6$.

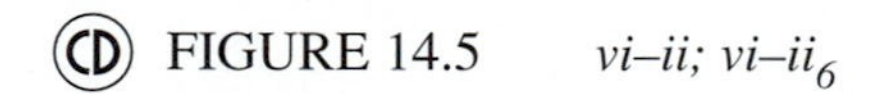

FIGURE 14.5 *vi–ii; vi–ii₆*

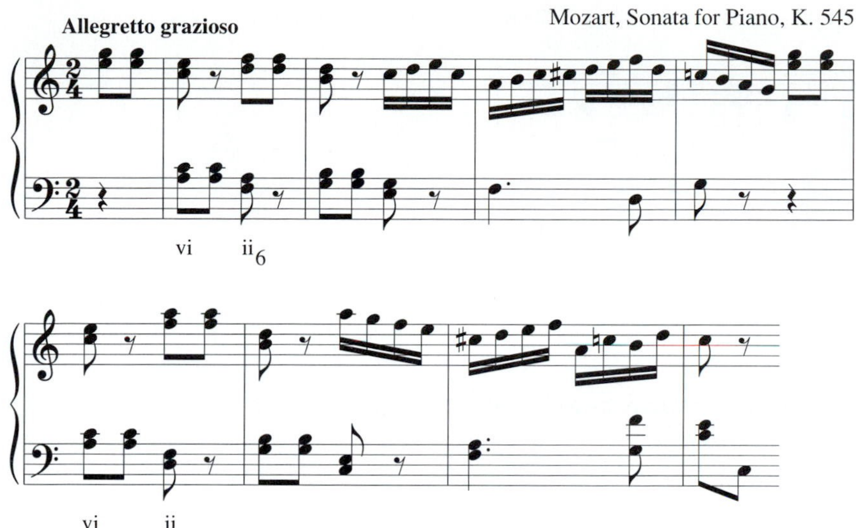

Progression from iii to vi (Figure 14.6) should be common, considering its root movement by fifth, yet it is far less common than root movement by second, iii–IV (Figure 14.12).

FIGURE 14.6 *iii–vi*

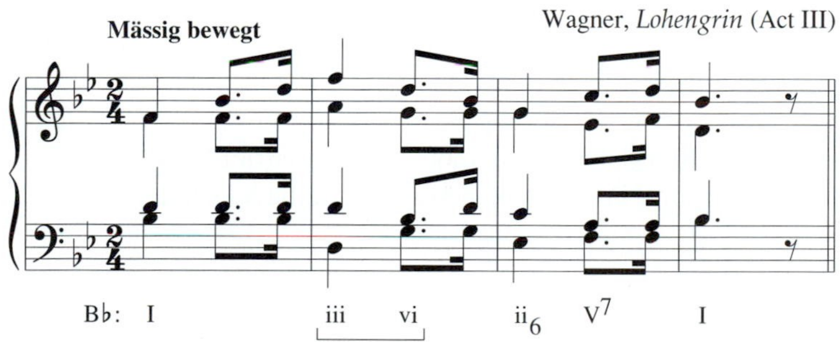

Root Movement by Seconds: the Deceptive Cadence

The *deceptive cadence* (V–vi) is one of the most dramatic of any individual chord progression. The reason for its name is obvious: The expected movement from dominant to tonic does not materialize; instead, we hear a submediant, more of a surprise than a deception. But the name describes the sensation vividly.

FIGURE 14.7 *V–vi*

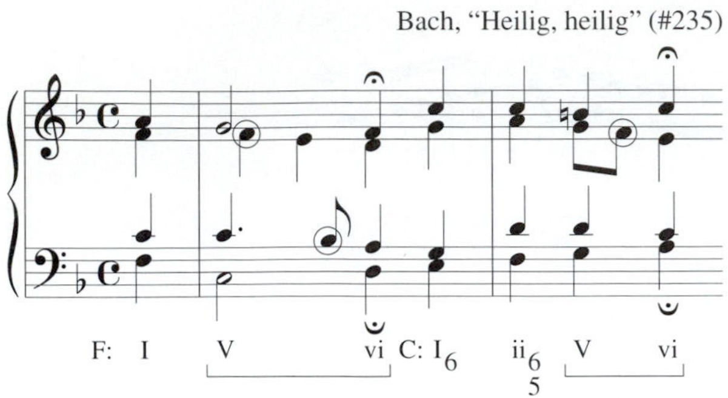

This progression may appear equally as well within the phrase.

FIGURE 14.8 *V–VI*

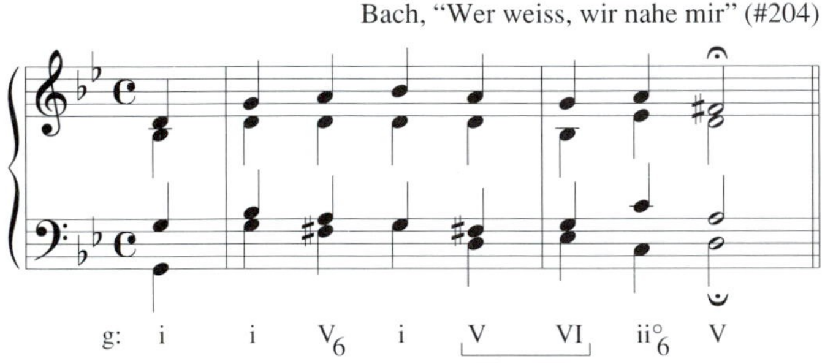

The deceptive cadence combined with nonharmonic tones can be particularly effective. In Figure 14.9, a double suspension occurs simultaneously with the VI triad.

FIGURE 14.9 *V–VI*

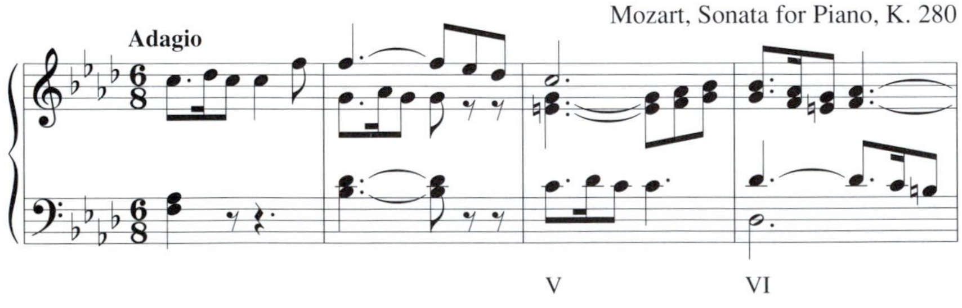

The deceptive progression is effectively used at the climactic moment in operatic arias or duets, as in the following duet for tenor and bass from an opera by Verdi. Note, beginning in measure 3, the root movement VII–III–VI–II–V, a series of downward fifths (but all major triads). These are secondary dominant chords, usually labeled V/V, V/ii, and so forth, the terminology and the symbol to be introduced in Chapter 18.

FIGURE 14.10

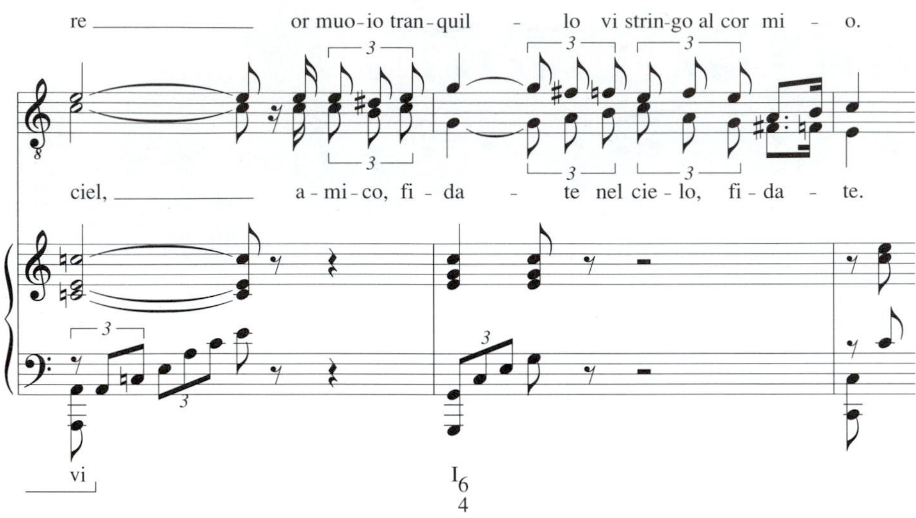

In Figure 14.11, by resolving down by step the submediant triad immediately reaches the dominant, thus bypassing the intermediate resolution of IV and/or ii.

FIGURE 14.11 *VI–V*

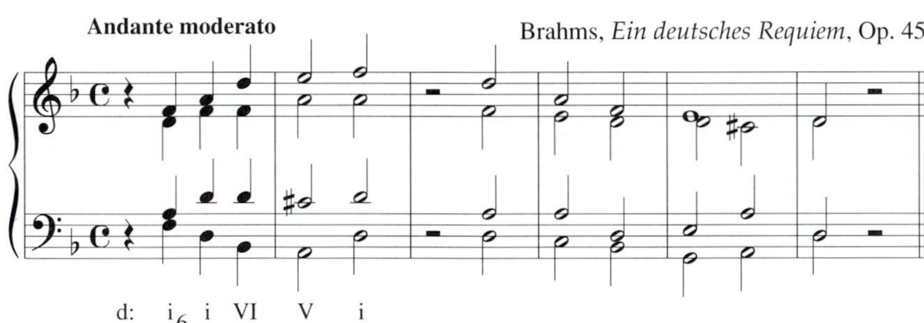

The most common use of the mediant triad, iii–IV, is particularly effective in harmonizing the descending scale line $\hat{8}$ $\hat{7}$ $\hat{6}$ $\hat{5}$, as in Figure 14.12. The roots of I–iii–iv–V in the bass produce a line in contrary motion to the melody. Brahms continues both lines one step further with V going to IV_6, the same bass stepwise as V–vi, so the aural effect is that of another deceptive progression.

FIGURE 14.12 *iii–IV*

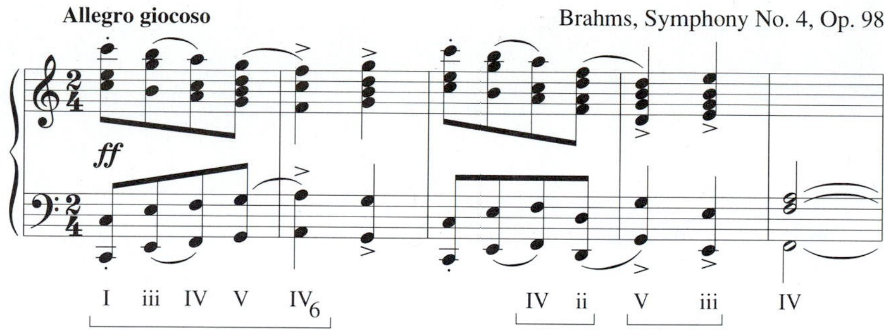

Also of interest in this figure are these two items:

1. IV–ii. Each of these triads has been studied separately. The root movement is by third, so the progression first appears in this chapter.
2. V–iii. An uncommon progression; the aural effect again is the same as that of the other deceptive procedures.

The vi–iii–IV Progression

A common progression is the vi–iii–IV (VI–III–iv in minor). Having vi precede iii is uncommon unless IV follows; this progression, vi–iii–IV, is the only one in the Table of Common Progressions (Figure 10.4) consisting of three items. Figure 14.13 shows the entire descending E♭ major scale harmonized, beginning with vi–iii–IV. The scale could have been harmonized starting with I–iii–IV, as in *b*.

FIGURE 14.13 *vi–iii–IV*

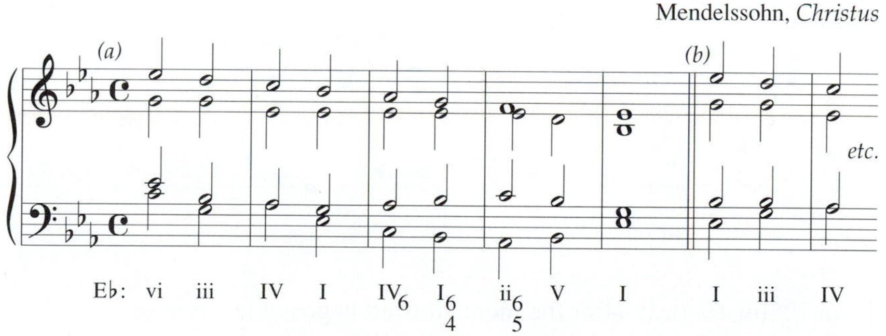

Could a simple eight-note melody include a harmonization of vi–iii–IV in two different places? Brahms does it in the *lied* in Figure 14.14. Here is a lesson in imaginative harmonization of a very simple melodic line.

FIGURE 14.14

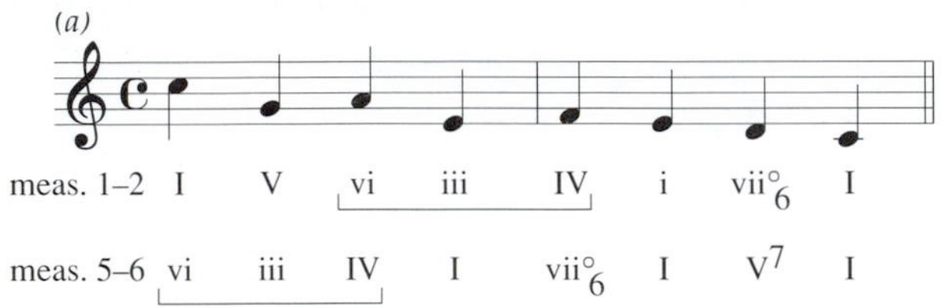

Brahms, *Romanzen aus Magelone*, Op. 33, "Liebe kam aus fernen Landen"

Substitution of ii_6 or ii°_6 for IV or iv after the mediant triad is possible because both progress to V and they have the same bass note. The following example in a minor key shows the progression VI–III–ii°_6 rather than the common VI–III–iv.

FIGURE 14.15 *VI–III–ii°₆*

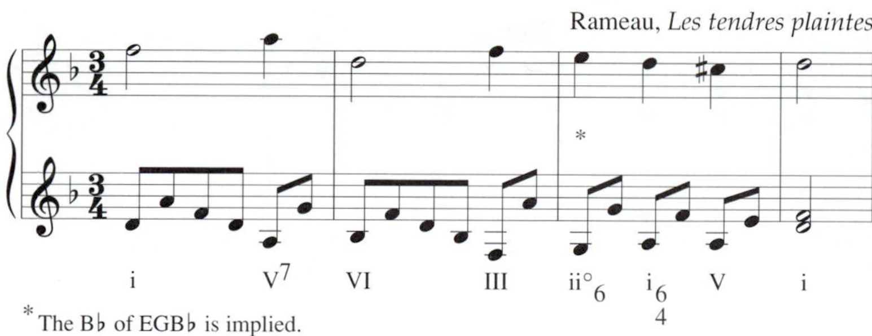

*The B♭ of EGB♭ is implied.

Inversions of the Submediant and Mediant Triads

Submediant and mediant triads are infrequent in first inversion and rare in second inversion. Each of the triads usually appears in first inversion only when the root of the preceding triad is the same bass note as the first-inversion note. There are just two practical possibilities: I–vi_6 and V–iii_6.

FIGURE 14.16

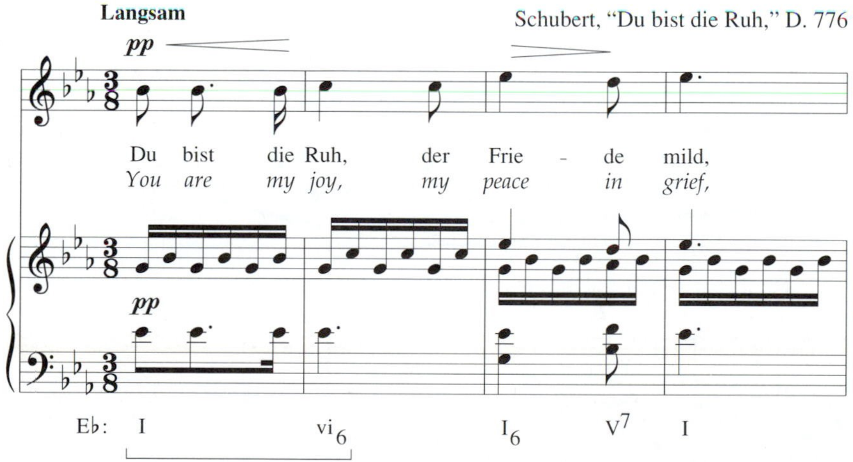

ASSIGNMENT 14.2 *Harmonic analysis.* Analyze the harmony and identify the nonharmonic tones of these excerpts.

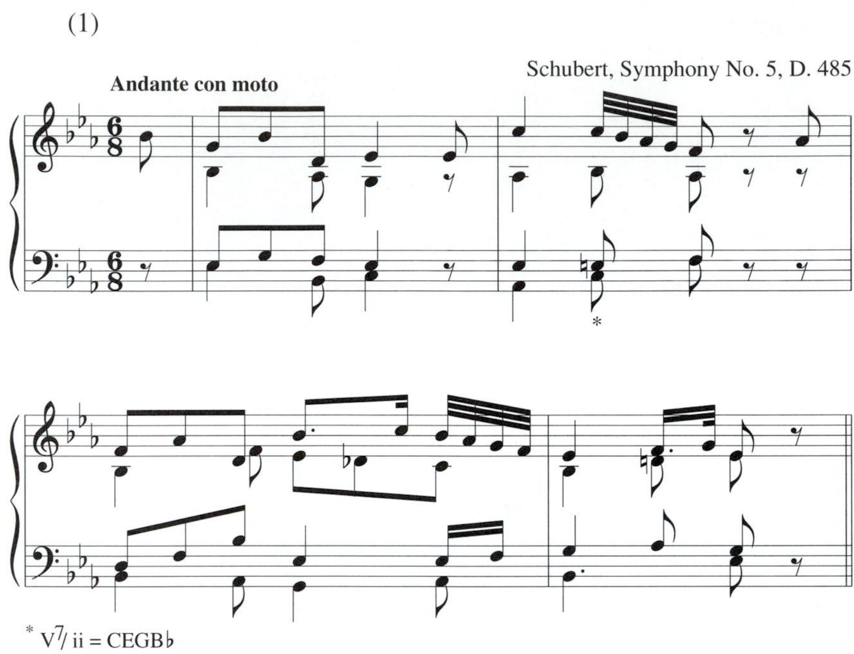
(1)
Schubert, Symphony No. 5, D. 485
Andante con moto
* V7/ ii = CEGB♭

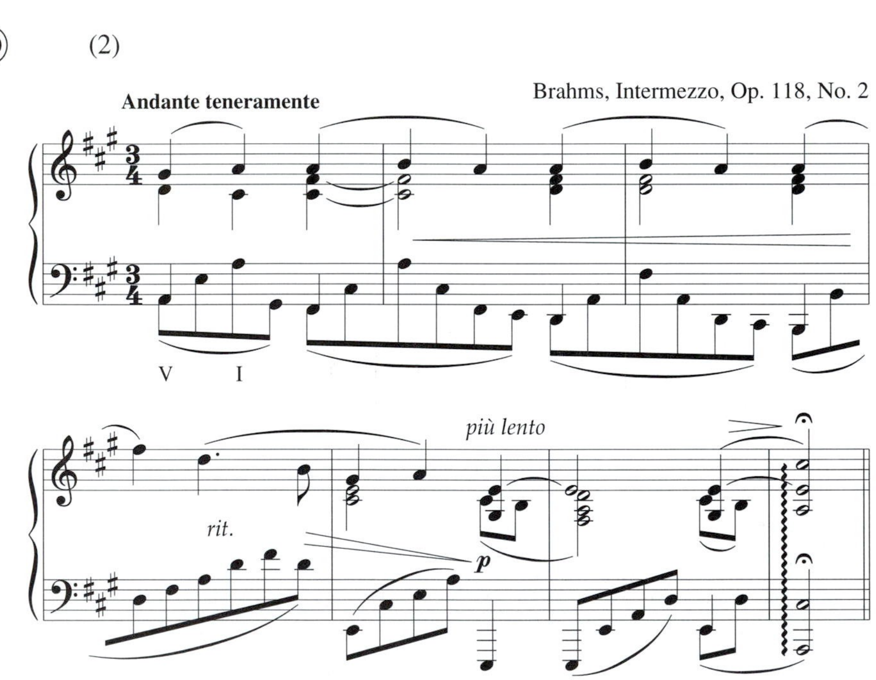
(2)
Brahms, Intermezzo, Op. 118, No. 2
Andante teneramente
V I
più lento
rit.
p

(3)

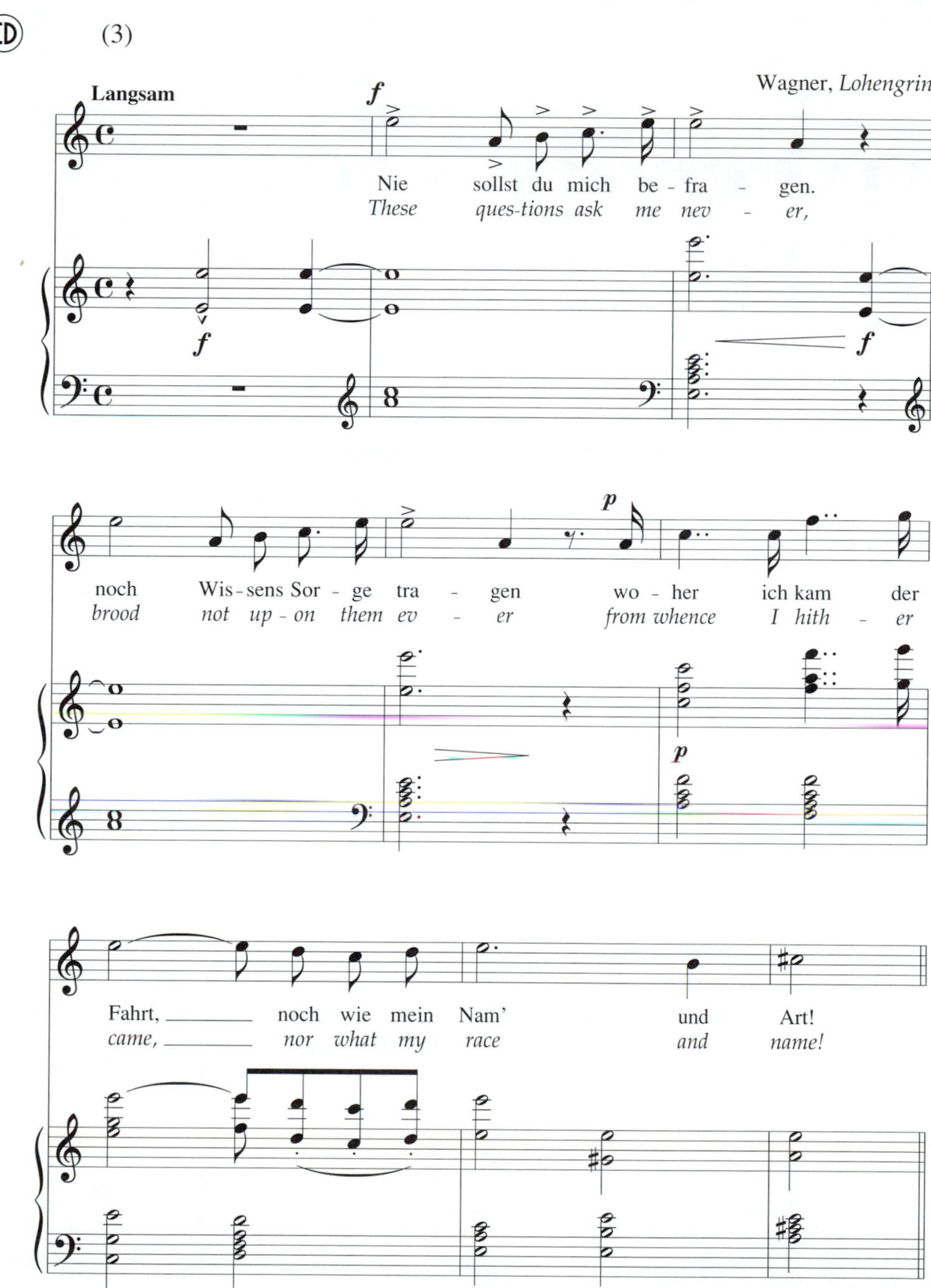
Langsam
Wagner, *Lohengrin*
Nie sollst du mich be - fra - gen.
These ques-tions ask me nev - er,
noch Wis-sens Sor - ge tra - gen wo - her ich kam der
brood not up - on them ev - er from whence I hith - er
Fahrt, noch wie mein Nam' und Art!
came, nor what my race and name!

(4)

Schubert, Sonata for Piano, D. 664

* Is the soprano note at each of these points a chord tone or a nonharmonic tone?

(5) Be sure to check the cadence before beginning your analysis.

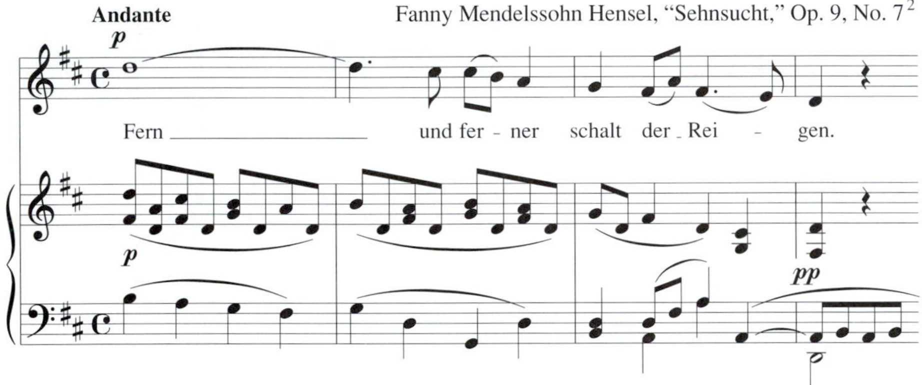

Fanny Mendelssohn Hensel, "Sehnsucht," Op. 9, No. 7[2]

Writing the Submediant and Mediant Triads

Most progressions in root position can be written with the conventional procedures already studied. When either triad is inverted, use the conventional procedure for approaching and resolving the doubled tone.

1. Roots a fifth apart.

FIGURE 14.17

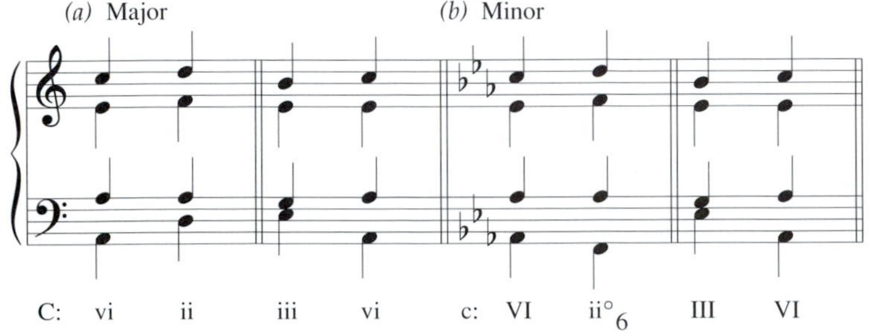

[2] Fanny Mendelssohn Hensel was the sister of Felix Mendelssohn.

2. Roots a second apart.

FIGURE 14.18

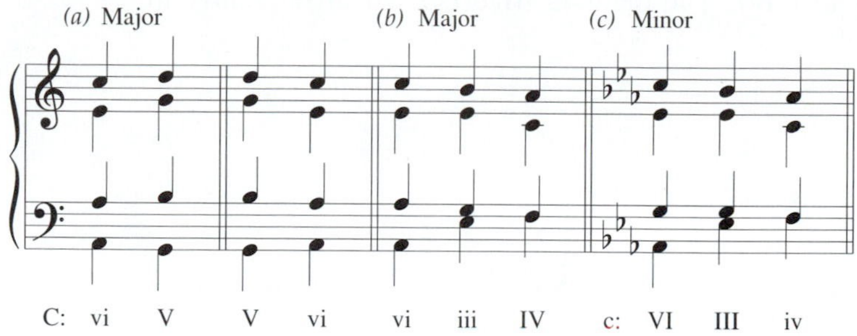

When roots are a second apart and the soprano and the bass move in the same direction, as in V–vi or vi–V, the conventional procedure will not work, because parallel fifths, octaves, and/or augmented seconds usually result. In this situation, an alternative procedure is used: Double the third in the submediant triad, as demonstrated in Figure 14.19*a–e*.

This procedure can be used in similar situations where use of conventional procedures is awkward or impossible, and is especially effective when the doubled note is the tonic, subdominant, or dominant note of the key. The I–ii progression in Figure 14.19*f* is a good example.

FIGURE 14.19

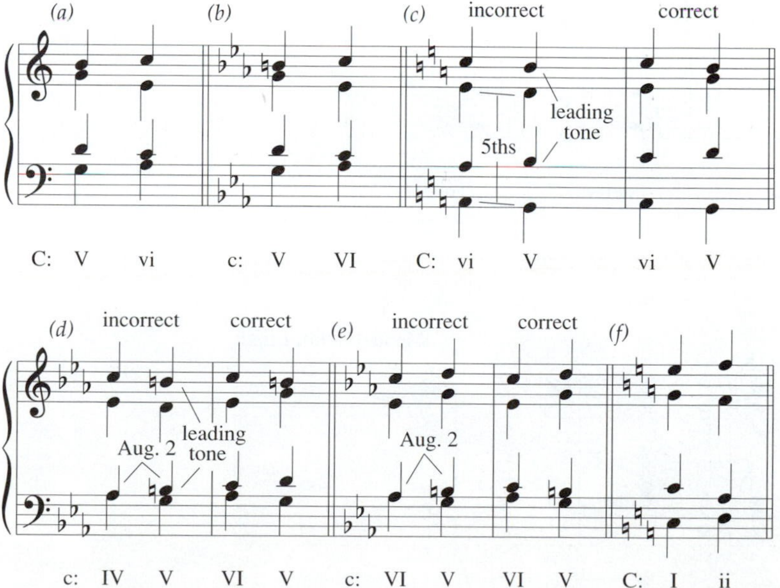

3. Roots a third apart. Although this is the last of the conventional root movements, its part-writing is actually the easiest. Triads with roots a third apart in the bass have two tones in common. Usually it is necessary only to hold these two tones and move the other voice by step. This procedure is useful in the progressions I–iii (i–III), I–vi (i–VI), IV–ii, and vi–IV (VI–iv). The mediant triad is used infrequently in inversion.

FIGURE 14.20

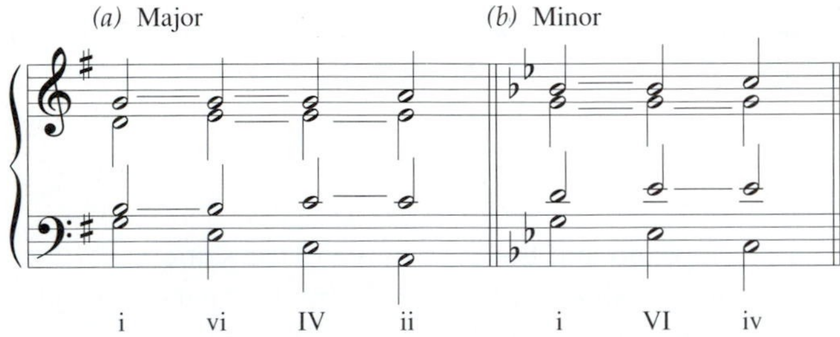

Should the melody line skip a third or more when the roots move by third, there is no conventional procedure. Simply make sure that there are no parallels and that the voices are in range.

FIGURE 14.21

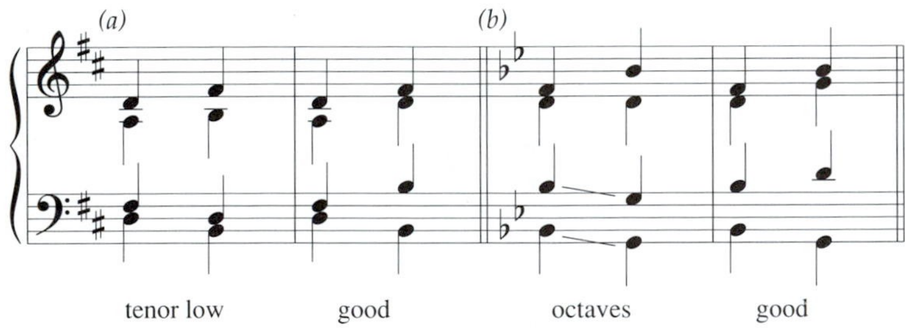

FIGURE 14.22

Once again you are reminded of the "mediant" triad caused by an accented non-harmonic tone, as shown in Figure 12.41 (page 274) and its discussion, and shown again below. Its figuration is 6 5.

FIGURE 14.23

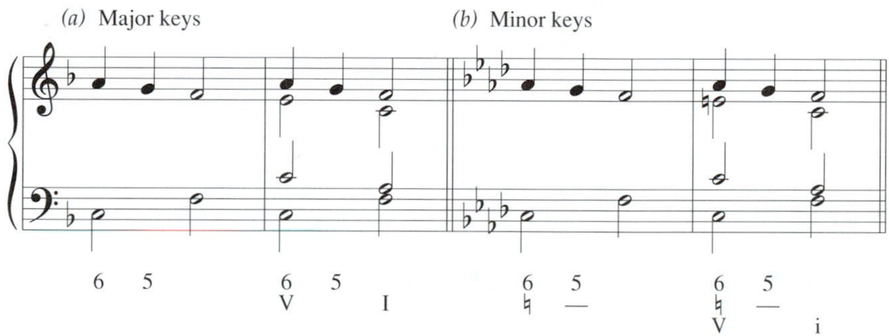

ASSIGNMENT 14.3 *Part-writing.* Write exercises showing various uses of the submediant triad. Fill in inner voices and make a harmonic analysis of each example.

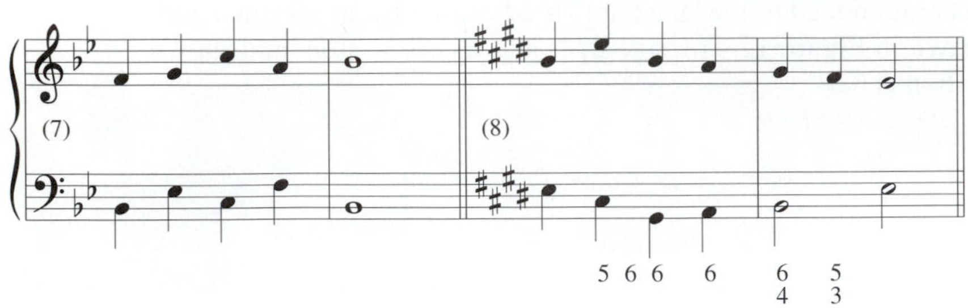

In exercises 9–11, the last triad is submediant.

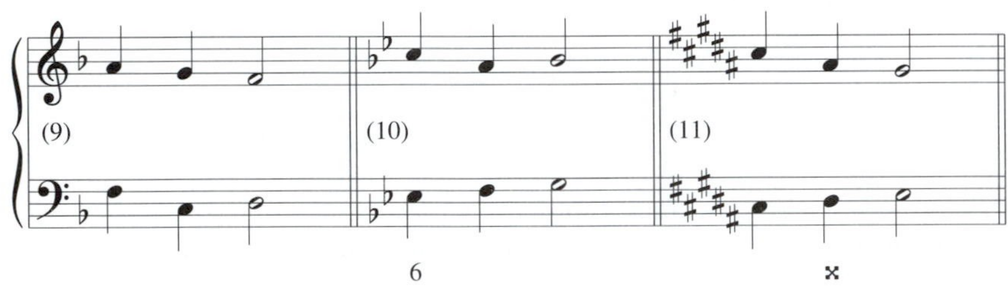

In Appendix E: Answers to (2), (4), (6), and (10) are given.
In the Workbook: Answers to the entire assignment are given.

ASSIGNMENT 14.4 *Part-writing.* Write exercises showing use of the mediant triad. Fill in inner voices and make a harmonic analysis of each example.

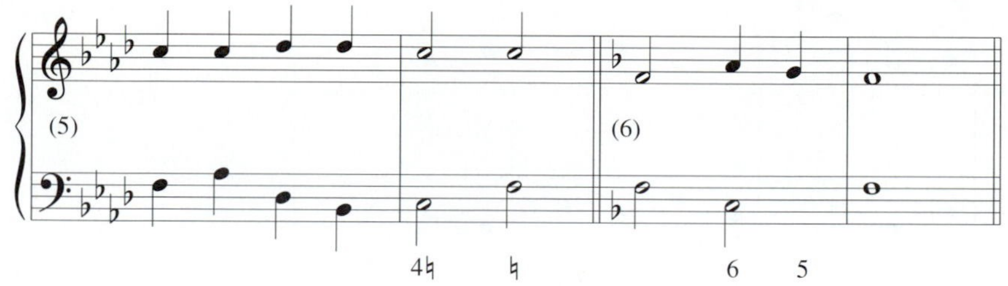

In Appendix E: Answers to (2) and (5) are given.
In the Workbook: Answers to the entire assignment are given.

ASSIGNMENT 14.5 *Extended exercises in part-writing.* Complete each exercise by filling in the alto and tenor voices. Solve some of these exercises using open score with C clefs, as assigned. Make a harmonic analysis and identify all nonharmonic tones.

(2)
♯ ♯ 6 ♯ 6 ♯
6 ♯ 6 6 6 6 ♯ 5
(3)
♮ 6 6 6 6 6 6 ♮ 6
6 ♮ 5 — 6 5 8 6 4 — — 2 — 5 ♮ 7 — —

(4)
7 6 8 9 8 7 4 3 ♯ 8 9 6 5 6 6 8 7
6 — 4 5 ♯—
3
(5)
6 4 3 7 6 6 4 3 3—8 7 9 8 8—7
3 2 4 3—
(6)
8——7 8 7 8 ——— 7 6
4 2 3— 5 —— 8 —
4 3 2 3 —
7 6 5 6 — 9 8 7 6 8 7
3 6 5 —
3 —

ASSIGNMENT 14.6 *Part-writing, bass line only given.* Make a harmonic analysis. Write a soprano line, and fill in inner voices.

Keyboard Harmony

ASSIGNMENT 14.7 Play the deceptive cadence. Notice in *b, c,* and *d* the use of the doubled third in vi (VI) to avoid parallels and the augmented second.

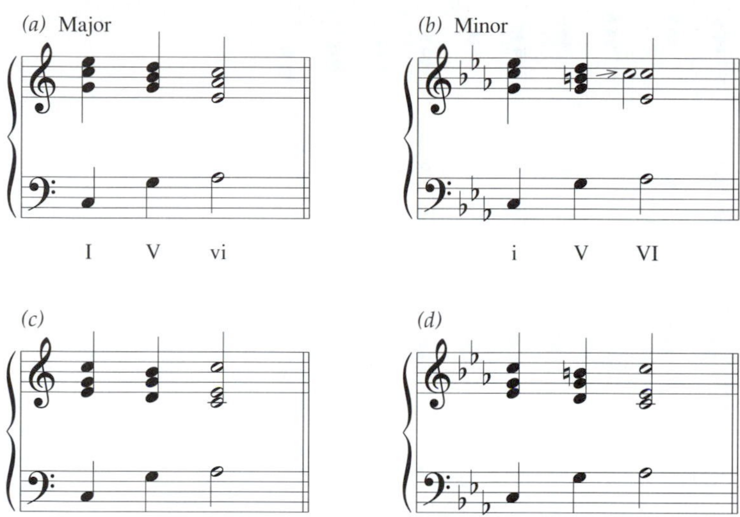

ASSIGNMENT 14.8 Play progressions using the submediant and mediant triads. Two examples are written out for you. Play others in a similar manner and in various keys.

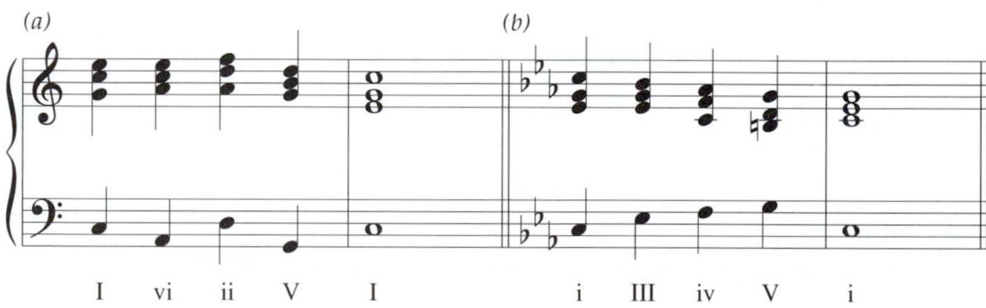

Major keys	***Minor keys***
I vi IV V I	i VI iv V i
I vi IV ii V I	I VI ii°_{6} V i
I iii vi $ii_{(6)}$ V I	i III VI ii°_{6} V i
I vi iii IV V I	i VI III iv V i

ASSIGNMENT 14.9 Harmonize major and minor scales. One version each in major and minor is shown, using roots in the bass only (except vii°). Play these and the other versions of the scales in various keys, as assigned.

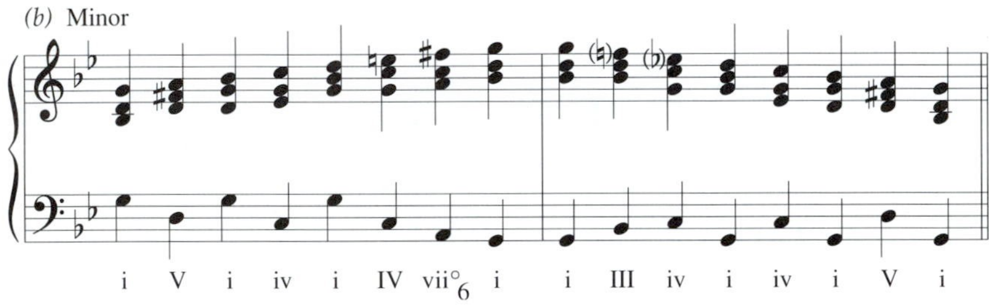

Major, ascending

$\hat{1}$	$\hat{2}$	$\hat{3}$	$\hat{4}$	$\hat{5}$	$\hat{6}$	$\hat{7}$	$\hat{8}$
I	V	I	IV	I	IV$_6$	V	I

Major, descending

$\hat{8}$	$\hat{7}$	$\hat{6}$	$\hat{5}$	$\hat{4}$	$\hat{3}$	$\hat{2}$	$\hat{1}$
I	iii	IV	I	ii$_6$	I$^6_4$	V	I
I	V	vi	iii	IV	I$^6_4$	V	I

Melodic minor, ascending

$\hat{1}$	$\hat{2}$	$\hat{3}$	$\hat{4}$	$\hat{5}$	$\hat{6}$	$\hat{7}$	$\hat{8}$
i	V	i	iv	i$_6$	IV	vii$^{\circ}_6$	i
i	V	i	iv	i$_6$	ii	V	i

Melodic minor, descending

$\hat{8}$	$\hat{7}$	$\hat{6}$	$\hat{5}$	$\hat{4}$	$\hat{3}$	$\hat{2}$	$\hat{1}$
i	III	iv	i	ii$^{\circ}_6$	I$^6_4$	V	i
i	III	iv	V	iv$_6$	I$^6_4$	V	i

Melody Harmonization Harmonizing melodies at the keyboard using submediant and mediant triads will be found as Assignment 15.3, page 338.

Summary

The *submediant* triad has many uses, in contrast to the *mediant,* which is less frequently used.

The submediant (vi or VI) progresses easily to all triads except vii° or iii (although the three-chord progression vi–iii–IV is quite common).

V–vi (or VI) is a "deceptive" progression, vi replacing the expected tonic triad. At a cadence point, this progression is known as a *deceptive cadence.*

The mediant (iii or III) most frequently progresses to IV, and often to vi and ii$_6$. This triad is effective in harmonizing $\hat{7}$ of a descending major scale line.

VI and iii are found in first inversion when the bass note is the same as the bass note of the preceding chord (as in I–vi$_6$).

New conventional part-writing procedures are

1. Roots a third apart: Hold the two common tones.
2. Roots a second apart, soprano moving in the same direction: Double the third in the second of the two triads.

15

The Melodic Line II

form, continued;
melody harmonization, continued;
melody writing

Music of the tonal era has often been called "square," and not without some justification, since the rhythm of the era consists largely of regularly recurring accents in groups of two, three, and four. (For a contrast, read the article "Another Metrical Concept" on page 343.) In the study of form, we have noted the extensive use of four-measure phrases and eight-measure periods. In fact, we stated in Chapter 7 that the four-measure phrase could be considered a standard with which other phrase lengths can be compared.

It is these other lengths that will engage our attention in the first part of this chapter, followed by forms larger than the eight-measure period.

Melodic Extensions

Modification of the "standard" phrase length can be found in most music literature, including both composed and folk music. In modifying a phrase, it is not enough to simply string a succession of notes through an odd number of measures in a formless manner; rather, the four-measure phrase is extended through creative adjustment. Some ways of doing that are presented here.

1. Repeat a part of a phrase.

FIGURE 15.1

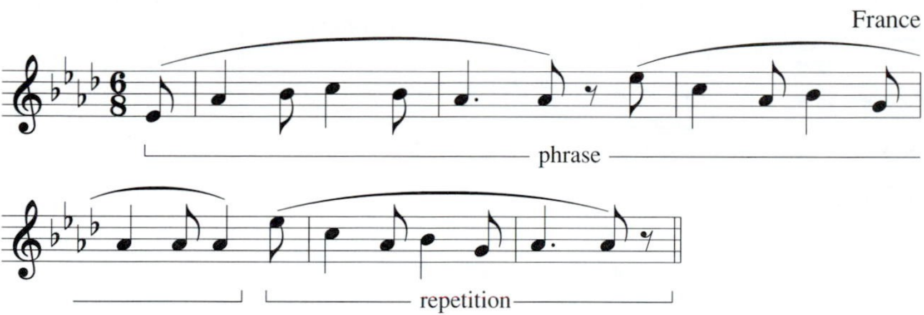

Exact repetition of an *entire* phrase is not extension. Since a phrase and its repetition are considered a single phrase, they cannot be considered a period.

2. Evade the cadence at the end of the phrase, allowing the melody to continue further to the ultimate cadence.

FIGURE 15.2

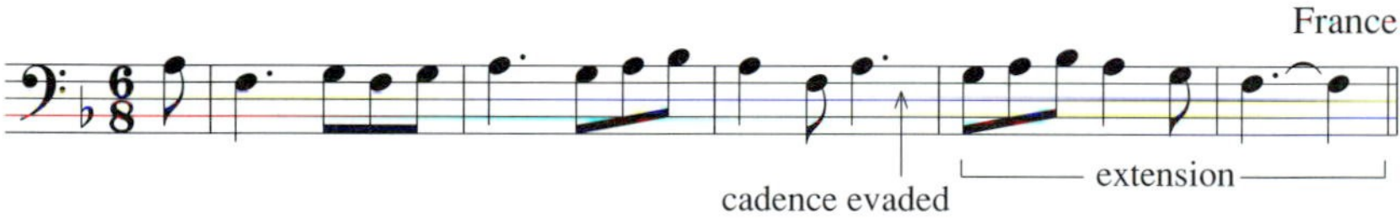

Without the evasion and extension, this phrase might have appeared as a normal four-measure phrase.

FIGURE 15.3

3. Use a sequential pattern during the course of the phrase.

FIGURE 15.4

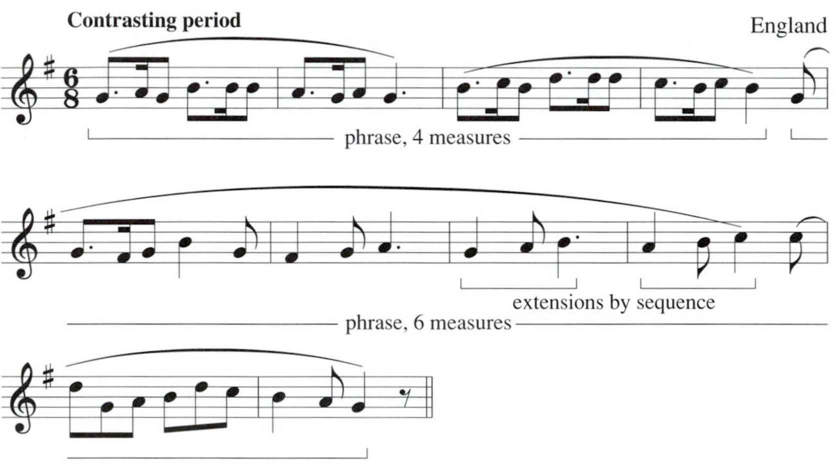

Without the two measures of sequence, the consequent phrase would be a four-measure phrase.

FIGURE 15.5

Observe, however, that a sequence in itself does not necessarily indicate the presence of an extension. A "normal" four-measure phrase may contain a sequence, as shown in Figure 7.10.

4. Lengthen by adding measures.

FIGURE 15.6

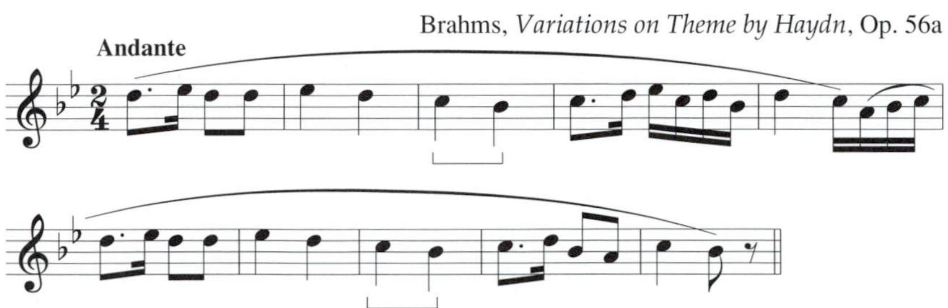

5. Add another motive to the phrase.

FIGURE 15.7

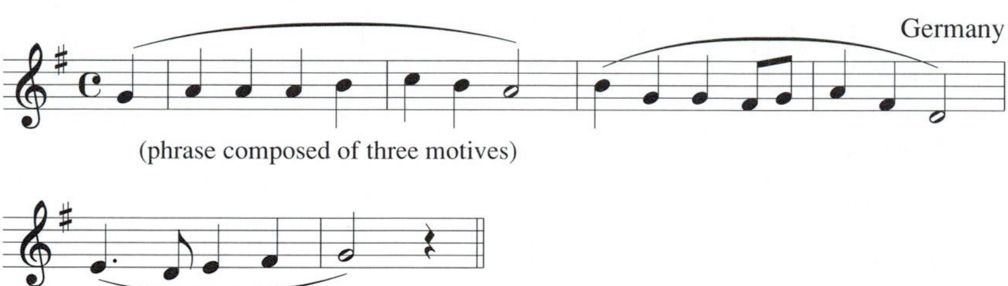

6. Occasionally, phrases may be more or less than four measures in length. The following is a six-measure phrase, made up of two three-measure motives.

FIGURE 15.8

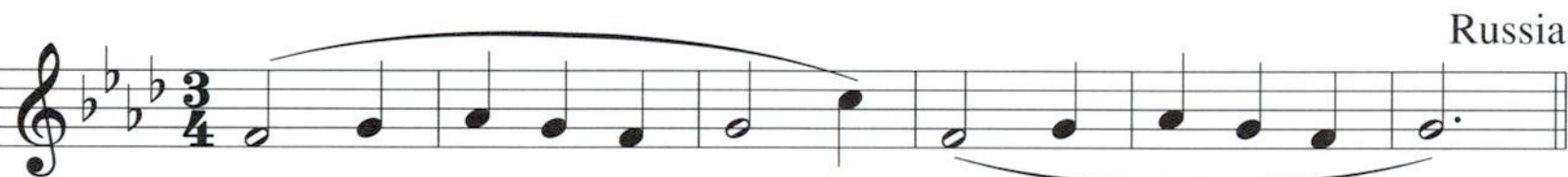

In some instances, a two-measure phrase or an eight-measure phrase may be considered a regular phrase length.

a. When the tempo is very fast or when each measure contains only a few notes, an eight-measure phrase may be considered regular. The extremely rapid tempo of Figure 15.9 (one beat to the measure) produces a phrase of only eight beats in eight measures, comparable in sound to four measures of two beats each.

CD FIGURE 15.9

b. When the tempo is very slow or when each measure contains many notes, a two-measure phrase may be considered regular. In Figure 15.10, the extremely slow tempo allows the completion of a phrase in a two-measure span.

FIGURE 15.10

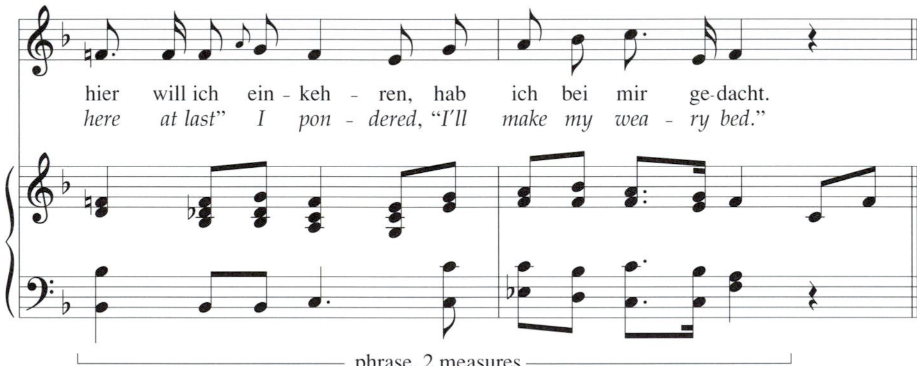

The Phrase Group and the Double Period

Two other forms, each larger than the period, can be constructed by the addition of phrase lengths.

1. The *phrase group* consists of three or more phrases (very often three), each of which differs melodically from the others. Usually, each of the first two phrases ends with a half cadence or an imperfect cadence, and the last phrase ends with a perfect cadence. Any or all phrases of a phrase group may be lengthened by extension.

FIGURE 15.11

2. The *double period* consists of two periods. From its name, you might guess that each of the periods is the same as the period you have already studied, but that is not the case. In the double period, there is but one perfect cadence, at the very end of the form.

The first eight-measure group (two phrases) looks and sounds like a period until its cadence, which is an imperfect or a half cadence. Of course, this temporary stop is necessary or there would be no double period, only two successive periods. The beginning of the second period is usually the same as or similar to that of the first period, and the last phrase can recall the second phrase or show all new material.

Figure 15.12 is a diagram of the music in Figures 15.13 and 15.14.

FIGURE 15.12

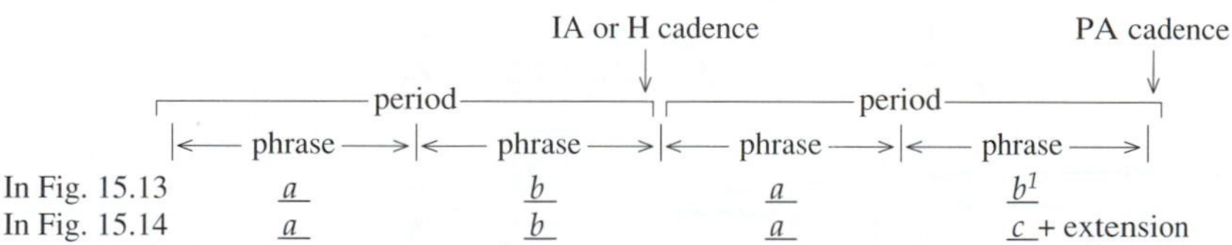

The italicized letters denote similar and dissimilar phrases. The two *a*'s indicate that those two phrases are identical, and the letter *b* indicates different material from *a,* with *b′* differing slightly from *b*. In this particular double period (Figure 15.13), measure 8 shows the "connecting link" between phrases (compare with Figure 7.6).

FIGURE 15.13

The double period of Figure 15.14 follows the basic structure just shown but with a difference: The fourth phrase is new material, marked *c,* and includes an extension.

FIGURE 15.14

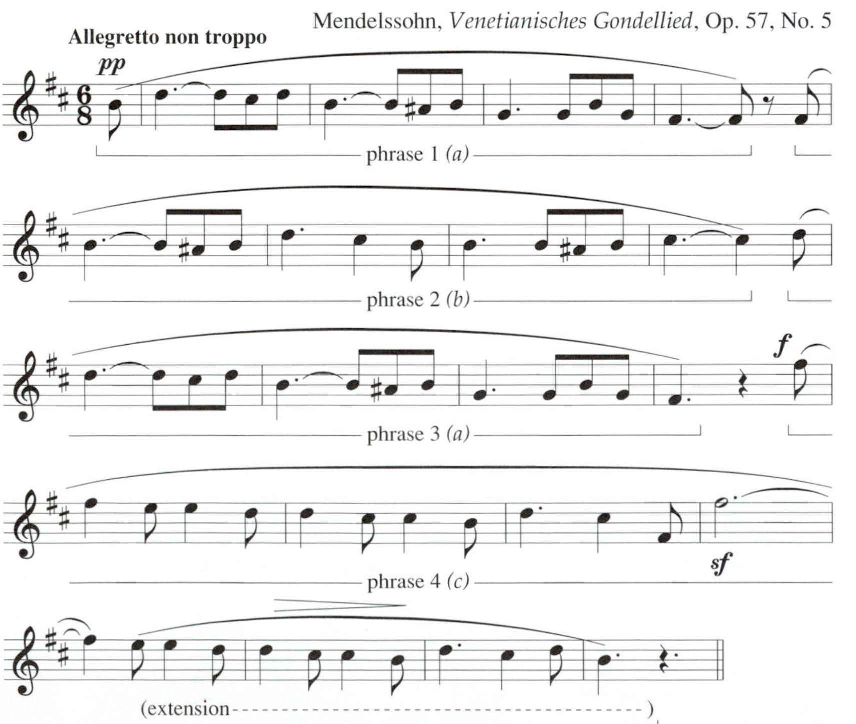

Extension in Motivic Development

Extensions are often used for the development of a melodic idea from the principal part of the phrase. In the next example, from Haydn's *Quinten* (*Fifths*) Quartet, the consequent phrase of the period shows a rather long extension, used to develop a motivic idea from measure 3. First this three-note idea is repeated in sequence, either exact or modified. The climax note, d^3, then turns down stepwise, as a two-note figure. This figure, in turn, is repeated four times, leading to the final two measures of the basic four-measure phrase.

FIGURE 15.15

ASSIGNMENT 15.1 *Analysis of form.* Analyze the form of each of the following examples. After placing phrase marks over each phrase or motive, supply the following information:

1. The beginning and the ending of each phrase
2. The form of the entire melody
3. The location and description of extensions
4. The location of any phrases other than those of four-measure length
5. The location of any idea later developed and a description of the process of development

(1)

Germany

(2)
Poland
(3)
England
(4)
Haydn, Sonata in E Minor for Piano, Hob. XVI:30
Molto vivace
(5)
Tchaikovsky, Piano Trio, Op. 50
Andante con moto
p

(6)

Mendelssohn, Symphony No. 3 (Scottish), Op. 56
Andante con moto
p
sf
p
p
sf
p
dim.
pp

(7)

Mozart, Trio in B♭, K. 502
Allegretto
p
f

(8)

In Appendix E: Answers to (1) and (2) are given.

Harmonizing a Melody without Lead Sheet Symbols

Up to this point, you have studied the harmonization of a folk-type melody in two ways.

1. At the keyboard, you have used lead sheet symbols. Since the harmony was given and a harmonic tone was found on each strong beat, little or no attention to the function of the nonharmonic tones was necessary.
2. In written work in chorale style, you have chosen the harmony, one chord for each melody note.

The object of the next study is to develop the ability to choose for yourself a satisfactory harmonization for melodies other than those in chorale style and without the assistance of lead sheet symbols. To help accomplish this, you must consider two factors, *tempo* and *harmonic rhythm.* Then you must determine whether certain melody tones are more satisfactory as harmonic tones or as nonharmonic tones in relation to the chosen accompanying harmony.

Tempo How fast or how slow should this tune be performed? You might think that slower would be easier, but that is not necessarily so. The slower the tempo, the more chords per measure (usually) will be required; the faster the tempo, the fewer will be required. In Figure 15.16, the melody to be harmonized has been given three different tempo markings to illustrate the effect on chord selection. If this melody is marked *very slow,* as in *a,* then the tempo is felt as six beats per measure, indicating the desirability of changing the chord on each of those beats where a change of melody note occurs. In the more common moderate tempo, *b,* the chord changes are more likely to occur on the strong beats of the measure, in this case two beats per measure. When the tempo is rapid, one chord per measure often suffices, as in *c.*

CD FIGURE 15.16

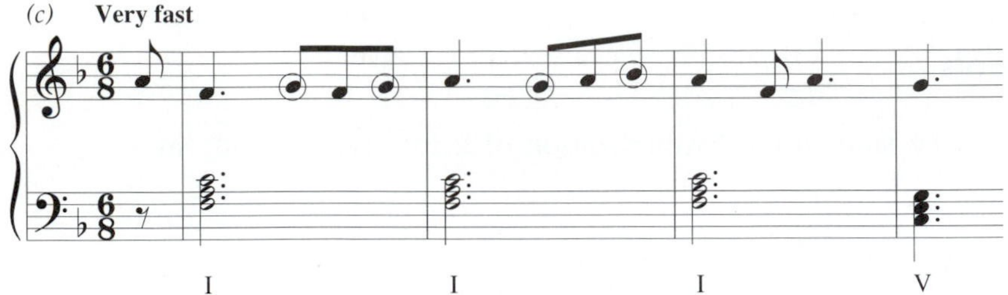

It cannot be specifically stated how slow or fast the tempo must be before the frequency of chord changes can be determined. This can be determined only by careful study of the melody and applying one's own aesthetic judgment.

Harmonic Rhythm Harmonic rhythm is the rhythmic pattern established when the durations of the chords are expressed as note values. In Figure 15.17, each chord in the chorale has a duration of one beat in $\frac{4}{4}$ time, so the harmonic rhythm pattern is simply a series of quarter notes.

FIGURE 15.17

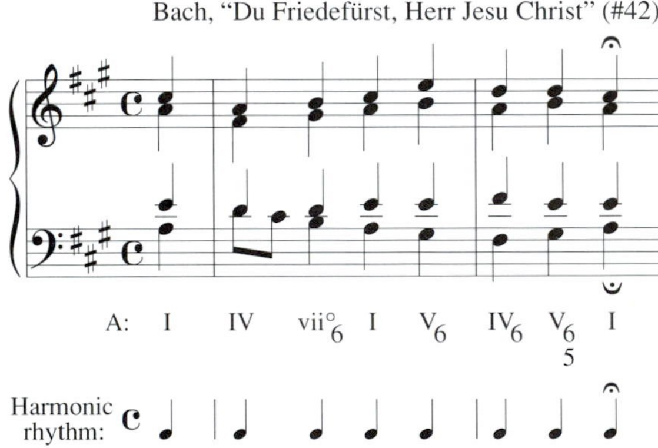

It is also possible for music to cover several measures with no change of harmony at all, resting in a harmonic rhythm pattern of a single long-held note.

FIGURE 15.18

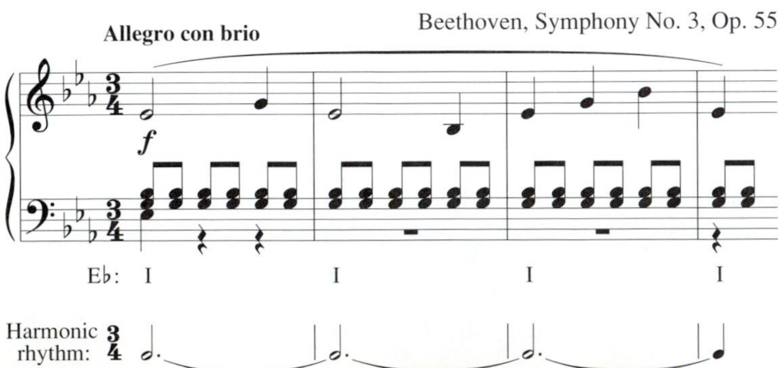

These are extremes in the application of harmonic rhythm. More common are patterns in which the harmonic rhythm changes in a more irregular manner.

FIGURE 15.19

Typical harmonic rhythm patterns show these characteristics:

1. Chords may be changed on any beat of the measure.
2. When a change of chord appears on a strong beat of the measure, it may extend into following beats.
3. When a change of chord appears on a weak beat or part of a beat, it should not be repeated on the following stronger beat; instead, a new chord should appear.
4. When a change of bass note appears on a weak beat of a measure, this note is not repeated on the following strong beat even for a new chord (Figure 15.20).

FIGURE 15.20

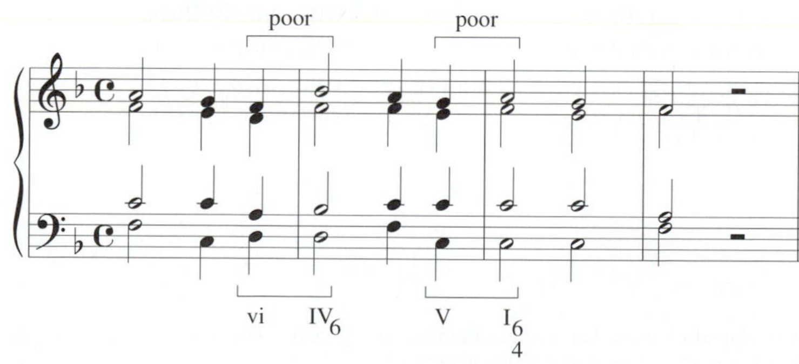

An exception occurs when a new phrase or motive begins on a strong beat, in which case the harmony of the previous weak beat may be repeated.

FIGURE 15.21

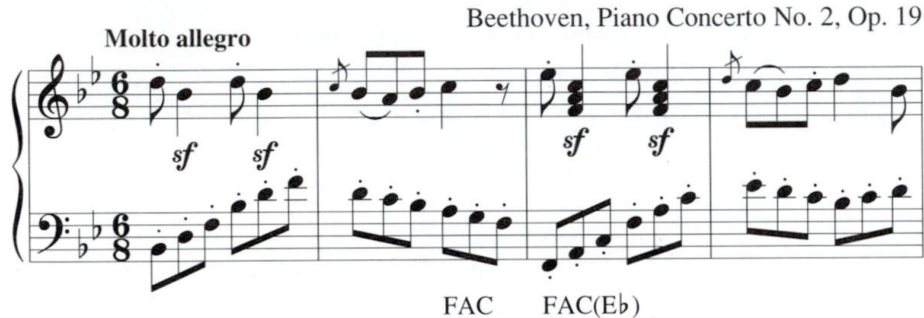

The *upbeat* to a phrase is treated in a special way. Commonly, there is no harmony at all.

FIGURE 15.22

But if the upbeat to the phrase is harmonized, the harmony may be repeated or changed on the strong beat that follows.

The following melody has been harmonized in two different ways to show the effect of both incorrect and correct applications of the principles of harmonic rhythm. Although the chord succession in both is satisfactory, observe how in harmonization *a* several chords appearing for the first time on weak beats are held over into strong beats, creating a rhythmic effect called *syncopation,*[1] which is generally avoided in harmonic rhythm.

[1]Syncopation results when stress is placed on weak beats rather than on strong beats. This is often accomplished by accenting a weak beat or tying a weak beat into a strong beat.

FIGURE 15.23

Differentiating Chord Tones and Nonharmonic Tones More often than not, a specific chord tone will appear on each strong beat of the measure, with nonharmonic tones between. In choosing the harmonic movement from chord to chord, be sure to use the chart of chord progressions on page 208. At times though, an accented nonharmonic tone will appear.

The melody line of Figure 15.24, the second phrase of a folk tune, demonstrates this problem. Here, on the first beat of each measure, we have chosen a chord that includes the soprano note. The result is less than successful. Why? (1) The V–IV progression is less effective than the common V^7–I. (2) Although escaped tones can be acceptable, they are not commonly used. (3) The approach and resolution of an escaped tone in the same direction, rather than the usual change of direction, makes their use even less desirable.

FIGURE 15.24

Since I is a better resolution for V^7, the *first* note of measure 2 must be a nonharmonic tone, and it is—an appoggiatura, repeated in measure 3, as in Figure 15.25.

FIGURE 15.25

When harmonizing a melody, always try different solutions. Often you will find that a note can be either harmonic or nonharmonic, as in Figure 15.26.

FIGURE 15.26

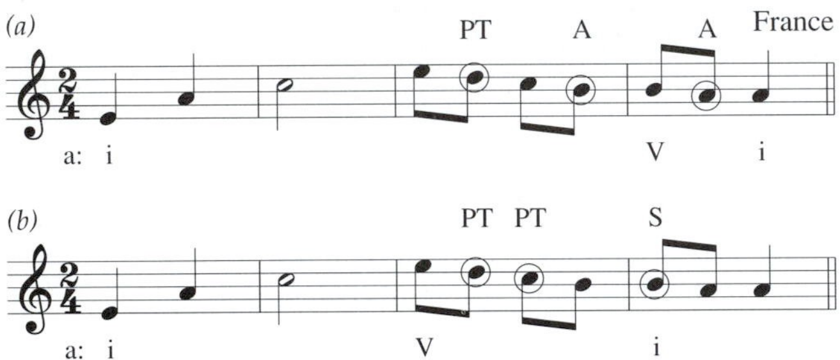

Application to the Keyboard

When you have determined the harmonic background of a melody, you can play it as though the lead sheet symbols were given. But what do you play when an accented nonharmonic tone sounds simultaneously with the strong beat of the measure?

Figure 15.27, which is the keyboard harmonization of Figure 15.25, shows how this is done. Usually the note after the dissonance is the chord tone. Choose the two notes that added to the melody triad tone will complete the desired triad. In measure 2 of Figure 15.27, the B♭ on the strong beat resolves to A. Since the triad is F A C, play the F and C of the triad with the B♭ of the melody. When the B♭ moves to A, the F A C will be complete.

FIGURE 15.27

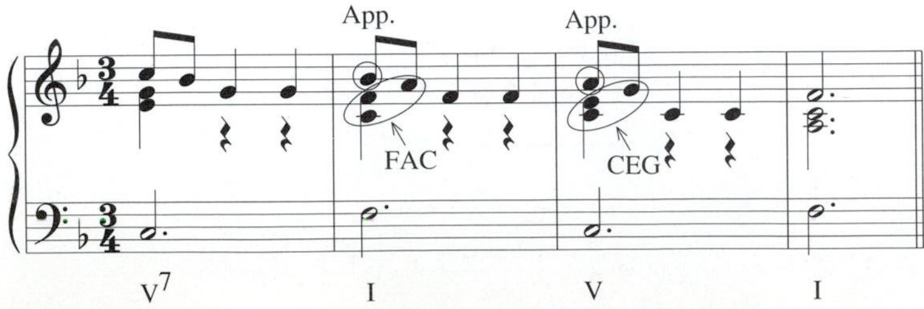

Here are the last two measures of Figure 15.26*b*.

FIGURE 15.28

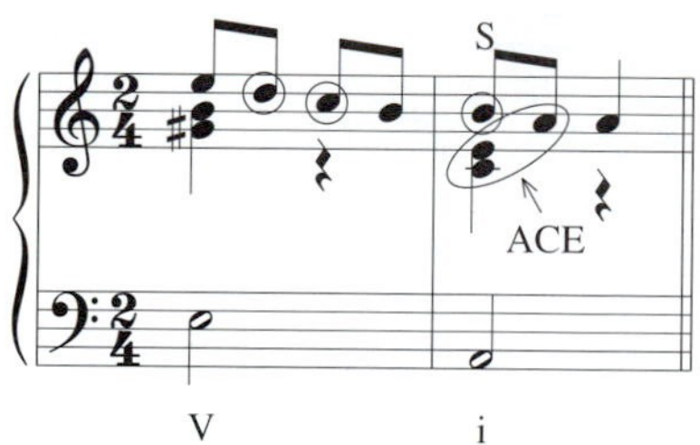

ASSIGNMENT 15.2 *Melody harmonization without lead sheet symbols.* These melodies are especially written to demonstrate nonharmonic accented tones, and each can be harmonized with I, IV, and V only. Assume that each melody is in a moderate tempo, each measure with the number of principal accents indicated by the time signature. Write the chord symbols below the melody. Circle and identify each nonharmonic tone.

Considerations for melody 1

Upbeat. No harmonization.

Measure 1. First note, F♯, does not imply IV as the following three notes imply I. F♯ is an upper neighbor.

Measure 2. For the first four notes, there are three choices: (1) V, each A is an UPT; (2) I, B is an UN and G♯ is a LN; (3) IV–I–V, B is an UN in IV, and A is an UPT in I progressing to B (V).

Measure 3. First note, G♯ does not imply V, since the following two notes would be a skip between dissonances. G♯ is a LN, and D is an App in I. In the last two beats, we need a V for the authentic cadence, so C♯ is a S and A is an APT.

In Appendix E: Answers to (1) and (2) are given.

ASSIGNMENT 15.3 Harmonize melodies using triads in addition to those of Assignment 15.2. Be sure that your choice of a harmony and its relation to its preceding and following chords adds up to a good harmonic progression (do not choose a chord only because it includes the melody tone).

The location of any of these—ii, iii, vi, and vii°—may not be obvious when a simpler harmony can be used at the same point. This melody, for example, can be harmonized with I and V only,

but a vi triad and ii, ii$_6$, or ii$^6_5$ can also be used.

For melody (1), the following are effective locations for vi, iii, and ii.

Measures 2–3: Do you remember learning about a good chord progression (other than I–V) for harmonizing $\hat{1}$–$\hat{7}$? (Review page 302.) That progression is I–iii. Following iii, harmonizing G with IV is a logical choice, making possible a plagal cadence. Also, measure 2 might be harmonized with vi, introducing the vi–iii–IV progression.

Measures 5–6: After the V^7 of measure 6, must we progress to I? Here is a place for the deceptive progression V–vi.

Measure 7: There are three E's. Three dominant chords would be correct but dull. What progression is commonly used to harmonize $\hat{2}$– $\hat{1}$ at the cadence? The progression is ii$^6_5$–V–I.

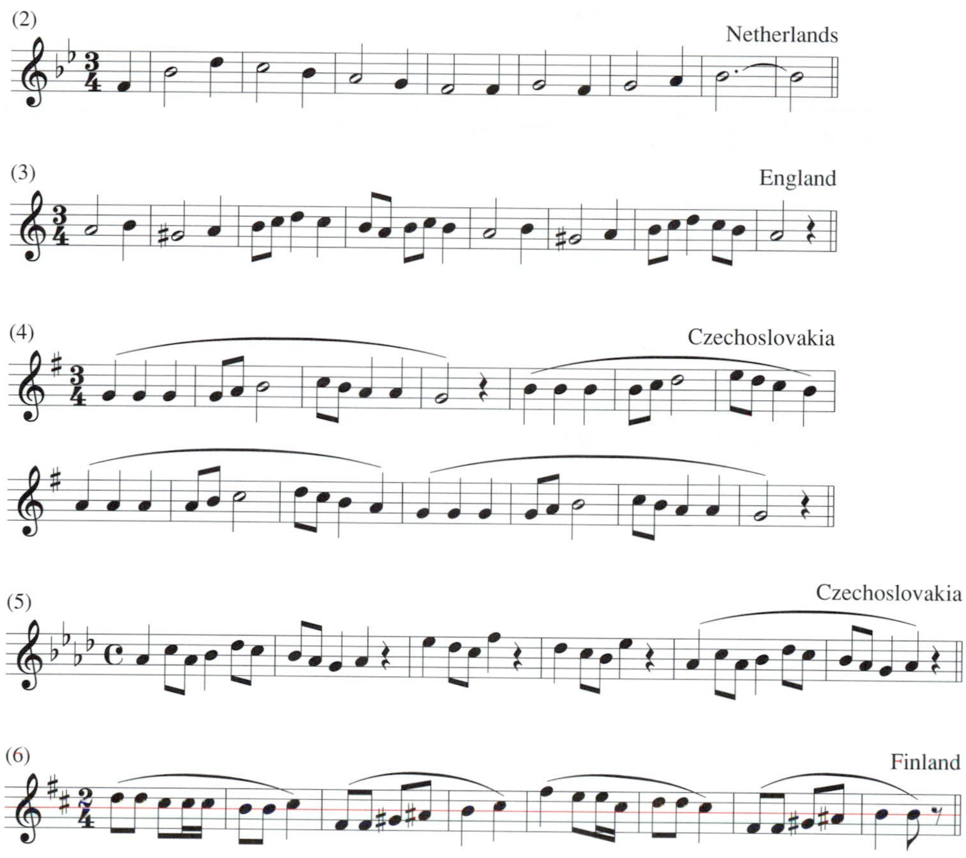

In Appendix E: The answer to (1) is given.

Melody Writing

In previous study and practice in melody writing (Chapter 7), you were limited to the simple phrase and period, and to the use of tonic and dominant implied harmony. The larger forms in this chapter, the addition of most of the diatonic triads, and your more complete knowledge of nonharmonic tones make possible the composition of melodies of considerably more musical interest.

Before beginning to write a melody, you should decide on the tempo. Will it be fast, medium, or slow? You will not be able to judge the harmonic implication of your melody without this pre-set condition. Knowing the tempo will also be a guide for the harmonic rhythm of your implied harmony.

In choosing the implied harmony, you should let the Table of Common Progressions (page 208) be your guide. If it will help, actually write the harmony, either by chord numbers or by block chords, on an extra bass staff.

Intervals larger than scale steps can now have several analytical implications:

1. The interval(s) may outline a chord. In most melodies, scale steps and small intervals predominate, as in Figure 15.29, which includes intervals implying the ii triad and the V^7 chord.

FIGURE 15.29

2. Melodies consisting predominantly of intervallic leaps can also be musically satisfactory. Note the use of sequence in this fugue subject.

FIGURE 15.30

3. Each note of the interval can represent a different chord (a chord change occurs as the interval is sounded).

FIGURE 15.31

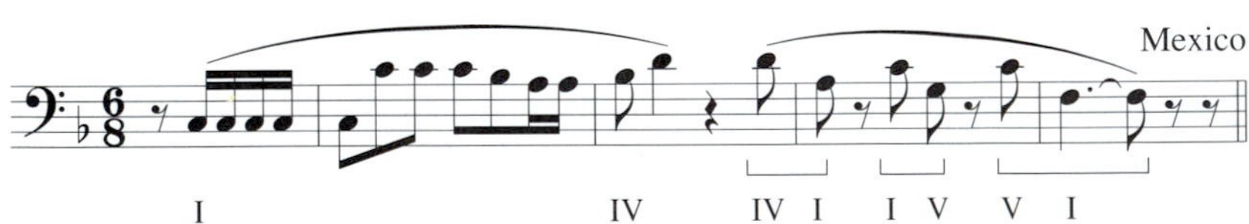

Two such leaps in the same direction are not common, but they can occur.

FIGURE 15.32

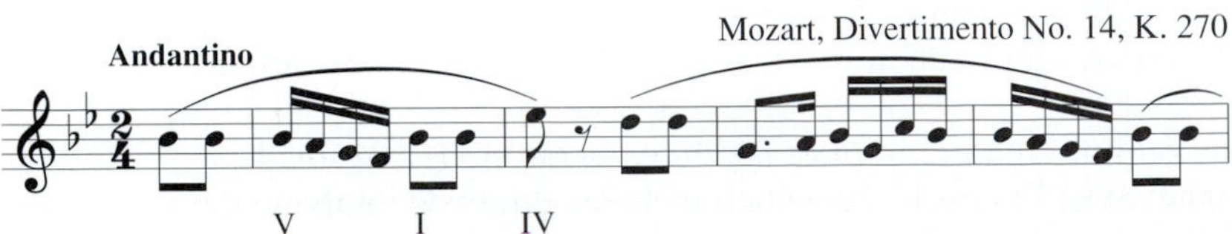

4. The interval may be a leap from a chord tone to a nonharmonic tone,

FIGURE 15.33

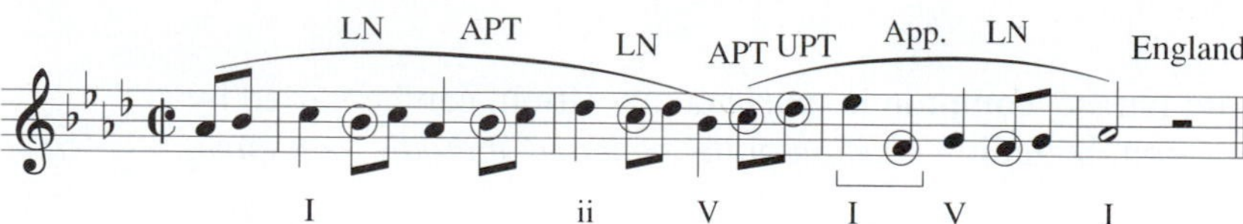

or, in the case of an escaped tone, from a nonharmonic tone to a harmonic tone.

FIGURE 15.34

5. In the melodic sequence, the same leap in successive figures may hold differing implications.

FIGURE 15.35

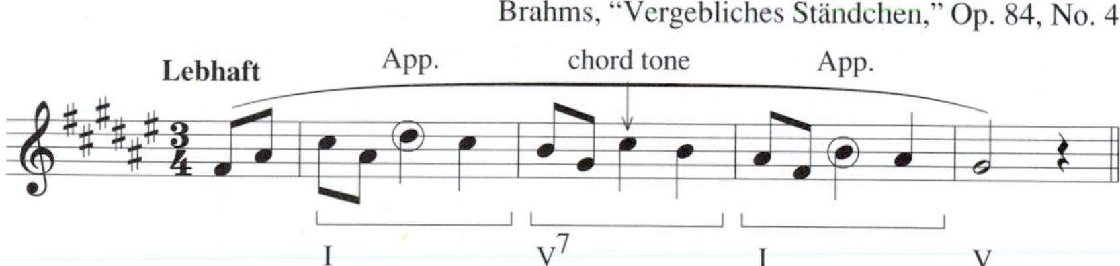

Extension in melodic writing is particularly important in that it helps to avoid the monotony of a constant four-measure metric repetition. When writing, review the various devices for extending a phrase as shown in the early pages of this chapter.

ASSIGNMENT 15.4 *Melody writing.* Write original melodies in various forms, as assigned. Use extensions and/or development of motive as studied in this chapter. Make a *complete analysis,* including *(a)* an analysis of the form, as shown in Figure 15.4; *(b)* an analysis of the implied harmony, as shown in Figure 15.33; *(c)* identification of nonharmonic tones; and *(d)* a description of any developmental procedures used.

If you are a "noncomposer," try making your melodies simple and folklike. Do not try for many ideas in a short space; one idea is usually enough—for example, a good melodic sequence will supply sufficient interest to a four-measure phrase. Do not be discouraged by early efforts. Unless you are lucky, some or much rewriting is usually necessary—even Beethoven had to do it!

Summary

Form The four-measure phrase, common in music composition, can be varied by several methods of extension, including *evasion of the cadence, melodic sequence,* and *added motives.*

The development of an idea found within a phrase often leads to a lengthy extension of that phrase.

Phrases may also be composed of two three-measure motives or three two-measure motives.

The *phrase group* usually consists of three phrases, each melodically different, and with a perfect authentic cadence at the end of the third phrase.

The *double period* consists of two periods (four phrases). Unlike a single period, the first period of a double period ends with a cadence other than a perfect authentic cadence. The third phrase is often the same as or similar to the first phrase, and the fourth phrase, similar to or different from the second phrase, ends with a perfect authentic cadence.

Melody Harmonization and Composition Successful melody harmonization depends upon knowing which tones are harmonic and which are nonharmonic. The tempo chosen for the harmonization will influence chord choice, and chord choice in turn must meet the requirements of good harmonic rhythm.

Harmonic rhythm is defined as the rhythm pattern established when the durations of the chords are expressed as note values.

Success in melody writing also depends upon consideration of the tempo and the rhythm of the implied harmony. Application of newly gained knowledge of harmonic and nonharmonic materials will aid in producing original melodies of greater musical interest than heretofore.

ARTICLE #11

Another Metrical Concept

If one were accustomed only to music in the style of the common practice period and acquainted with meter and rhythm only as they are presented in Chapter 3 of this text, one might believe that all music is made up of regularly recurring measure lengths, each with regularly recurring strong and weak beats. Although such metrical patterns have been used since early times in music meant for dancing or marching, compositions of the greatest composers of the fifteenth and sixteenth centuries often display a metrical system markedly different from these.

These composers, who were to their period what Bach and Beethoven were to the Baroque and Classical periods, made their greatest accomplishments in vocal contrapuntal music. This style is based on the simultaneous sounding of two to eight, and sometimes more,* independent melodic lines. In pre-seventeenth-century practice, each of these lines was written as a separate score, as are band and orchestra parts today. Also, these voice lines were written without bar lines, as shown in this example of the beginning of the bass and tenor lines from a three-voice work by Palestrina.

Palestrina, Missa, *O Regem coeli*

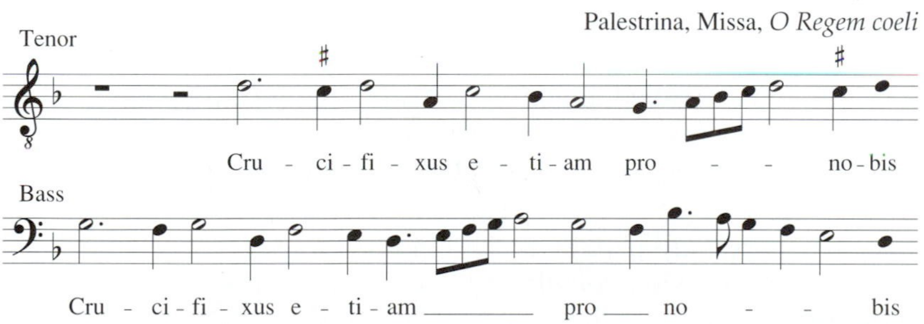

Vocal performers in the fifteenth and sixteenth centuries, like instrumental musicians today, read their parts without visual reference to the parts for other voices; this is in contrast to today's full choral scores. And yet, without such reference and without bar lines, how was the meter determined by the performer? It was done by observing the natural accents of the text.

> Crú- ci- fí- xus é- ti- ám pro nó- bis
> (He was crucified for us)

In the music, each of these implied accents marks the beginning of a metrical group, and each group may be of like or different length from the previous or following group. If we place a bar line and an appropriate time signature

*For instance, the motet *Spem in alium,* by Thomas Tallis (ca. 1550), is written for eight five-voice choirs, for a total of forty independent melodic lines.

before each accented note, each voice will consist of measures showing differing numbers of beat durations (and hence differing time signatures), and the resulting bar lines of the two voices will not always coincide.

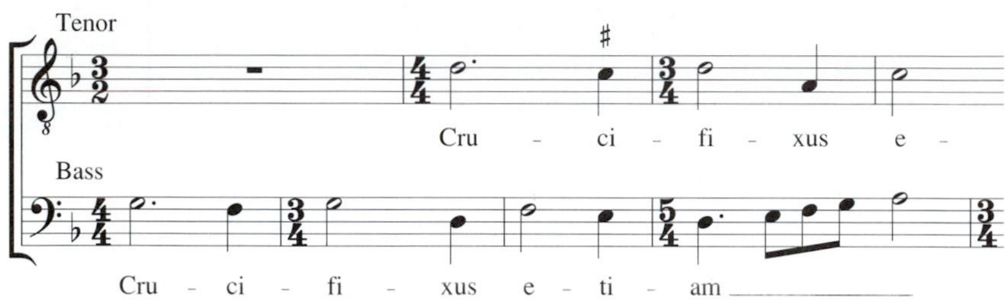

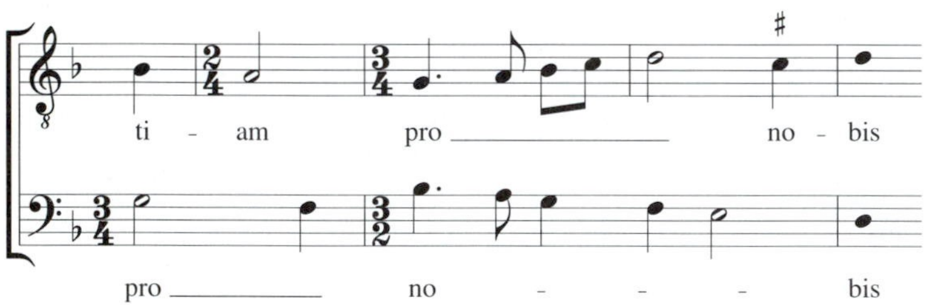

Observe that the accented syllables usually appear on a longer note value or at the beginning of a *melisma* (a group of notes on one syllable) longer than the previous note value. Accents such as these are caused by the relationship of long and short note values and are called *agogic* accents. In the preceding illustration, the only exception is the penultimate note in the tenor voice, a strong syllable on a metrically weak note to allow for a cadence on the next beat.

Modern editions of this early music are usually barred in the same way as today's music, that is, in measures of equal length. In the complete score for three voices shown below, one can see that the bar lines are at odds with the actual fluctuating meters, thus often giving the impression of syncopation (and, unfortunately, often performed as such). Look now at the alto voice to determine the location of the accents and the duration of each metric group. Also, observe the rhythmic freedom of each individual voice line and the

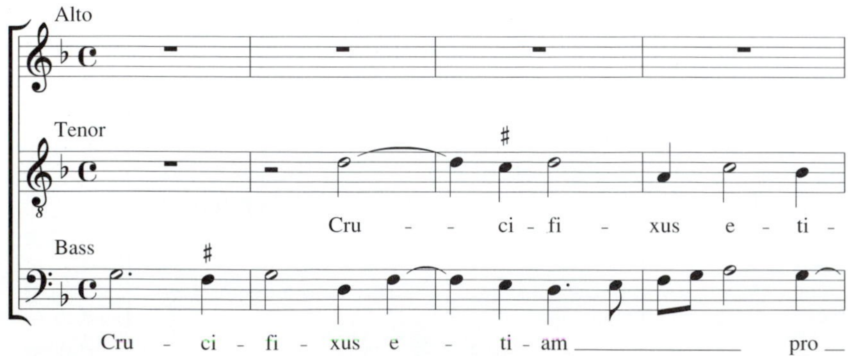

nonconformity of the agogic accents in all the voices, which give this music its particular charm in a performance and lend it an effect generally absent from most of the music of the seventeenth through nineteenth centuries.

The accidentals *above* certain notes in this example are indications of *musica ficta (false music).* Before the sixteenth century, many chromatic alterations were not written in the music on the assumption that the performer knew where they were needed. In modern editions of this early music, accidentals are placed above the notes to indicate the probable use of *musica ficta.*

Use of the regularly recurring bar line, so common in music of the seventeenth through nineteenth centuries, is often referred to as the "tyranny of the bar line." Harking back to sixteenth-century rhythmic practice, twentieth-century composers have broken this tyranny in many ways, one of them being the use of successions of measures in differing time signatures. Another method, as shown in the following example, is the use of beaming and dynamic markings. Time signatures have been added in parentheses above the staff to show an interpretation of the actual meter changes.

Bartók, Quartet No. 4
f sf
sf
sf
sf
simile
sf
sf
sf
sf
sf
sf
sf

16

The v and VII Triads; the Phrygian Cadence

The v and VII triads, together with the little-used vi° and III+, the last of the diatonic triads, occur exclusively in the minor mode. The Phrygian cadence also finds more use in minor than in major.

The Minor Dominant Triad (v)

Since you are now well informed about the function of the sixth and seventh scale steps in minor, the reason for the triad spelling D F A in G minor seen in Figure 16.1 should be quite clear to you. The descending line in the alto, $\hat{8}\,\hat{7}\,\hat{6}\,\hat{5}$, requires the spelling G F E♭ D. Therefore, when the descending F (♭$\hat{6}$) coincides with the dominant triad, the result is a minor dominant triad or minor-five, D F A.

FIGURE 16.1

Since v includes ♭7, the chord following v must contain ♭6, usually VI or iv. If the progression were v–i, ♭$\hat{7}$ would ascend, a characteristic not of the minor mode but of three of the medieval modes (see Appendix D).

In Figure 16.2, the line $\hat{7}\,\hat{6}\,\hat{5}$ is in a different voice, which you should be able to locate easily. Also, measures 1–2 are obviously in D minor (i). How do you analyze the nonharmonic tones in the piano right hand?

FIGURE 16.2

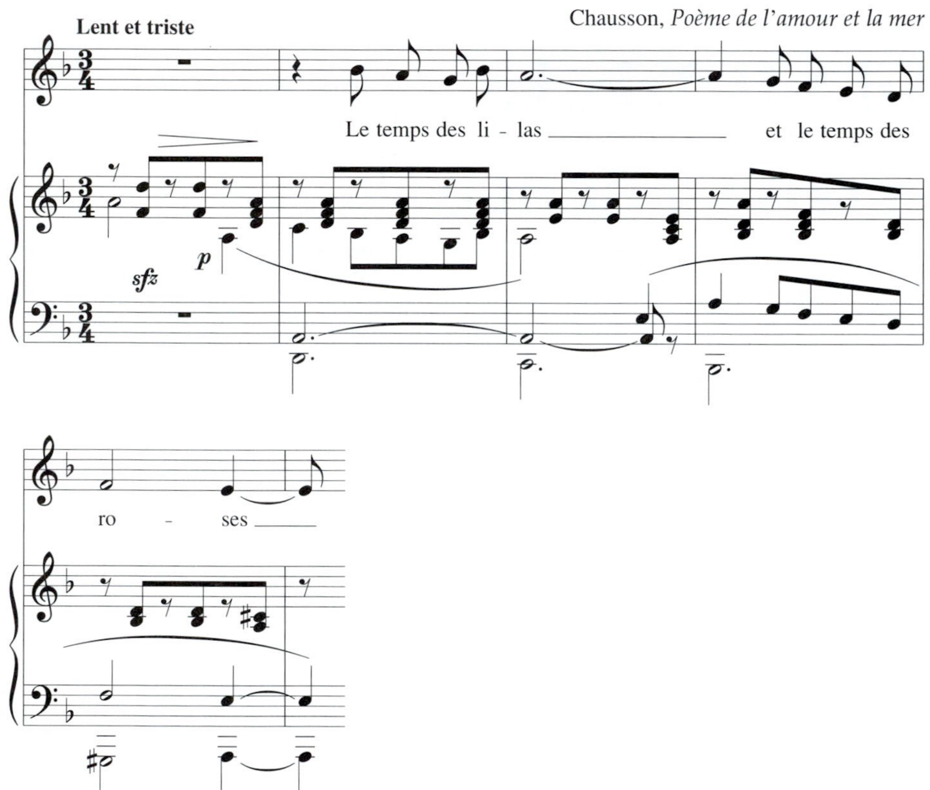

An interesting sonority includes the use of ♯$\hat{7}$ and ♭$\hat{7}$ simultaneously. This can occur when two voice lines, both using $\hat{7}$, move in contrary motion. In Figure 16.3, the descending appoggiatura F♮ sounds at the same time as the ascending triad tone F♯.

FIGURE 16.3

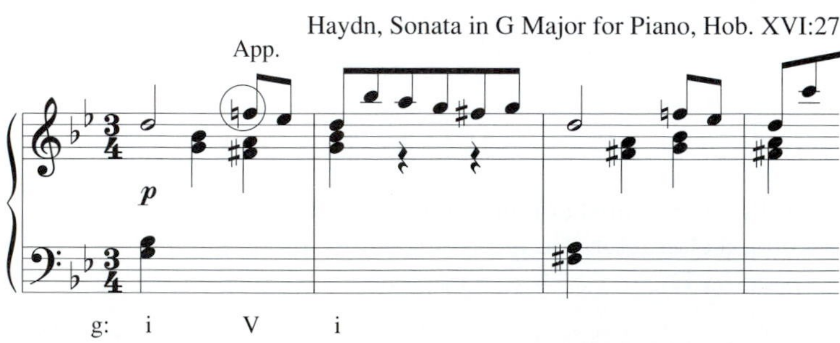

In a more unusual instance (Figure 16.4), both ♯$\hat{7}$ and ♭$\hat{7}$ could be considered chord tones. The dissonance of the sonority is compounded by the use of tonic pedal.

FIGURE 16.4

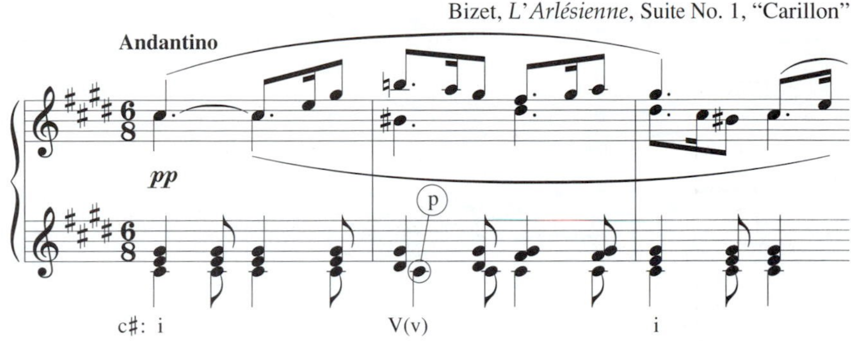

Passages employing ♯6 and ♭6 simultaneously are far less frequent. In Figure 16.5, we see this usage in E minor. While C (♭$\hat{6}$) is held, C♯ (♯$\hat{6}$) in the ascending scale line sounds against it. Since the second violin can sustain the sound of C♮, the clash against C♯ will be distinctly audible. The harmony is V^9 (B D♯ F♯ A C). In this case, the dissonance, C, can be considered an appoggiatura against the passing tone C♯.

FIGURE 16.5

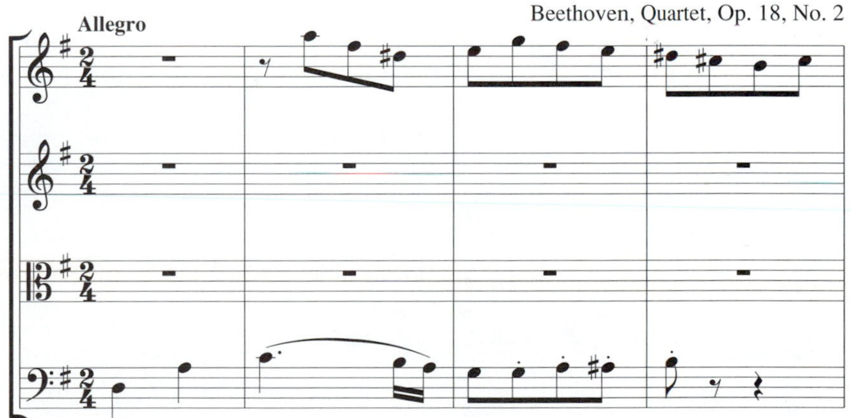

The Subtonic Triad (VII)

In minor keys, the triad built on the subtonic, ♭7̂ (C minor: VII = B♭ D F), does not function as does vii°, built on the leading tone. Usually the root of VII moves down a perfect fifth to III. Play or listen to Figure 16.6 where VII begins a progression whose roots are a fifth apart, VII–III–VI–ii°, and, with an interrupting tonic, to V. Play again, stopping at the third chord. Does this III sound as if it might be tonic? That is because VII–III has the same property as V–I, a root movement down a perfect fifth from a major triad to another major triad (or to a minor triad).

FIGURE 16.6

Now review Figures 10.2 and 10.3 (pages 206 and 208). How many pairs of successive triads have this same characteristic? VII–III and III–VI in minor keys are the only ones, except for V–I(i).

When a chord progression other than V–I(i) suggests that its second triad could be tonic (however briefly), the first triad is called a *secondary dominant.* This term is ordinarily used when a triad other than a major triad is altered to become a major triad, such as C: D F♯ A–G B D, where, in a process called *tonicization,* the first triad assumes a dominant-like function to tonicize the second triad. The study of secondary dominants is continued in Chapter 18.

So VII–III and III–VI present dual auditory impressions: (1) a simple diatonic progression in a key and (2) a tonicizing of the second triad. The use of VII as shown in Figure 16.6 is much less common than its use in a harmonic sequence (Chapter 17) or in a change of key, called *modulation* (Chapter 18). Note in the Handel example that the composer could have chosen to stay in F major from the third chord onward by considering the F major triad as tonic.

The Progression iv–VII

In a minor key, the root of iv is a perfect fifth above the root of VII, as indicated in the Table of Harmonic Progressions, Figure 10.3. Thus, iv is useful both in a iv–VII progression and in the common iv–V and IV–vii° progressions. Most commonly, iv–VII is used in the harmonic sequence, as shown in Figure 17.3b, but look for an example in Assignment 16.2.

The Triads vi° and III+

The use of vi° is very limited. In Figure 16.7, it harmonizes ♯$\hat{6}$. As a diminished triad, its use is in first inversion, and here it is found in a series of first inversions, i_6–vi°_6–vii°_6.

FIGURE 16.7

The only remaining triad, III+, is an augmented triad (C minor: E♭ G B). In most triad formations appearing to be augmented, the fifth (♯$\hat{7}$) is almost invariably and clearly a nonharmonic tone. An example of III+ used as a harmony can be seen in Figure 17.10.

Half Cadences; the Phrygian Cadence

Any diatonic triad except vii° and VII can precede the V triad to create a half cadence at an appropriate cadential point. Common are ii–V and IV–V, in both major and minor. One of these, iv_6–V, carries a special designation, the Phrygian cadence. In this cadence, the soprano ascends by whole step while the bass descends by half step, a characteristic of the Phrygian mode (Figure 16.8*a* and Appendix D). The cadence is shown in two versions in Figure 16.8*b* and *c*. The cadence at *c* is considered Phrygian even though the half- and whole-step arrangment is reversed.

FIGURE 16.8

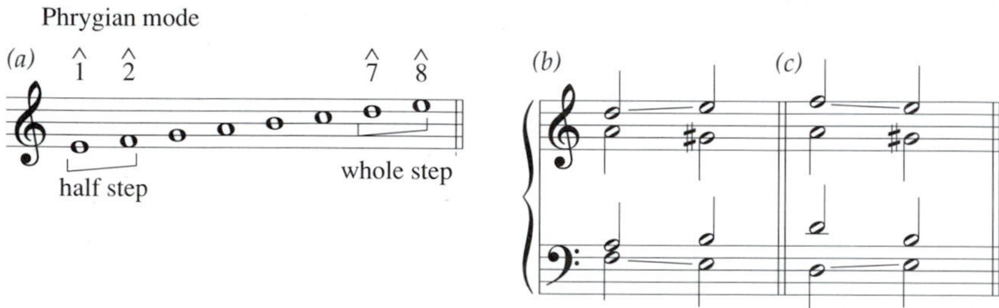

FIGURE 16.9

The part-writing of measure 1 in Figure 16.9 is worth noting. The soprano and tenor voices are mirror images of each other, each using the same contour but in opposite directions. Also, the alto and the tenor are in thirds for three beats, then immediately the bass is in thirds with the alto. The part-writing uses unconventional procedures to accommodate the superior interest of the melodic lines.

Figure 16.10, written in the Phrygian mode, shows the cadence of Figure 16.8*c* used as the final cadence of a chorale. To most people, whose ears are accustomed to major and minor tonality, this final cadence sounds incomplete.

FIGURE 16.10

The Phrygian cadence exists also in a major key as ii_6–III. The III triad in a major key is usually considered a secondary dominant chord (Chapter 18), but as a member of the Phrygian cadence it usually returns directly to tonic.

FIGURE 16.11

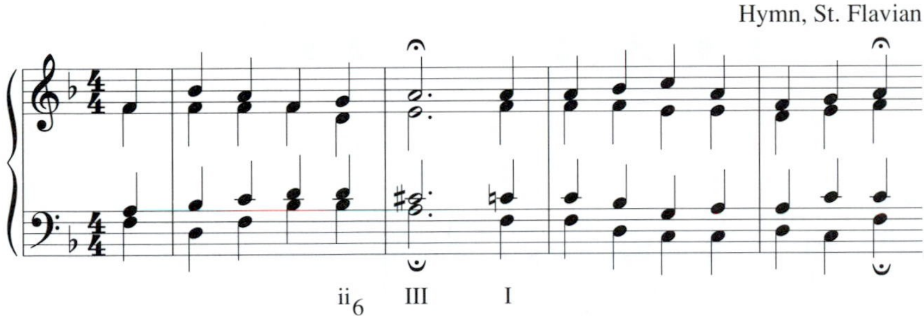

ASSIGNMENT 16.1 Spell the v triad and the VII triad in each minor key.

In the Workbook: Answers to the entire assignment are given.

ASSIGNMENT 16.2 *Harmonic analysis.* These excerpts contain examples of v, VII, and the simultaneous use of $\sharp\hat{7}$ and $\flat\hat{7}$. Discuss any other features of interest you may find.

(1)

(2)

Schubert, Waltz, D. 146, No. 15

(3)

Schubert, Sonata in B♭ Major for Piano, D. 960

(4) In measure 3, what is the complete spelling of the triad above each bass note?

Haydn, Sonata in B♭ Major for Piano, Hob. XVI:2

(CD) (5)

(CD) (6) In addition to the v and VII triads, look for III and for an uncommon use of the major tonic triad in a minor key. Also discover the various ways in which a series of first inversions is used, including the use of chromatic nonharmonic tones.

Writing the v and VII Triads in a Minor Key

No new part-writing procedures are required for either of these triads. Each triad contains a lowered seventh scale step. In the dominant minor triad (v), this tone must descend. In the VII triad, the lowered seventh scale degree assumes the role of the root of a secondary dominant chord; therefore, its properties are the same as those of the root of the dominant triad.

FIGURE 16.12

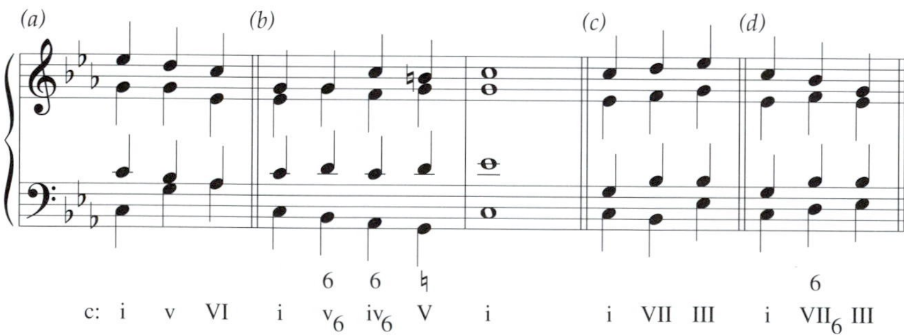

ASSIGNMENT 16.3 *Part-writing v and VII triads.* Fill in the alto and tenor voices. Make a harmonic analysis.

In Appendix E: Answers to (2), (6), and (7) are given.
In the Workbook: Answers to the entire assignment are given.

Writing the Phrygian Cadence

In the Phrygian cadence, the iv_6 triad can be written with any doubling.

FIGURE 16.13

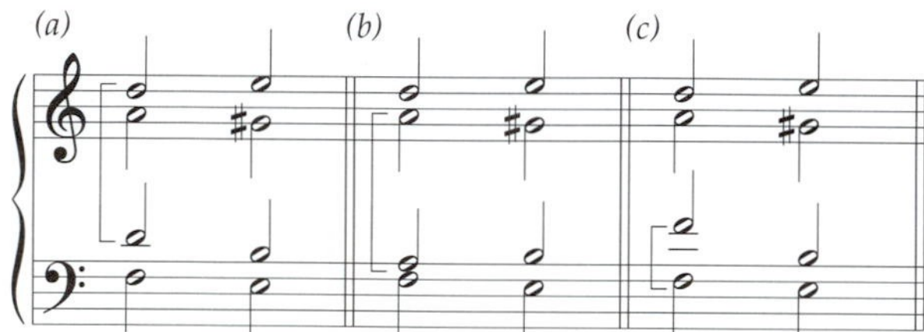

ASSIGNMENT 16.4 Write examples of Phrygian cadences. Try each of the doublings in Figure 16.13.

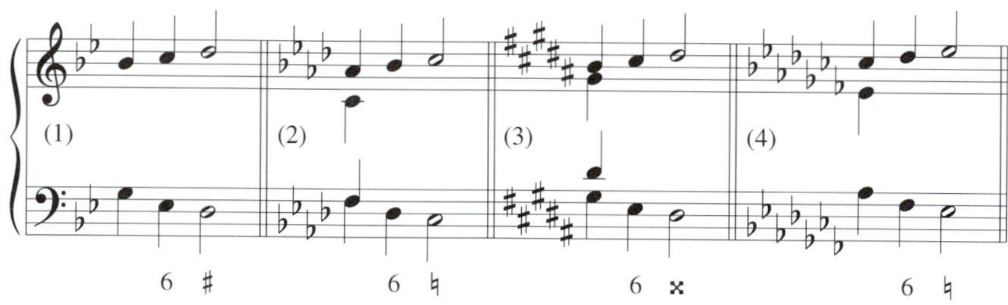

In Appendix E: Three versions of (1) are given.
In the Workbook: Answers to the entire assignment are given.

ASSIGNMENT 16.5 *Part-writing.* These exercises contain examples of many of the chord progressions and part-writing procedures studied up to this point. Fill in inner voices and make a harmonic analysis. Solve the exercises in open score, as assigned.

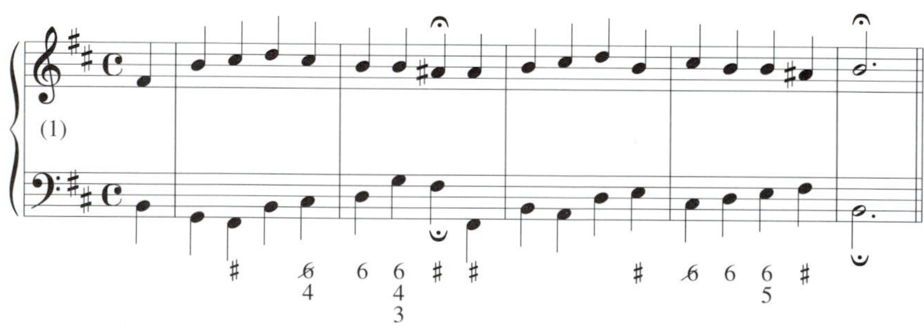

(2)
6 6 ♮ 6 6 4 ♮
♮ 8 6 ♮ 7 5 —
(3)
8 7 9 8 6 ♯ 5 — 7 6 5 6 ♯ 6
9 8 9 8 6 6 5 6 4 6 8 5 ♯ 7 4 —

(4)
6 9 8 4 3 9 5 6 — ♮ 6
♮ 4 3
9 8 8 7 8 7 5 6 5 — ♮
4 3 4 ♮ ♮ 4 — ♮
(5)
8 9 8 7 9 8 6 5 8 3 6 5 ♯
3 4 3 2 ♯ — 3 5
5 4 8 7 7 8 5 6 8 — — 7 ♯
3 2 3 2 5 6 6 7 5 4
♯ — 4 5 ♯ —

ASSIGNMENT 16.6 *Part-writing.* The bass voice only is given. Add soprano, alto, and tenor lines. Try for interesting inner voice lines, using part-writing procedures as required.

(2)
(3)

ASSIGNMENT 16.7 *Part-writing an unfigured bass.* In this type of problem, the bass line only is given, without figuration. It must be determined which triads are in inversion and which have the root in the bass. Many solutions are possible for each exercise, so try several and compare them with one another, finally selecting the most musical. Below are three of the possible figurations for the first two measures of exercise 1.

Keyboard Harmony

ASSIGNMENT 16.8 Play each of the following progressions in each minor key.

i–v–VI–iv(ii$^{\circ}_{6}$)–V–i
i–v$_6$–iv$_6$–V–i
i–VII–III–iv–V–i

ASSIGNMENT 16.9 Play this scale in any minor key.

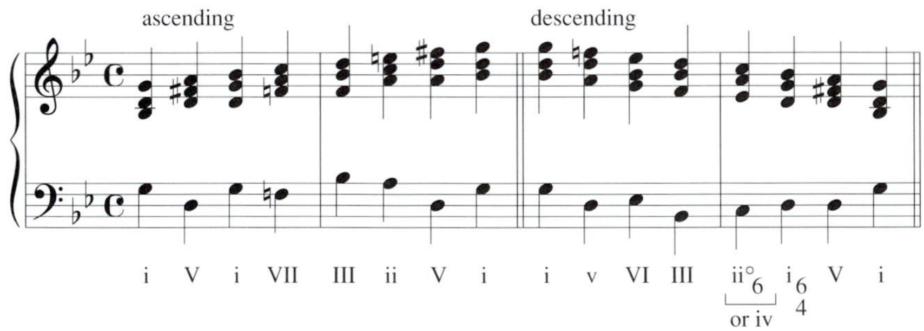

ASSIGNMENT 16.10 *Melody harmonization.* Three melodies are provided, one each for the v and VII triads and one for the Phrygian progression.

Summary

The *minor dominant triad* (v) is used in a minor key when $\flat\hat{7}$ in a voice line occurs at the same time as a dominant triad. Its usual resolution is to VI rather than to the tonic.

The VII triad is built on the $\flat\hat{7}$ of the minor scale. Its usual function is that of a dominant to III.

Other triads using $\hat{6}$ and $\hat{7}$ are vi° and III+. Both are used infrequently.

The progression iv$_6$–V in a minor key is known as a Phrygian cadence. The two outside voices of the cadence are the same as $\hat{2}$–$\hat{1}$ and $\hat{7}$–$\hat{8}$ of the Phrygian scale.

17

Harmonic Sequence

Mozart's arpeggiated passage in Figure 17.1 displays to perfection two important elements in tonal composition. One you already know, and the other you will probably guess from the title of this chapter. The chord symbols reflecting this harmonic progression are the clues to both.

FIGURE 17.1

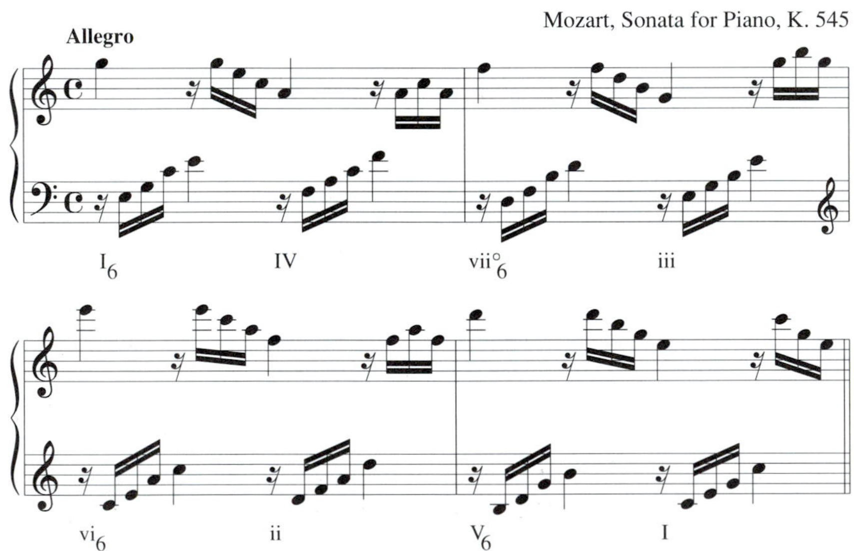

First, have you seen the progression before? It is the Harmonic Progression by Fifths in Major, Figure 10.2 (in minor, Fig. 10.3). The root movement in Figure 10.2 is identical to that in Figure 17.1.

Second, the Mozart example illustrates *harmonic sequence,* defined as a series of chords with a repeating pattern of root movements. Mozart's repeating pattern shows roots down a fifth, up a fourth, down a fifth, and so on.

FIGURE 17.2

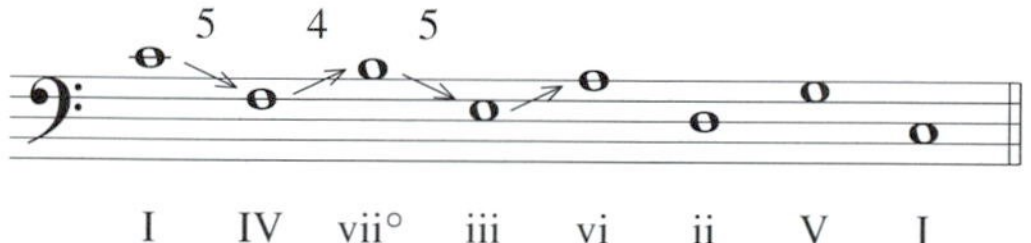

Have we described the same thing twice? Well, yes and no. The two analyses, root movement by fifth down and sequence by roots down a fifth and up a fourth, are a coincidence, since the fourth is the inversion of the fifth. This coincidence will not occur in other sequences.

Note also in Figure 17.1 that each pair of descending fifths—C–F, B–E, and so forth—is a second lower than the previous pair. We can identify this movement as a *sequence descending by seconds.*

Before investigating specific types of sequences, here are the general characteristics you should look for in harmonic sequences.

1. A minimum length for a harmonic sequence is four chords, the given intervallic relationship and one repetition.
2. The intervals of root movement refer to their letter-name sizes. Down a fifth from F could mean either B or B♭, according to the key.
3. Root movements not common otherwise are used freely, such as ii–vi and vii°–IV.
4. Any diminished triad may be used with its root in the bass.
5. In a minor key, use of the minor dominant (v) and the major subtonic (VII) is common.
6. The sequence need not begin or end on the tonic, though it frequently does.
7. Inversions may be used as long as the bass line itself displays a melodic sequence. In Figure 17.1, first inversion alternates with root position, so the bass line is always up a second and down a third.
8. The harmonic sequence is usually accompanied by melodic and rhythmic sequence in the upper voices.

The sequences to be described are the most common ones, but others do exist and are based on the same principles.

Sequence: Roots Down a Fifth and Up a Fourth (Descending by Seconds)

This is the sequence of Figure 17.1, shown in Figure 17.3 in block chords, roots in the bass. You should use these examples for keyboard practice.

FIGURE 17.3

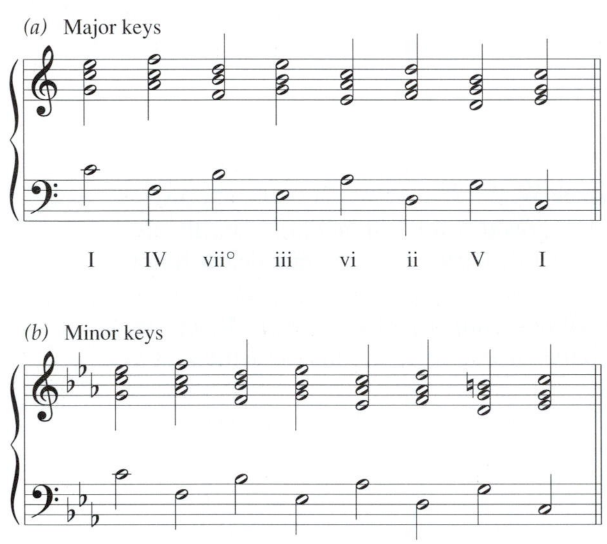

This sequence, highly developed in the Baroque era, has been an effective harmonic progression for centuries. Even today, if you listen carefully you will hear it in movie and TV scores, as well as in much popular and commercial music.

Figure 17.4, the same sequence in minor, shows a melodic bass line, the chord roots appearing at each first and third beat. Note also in measures 3 and 4 that there is a new melodic sequence in the treble clef, a feature of which is the highly decorated suspension in both upper voices.

FIGURE 17.4

Bach, *Well-Tempered Clavier*, Vol. 1, No. 2, BMV 847

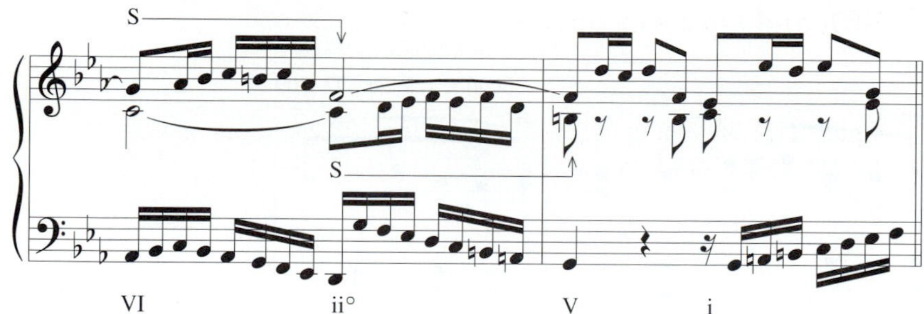

Sequence: Roots Up a Fifth and Down a Fourth (Ascending by Seconds)

This sequence is the reverse of the previous one. In fact, it is the movement *backward* through Harmonic Progressions by Fifths.

In minor keys, sequences other than down a fifth, up a fourth usually encounter difficulty at some point because of the conflict between the sixth and seventh scale steps. This sequence, up a fifth, down a fourth, is best limited in minor to that portion from VI to i.

FIGURE 17.5

(a) Major

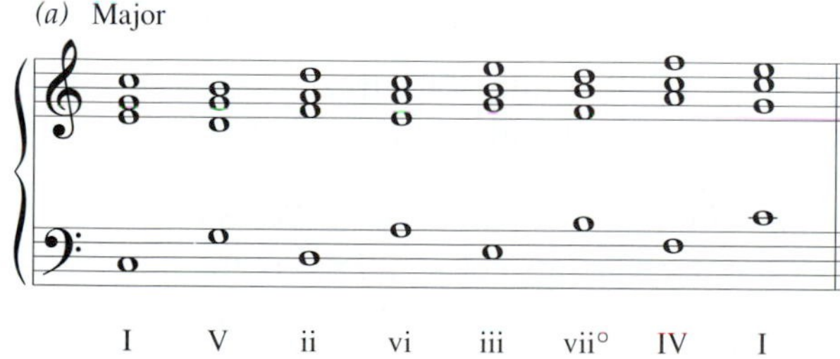

(b) Minor

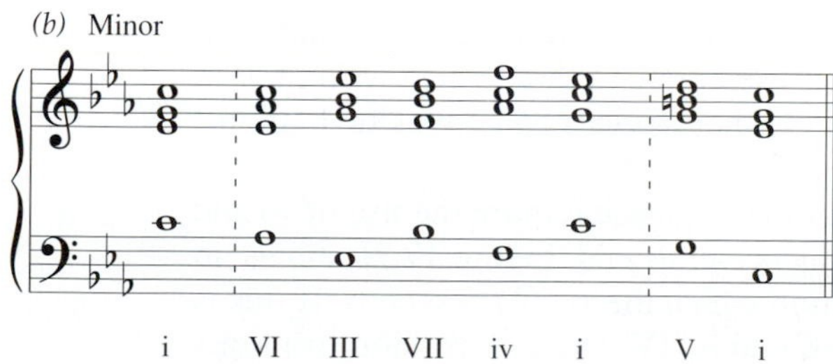

FIGURE 17.6

Sequence: Roots Down a Third and Up a Fourth (Ascending by Seconds)

This sequence is often called an "ascending 5 6" sequence: The fifth of the triad moves up a step, followed by the two remaining tones up a step. (If all three notes moved together, the result would be parallel fifths.) It is in this manner that this sequence is generally used—that is, root position alternating with first inversion. The complete series is a long one, requiring in major fourteen root movements before all possibilities are shown. Of course, in actual practice, only sections of such a sequence could be used.

Writing this sequence in four voices produces what looks and sounds suspiciously like hidden octaves on a continuing basis; in our example, they are between tenor and bass. For this reason, the sequence is used more in three-voice writing or in instrumental styles, in which arpeggiation and other devices can cover such an impression (see Figure 17.8).

In minor, the ascending melodic lines of the sequence require the use of $\sharp\hat{6}$ and $\sharp\hat{7}$. Once a $\flat\hat{6}$ is sounded in any voice, the sequence must end. Figure 17.7*b* shows, in three voices, the sequence ending at iv–ii°, from which the $\flat\hat{6}$ (A♭) descends. If this is not the desired end of the sequence, the iv should be IV. The progression from this point would then be IV–ii–V–III+–VI. Since VI includes $\flat\hat{6}$, the sequence ends, or vi° instead of VI at this point will again allow the sequence to continue. These complications limit the use of this sequence.

FIGURE 17.7

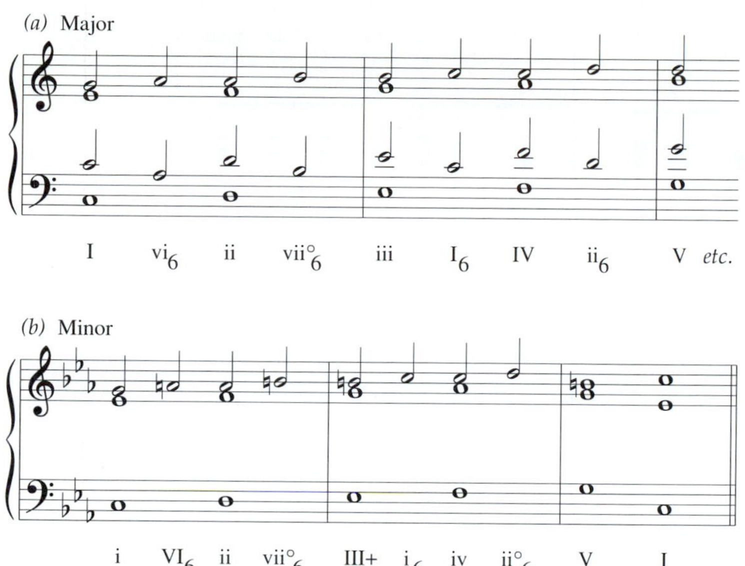

This sequence in major is well demonstrated by the famous "catalogue aria" from *Don Giovanni* (Figure 17.8), where, starting at measure 3, the first six chords, I–vi–ii–vii°–iii–I, are utilized.

FIGURE 17.8

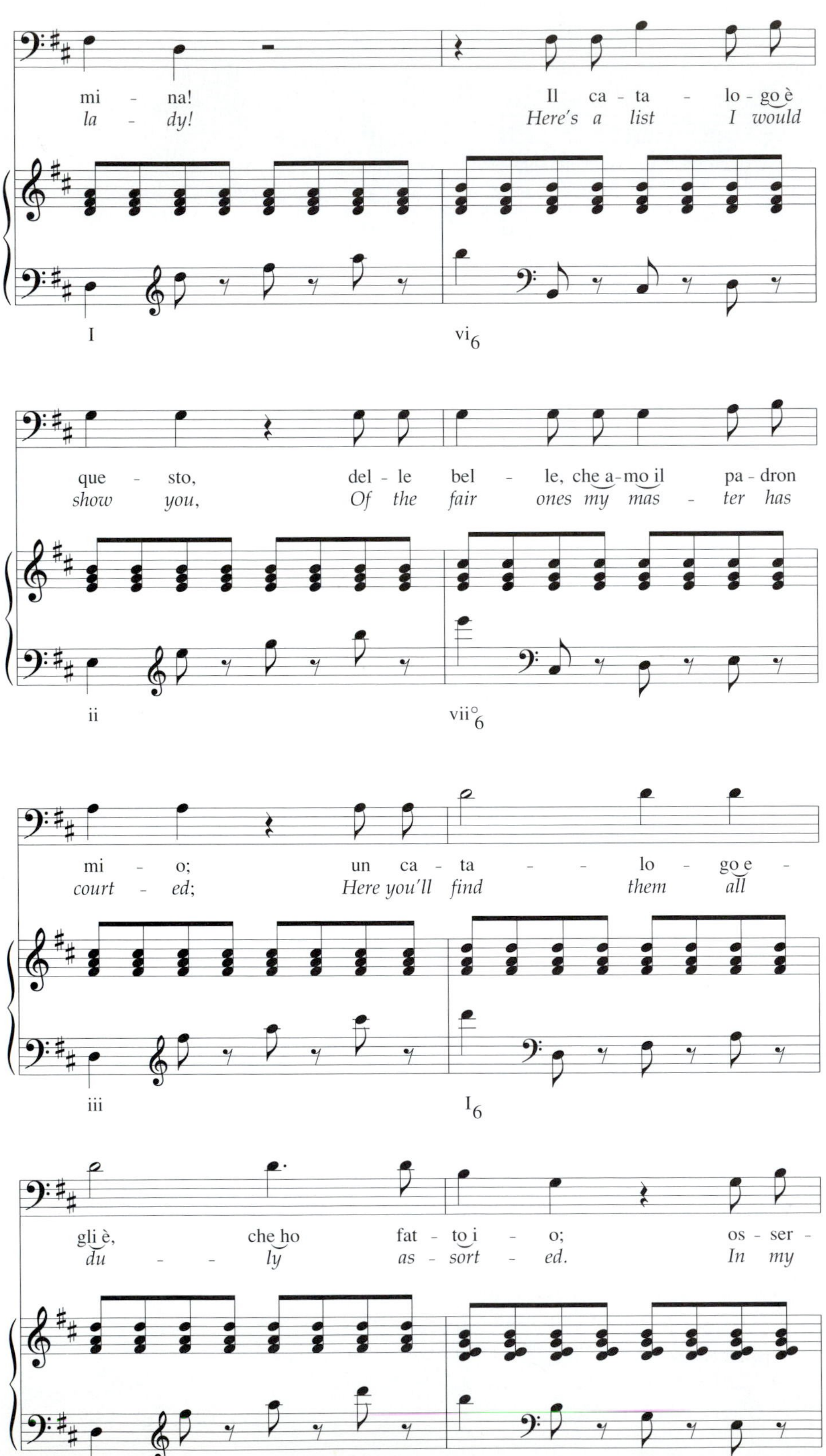
mi - na! Il ca - ta - lo - go è
la - dy! Here's a list I would
I
vi6
que - sto, del - le bel - le, che a - mo il pa - dron
show you, Of the fair ones my mas - ter has
ii
vii°6
mi - o; un ca - ta - lo - go e -
court - ed; Here you'll find them all
iii
I6
gli è, che ho fat - to i - o; os - ser -
du - ly as - sort - ed. In my

In the example in minor, Figure 17.9, Bach cleverly and masterfully solves the problem of the melodic $\hat{6}$ and $\hat{7}$ by following ♭$\hat{6}$ with ♮$\hat{6}$ and ♭$\hat{7}$ with ♮$\hat{7}$. In leaving iv, ♭$\hat{6}$ is maintained in the ii° triad and then replaced by ♮$\hat{6}$ in the ii triad, as shown in the implied harmony below the staff. The continuing sequence finds ♭$\hat{7}$ replaced by ♮$\hat{7}$ in v–III–III+. Upon reaching the ♭$\hat{6}$ in the VI triad, the sequence ceases.

FIGURE 17.9

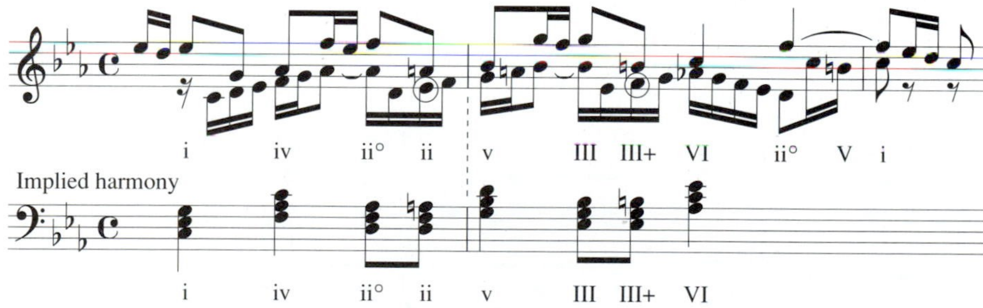

In the "implied harmony" of Figure 17.9, there appear to be chromatic half steps, ♭$\hat{6}$–♮$\hat{6}$ and ♭$\hat{7}$–♮$\hat{7}$. Observe in Figure 17.10 how Bach avoids these. The second note of each pair is a chord tone appearing in a different voice from the other. The alto A♭ leaps down to make way for the soprano leap down to A, followed by a similar treatment of B♭ and B.

FIGURE 17.10

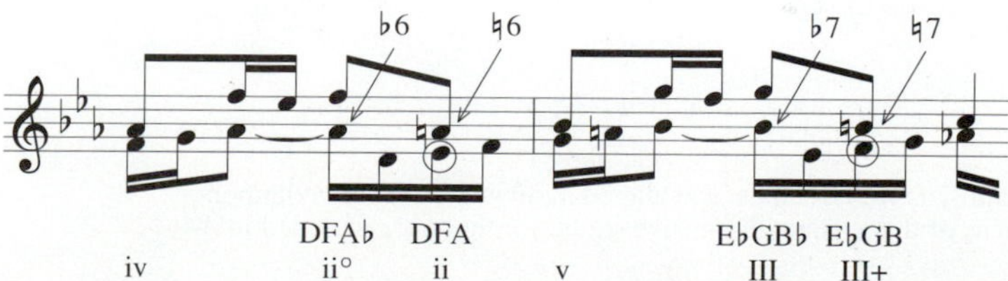

Sequence: Roots Down a Third and Up a Second (Descending by Seconds)

This sequence can be played in either major or minor. It is best used in minor, though in major it can be effective if vii°–V is avoided (for example, starting on V: I–V–vi–IV, etc.).

FIGURE 17.11

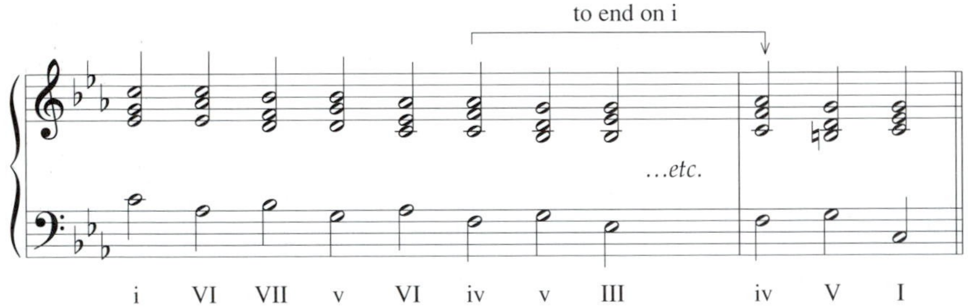

Although our example from Fauré (Figure 17.12) uses alternating triads and seventh chords,[1] the triad version can be heard simply by placing each seventh a step higher (making it the root of the triad).

CD FIGURE 17.12

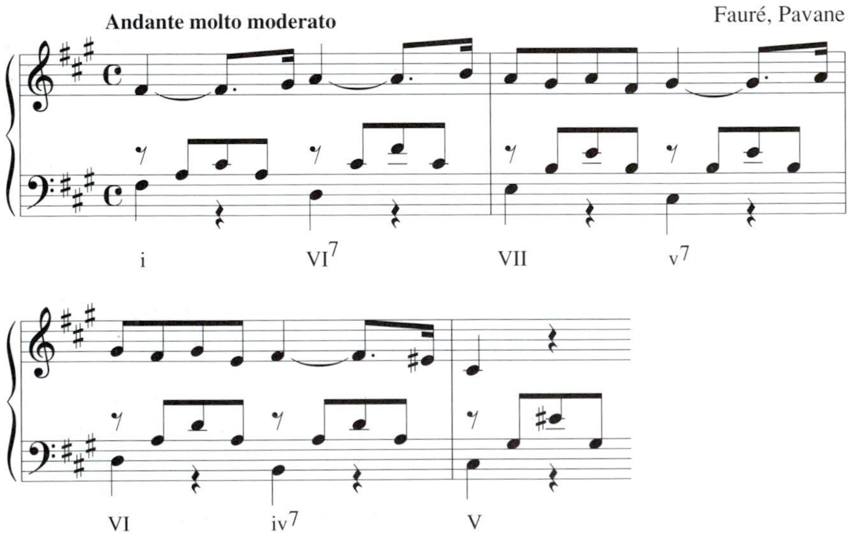

[1]Sequences containing many sevenths, as well as ninths and altered harmonies, are very common—more so than the diatonic triadic sequences of this chapter. Extensive studies of these are included in *Advanced Harmony.*

As written by Fauré, each seventh is a suspension in a chain of 7 6 suspensions above the bass line (review Figure 12.10).

FIGURE 17.13

		Ⓢ		Ⓢ		Ⓢ	
	C♯	C♯	B	B	A	A	G♯
bass:	F♯	D	E	C♯	D	B	C♯
	i	VI	VII	v	VI	iv	V

Sequence: Roots Down a Fourth and Up a Second (Descending by Thirds)

Shown in Figure 17.14 is the most commonly used section of this particular series of root movements. When the pattern continues, the next tonic triad appears eight triads later and in either major or minor includes diminished triads in awkward relationships to their previous and following triads.

FIGURE 17.14

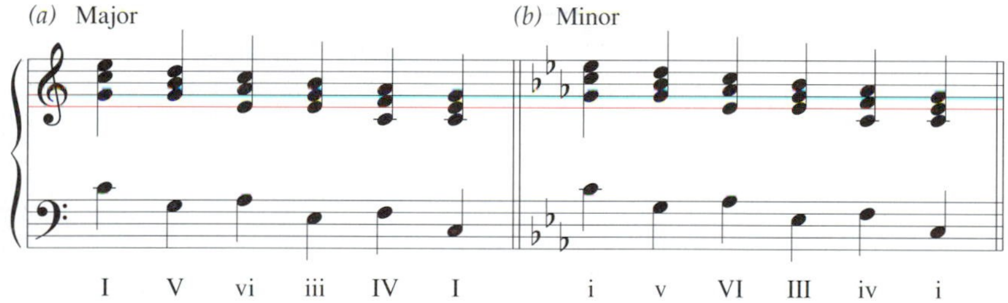

In Figure 17.15, measure 2, Beethoven avoided the progression i–ii°–VI by altering E G B♭ to E♭ G B♭. This major triad could be identified as ♭II. Instead, it is commonly called a *Neapolitan* chord, symbolized by N, or, in its most common usage, the *Neapolitan Sixth,* N_6.

FIGURE 17.15

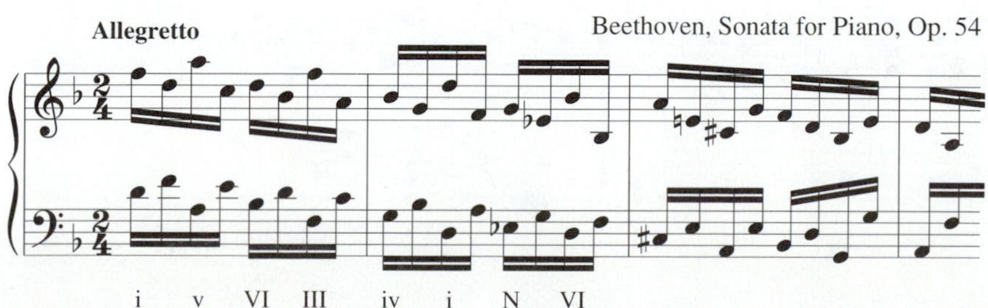

Bach's variant on this sequence, Figure 17.16, is the repetition of the first pair of triads as I–V_6–I–V, continued in the same manner for the following pairs, vi–iii and IV–I. The emphasis given the strong beats, 1 and 3, produces the effect of a progression by downward thirds: I–vi–IV–ii–V–I.

FIGURE 17.16

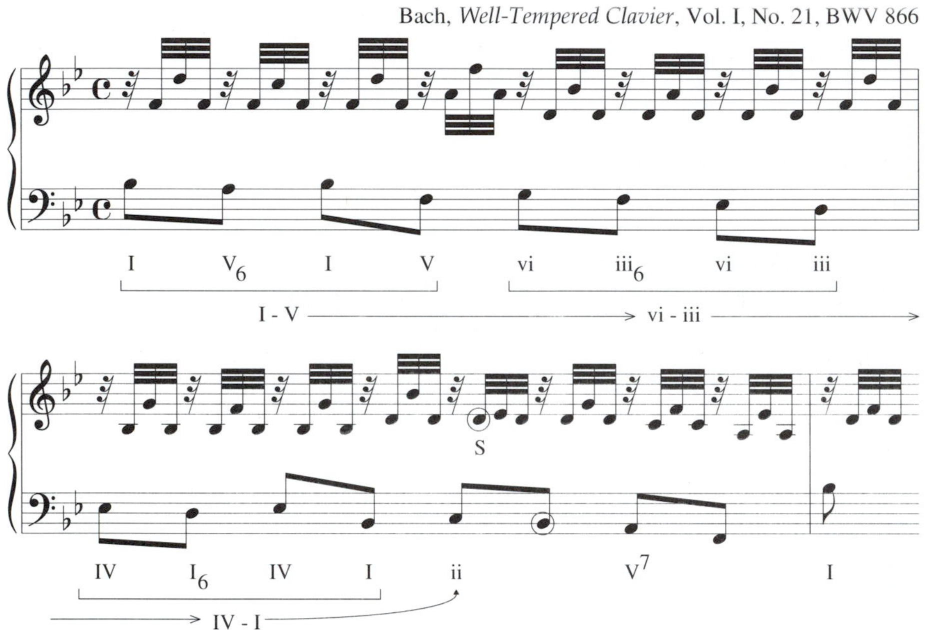

First Inversion in Series

Writing triads in parallel first inversion is, in a way, allied to the concept of harmonic sequence, in that repetition of an idea is involved. Obviously, no consideration of chord succession is necessary. In four-voice writing, the procedures already learned for successive first inversions will apply.

FIGURE 17.17

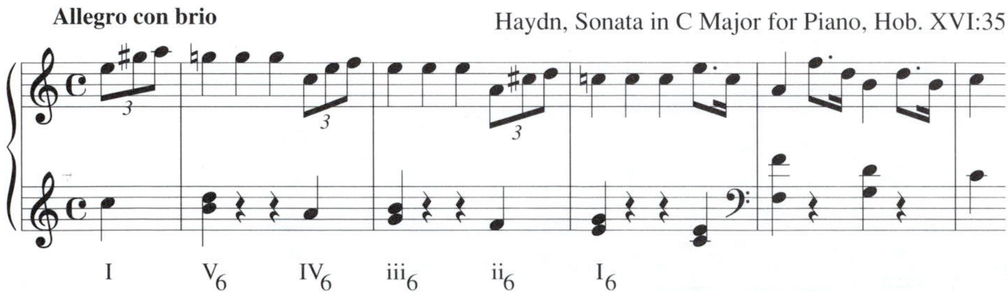

ASSIGNMENT 17.1 *Harmonic analysis.* In your harmonic analysis of these examples, describe the sequential root movement both by intervals between roots and by the inversions actually used (if any). Also, use brackets to designate the sequential melodic movements in the upper voices.

(1)

Schumann, *Albumblätter*, Op. 124, No. 4

Animato

p

CD (2)

Purcell, *Abdelazar*, or *The Moor's Revenge*

(3)

Handel, *Messiah*

(4)

Bach, *French Suite V*, BWV 813, Gavotte

(5)
Vivace
Beethoven, Sonata for Piano, Op. 79
(6)
Handel, Suite in C Major, Chaconne

(7)

Writing Sequences

ASSIGNMENT 17.2 Write out in various keys as assigned the harmonic sequences shown in Figures 17.3, 17.5, 17.7, 17.11, and 17.14.

ASSIGNMENT 17.3 Complete the following sequences. The three chords given outline the root movement. For example, in sequence 1, the root movement is down a fifth and up a fourth (B♭–E♭–A). When more than three chords are given, the three bracketed indicate the sequence.

Copy out the given chords and continue the sequence until you arrive at a final cadence. If the tonic falls on a weak beat, continue with IV–V–I, ii_6–V–I, or any similar progression to place the tonic on a strong beat.

Experiment by repeating an exercise with a change of accent. For example, sequence 1 in $\frac{4}{4}$ begins with beats 4 | 1 2. Play again, considering the three given chords as $\frac{4}{4}$ 1 2 3.

In a minor key, observe these special considerations:

1. $\hat{6}$ and $\hat{7}$ are usually lowered until reaching the cadential V–i or vii$^{\circ}_{6}$–i.
2. To continue through and past the dominant–tonic progression, use v–i or VII–i.

These exercises may also be written in other keys, as assigned, and may also be used for keyboard practice.

In Appendix E: Answers to (1), (5), and (7) are given.

ASSIGNMENT 17.4 *Melody harmonization.* Find the harmonic sequence that can be accommodated by the melody line. Harmonize with block chords or experiment with a simple keyboard accompaniment.

(1)

Bach, Prelude and Fugue in C Major, BWV 55:

(2)

(3) Each triad lasts the duration of eight sixteenth notes. Circle passing tones and indicate with "S" the dissonant note of each suspension.

(4) Add a middle voice to create a "5 6" sequence (measures 1–2).

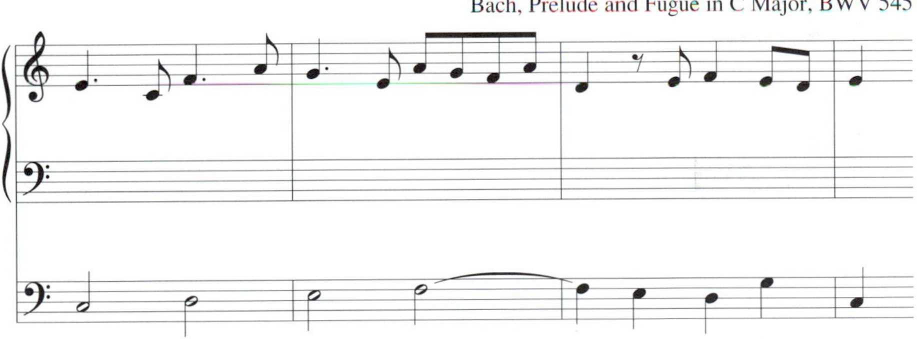

In Appendix E: Answers to (1) and (2) are given.

Summary

The *harmonic sequence* is a series of chords with a repeating pattern of root movements. Like a melodic sequence, the harmonic sequence provides variety along with the stability of repetition.

The most common series displays root movements down a fifth, up a fourth, down a fifth, and so forth. Any combination of interval movement in the bass can be utilized, however, such as up a fifth, down a fourth; down a third, up a fourth; and down a third, up a second.

Devices uncommon elsewhere can be used freely in sequence, including uncommon chord progressions, the diminished triad with root in the bass, and v and VII in minor.

Triads in a sequence may be in inversion as long as a melodic sequence in the bass in maintained.

Harmonic sequence has been a popular compositional device from the Baroque period to the present day.

18

Secondary Dominant Chords; Elementary Modulation

Chromaticism

The term *chromaticism* refers to the use of tones not belonging to the diatonic scale in which they are found. In this definition, the two forms of $\hat{6}$ and $\hat{7}$ in minor keys are *not* included. We have already seen a number of examples of chromaticism in nonharmonic tones, ranging from a single tone, first described in Figure 14.2, to the chromatic scale line of Figure 11.7.

Chromaticism also finds its place in harmonic structures. A chord can be altered by changing one or more of its tones by a chromatic half step (same letter name); for example, we can change D F A to D F♯ A, or D F A to D F A♭. Since raised tones usually resolve upward, and lowered tones downward, an altered chord is more limited in its choice of resolution than the unaltered version, and thus the function of the chord is redefined.

This restriction is particularly evident in the chords of this chapter. These, the most common type of altered chords, are termed *secondary dominants* or *applied dominants,* so called because each functions as a dominant to a major or minor triad other than the tonic.

Secondary Dominant Chords

In the music of Figure 18.1 (reduced to block chords in Figure 18.2), the chromatic tone C♯ in C major alters the triad A C E to A C♯ E, and is followed immediately by D F A. If you play only these two triads, the aural impression is that of V–i in D minor with the altered tone C♯ now functioning as a leading tone to the presumed key of D minor. This alteration and its function as a leading tone to a chord a perfect fifth down is typical of all secondary dominant chords.

Playing Figure 18.1 or 18.2 in its entirety proves the aural impression of D minor created by the secondary dominant triad to be momentary; the effect is dispelled immediately, since the phrase ends in C major.

FIGURE 18.1

FIGURE 18.2

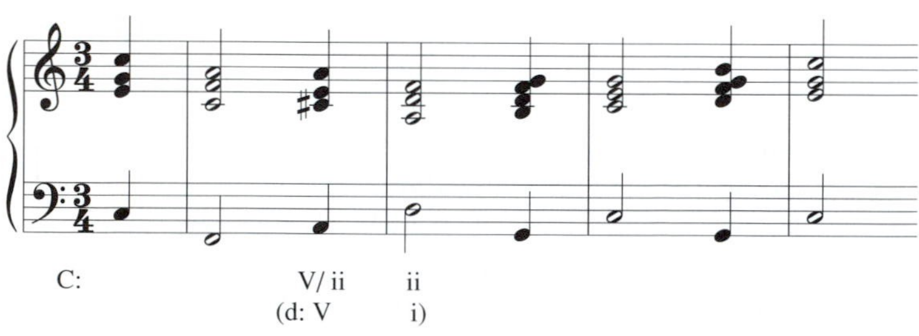

The process of a secondary dominant's endowing its following chord with the property of tonic, however momentary, is called *tonicization.* The secondary dominant is symbolized as V/–. In Figure 18.1, ii is tonicized, so its secondary dominant is V/ii, spoken "five of two."

Any major or minor triad may be preceded by its secondary dominant triad or seventh chord. Since diminished and augmented triads cannot assume the function of tonic, they have no secondary dominants. Figure 18.3 shows each of the possible secondary dominants for diatonic triads in major and minor keys.

FIGURE 18.3

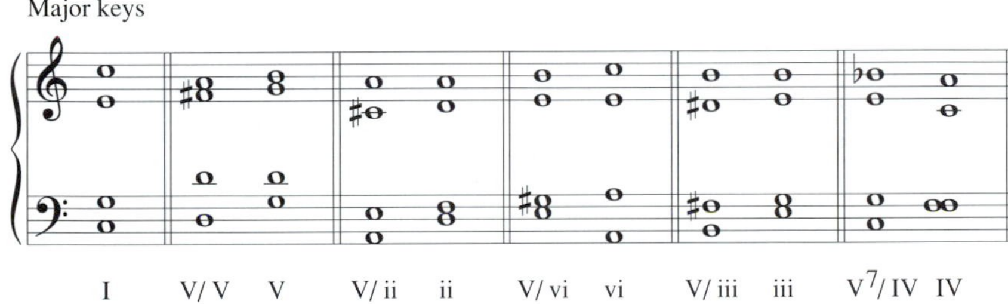

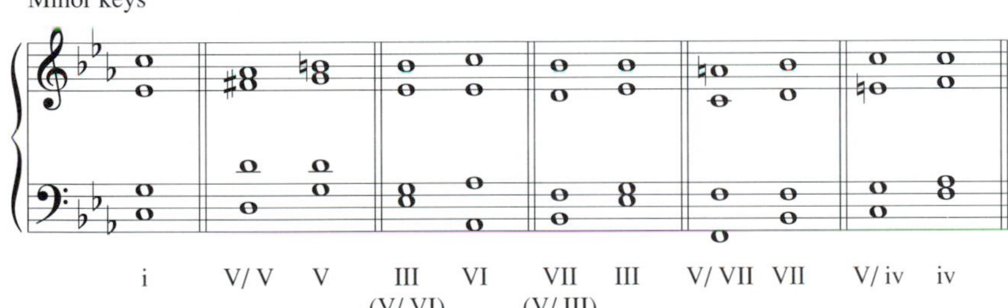

A few special explanations about the use of secondary dominant chords follow.

1. Each secondary dominant triad may also be changed to a seventh chord by adding a minor seventh above the root (C: V/V = D F♯ A; V^7/V = D F♯ A C). In actual practice, the seventh chords are the more frequently used, just as the diatonic V^7 is more common than the V triad (Figure 18.4).

FIGURE 18.4

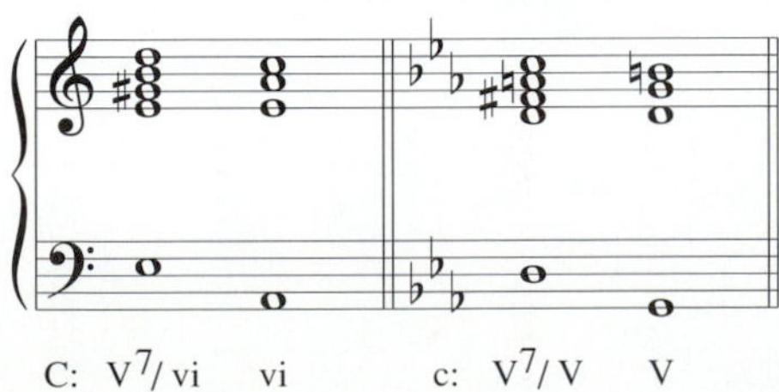

2. In major, the I of I–IV is not considered V/IV because there is no chromatic alteration and because I–IV is a diatonic progression, anyway. But placing a minor seventh above the tonic (C major: C E G B♭) creates a secondary dominant (V^7/IV).
3. In minor, the major tonic triad (I) *can* be considered a secondary dominant (V/iv). The ambiguous functions of VII–III and III–VI have already been discussed in a previous chapter (page 350). Secondary dominant symbols generally are not used for these two diatonic progressions.
4. Secondary dominant triads and seventh chords may be found in succession, such as V/vi followed by V/ii. This particular progression can be symbolized V/→V/ii (five of five-of-two).

When in a series of two or more secondary dominants the second chord of any pair is V^7/, that chord is considered to be a tonicized chord, even though a seventh chord can hardly be said to sound like a tonic triad. In some situations, such as in a long series, analysis may be clearer if the full symbol is used, as discussed on page 394.

Spelling Secondary Dominants

All secondary dominants are major triads or major–minor seventh chords (dominant sevenths). To spell any such triad, first spell the root of the tonicized triad, count up five steps from that note, then spell a major triad. For example, for V/ii in A major:

1. The root of ii is B.
2. Five scale steps up is F♯.
3. The major triad on F♯ is F♯ A♯ C♯.

The secondary dominant seventh chord includes a minor seventh above the root, exactly the same as the diatonic V^7; for example, A major: V/ii = F♯ A♯ C♯, so V^7/ii = F♯ A♯ C♯ E.

The seventh will be a pitch name diatonic in the key, but with two exceptions: In the V^7/IV in major and the V^7/VI in minor, the seventh is lowered in relation to the key. Examples: C major: V^7/IV = C E G B♭; C minor: V^7/VI = E♭ G B♭ D♭.

ASSIGNMENT 18.1 Practice spelling secondary dominant triads and seventh chords. Choose a key and spell each secondary dominant relationship listed in Figure 18.3

ASSIGNMENT 18.2 Check your ability to spell secondary dominants by filling in the blanks.

(1) C major V/ii ____ ____ ____

(2) A major V^7/V ____ ____ ____ ____

(3) B♭ major V/iii ____ ____ ____

(4) E major V^7/IV ____ ____ ____ ____

(5) D♭ major V^7/vi ____ ____ ____ ____

(6) F♯ major V/V ____ ____ ____ ____

(7) C♯ major V^7/ii ____ ____ ____ ____

(8) G♭ major V/iii ____ ____ ____

(9) D minor V/V ____ ____ ____

(10) G minor V^7/iv ____ ____ ____ ____

(11) D♯ minor V^7/V ____ ____ ____ ____

(12) F minor V^7/VI ____ ____ ____ ____

In Appendix E: Answers to the entire assignment are given.
In the Workbook: Do Assignment 18.2a. Answers are given.

Use of Secondary Dominants

Figure 18.5 is a simple folk song of four phrases *aaba′* (*a* differs from *a′* in only a few notes in measure 15). Each of the three *a* phrases has been harmonized differently; the first uses diatonic chords only and the other two include V^7/V.

In measures 2–3 of the first phrase, a simple ii–V is used. How is this changed in the repetition, measures 6–7?

More changes occur in measures 13–15. What is the new harmony? What is the beat location of V^7/V–V compared with the previous phrase? (The bracket under these measures and the term *hemiola* are discussed in Article 12, immediately following.)

Does the *c* phrase, even though its final chord is tonicized by V/V, really sound like tonic, even temporarily? How did Brahms dissipate the tonic sound of D major?

Finally, compare all the V^7/V harmonies. Are they the same? How do they differ?

(CD) FIGURE 18.5

The entire folk song is set with the simplest of harmonies. Even the more exotic harmonization in the final phrase consists only of chords and nonharmonic tones you have already studied. By making subtle changes in the simplest material, such as three different bass positions of V^7/V, Brahms has raised the level of the harmonization from a common "oompah-pah" to a minor masterwork. Review this composition for its outstanding combination of simplicity and variety whenever harmonization of a melodic line seems to elude you.

ARTICLE #12

The Hemiola

The *hemiola* is a metric device in which two groups of three notes are performed as three groups of two notes. It can occur in any meter in which note values are grouped in threes.

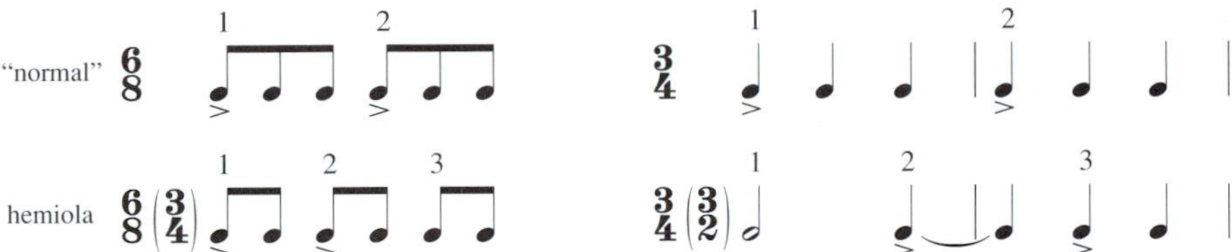

In Figure 18.5, the hemiola is in the piano part in measures 13–14, in which the bass and alto lines clearly delineate the placement of the accents as in the $\frac{3}{4}$ ($\frac{3}{2}$) example above. But note that the folk tune remains in a "normal" $\frac{3}{4}$ meter, resulting in two meters sounding simultaneously.

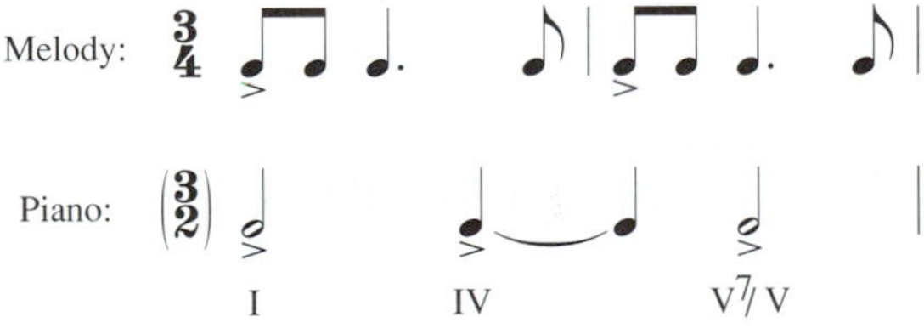

As if that were not enough, Brahms has written the upper voice of the piano part as a chromatic scale line, D–D♯–E–E♯–F♯–G, so that the passing tones D♯ and E♯ momentarily produce the sound of augmented triads G B D♯ and A C♯ E♯.

The hemiola was a favorite rhythmic device from the fifteenth century through the Baroque, and not uncommon in later periods. Here are some well-known works from the eighteenth to twentieth centuries in which examples may be found.

Handel, *Messiah,* No. 4, "And the Glory of the Lord," measures 9–10
Mozart, Symphony No. 40 in G Minor, K. 550, third movement, measures 1–2
Schumann, Symphony No. 3, Op. 97, first movement, measures 1–4
Bernstein, *West Side Story,* "America"

A most striking example of a secondary dominant is in the opening of Beethoven's Symphony No. 1 (Figure 18.6), which evoked much caustic comment at its premiere in 1800 because its first harmonic progression, C E G B♭–F A C, sounds like V–I in F major, a startling opening in its time for a work in C major.

FIGURE 18.6

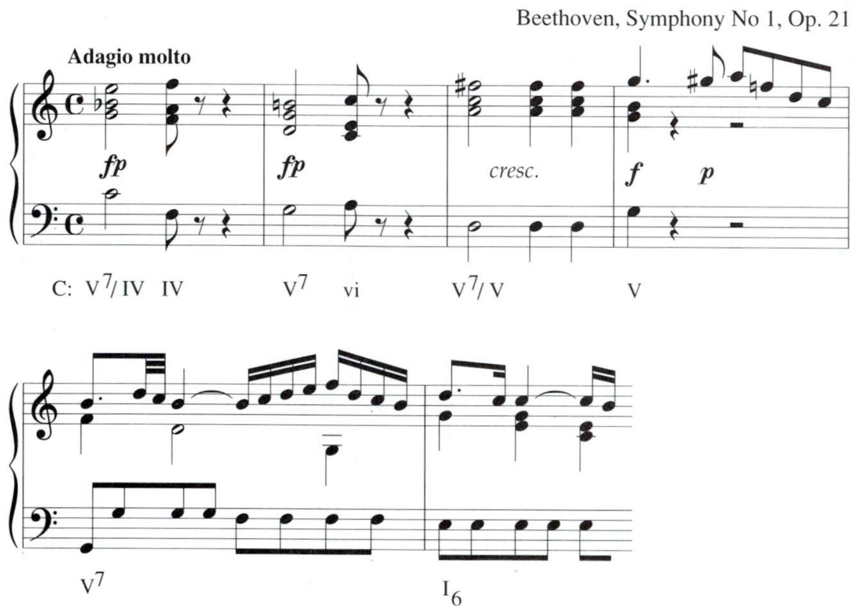

Not frequently seen is the major tonic triad in a minor key used as a secondary dominant, V/iv. Following in close succession, the functions of the A C E (i) and A C♯ E (V/iv) triads are clearly delineated.

FIGURE 18.7

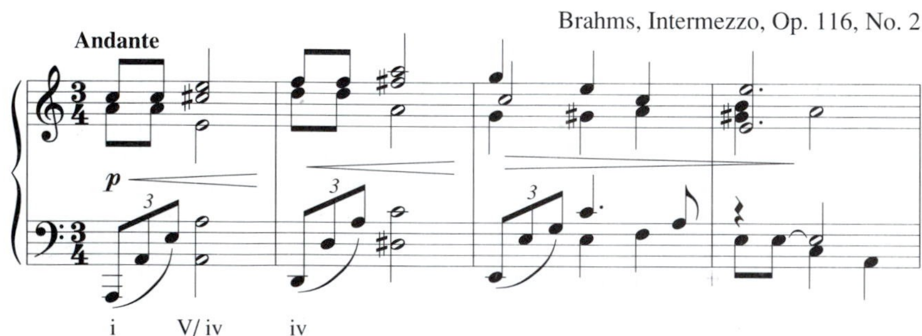

Before examining the next example, be sure you can spell the V^7 and the V^7/V in G♯ minor! Of interest here is the treatment of the "secondary leading tone." In this common exception, the secondary leading tone resolves downward by chromatic half step to the seventh of the following chord, either directly, or indirectly as in Figure 18.8. Here the secondary leading tone of C𝄪 of A♯ C𝄪 E♯ G♯ slips down a half step to C♮, the seventh of D♯ F𝄪 A♯ C♮. This movement can occur in any voice.

FIGURE 18.8

Bach, *Well-Tempered Clavier*, Vol. 2, No. 18, BWV 887

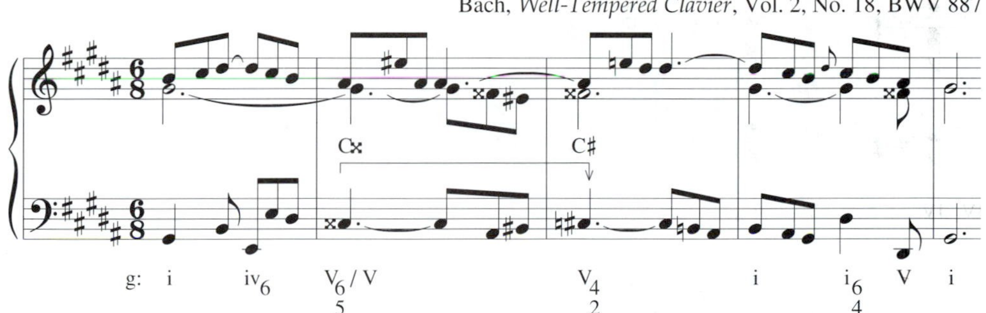

What would ordinarily be the final cadence in Figure 18.9 (a Picardy third in B♭ minor) becomes a secondary dominant seventh by the addition of A♭ to the B♭ D F triad, which progresses to iv over a pedal and then on to tonic. A brief excursion into the subdominant after a "final" authentic cadence is frequent in the Baroque period and shows up regularly in later music, especially in the music of Brahms.

FIGURE 18.9

Bach, *Well-Tempered Clavier*, Vol. 1, No. 22, BWV 867

The Deceptive Progression

Like the deceptive progression V–vi, the root of the secondary dominant can move up stepwise in its own deceptive progression, as in Figure 18.10, in which the root of

V^7/vi moves up stepwise to IV. Were the root of the secondary dominant identified by its scale-step number, the progression would be seen to be the common progression vi–III–IV.

FIGURE 18.10

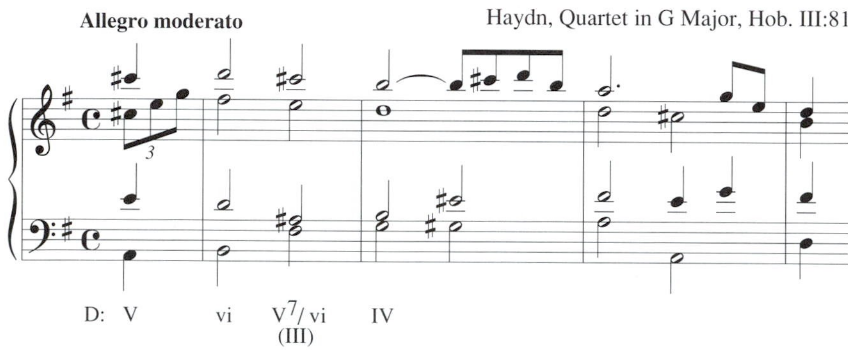

Secondary Dominant Chords in the Harmonic Sequence

The effectiveness of the familar and much-used device of harmonic sequence can be enhanced through the additional opportunities for variety when using secondary dominant chords. We have already seen such a sequence in Figure 14.10, page 301, using only secondary dominants. Each was identified by a single uppercase roman numeral representing a major triad and the location of the chord root, thus avoiding an awkward V/→V^7/→V^7/→V/→V^7–vi (awkward because of the difficulty of quick identification or chord spelling of a particular V/ symbol). In this case, either the symbols of Figure 14.10 or a series of V/ (without arrows) is easier to comprehend (review page 388). Symbols should be chosen for their simplicity and clarity.

In Figure 18.11, after the Phrygian cadence of the first phrase, the sequence in the second phrase is interrupted by vi following V/ii. Note that the E major triad at this point is symbolized by V/ii, not by V/→.

FIGURE 18.11

An interesting variant from an early-eighteenth-century work by Stamitz is shown in Figure 18.12. The basic harmony of measures 1–6 is the ordinary progression I–IV–V–vi. But both V and vi are preceded by *two* secondary dominant chords:

	V7/⟶V/⟶V and V7/⟶V/⟶vi					
Roots	B	E	A	C♯	F♯	B

FIGURE 18.12

The V/V at the Cadence

As you listened to the cadence in measures 11–12 in Figure 18.5, analyzed as V/V–V in G major, it may have occurred to you that this could be a V–I cadence in D major. As you listen again from measure 9, you can easily hear the sound of the harmonic progression as D: IV–I_6–V^4_3–I. Should that be what you hear, you would say that there had been a *modulation* from G major to D major, the term *modulation* meaning the process of going from one key to another. If this *is* a modulation, the life of the new key is as short as possible, since the introduction of C♮ on the next eighth note takes us back to the key of G.

FIGURE 18.13 *Measures 9–12 of Figure 18.5*

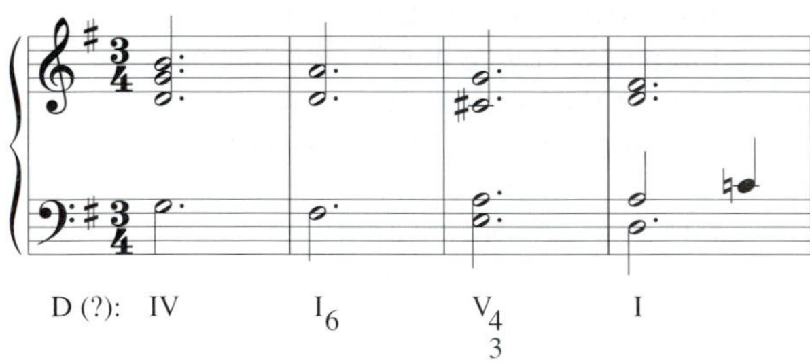

Listen to another example (Figure 18.14). The music starts in A major, then arrives in measure 8 at a cadence on V, preceded not only by its V but also by an even stronger I^6_4–V progression.

FIGURE 18.14

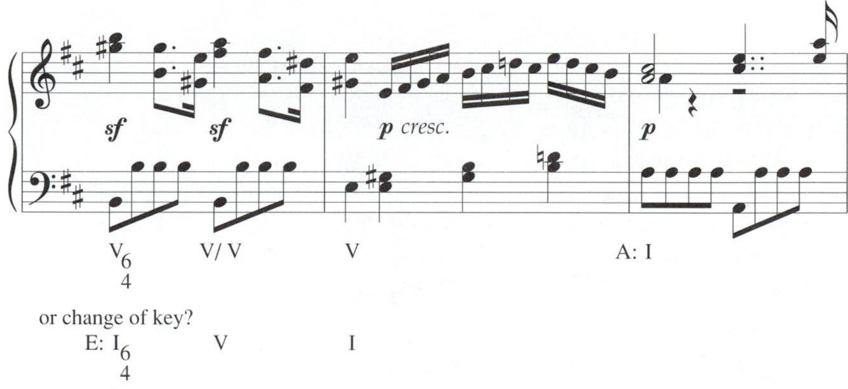

In both cases (Figures 18.5 and 18.14), we have arrived at a cadence with a harmonic analysis that could indicate possible arrival at a new key center. Whether these cadences are heard as new tonics or as the dominants of the original keys is strictly a subjective evaluation on the part of the listener. In Figure 18.5, most people will experience no change of key, whereas in Figure 18.14, some will feel that the presence of the six-four helps establish E major, however temporarily. Only when it is certain that a new key center has been established is the process described as modulation. The mere presence of V/V–V at the cadence usually does not justify analysis of a new key; but the more harmonic activity preceding the cadence that can be ascribed to a new key, the greater the possibility that a new key has indeed been created.

The cadences we have just studied have been described variously by theorists, using terms such as "progressive cadences" and "transient modulations," indicating the degree of difficulty one has in evaluating them. In contrast, the next excerpt, Figure 18.15, reaches the goal of the cadence on the dominant three successive times. Again you are asked to listen and determine for yourself: At the end of the excerpt, is the sound that of A major, or do those three cadences on A fail to pull you away from a feeling for the key of D major? Here again, there will be no consensus, but the case for modulation to A major is much stronger. The analyses of Figures 18.14 and 18.15 as modulations will be explained in the next section.

FIGURE 18.15

Modulation

Progressing to a key other than the dominant poses far fewer aural problems than those just described. In Figure 18.16, the harmony begins in E minor and modulates to G major. In listening, you will probably not feel the same urge to return from G major to the original tonic that you did when you arrived at the dominant in the earlier examples.

FIGURE 18.16

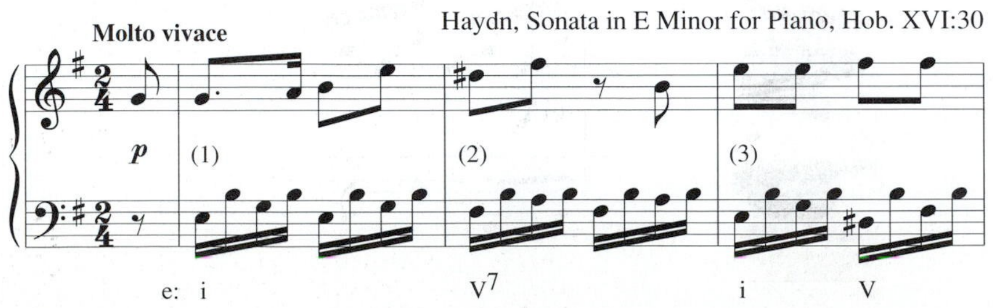

The modulation in Figure 18.16 has been effected through the use of a *pivot chord.* The harmonic analysis iv = ii indicates that the A C E triad functions simultaneously as the iv triad in E minor and the ii triad in G major.

measure 6	E minor: i	iv =		
	G major:	ii	V	I

To prove the location of this pivot, play up to and including the pivot, but no further. At this point, the music could easily have continued in E minor as shown in Figure 18.17 (not by Haydn!), where we start at the pivot, calling it iv only, and continue to a cadence in E minor.

FIGURE 18.17

Next, start at the pivot, measure 6, and play the remaining measures as written by Haydn. Now the A C E triad sounds like ii in G major.[1]

[1]It is possible to consider measure 5 as the pivot, e: i = G: vi, though it is further away from the new V–I. But the progression from measure 5 to the cadence, vi–ii–V–I, is logical, so the pivot at that point is acceptable.

How does one determine which chords can be pivots? Any chord that is spelled identically in the two keys of a modulation can act as a pivot, though two other considerations do apply.

1. The pivot usually immediately precedes one of these progressions or cadences in the new key: V–I, I^6_4–V–I, IV–V–I, or ii–V–I, just as in Figure 18.16 the pivot iv = ii preceded V^7–I of the new key.
2. A pivot that includes V or vii° is usually avoided. The strength of each of these in relationship to a tonic makes it difficult to aurally comprehend a relationship to a different tonic.

By lining up the triad spellings of the two keys, we can see what is available, as marked with an x to indicate a spelling common to both keys. Note that the pair that includes V is not useful.

E minor:	i	ii°	III	iv	V	VI	vii°	i	ii°
G major:			I	ii	III	IV	V	vi	vii°
			x	x		x		x	

Thus, to modulate from a minor key to its relative major, as above, there are four possible pivots, as shown from C minor:

C minor:	i	=	E♭ major:	vi	(C E♭ G)
	III	=		I	(E♭ G B♭)
	iv	=		ii	(F A♭ C)
	VI	=		IV	(A♭ C E♭)

When lining up the triads of a major key and its dominant key, we find three possible pivots.[2] In D major, they are

D major:	I	=	A major:	IV	(D F♯ A)
	iii	=		vi	(F♯ A C♯)
	vi	=		ii	(B D F♯)

For an example of the pivot in a modulation from a major key to its dominant key, return to Figure 18.14. Considering that a modulation has occurred, note that I^6_4–V–I of the new key is preceded by F♯ A C♯, vi in A and ii in E, so the pivot is vi = ii. Also, in Figure 18.15, ii–V–I of the new key is preceded by D F♯ A, I in D and IV in A, pivot I = IV.

For this chapter, we will consider just the two modulations described, major key to its dominant and minor key to its relative major, which are two of the most frequently encountered. Abstract progressions showing each of the usable pivot chords can be seen in the "Keyboard Harmony" section, Assignment 18.13.

[2]Should you modulate from C♯ major to its dominant key, the new key will be G♯ major, eight sharps, for which there is no key signature. The leading tone in G♯ major is F𝄪 and is placed in the music where needed. See the Prelude and Fugue in C♯ Major in each of the two volumes of Bach's *Well-Tempered Clavier.* Some composers substitute the enharmonic key of A♭ major for G♯ major.

Return to the Original Tonic Key

Once a new key is achieved, there may be an immediate return to the old key—a very common occurrence—or the music may continue for a variable length of time in the new key or in other keys before making the return. For our purposes at present, we will consider only the *direct return* to the original key. After a modulation to a new key, return to the original tonic is accomplished simply by beginning the next phrase with I, V–I, or some other basic progression in the original key. In the final cadence of Figure 18.14 (modulation to the dominant), a minor seventh (D) is added to the E major triad, allowing the next phrase to begin with the tonic triad in the original key of A major.

ASSIGNMENT 18.3 *Spelling pivot chords when modulating from a major key to its dominant.* Spell the three possible pivot triads. Example: G major to D major: I = IV, G B D; vi = ii, E G B; iii = vi, B D F♯.

In the Workbook: Do Assignment 18.3a. Answers are given.

ASSIGNMENT 18.4 *Spelling pivot chords when modulating from a minor key to its relative major.* Spell the four possible pivot triads. Example: D minor to F major: III = I, F A C; iv = ii, G B♭ D; VI = IV, B♭ D F; i = vi, D F A.

In the Workbook: Do Assignment 18.4a. Answers are given.

ASSIGNMENT 18.5 Write in the pivot chord symbols or spell the pivot chord, as required by the blank spaces.

(1) D major to A major	I	=	IV	____	____	____
(2) E♭ major to B♭ major	vi	=	ii	____	____	____
(3) A♭ major to E♭ major	____	=	____	F	A♭	C
(4) B major to F♯ major	____	=	____	B	D♯	F♯
(5) G minor to B♭ major	iv	=	ii	____	____	____
(6) F♯ minor to A major	____	=	____	F♯	A	C♯
(7) B♭ minor to D♭ major	VI	=	IV	____	____	____
(8) C♯ minor to E major	____	=	____	F♯	A	C♯
(9) F♯ major to C♯ major	vi	=	ii	____	____	____
(10) A♭ minor to C♭ major	____	=	____	D♭	F♭	A♭

In Appendix E: Answers to the entire assignment are given.

ASSIGNMENT 18.6 *Harmonic analysis.* Analyze each example for harmony and nonharmonic tones. Be sure to identify the pivot chord and its function in each key. These excerpts include examples of both secondary dominant chords and modulation.

(1)

Gluck, *Alceste*, "Ah! malgré moi"

Lentemente

Vos ten - dres pleurs, _ vos re - grets si tous _ chants; _

(2)

Chopin, Waltz, Op. 64, No. 2

Tempo giusto

(3)

Mozart, Sonata in C Major, K. 330

Andante cantabile

pp

f
p

(4)

Moderato
Mussorgsky, *Khovantchina*, Act II
p
pp

(5)

Moderato
Maria Szymanowska (1789–1831), Nocturne
p
dolce
(vii°7/ ii)

(6)

Beethoven, Sonata for Cello, Op. 69

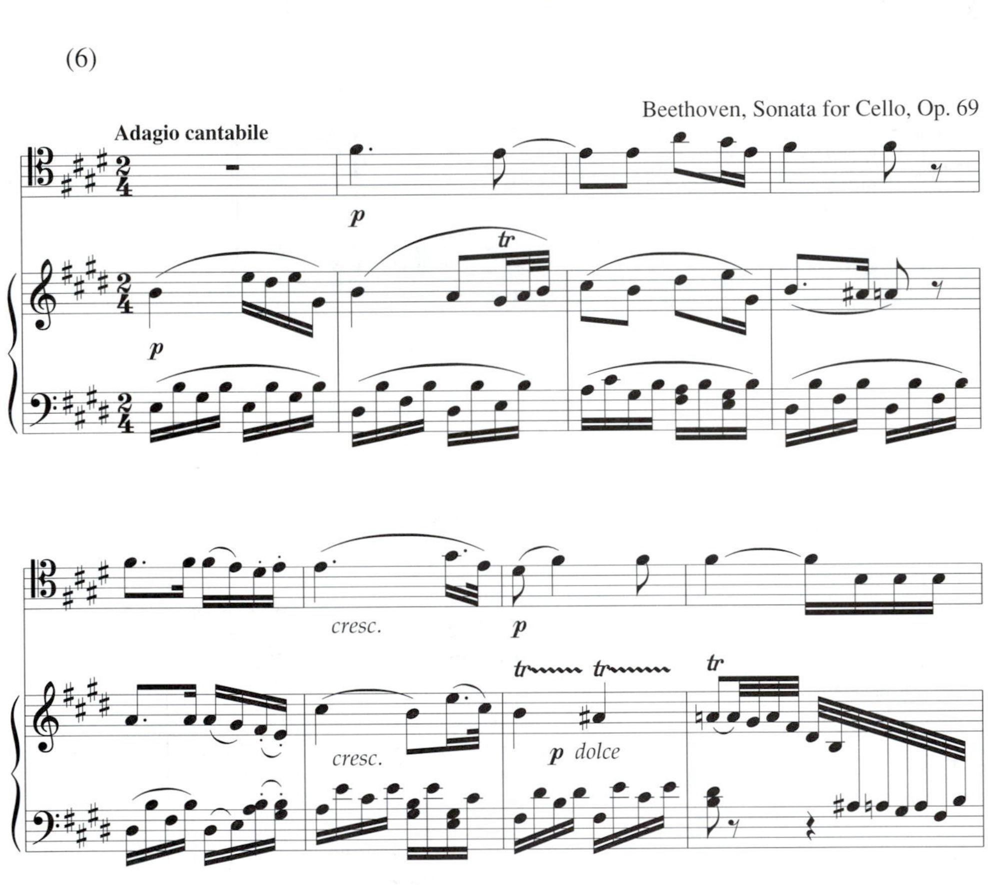

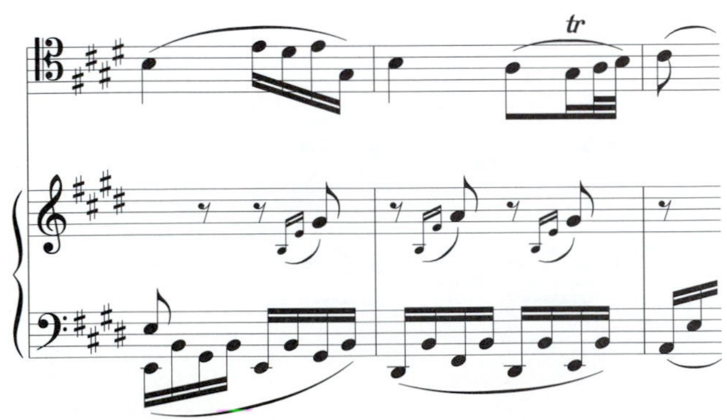

(7)

Bach, *French Suite II*, BWV 813

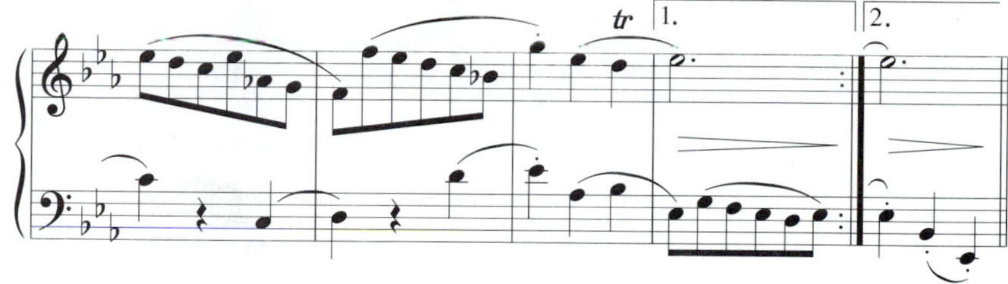

(8)

Haydn, Quartet, Hob. III:67

(9)

con molto express.
Largo
Verdi, Requiem
La - cry - mo - sa di - es il - la! Qua re -
p
sur - get ex fa - vil - la Ju - di - can - dus ho - mo

re - us Hu - ic er - go par - ce De - us.

(10)

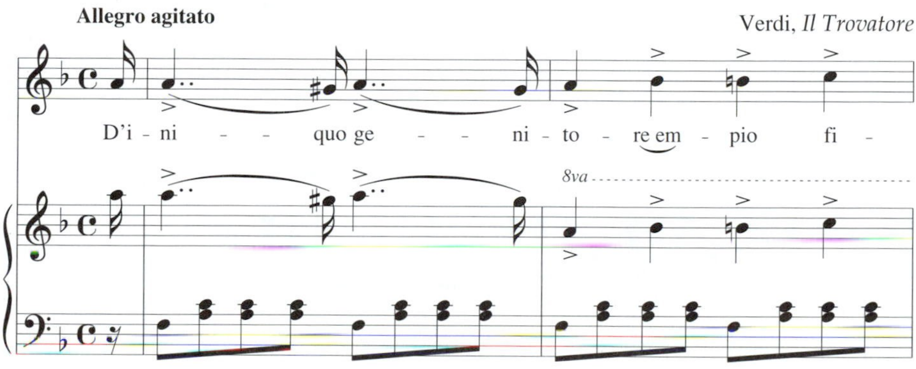
Allegro agitato
Verdi, *Il Trovatore*
D'i - ni - - quo ge - - ni - to - re em - pio fi -
8va

declamato ppp
gli iol peg - gio - re, tre-ma! v'è Dio pei
8va
ppp

mi - se-ri, v'è Dio pei mi - se - ri, tre-ma!
f
tre - - ma! v'è Di - o, e Dio ti pu-ni - rà!
8va

(11)

Allegro, ben ritmico
Bizet, *Carmen*
f
With the guard on du - ty go - ing sound trum - pets
March - ing on - ward, here we are
p

* Review page 351.

Modulation or Secondary Dominants in the Melodic Line

In a melody, a modulation or a secondary dominant becomes apparent when the implied harmony forms a cadence or a cadential progression. Very often the location is obvious because of the presence of an altered tone in the melody. In Figure 18.18, the altered tone D♯ is part of the line B C♯ D♯ E, in which it functions as a leading tone to E, confirmed by the V–I cadence in E major.

Two analyses are possible, depending on the tempo. Below the music is a possible analysis in a slow tempo. In a fast tempo, the pivot I = IV can appear in measure 4, followed by V for all of measure 5. C♯ and D♯ are then passing tones.

FIGURE 18.18

It is not always possible to depend upon the appearance of an altered tone in the melody. In Figure 18.19, *only* the implied harmony locates the secondary dominant or the modulation. The leading tone, C♯, will be in a lower voice. The two analyses given are first for a slow tempo and then for a fast tempo.

FIGURE 18.19

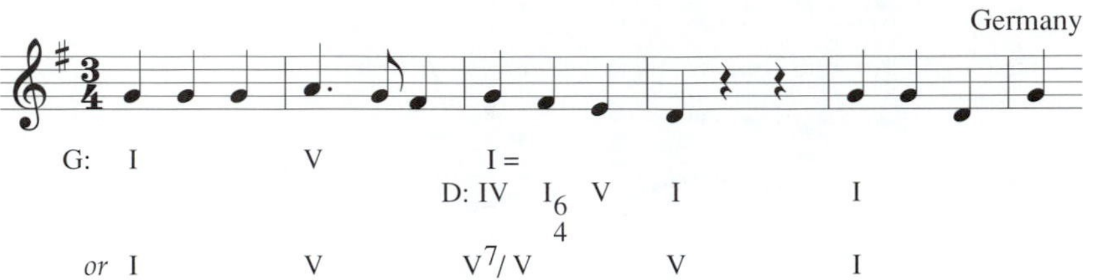

ASSIGNMENT 18.7 Make a complete analysis of the harmony implied in these melodies. Each will include modulation and/or secondary dominant chords. Use Figures 18.18 and 18.19 as models.

(1)

(2)

(3)

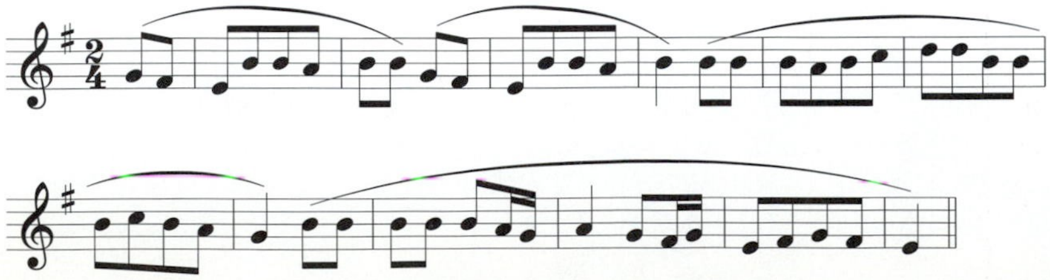

(4)

Writing Secondary Dominant Chords

The secondary dominant functions in the same way as the diatonic V or V^7; therefore, its leading tone (the third of the chord) ordinarily ascends (Figure 18.20), except that it may descend a half step, *using the same letter name,* to the seventh of the following chord (Figure 18.21; review Figure 18.8).

FIGURE 18.20 FIGURE 18.21

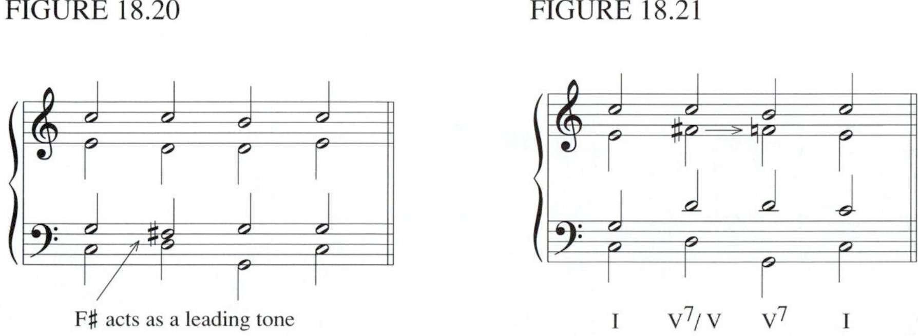

In a minor key, the fifth of V/V is $\sharp\hat{6}$, but in relation to its tonicized chord it is $\hat{2}$, and may therefore descend (Figure 18.22).

FIGURE 18.22

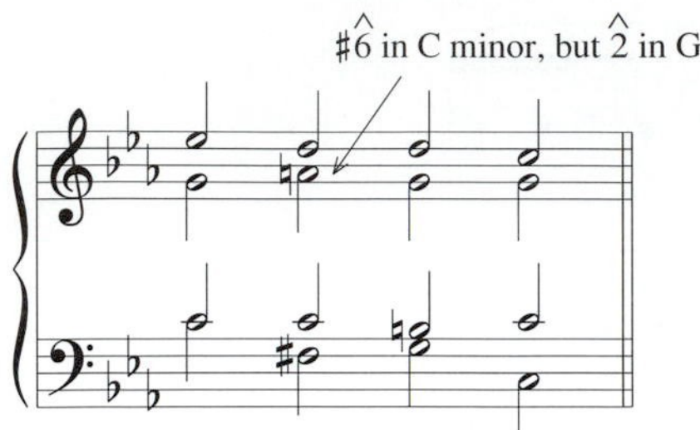

The *cross-relation* occurs when a member of a chord is also found in the following chord but in a different voice and with a different chromatic inflection. It is usually avoided because of its unpleasant sound.

FIGURE 18.23

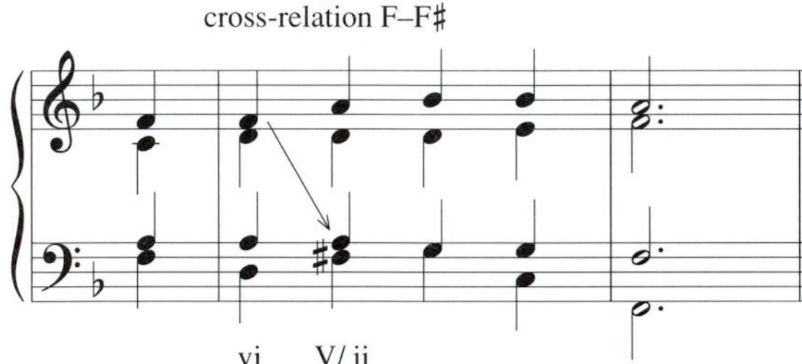

The cross-relation can be avoided by keeping the two notes in the same voice line, or its effect can be eliminated simply by adding a seventh to the second of the two chords. Compare the following examples with Figure 18.23.

FIGURE 18.24

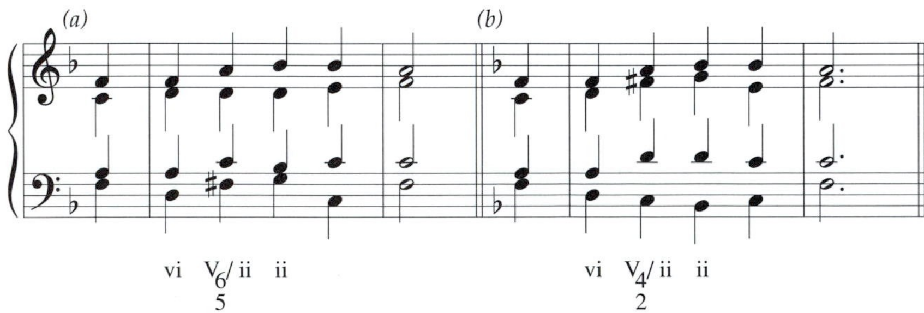

FIGURE 18.25

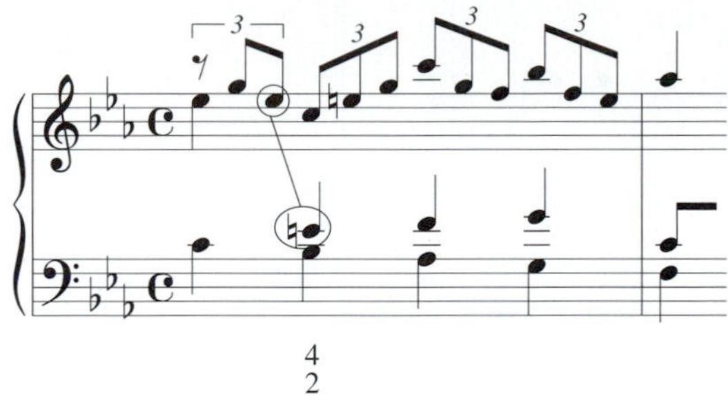

ASSIGNMENT 18.8 Write examples of the V/V and V⁷/V. The part-writing techniques involved can be applied to any secondary dominant triad or seventh chord.

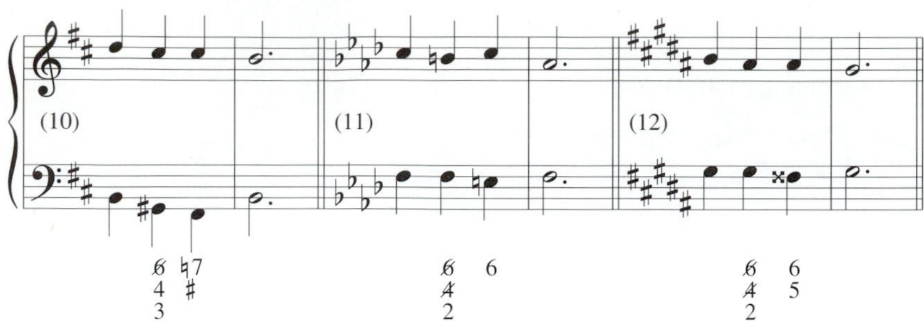

In Appendix E: Answers to (1), (6), (9), and (10) are given.
In the Workbook: Answers to the entire assignment are given.

ASSIGNMENT 18.9 *Part-writing modulations to the dominant or to the relative major.* Add nonharmonic tones if so assigned. Where no figured bass is given, add your own figured bass before filling in the inner voices.

Occasional exceptions to basic part-writing procedures may be necessary. These include incomplete triads and overlapping voices. Avoid, of course, parallel fifths and octaves, and exercise the usual care with leading tones.

In Appendix E: For exercise 2, the original chorale as written by Phillip Nicolai in 1599 is given. For Bach's harmonization of the same melody, see number 179 in The 371 Chorales.

ASSIGNMENT 18.10 *Part-writing secondary dominant harmony.* These exercises include a wide variety of secondary harmony usages other than the V/V. For (1)–(3), fill in inner voices; for (4)–(5), the bass line and an optional first soprano note are given.

(2)
(3)
(4)

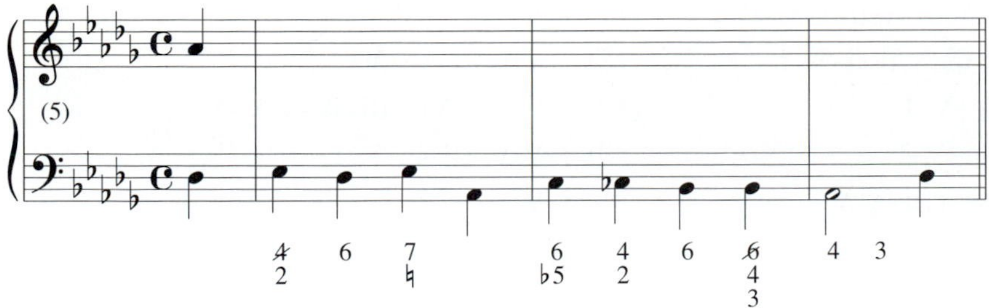

ASSIGNMENT 18.11 Harmonize these melodies: the first with a modulation to the dominant, and the second with a modulation to the relative major.

Keyboard Harmony

ASSIGNMENT 18.12 *Playing secondary dominant progressions.* Use these examples for practice. Play as written or with a seventh added to the secondary dominant chord.

(1) I–V/V–V–I
(2) I–V/ii–ii–V–I
(3) I–V/ii–V/V–V–I
(4) I–V/vi–vi–ii–V–I
(5) I–V/vi–vi–V/V–V–I
(6) I–V/vi–V/ii–V/V–V–I
(7) I–V/vi–IV–V–I
(8) I–vi–V/iii–iii–vi–ii–V–I
(9) I–vi–V/iii–iii–V/ii–ii–V–I
(10) I–vi–V/iii–iii–vi–V/V–V–I

(11) I–IV–V/iii–V/vi–V/ii–V/V–V–I
(12) I–IV–V/iii–iii–V/ii–ii–V–I
(13) I–V^7/IV–IV–V–I
(14) I–IV–V/ii–ii–V–I
(15) I–V^7/IV–IV–V/ii–ii–V–I
(16) i–V/V–V–i
(17) i–V^7/iv–iv–V–i
(18) i–VII–III–VI–V/V–V–i
(19) i–V/VII–VII–III–iv–V/V–V–i
(20) i–V/V–III–iv–V–i
(21) i–V/iv–iv–V–i
(22) i–V–VI–V/V–V–i

ASSIGNMENT 18.13 Play at the keyboard the following modulation formulas, beginning in any major or minor key, as instructed. You may start any example with any soprano position of the initial tonic triad, then continue the formula using basic part-writing procedures.

Major to Dominant

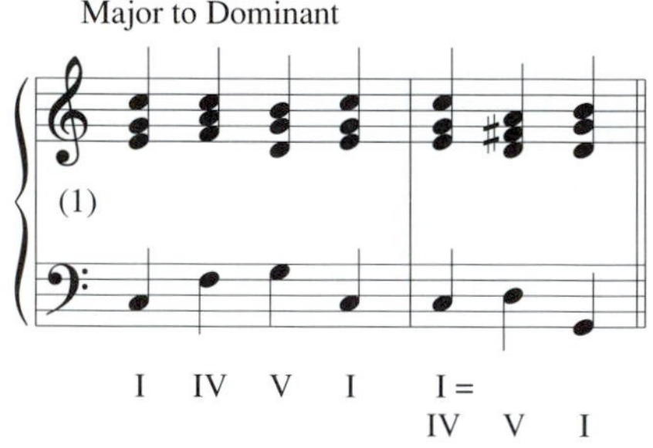

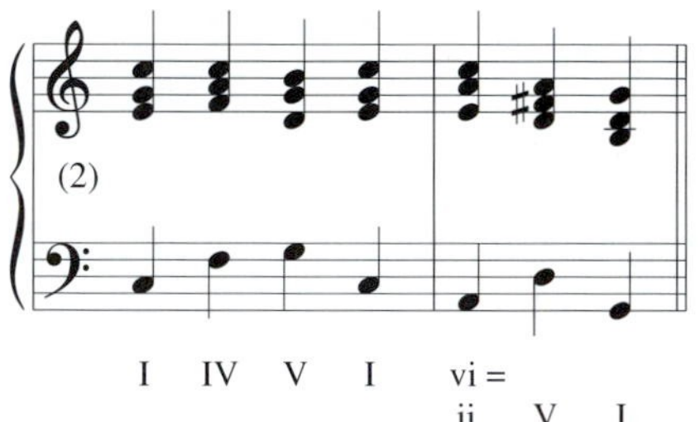

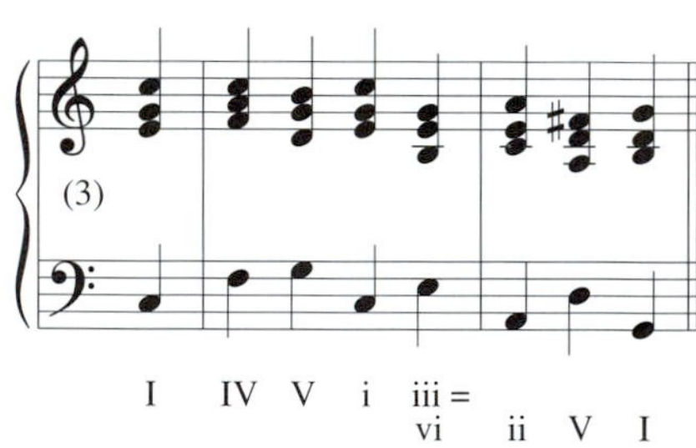
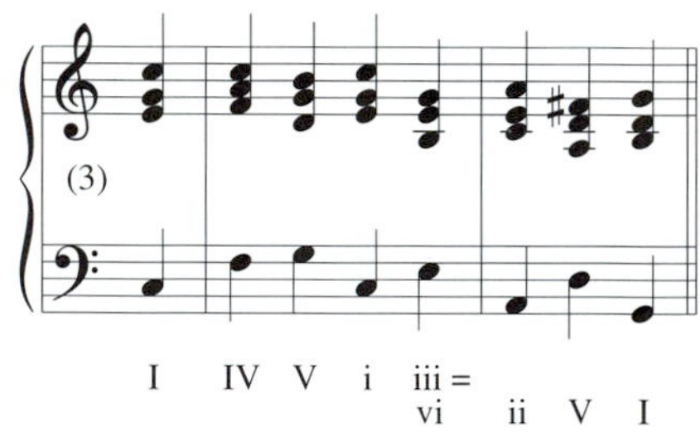

Minor to Relative Major

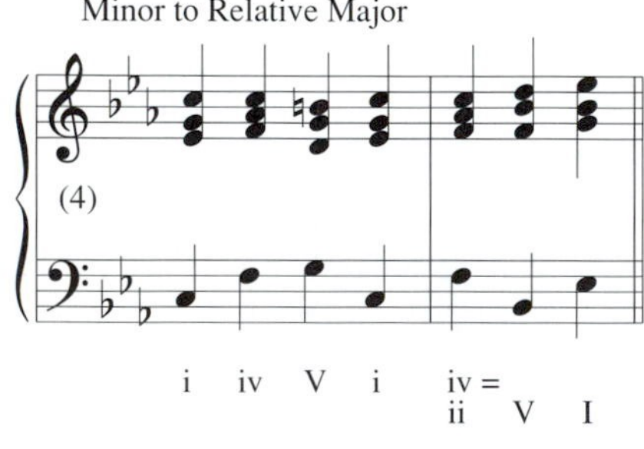

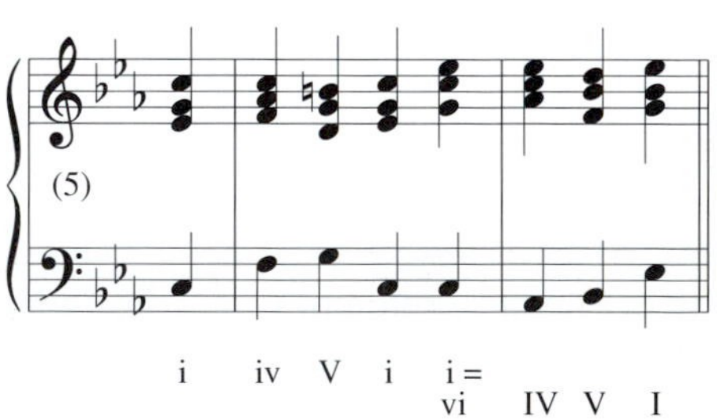

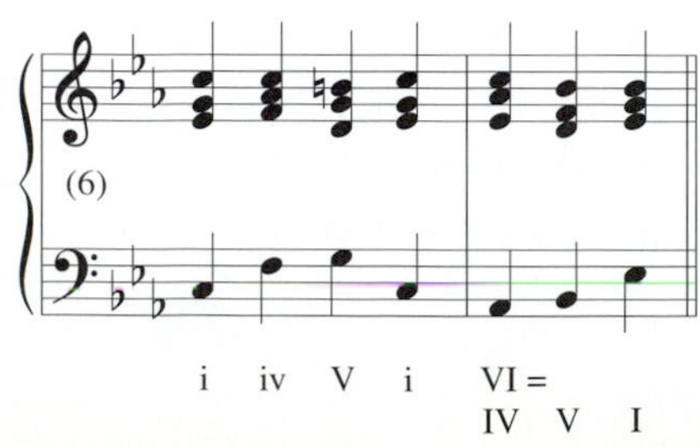

Summary

A *secondary dominant chord* is one that functions as a dominant to a chord other than the tonic of the key. Endowing a chord other than the tonic with the property of a tonic chord is called *tonicization.*

Secondary dominants (triads or major–minor seventh chords) may precede any major or minor triad, or any seventh chord with dominant or secondary dominant function. A *deceptive resolution* is also possible, the root of the secondary dominant resolving up a step to the following triad.

A harmonic sequence, roots down a fifth and up a fourth, may include secondary dominant chords in whole or in part.

Modulation is the process of harmonic movement from one key to another. It is most often accomplished by means of a *pivot chord,* one that is spelled identically in the two keys.

A harmonic progression including $V^{(7)}/V$ at the cadence often displays the characteristics of modulation to the dominant but leaves the aural impression of a half cadence in the original key. Analysis in this case is subjective, since the aural impression varies from person to person.

Modulation in a melodic line, even when no accidental is included, is discovered through the line's harmonic implication.

APPENDIX A

The Essentials of Part-Writing

conventional procedures

These essentials represent the basic procedures of part-writing. They are not intended to include the countless variations in part-writing techniques that can and do exist.

The Single Chord

Approximate range of the four voices

Soprano: d^1–g^2
Alto: a–c^2
Tenor: e–g^1
Bass: G–d^1

Triad Position In *open position,* the distance between the soprano and the tenor is an octave or more. In *close position,* the distance between the soprano and the tenor is less than an octave. The distance between adjacent voices usually does not exceed an octave, although more than an octave may appear between bass and tenor.

Usual Doubling The tonic, subdominant, and dominant tones in a key can ordinarily be doubled freely. To go beyond this generalization, some common doubling procedures are listed here.

Diatonic major and minor triads

1. Root in bass: Double the root.
2. First inversion: Double the soprano note.
3. Second inversion: Double the bass note.
4. Exception: Minor triads, root or third in bass. The third of a minor triad is often doubled, particularly when this third is the tonic, subdominant, or dominant note of the key.

Diminished triad (usually found in first inversion only): Double the third; however, when the fifth is in the soprano, the fifth is usually doubled.

Augmented triad: Double the bass note.

Seventh chord: Usually all four voices are present. In the major–minor seventh chord, root in bass, the root is often doubled and the fifth omitted.

Altered triad: Same doubling as nonaltered triads; avoid doubling the altered note unless that note is the root of a chord.

Chord Connection

The objective of part-writing is the connection of a series of chords in such a way that each of the voice lines is an acceptable melodic line and that any pair of voice lines sounds well together. The general procedures listed here should always be a consideration when working with any of the more specific procedures that follow shortly.

1. Move each voice the shortest distance possible.
2. Move the soprano and the bass in contrary or oblique motion if possible.
3. Avoid doubling the leading tone, any altered tone (including ♯$\hat{6}$ and ♯$\hat{7}$ in minor), any nonharmonic tone, and the seventh of any seventh chord.
4. Avoid parallel fifths and parallel octaves between any two voices, and the augmented second in a melodic line.

The more specific conventional procedures that follow help to ensure the production of satisfactory melodic lines while avoiding the objectionable items listed above. But they do not rule out the use of more creative melodic lines, the procedures for which are unique in any given situation (review page 245). Each conventional procedure following includes a page reference locating its initial presentation in the text.

Triads with Roots in the Bass

These procedures refer to two successive triads, each with its root in the bass.

Repeated Roots When roots in the bass are repeated, the two triads may be written in the same position (open or close) or they may be in different positions (page 89). Triad positions should be changed

1. when necessary to keep voices in correct pitch range;
2. when necessary to maintain a voice distribution of two roots, one third, and one fifth;
3. to avoid large leaps in an inner voice.

Roots a Fifth Apart

1. Retain the common tone; move the other voices stepwise (page 92).
2. Move the three upper voices in similar motion to the nearest triad tones (page 92).

3. At the cadence, the root of the final triad may be tripled, omitting the fifth (page 95).
4. Move the third of the first triad by interval of the fourth to the third of the second triad. Hold the common tone and move the other voice by step (page 95).

Roots a Second Apart Move the three upper voices in contrary motion to the bass (page 119).

Roots a Third Apart Hold the two common tones; the other voice moves stepwise (page 310).

General Exception When it is impossible or undesirable to follow conventional procedures, double the third in the second of the two triads; however, if this third is the leading tone or any altered tone, double the third in the first of the two triads (page 309).

Triads in Inversion

One of the Two Triads Is in Inversion Write to or from the doubled note first, using oblique or contrary motion if possible, and then fill in the remaining voice (page 181).

Both Triads Are in Inversion Each triad must have a different doubling to avoid parallel octaves and/or fifths, or the same doubling may appear in a different pair of voices. Avoid doubling the leading tone or any altered tone. Approach and leave each doubled tone as above (page 184).

Nonharmonic Tones

A nonharmonic tone temporarily replaces a harmonic tone. Approach and leave any nonharmonic tone according to the definition of the nonharmonic tone being used. Consider an accented nonharmonic tone as one of the chord tones, so that when it resolves the chord displays conventional doubling (page 241).

Seventh Chords

The seventh of a seventh chord, its note of approach, and its note of resolution constitute a three-note figure similar to these nonharmonic tone figures: passing tone, suspension, appoggiatura, and upper neighbor. The seventh usually resolves down by step (page 278).

APPENDIX B

Instrumentation

ranges; clefs; transposition

Range

For each instrument, the range written in whole notes is satisfactory for use in the exercises in this text. The lowest note for each instrument is given, and a dotted line connects the upper whole note with the actual highest note in that instrument's range.

Clef

Each instrument regularly uses the clef or clefs found in the musical illustrations under "Range." Exceptions or modifying statements are found under the heading "Clef."

Transposition

Unless otherwise indicated under this heading, pitches given under "Range" sound concert pitch when played (concert pitch: a^1 = 440 vibrations per second; the note a^1 on the piano keyboard is concert A). All transposing instruments sound their name when written C is played; for example, a clarinet in B♭ sounds B♭ when it plays a written C.

String Instruments

Violin

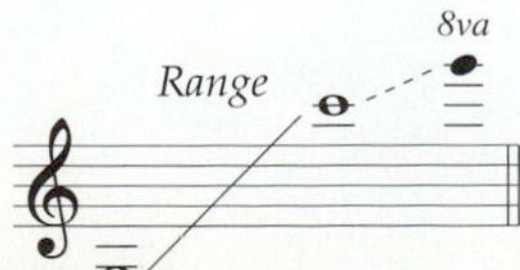

Viola

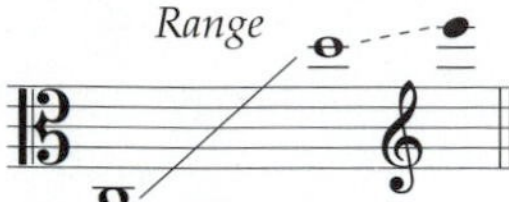

Clef. Alto clef is used almost exclusively. Treble clef is used occasionally for sustained high passages.

Violoncello (Cello)

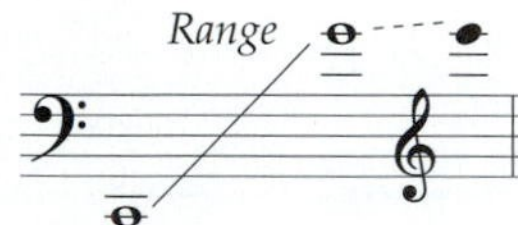

Clef. Bass clef is ordinarily used. Tenor clef is used for extended passages above small A. Treble clef is used for extreme upper range (not shown).

Double Bass (Bass Viol, Contrabass)

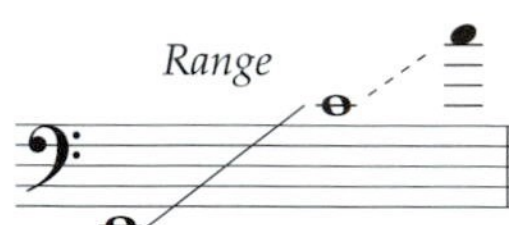

Transposition. Notes sound an octave lower than written.

Woodwind Instruments

Flute

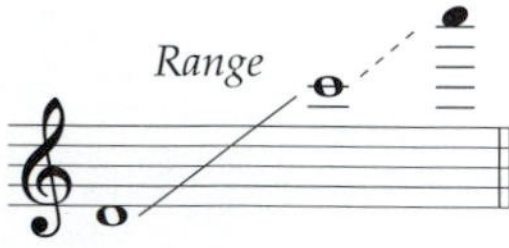

Oboe

English Horn (Cor Anglais)

Transposition. Notes sound a perfect fifth lower than written. Use signature for the key a perfect fifth *above* concert pitch.

Clarinet: B♭ and A

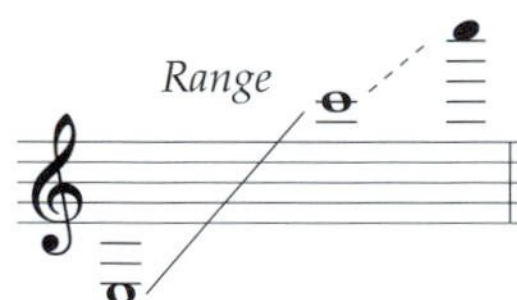

Transposition

1. Clarinet in B♭. Notes sound a major second lower than written. Use signature for the key a major second *above* concert pitch.
2. Clarinet in A. Notes sound a minor third lower than written. Use signature for the key a minor third *above* concert pitch.

Bassoon

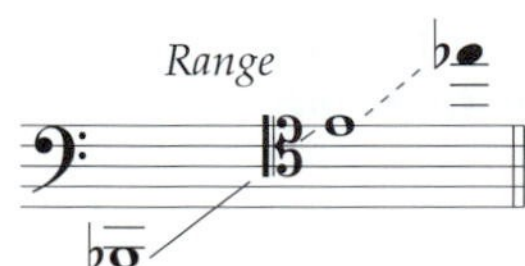

Clef. Bass clef is ordinarily used. Tenor clef is used for upper range.

Saxophone: E♭ Alto, B♭ Tenor, and E♭ Baritone

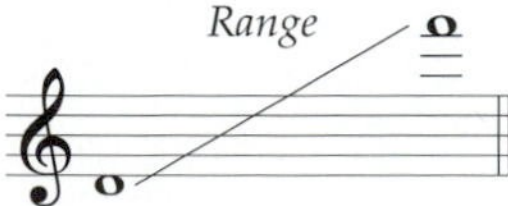

Transposition

1. **1.** E♭ alto saxophone. Notes sound a major sixth lower than written. Use signature for the key a major sixth *above* concert pitch.
2. **2.** B♭ tenor saxophone. Notes sound a major ninth (an octave plus a major second) lower than written. Use signature for the key a major second *above* concert pitch.
3. **3.** E♭ baritone saxophone. Notes sound an octave plus a major sixth lower than written. Use signature for the key a major sixth *above* concert pitch.

Brass Instruments

Horn (French Horn)

Clef. Treble clef is commonly used.
Transposition. Horn parts are written in F, E, E♭, and D.

In F: Notes sound a perfect fifth lower than written.

In E: Notes sound a minor sixth lower than written.

In E♭: Notes sound a major sixth lower than written.

In D: Notes sound a minor seventh lower than written.

Traditionally, horn parts have been written without key signatures, requiring accidentals to be placed before notes as needed. In recent practice, key signatures are given.

Trumpet or Cornet: B♭ and C

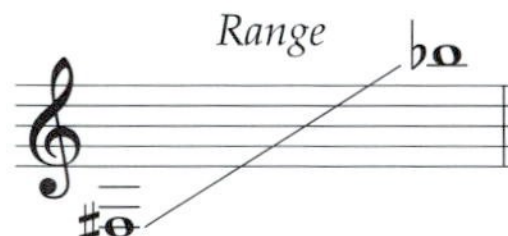

Transposition

1. **1.** Trumpet or cornet in B♭. Notes sound a major second lower than written. Use signature for the key a major second *above* concert pitch.
2. **2.** Trumpet or cornet in C. Nontransposing—sounds as written.

Trombone

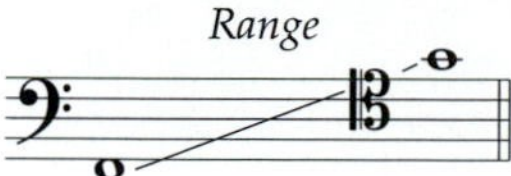

Clef. Both tenor and bass clefs are commonly used.

Tuba

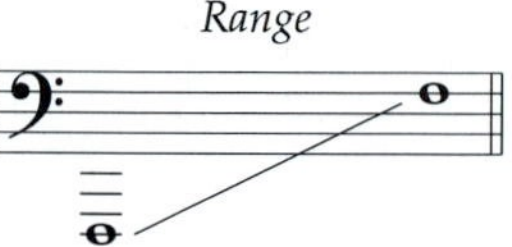

APPENDIX C

Elementary Acoustics

Sound occurs as the result of a three-stage process. First, an object must be set in vibration. Among such vibratory objects in music are a timpani head, a violin string, a clarinet reed, and the human vocal cords. Second, a transmission medium is necessary. Air serves this purpose by carrying vibrations from their source to the receiver. Third is the hearing process, carried out by the human or animal auditory system, in which the ear receives the vibrations and sends their message to the brain, which instantly interprets the message as sound. The study of this three-stage process—vibrating source, transmission medium, and receiver—is known as *acoustics.*

Frequencies

To produce vibrations, an object must be struck or in some other way set in motion. Vibrations are the back-and-forth motions of the object (vibrating body) after having been set in motion. These vibrations are usually measured by number per second (*frequency* of vibration), which can range from less than one (but more than zero) per second to many thousands per second. Frequencies ranging between approximately 16 and 20,000 per second can usually be perceived by the human auditory system, although in many animals the range can be much higher. The piano produces a range of approximately 30 to 4,000 vibrations per second from its lowest to its highest pitch.

A vibrating object will set the surrounding air in motion, so that it vibrates at the same rate as the original vibrating body. The vibrations are thereby transmitted from the object to the ear.

When counted, the vibrations of the original object and of the surrounding air were originally expressed as *cycles per second,* abbreviated *cps.* In recent times, the term *cps* has been replaced by *Hz,* in honor of Heinrich Hertz (1857–1894), discoverer of radio waves, but the two terms have the same meaning. Figure C.1 represents 2 cycles per second, or 2 cps, or 2 Hz. The horizontal line in the center represents a duration of time—in this case, 1 second—and the curved line represents the back-and-forth movement of the vibrating object. 2 Hz cannot, of course, be heard, but perhaps you can visualize a similar diagram for middle C, with approximately 256 vibrations per second. (If the horizontal line represented 1/128 of a second, Figure C.1 would represent 256 Hz.)

FIGURE C.1

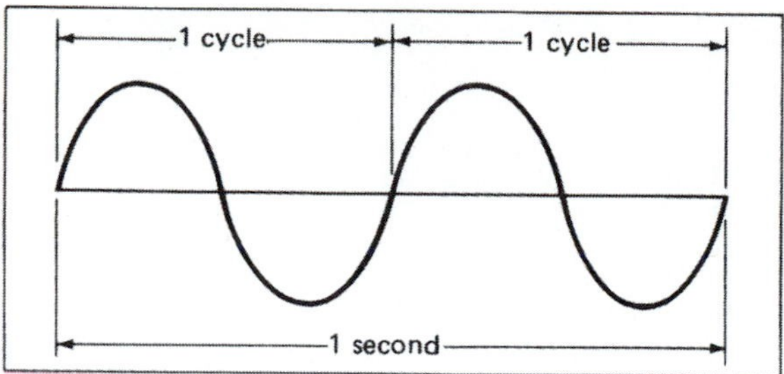

Pitch

When we hear a musical sound and think of it as being a "high" sound or a "low" sound, we are actually using these terms to express a property of sound: its *pitch.* The pitch of a sound is specifically related to its frequency of vibration: the greater the number of vibrations per unit of time, the higher the pitch; the fewer the number of vibrations for the same unit of time, the lower the pitch. Further, the two pitches of an interval can be expressed as a ratio of their frequencies. For example, for the interval of the octave, the upper note will have twice the number of vibrations of the lower note. If middle C is 256 Hz, the C one octave higher is 512 Hz, the next octave higher is twice 512, or 1,024 Hz, and so forth. The ratios for the five simplest intervals are shown in Figure C.2.

FIGURE C.2 *Intervallic ratios*

Interval name	***Perfect octave***	***Perfect fifth***	***Perfect fourth***	***Major third***	***Minor third***
Ratio	1:2	2:3	3:4	4:5	5:6

	1	2	3	4	5	6
Example 1 = 90 Hz	↑ 90	↑ 180	↑ 270	↑ 360	↑ 450	↑ 540

The Overtone Series

This series of ratios is also found in another phenomenon, the *overtone series.* Simply stated, when any pitch is sounded, a series of higher frequencies is also created, sounding simultaneously but usually inaudible to the human ear. Figure C.3 shows an overtone series on the pitch F. Although this example stops at 16, the series continues indefinitely, each successive interval becoming smaller and having less intensity.[1]

FIGURE C.3

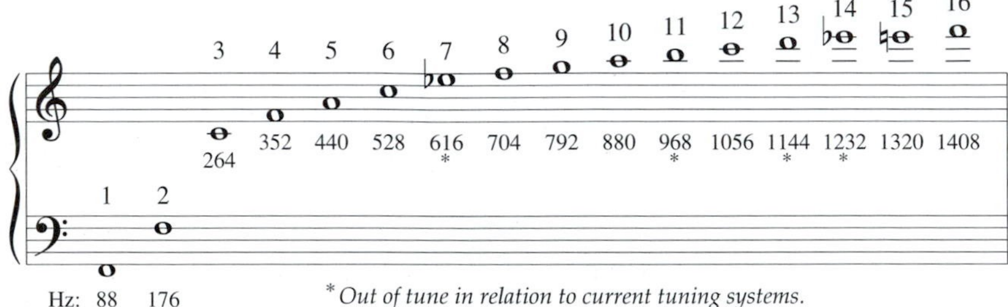

The intervallic ratios of the intervals in the table in Figure C.2, as well as all additional intervals, can be found in the overtone series. For example, 15:16 represents the minor second.

Members of the overtone series are usually known as partials. The lowest tone is the first partial, the tone an octave higher the second partial, and so forth. However, the members of this series are also known as overtones. In this terminology, the lowest tone is the fundamental, its octave the first overtone, and so forth. These terms describe the first four notes of the series seen in Figure C.3:

F:	first partial	fundamental
f:	second partial	first overtone
c^1:	third partial	second overtone
f^1:	fourth partial	third overtone

Intensity

The *intensity* of a pitch, its loudness or softness, is determined by the *amplitude,* or size, of its vibration. In Figure C.4, the two examples sound the same pitch (assuming that 2 Hz could be heard), but at *a* the pitch is softer because the amplitude of the vibrations is less than that at *b.*

[1]Similar acoustical properties are shown in the division of a string. See the article "The Theory of Inversion," page 196.

FIGURE C.4

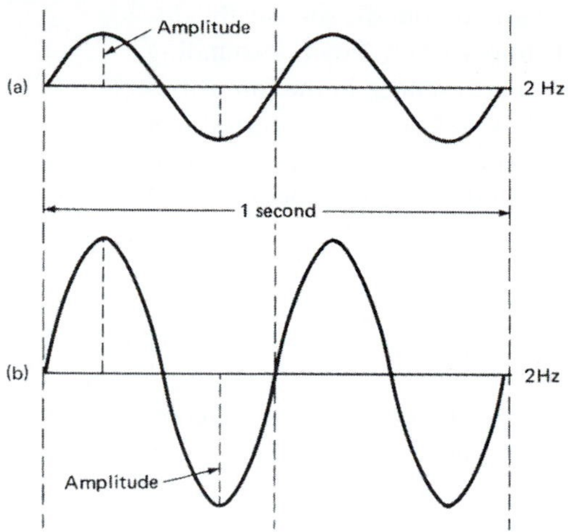

In Figure C.5, the tone at *a* is both higher (more vibrations per second) and louder (greater amplitude of vibrations) than the tone at *b*.

FIGURE C.5

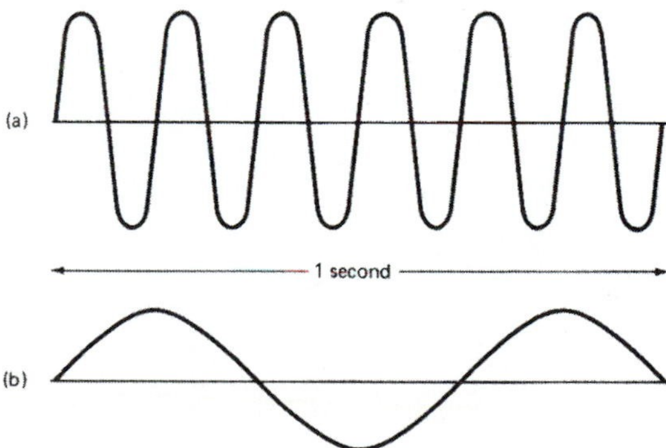

Timbre

The term *timbre* describes the difference in quality of various sounds, such as the difference between the sound of an oboe and that of a trumpet when they are sounding the same pitch. Differences in timbre are caused by (1) differences in the intensities of various partials produced by the vibrating body, (2) a lack of certain partials, or (3) a combination of these factors. For example, the clarinet tone includes only odd-numbered partials, the oboe tone most of the partials, and the flute tone only the first two partials.

Duration

The temporal length of a sound, or its *duration,* is under the direct control of the composer and the performer. Studies in duration are begun in Chapter 3 of this text.

APPENDIX D

The Medieval Modes

Music from medieval times to the seventeenth century was characterized by the use of six scale patterns, or modes, rather than the two, major and minor, in use in the tonal period. These are like the major and minor modes in that all consist of seven scale steps, but each mode begins on a different letter name and uses only pitches from the "white notes" of the keyboard. Therefore, the location of the half steps and whole steps differs in each mode, as seen in the following table. The first scale step in any mode is known as its *final.* When the range of the melody is generally between the final and its octave, the mode is said to be *authentic,* and when the range is generally between the fifth of the scale and its octave, it is *plagal.* For the latter, the prefix *hypo-* becomes part of the name of the mode—for example, *hypodorian.*

Authentic mode number	***Mode***	***Spelling/half steps***	***Plagal mode number***
I	Dorian	D E F G A B C D $\hat{2}$ $\hat{3}$ $\hat{6}$ $\hat{7}$	II
III	Phrygian	E F G A B C D E $\hat{1}$ $\hat{2}$ $\hat{5}$ $\hat{6}$	IV
V	Lydian	F G A B C D E F $\hat{4}$ $\hat{5}$ $\hat{7}$ $\hat{8}$	VI
VII	Mixolydian	G A B C D E F G $\hat{3}$ $\hat{4}$ $\hat{6}$ $\hat{7}$	VIII
IX	Aeolian	A B C D E F G A $\hat{2}$ $\hat{3}$ $\hat{5}$ $\hat{6}$	X
XI	Ionian	C D E F G A B C $\hat{3}$ $\hat{4}$ $\hat{7}$ $\hat{8}$	XII

A mode on B, called Locrian, is theoretical. Because it has a tritone from its tonic to its dominant, it was not considered practical or useful.

These modes can be related to the present major and minor modes for easy identification:

Dorian: Like natural minor with a raised sixth scale step
Phrygian: Like natural minor with a lowered second scale step
Lydian: Like major with a raised fourth scale step
Mixolydian: Like major with a lowered seventh scale step
Aeolian: Same as natural minor
Ionian: Same as major

The Kyrie following is an example of the Mixolydian mode. Note that the final is G but that F♮ is used throughout except for an F♯ at the cadence.

Palestrina, Missa, *Dies Sanctificatus*

The F♯ at the cadence is one example of a system known as *musica ficta,* or *false music.* The accidental, though not written in the music, was assumed to be present by both the composer and the performer (it is placed above the note in modern scores). The cumulative effect of the various rules of *musica ficta* was eventually to reduce the modes, except for the Phrygian, to major and minor. For example, changing the F in Mixolydian to F♯ creates a major scale.

Many of the Bach chorales are based on hymn tunes written in the modes that were common a century or more before Bach's time. One of the best known, "O Haupt voll Blut und Wunden" ("O Sacred Head Now Wounded"), a tune in the Phrygian mode, was originally the secular love song shown in the next example.

Hans Leo Hassler, *Mein Gmüth ist mir verwirret* (1601)

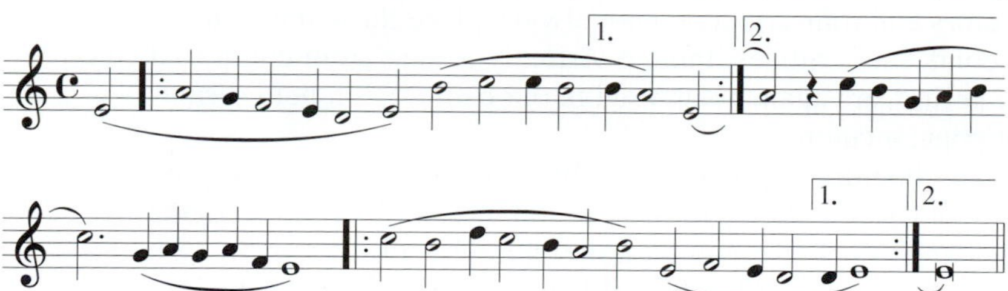

(Because of this girl, my feelings are all confused. I feel lost and heart-sick, and have no peace. Always I complain, and I weep in my sadness.)

Bach harmonized this tune both in Phrygian and in major, as shown in the following example by these two versions of the final phrase. Note how Bach changed the penultimate note of the melody.

(a) Bach, "O Haupt voll Blut und Wunden" (#89)

(b) Bach, "O Haupt voll Blut und Wunden" (#98)

Transposition of Modes

Before the seventeenth century, modes had been written only on the scale steps listed, or transposed a fifth lower (fourth higher), adding one flat to the key signature.

Dorian

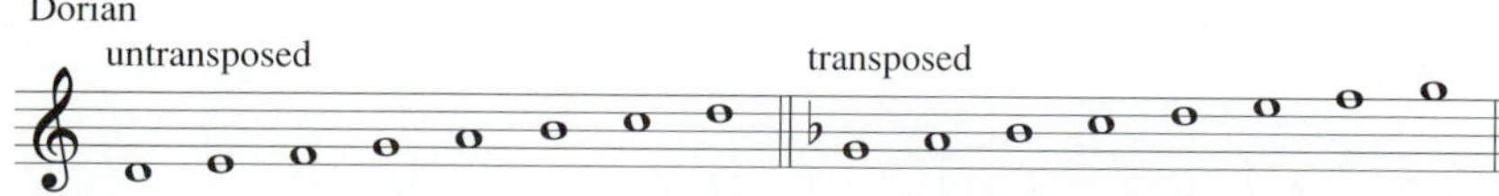

Other transpositions are useful for at least two reasons. First, much of the world's folk music is modal. Collectors and transcribers do not always place these tunes in untransposed modes. Second, these modes, though virtually absent from composed music during the tonal period, are again being used in our own time in both serious music and the music of popular culture.

Transposition to any beginning pitch is possible and can be done easily by recalling the relationship of each mode to either the major or the minor mode. In the preceding example, Dorian is similar to natural minor but with a raised sixth scale step. To transpose to G, spell a G natural minor scale and raise the sixth scale step, E♭, to E. To transpose to E, do the same, and the scale E F♯ G A B C♯ D E is the result.

To determine the mode of the melody, ask yourself: (1) Is the scale more like major or minor (check the third scale step)? and (2) Which scale step differs from this major or minor scale? Here is the well-known folk tune "Greensleeves."

1. The scale is more like minor (tonic, F; third, A♭).
2. The sixth scale step, D, is raised. Therefore, "Greensleeves" is in the Dorian mode.

In current practice, the key signature for a mode may be the same as that for the closest major or minor key, or it may include those accidentals used in that mode. As notated in the preceding example, "Greensleeves" shows a signature for F minor, with D♮ written in. The key signature could have been three flats.

Here are five modal tunes. Some signatures reflect only the accidentals of the mode, whereas other signatures are the same as the major or minor scale built on the mode's first scale step. All are transposed modes. Name the mode and spell the scale in the key of the example.

In Appendix E: Answers to the entire assignment are given.

APPENDIX E

Answer Key

Chapter 1

Basics Quiz #1

1. (1) b^1, (2) f^1, (3) a^2, (4) d^1, (5) g, (6) a^3, (7) f, (8) A, (9)BB, (10) g^1, (11) F, (12) e^1

2. (1) GG, (2) A, (3) b, (4) e^2, (5) d^3, (6) c^4

3. (1) whole, (2) half, (3) whole, (4) half, (5) half, (6) whole

4.

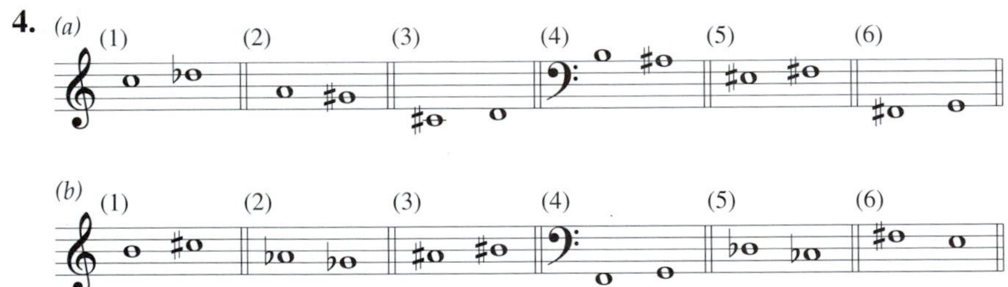

5.

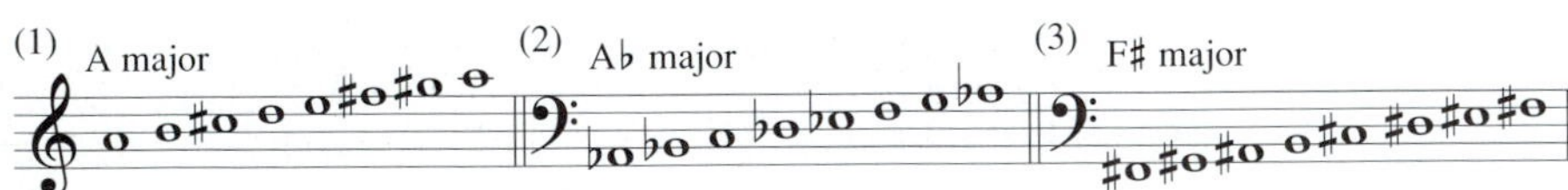

6. (1) B♭, (2) C♯, (3) D, (4) D♭, (5) B

7.

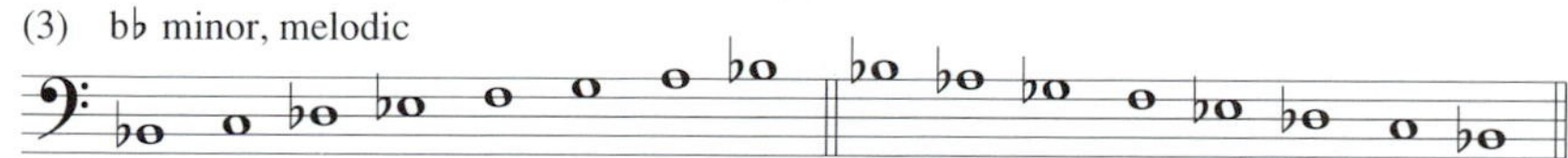

8. (1) g, (2) c♯, (3) b♭, (4) b, (5) a♭

9. (1) b, d, (2) c, e♭, (3) F, D, (4) B, none, (5) D, B, (6) f, a♭

10. (1) G♭, (2) C♯, (3) C♭

Chapter 2

Drill #1

Drill #2

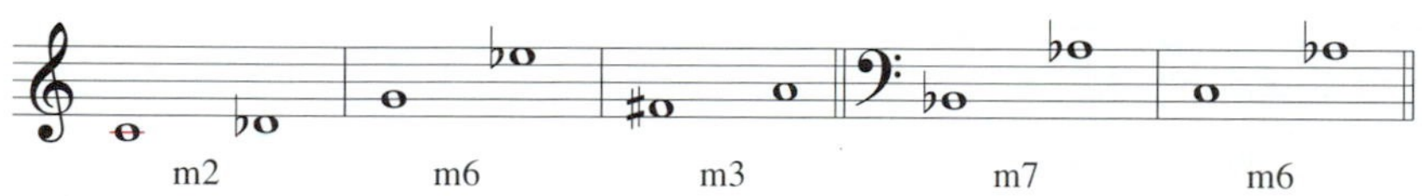

Drill #3

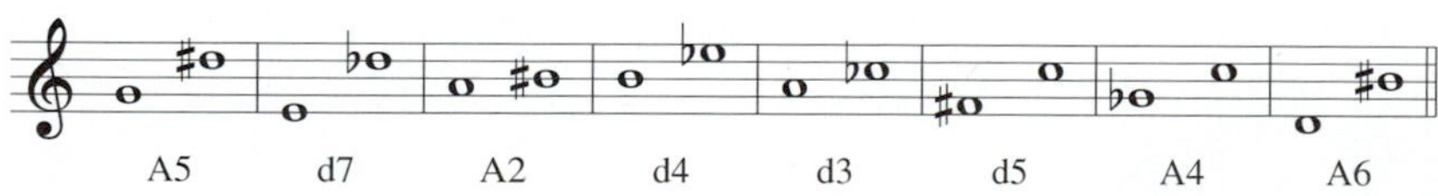

Drill #4

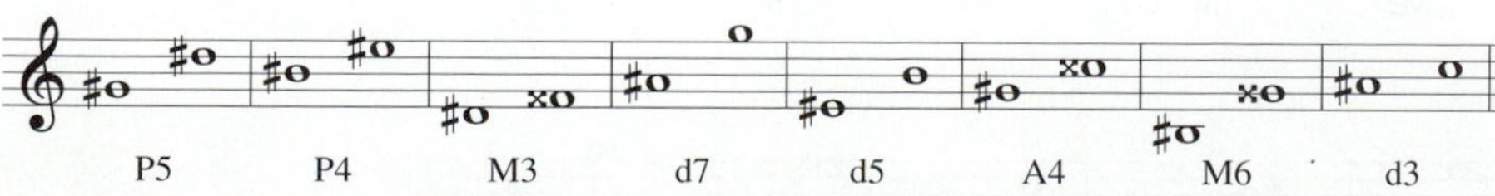

Drill #5

Drill #6

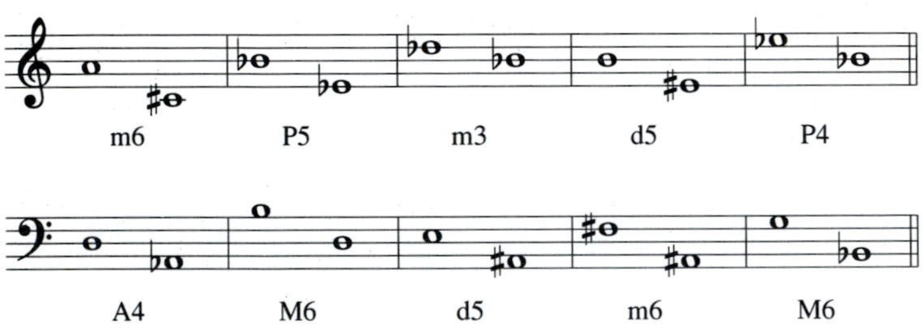

Basics Quiz #2

1.

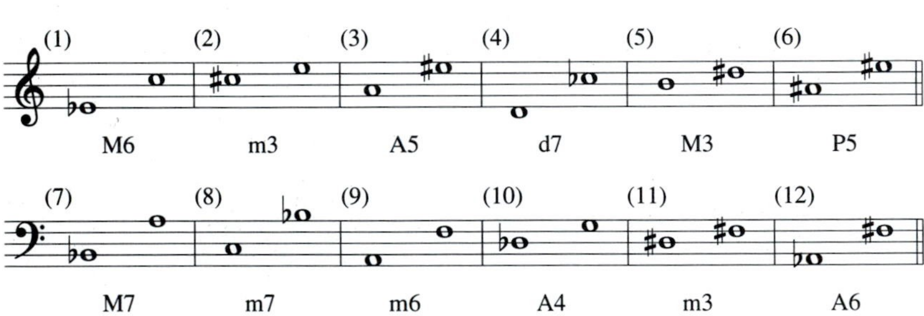

2. *a.* m6 *e.* m3
b. P4 *f.* m7
c. m2 *g.* A4
d. d5 *h.* d7

3.

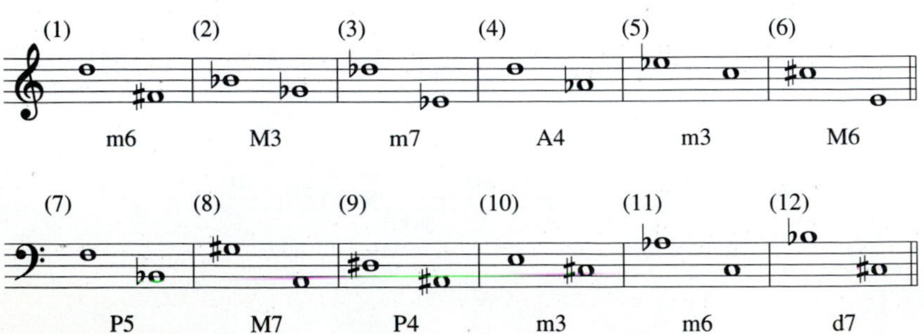

4. (1) d, (2) M, (3) A, (4) m, (5) A, (6) d, (7) M, (8) m

5. (1) V, (2) ii, (3) vii°, (4) IV, (5) I, (6) vi, (7) iii

6. (1) iv, (2) VI, (3) V, (4) IV, (5) ii°, (6) VII, (7) vii°, (8) III

Chapter 3

Basic Quiz #3

1.

2.

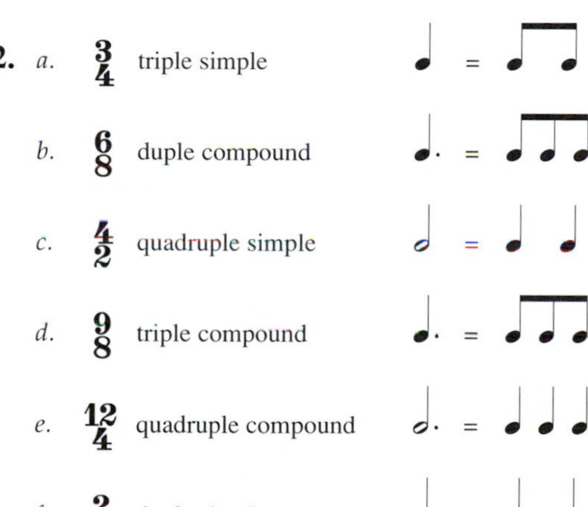

Chapter 4

Assignment 4.1

(a) Group I: F A C, F♯ A♯ C♯, F♭ A♭ C♭; G B D, G♯ B♯ D♯, G♭ B♭ D♭
Group II: D F♯ A, D♯ F𝄪 A♯, D♭ F A♭; E G♯ B, E♯ G𝄪 B♯, E♭ G B♭

(b) E G♯ B, G B D, D F♯ A, G♭ B♭ D♭, B♭ D F, D♯ F𝄪 A♯, A C♯ E, B𝄫 D♭ F♭, G B D, F♯ A♯ C♯

(c) F A C, E G♯ B, B D♯ F♯, D♭ F A♭, B♭ D F, C♯ E♯ G♯, E♭ G B♭, D♭ F A♭, A♯ C𝄪 E♯, C♭ E♭ G♭

Assignment 4.3

(1) F, PA, $\hat{7}$–$\hat{8}$; (2) B♭, IA, $\hat{5}$–$\hat{5}$; (3) A♭, PA, $\hat{2}$–$\hat{1}$; (4) F, H, $\hat{1}$–$\hat{2}$; (5) F, IA, $\hat{5}$–$\hat{5}$ *or* PA, $\hat{7}$–$\hat{1}$; (6) E♭, PA, $\hat{2}$–$\hat{1}$; and PA, $\hat{7}$–$\hat{8}$

Assignment 4.4

(a) A C E, B♭ D♭ F, B D F♯, C♯ E G♯, F♯ A C♯

(b) E G B, C E♭ G, G B♭ D, F A♭ C, G♯ B D♯

(c) B D F♯, C♯ E G♯, G B♭ D, E♭ G♭ B♭, D♯ F♯ A♯

Assignment 4.5

(1) a, PA, $\hat{2}$–$\hat{1}$; (2) d, PA, $\hat{7}$–$\hat{8}$; (3) g, H, $\hat{3}$–$\hat{2}$

Assignment 4.6

(1) b, PA, circle the note B; (2) g, PA, circle the note G; (3) D, IA, circle the note B in the alto, G in the soprano

Assignment 4.7

(1) at *, H, final, PA; (2) H; (3) IA; (4) at *, H, final PA

Assignment 4.8

(1) A, (2) B♭, (3) D♭, (4) E♯, (5) G♭, (6) C♭

Assignment 4.9

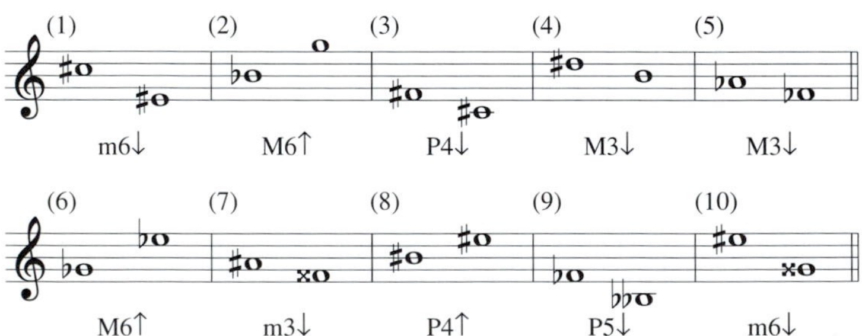

Chapter 5

Assignment 5.2

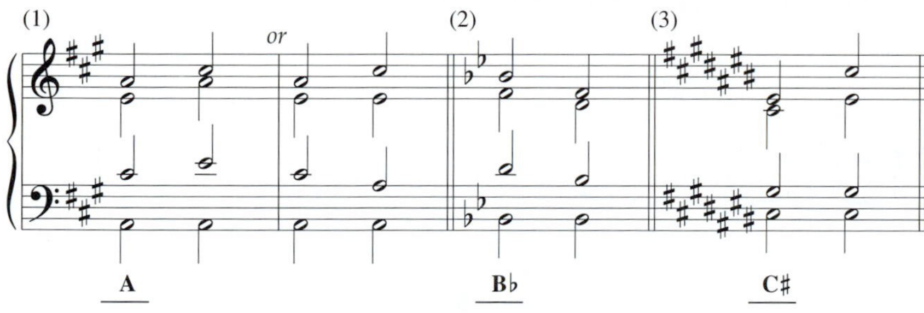

Assignment 5.4

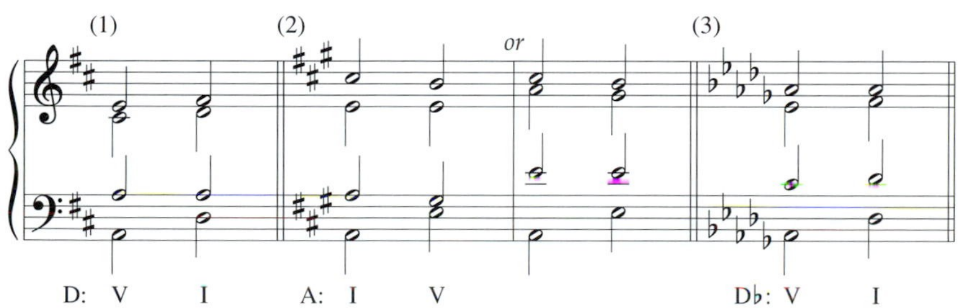

Assignment 5.8

Chapter 6

Assignment 6.3

(1) g, IP, $\hat{3}$–$\hat{2}$; (2) A, PP, $\hat{5}$–$\hat{5}$; (3) c♯, H, $\hat{2}$–$\hat{3}$; (4) f♯, IP, $\hat{1}$–$\hat{3}$; (5) g♯, IP, $\hat{6}$–$\hat{5}$

Assignment 6.4

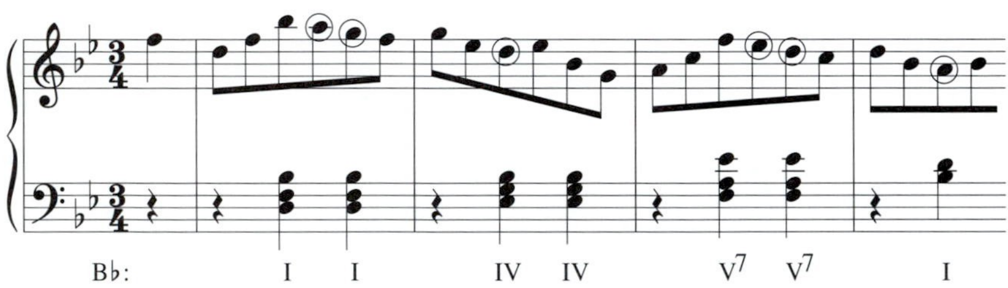

Assignment 6.10

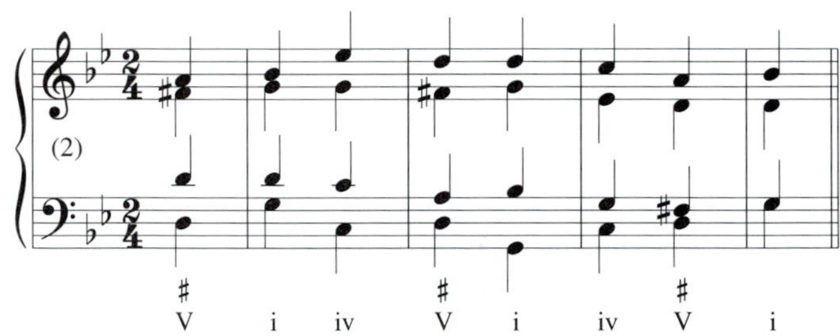

Chapter 7

Assignment 7.1

(1)
First phrase: weak beginning; strong ending; cadence, H ($\hat{1}$–$\hat{2}$)
Second phrase: weak beginning; weak ending; cadence PA ($\hat{2}$–$\hat{1}$)
Form: parallel period

(2)
First phrase: weak beginning; strong ending; cadence, H ($\hat{3}$–$\hat{2}$)
Second phrase: weak beginning; strong ending; cadence, PA ($\hat{2}$–$\hat{1}$)
Form: contrasting period

(5)
First phrase: strong beginning; strong ending, IA ($\hat{1}$–$\hat{5}$) with connecting link to
Second phrase: strong beginning, weak ending, PA ($\hat{7}$–$\hat{1}$)
Form: contrasting period

Assignment 7.2

(1)

Assignment 7.4

Chapter 8

Assignment 8.4

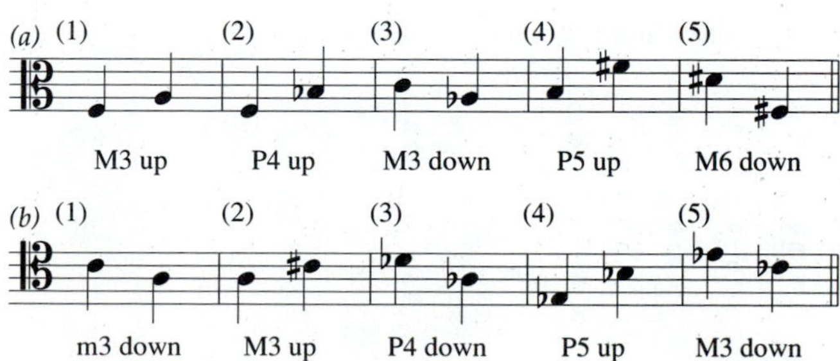

Assignment 8.5

(1)

Assignment 8.6

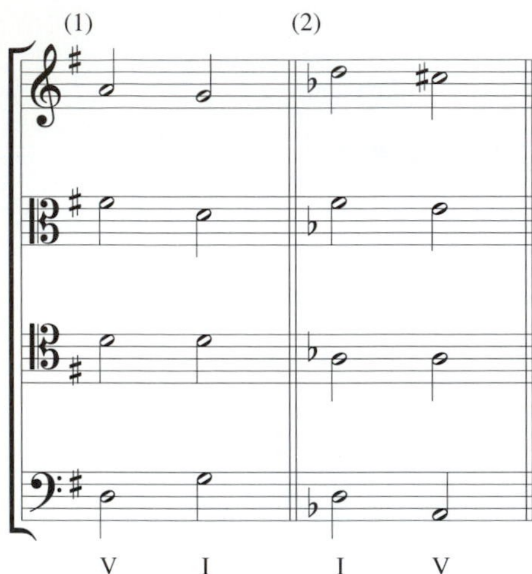

Assignment 8.7

(a) (1) E, (2) E, (3) D♭, (4) F, (5) B♭

(b)

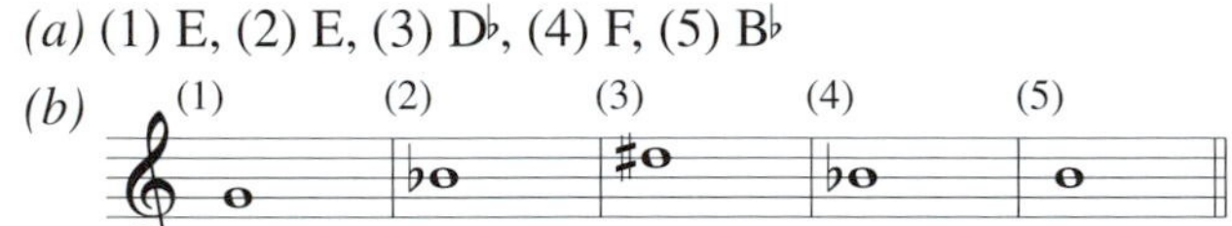

Chapter 9

Assignment 9.1

(1)

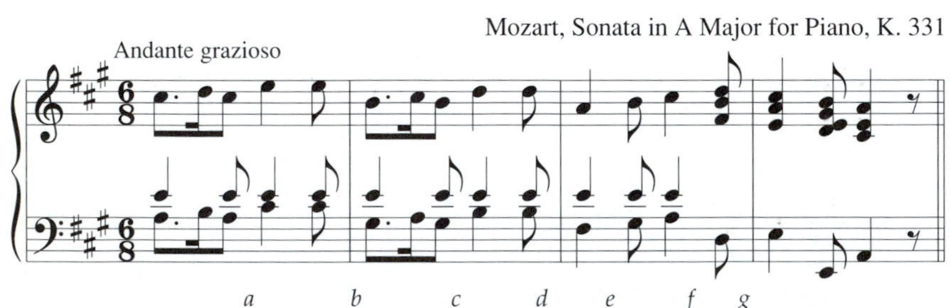

(a) Skip to first inversion in the same triad.

(b) Skip from first inversion of I to first inversion of V.

(c) Skip from first inversion of V to second inversion of V.

(d) Skip from second inversion of V to first inversion of IV

(e) Inversion in scale-line movement.

(f) Skip from root in bass line to first inversion.

(g) Cadential six-four chord.

Assignment 9.2

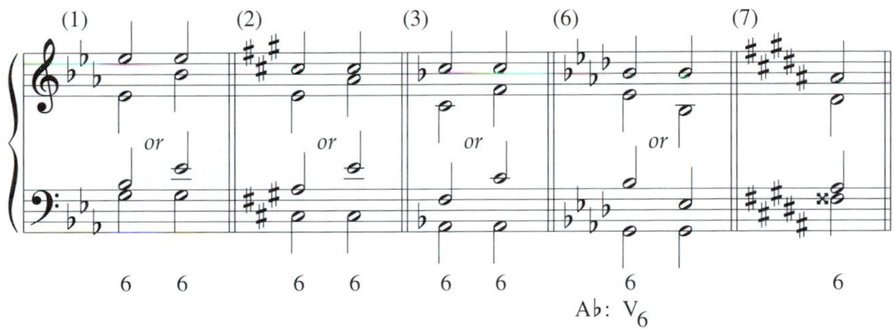

Assignment 9.3

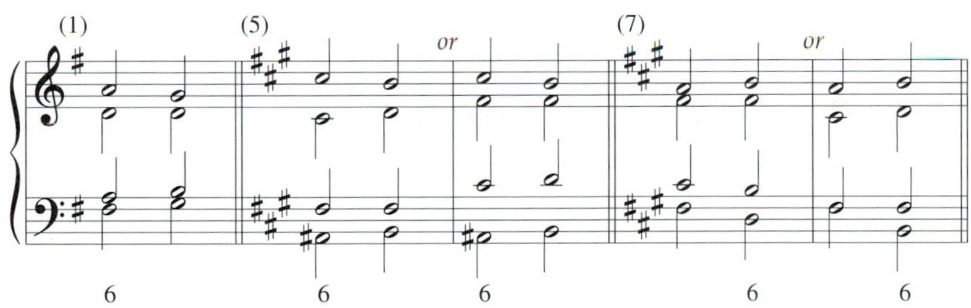

Assignment 9.4

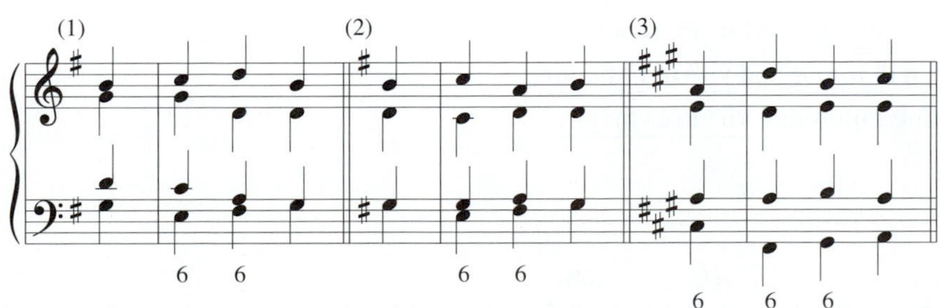

Assignment 9.5

Assignment 9.8

	C	S	O	S: 3rds and 6ths
Figure 9.5	7	4	1	4
Figure 9.7	5	1	1	1
Figure 9.11	3	3	1	3
Figure 9.17	2	3	2	2

Chapter 10

Assignment 10.2

(1) C E♭ G♭; (2) G B♭ D♭; (3) F♯ A C; (4) D♯ F♯ A; (5) E♯ G♯ B; (6) D F A♭

Assignment 10.3

a. D♯ F♯ A is vii° in E major and ii° in c♯ minor.
b. G B♭ D♭ is vii° in A♭ major and ii° in f minor.
c. A♯ C♯ E is vii° in B major and ii° in G♯ minor.
d. C E♭ G♭ is vii° in D♭ major and ii° in b♭ minor.
e. F♯ A C is ii° e minor and vii° in G major.
f. G♯ B D is vii° in A major and ii° F♯ minor.
g. E♯ G♯ B♯ is ii° in d♯ minor and vii° in F♯ major.
h. C♯ E G is ii° in b minor and vii° in D major.

Assignment 10.5

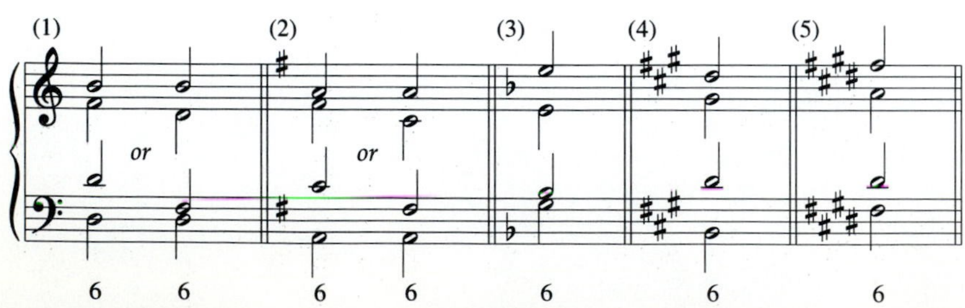

Assignment 10.6

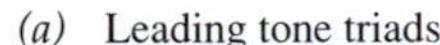

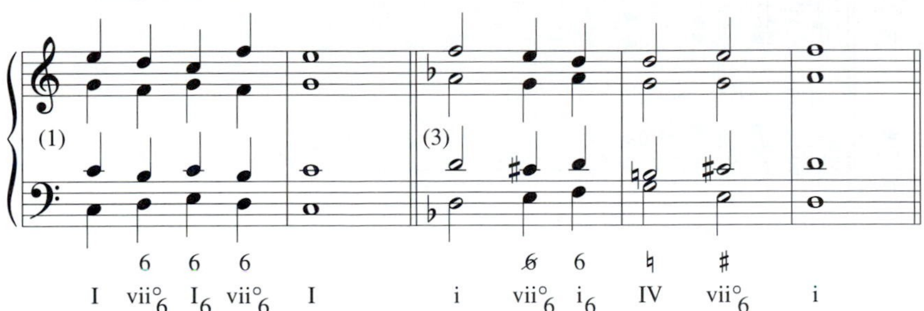

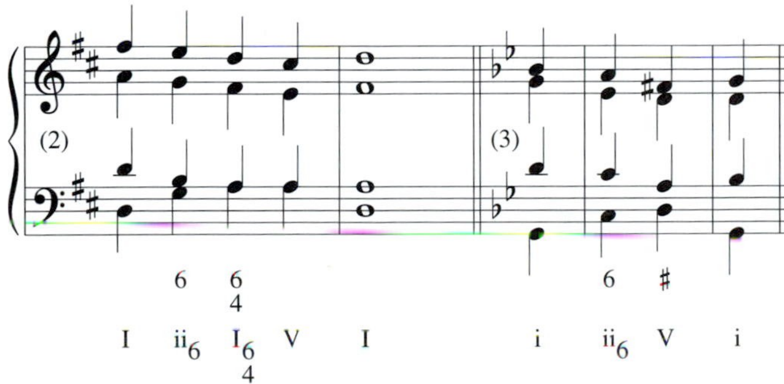

Chapter 11

Assignment 11.1

A. 1, B. 7, C. 5, D. 2, E. 8, F. 9, G. 3, H. 6, I. 4, J. 11, K. 10, L. 2, M. 8, N. 12

Chapter 12

Assignment 12.1

Suspension	*Example*	*Measure*	*Beat*
9 8	1	2	2
7 6	2	1	4
4 3	1	3	4
2 1	2	2	1
2 3	1	1	2

Assignment 12.3

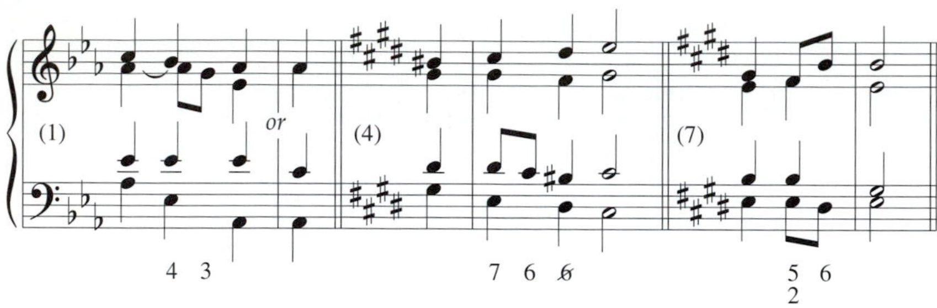

Assignment 12.4

Assignment 12.5

Nonharmonic tone	*Example number*	*Cue numbers*
Chain suspension	1	3–5
2 1 suspension	8	5
Suspension, change in bass, different chord	1	3, or 2 7
Successive neighbors	7	8–9
Ornamental resolution of suspension	4	6, or 7 13, 8 6
Anticipation	3	6
Double suspension	5	2
Appoggiatura	6	6
Escaped tone	4	5
Pedal	7	6–14
Double appoggiatura	2	5
Retardation	1	6

Assignment 12.6

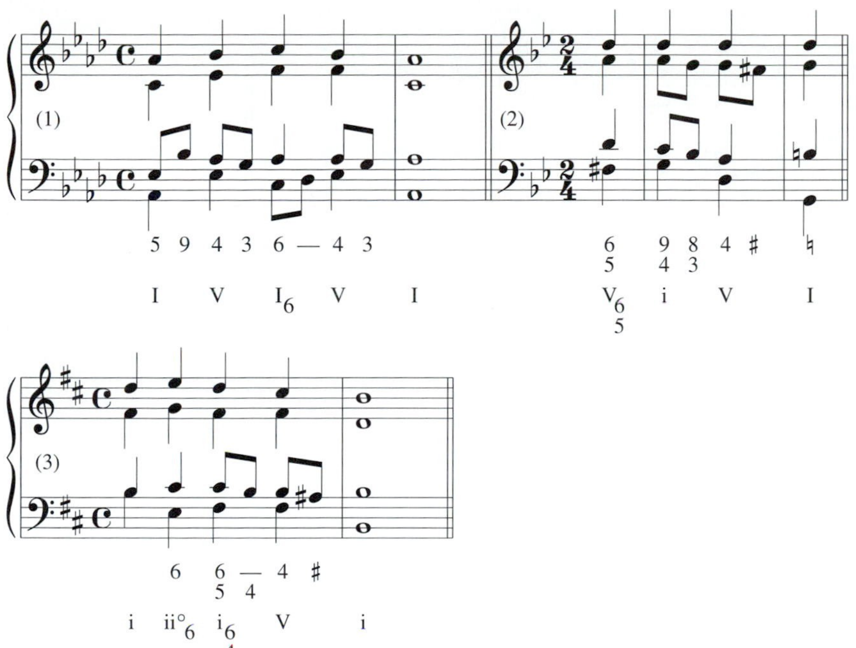

Chapter 13

Assignment 13.3

Assignment 13.4

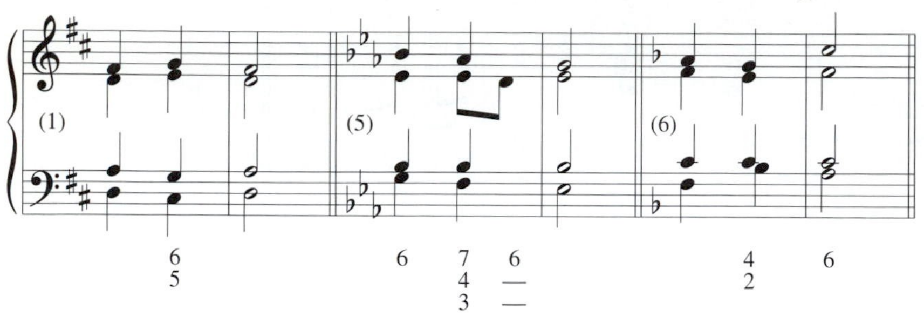

Assignment 13.5

Chapter 14

Assignment 14.3

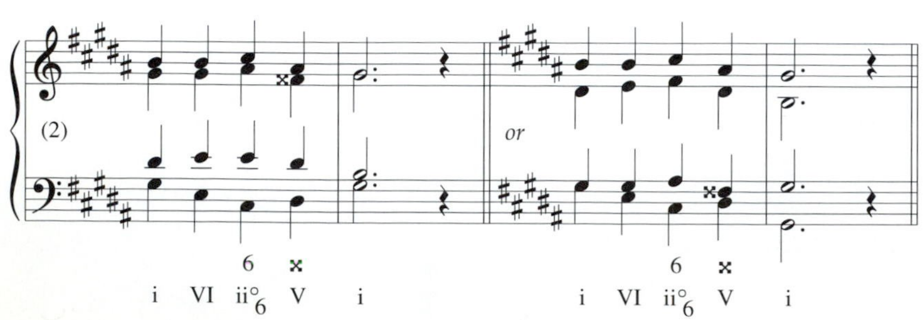

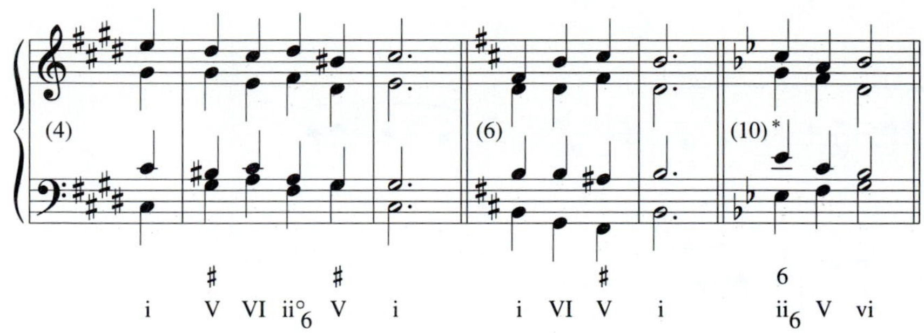

* C in tenor acceptable

Assignment 14.4

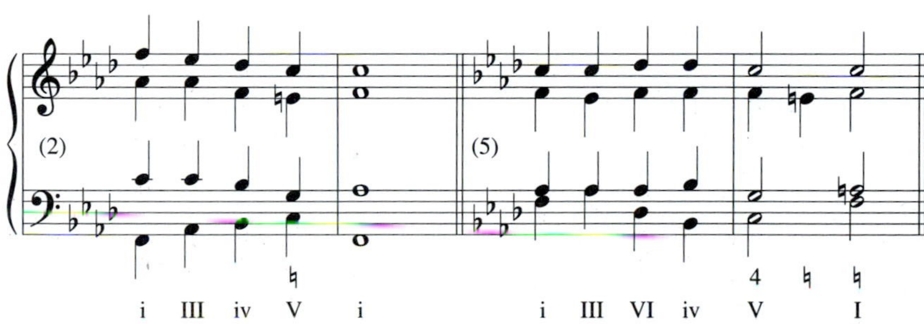

Chapter 15

Assignment 15.1

(1)

1. Phrase 1: ends in measure 4
   Phrase 2: ends in measure 9
2. Form: contrasting period, with extension
3. Extension: measure 6, added measure
4. Phrase lengths: (1) 4 measures, (2) 5 measures

(2)

1. Phrase 1: ends in measure 4
   Phrase 2: ends in measure 10
2. Form: contrasting period, with extension
3. Extension: measures 7–8, sequence
4. Phrase lengths: (1) 4 measures, (2) 6 measures

Assignment 15.2

Assignment 15.3

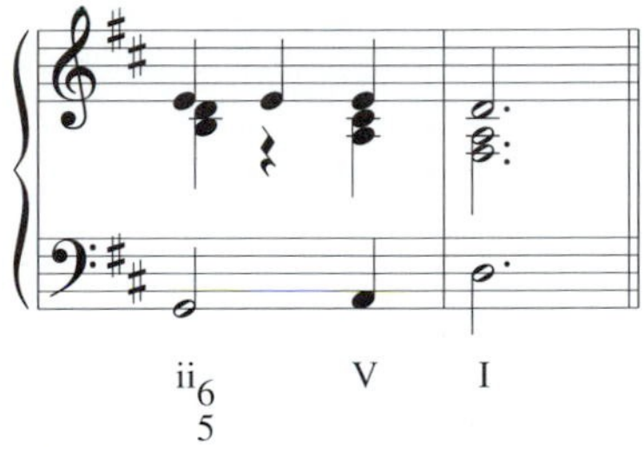

* Or use vi.

Chapter 16

Assignment 16.3

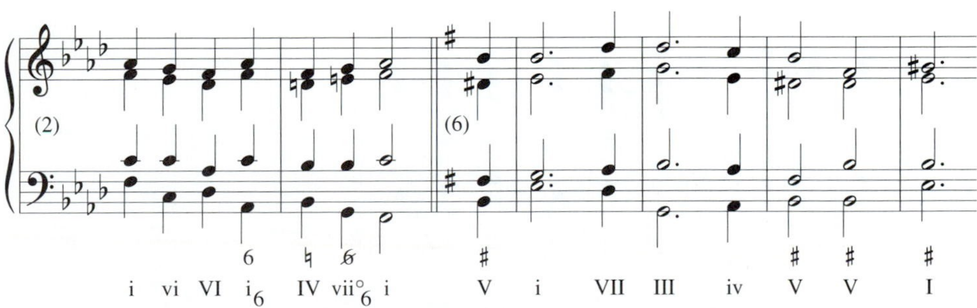

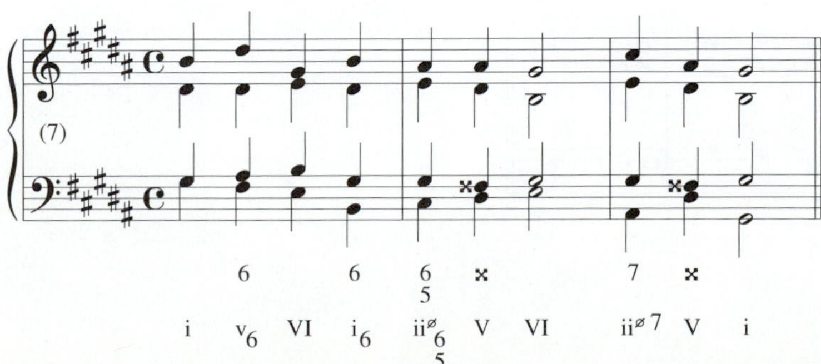

Assignment 16.4

Chapter 17

Assignment 17.3

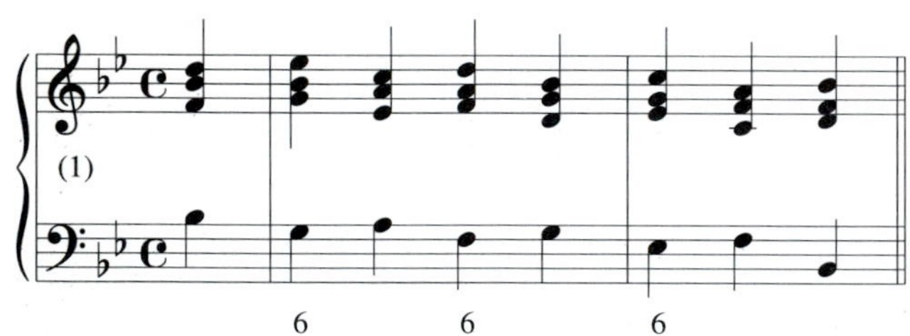

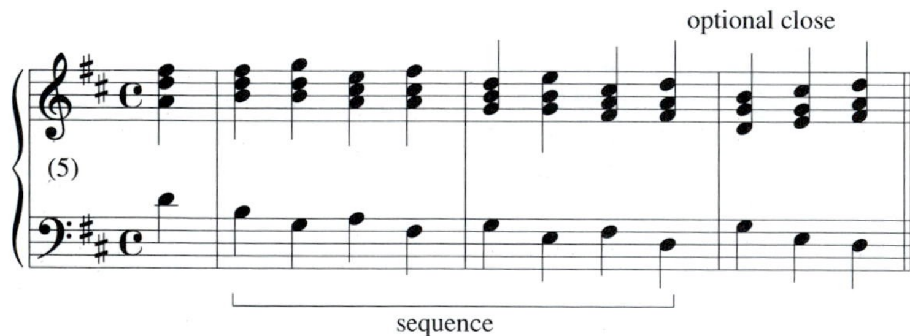

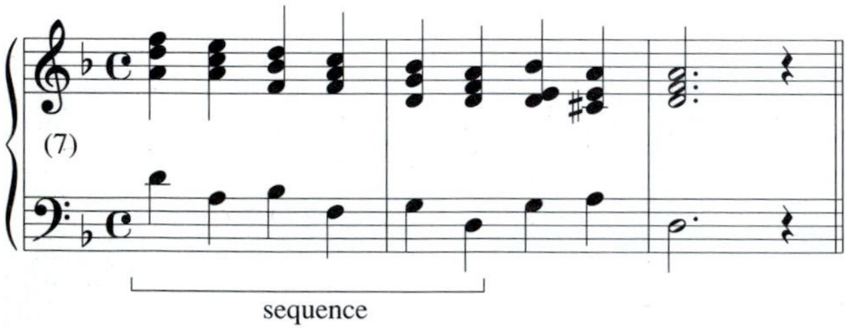

Assignment 17.4

Chapter 18

Assignment 18.2

(1) A C♯ E
(2) B D♯ F♯ A
(3) A C♯ E
(4) E G♯ B D
(5) F A C E♭
(6) G♯ B♯ D♯
(7) A♯ C× E♯ G♯
(8) F A C E♭
(9) E G♯ B
(10) G B D F
(11) E♯ G× B♯ D♯
(12) A♭ C E♭ G♭

Assignment 18.5

(1) D F♯ A
(2) C E♭ G
(3) vi = ii
(4) I = IV
(5) C E♭ G
(6) i = vi
(7) G♭ B♭ D♭
(8) iv = ii
(9) D♯ F♯ A♯
(10) iv = ii

Assignment 18.8

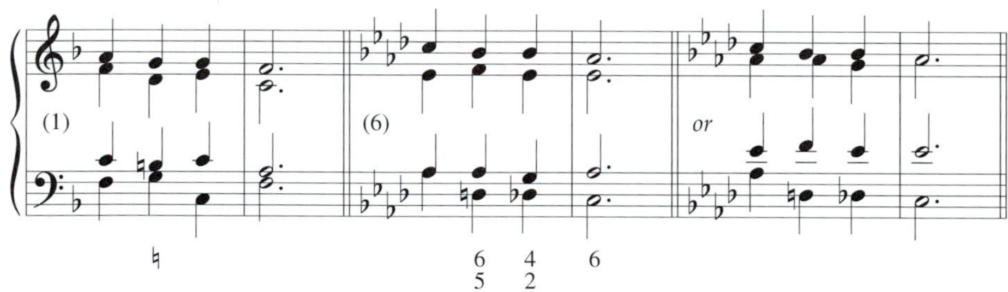

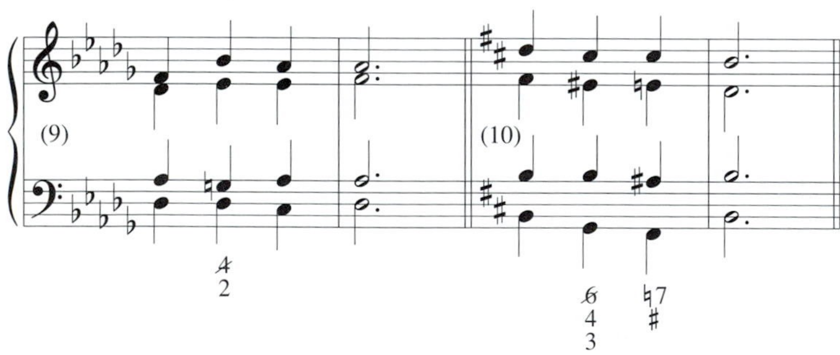

Assignment 18.9

Appendix D

Page 436

(1) Aeolian mode: G A B♭ C D E♭ F G

(2) Lydian mode: E♭ F G A B♭ C D E♭

(3) Phrygian mode: F♯ G A B C♯ D E F♯

(4) Mixolydian mode: F♯ G♯ A♯ B C♯ D♯ E F♯

(5) Dorian mode: B C♯ D E F♯ G♯ A B

Index of Compositions

Folk tunes, hymn-tunes, and "community" songs are not included.
The symbol "m" after a page number indicates a single melodic line only.

C

Subject Index